Paradoxes of
LEADERSHIP IN
POLICE MANAGEMENT

By Douglas W. Perez
and
Michael Barkhurst

DELMAR
CENGAGE Learning™

Australia • Brazil • Japan • Korea • Mexico • Singapore • Spain • United Kingdom • United States

DELMAR
CENGAGE Learning™

Paradoxes of Leadership in Police Management
By Douglas W. Perez and Michael Barkhurst

Vice President, Career and Professional Editorial: Dave Garza

Director of Learning Solutions: Sandy Clark

Senior Acquisitions Editor: Shelley Esposito

Managing Editor: Larry Main

Product Manager: Anne Orgren

Editorial Assistant: Danielle Klahr

Vice President, Career and Professional Marketing: Jennifer Baker

Marketing Director: Deborah S. Yarnell

Marketing Manager: Erin Brennan

Marketing Coordinator: Erin Deangelo

Production Director: Wendy Troeger

Production Manager: Mark Bernard

Senior Content Project Manager: Betty Dickson

Senior Art Director: Joy Kocsis

Production Editor: Sara Dovre Wudali, Buuji, Inc.

For product information and technology assistance, contact us at
Cengage Learning Customer & Sales Support, 1-800-354-9706

For permission to use material from this text or product, submit all requests online at **www.cengage.com/permissions.**
Further permissions questions can be e-mailed to
permissionrequest@cengage.com

Library of Congress Control Number: 2010934269

ISBN-13: 978-1-4354-8807-6

ISBN-10: 1-4354-8807-5

Delmar
5 Maxwell Drive
Clifton Park, NY 12065-2919
USA

Cengage Learning is a leading provider of customized learning solutions with office locations around the globe, including Singapore, the United Kingdom, Australia, Mexico, Brazil, and Japan. Locate your local office at:
international.cengage.com/region

Cengage Learning products are represented in Canada by
Nelson Education, Ltd.

To learn more about Delmar, visit **www.cengage.com/delmar**

Purchase any of our products at your local college store or at our preferred online store **www.cengagebrain.com**

Printed in the United States of America
1 2 3 4 5 6 7 14 13 12 11 10

For the men and women of American
policing who protect, serve, and
maintain order in their communities

CONTENTS

PART THREE

OFFICER BEHAVIOR 219

ABSTRACT

This text hopes to engage in the difficult task of discussing leadership with present and future leaders of the American police force. It attempts to make sense of what is at times an art and at times an inexact science. Drawing from classic works in the field of organizational theory and contemporary research into the areas of leadership and communications studies, this work seeks to provide a diverse collection of ideas for the consideration of three distinctive groups: experienced police leaders in managerial positions; first line supervisors, whether veterans or new leaders; and students of police management who are still involved in the university experience. The book makes liberal use of theory, but also utilizes practical examples throughout in order to illustrate the principles and ideas considered herein.

ACKNOWLEDGEMENTS

Our thanks go out to Stephen Sampson, John D. Blakeman, and Robert Carkhuff for insights into their cutting-edge work in the fields of leadership studies and modern interpersonal communications. The substance of their work has aided in the creation of this text, and their personal insights have also facilitated the process. For sharing their lifelong insights into the world of police studies, we thank Sandy Muir and Jerome Skolnick, as always.

Leaders in the field of police work who have allowed us access to their organizations over the years and who have equally shared with us about their personal journeys through the police leadership experience include Chief John Hart, Chief Dashel Butler, Chief John Terry, Chief Kevin Scully, Chief Norm Stamper, Chief Joseph McNamara, and Sheriff Richard Rainey. For their insights into the individual police officer experience, we have far too many practitioners to thank, but John Gackowski, Al Salerno, Nolan Darnell, Bill Moulder, Jim Simonson, Skip Stevens, and Joe Colletti must be singled out here.

To our hard-working, line-by-line editor Renee Eckhoff go our profound thanks for her many hours of polishing the manuscript. Also, from Cengage, Anne Orgren (Product Manager) and Shelley Esposito (Senior Acquisitions Editor) were instrumental in ensuring that the work was finalized. Without the hard work of each of these people the book would never have reached fruition. We must also thank the hundreds of students, athletes, and police officers who, over the course of more than 30 years, have helped us to hone our understandings of leadership and of the paradoxes of police work.

— *Douglas W. Perez and Michael Barkhurst*
May 2010

The authors and Delmar Cengage Learning would like to thank the following reviewers:

John DeCarlo
Chief of Police, Branford, Connecticut
Assistant Professor, University of New Haven

George R. Petersen
Sussex County College
Newton, New Jersey

Richard M. Hough, Sr.
University of West Florida and George Stone
    Criminal Justice Academy
Pensacola, Florida

Bobby B. Polk
Metropolitan Community College
Omaha, Nebraska

Stephen Kappeler
Eastern Kentucky University
Richmond, Kentucky

Donald S. Winger
Saint Mary's University of Minnesota
Minneapolis, Minnesota

Scott Lyons
Law Enforcement Coordinator, Duluth,
    Minnesota Police Department
Duluth, Minnesota

CHAPTER 1

Introduction

INTRODUCTION

The mission of this book is to provide assistance to current police leaders, and would-be leaders, as they attempt to accomplish a fascinating, complicated, engaging, confusing, rewarding, and frustrating task: leading a group of powerful individuals. Police officers are not like any other workers. The unique nature of who the police are and what they do, combined with the strength and solidarity of their ever-present **subculture**, makes police **leadership**—the capacity to lead and manage—different from leadership of any other kind. It can seem next to impossible to lead individuals who are as empowered as the police, and who tend to band together in order to brace themselves against outside interference. Leadership involves the exercise of power over subordinates, and police officers are people who are experts at manipulating others in interpersonal power relationships. All police officers must be leaders themselves, which creates numerous complications in leading them. At times, police personnel leadership can appear to be "like herding cats."

The experience of managing and leading police officers is replete with paradoxical dynamics that operate contrary to common sense. Sometimes, these paradoxes are so powerful that the endeavor seems to go beyond being merely difficult and takes on the feeling of absurdity (Farson, 1996). The paradoxes of the experience come at the police leader/manager from three different directions. There are those associated with the **management** of all complex organizations, those associated with the job that police officers are charged to accomplish on the street, and those associated with police management specifically. Our endeavor in this book will be to discuss police leadership and management in a way that takes cognizance of all three sets of paradoxes.

First, there are the paradoxes associated with management and leadership in organizations in general. Managers in the contemporary world are forever attempting to make something scientific and logical out of the process of leading their subordinates. But paradoxical dynamics present themselves to managers on a regular basis that operate contrary to how they might appear to operate. This makes leadership in *all* complex organizations not merely difficult, but impossible to conduct in a systematic manner. Many dynamics within organizations work in ways that are antithetical to what logic or common sense might dictate.

BOX 1.1

WHAT IS A PARADOX?

A paradox is a tenet or dynamic that operates contrary to contemporary wisdom or to accepted opinion. Also, it can be an assertion or sentiment seemingly contradictory or opposed to common sense, but that is true in fact.

Second, there are the paradoxes of the policing endeavor itself, experienced at every turn by every man or woman who goes out on the street attempting to enforce the law, maintain order, and provide services to their community. In Chapter 2, we will discuss these paradoxes and engage the idea that the policing experience is forever laced with circumstances under which the dynamics of the job operate contrary to intuition and logic. Taken together, these two sets of paradoxes make police management and leadership troublesome and almost impossible to accomplish in an effective manner.

But there is more. Presenting the police supervisor with a sort of "third tier" of paradoxes, the experience of leading police officers includes its own set of ironies and apparent absurdities that are not experienced by leaders in other types of organizations, lacing the experience with additional frustration and contradiction. These three layers of paradoxes tend to play off of each other, making the endeavor of police leadership difficult, bewildering, and (again) absurd. Our discussions hope to illuminate the reality of this three-tiered system—paradoxes operating upon paradoxes.

Policing the streets of a free society is like no other occupation. While many principles of general personnel management are applicable to the police, some are not. Some of the operational norms that are studied in generalized courses on personnel management quite simply *will not work* in the police world. In this book, we will draw from general management principles at times, but will stop to take note of how the police endeavor can frustrate, thwart, and even defeat leaders who do not take care to note police work's unique nature.

We will begin our introductory discussion with some reminders about the paradoxes of leadership. A central theme throughout the book is that for as much as managers in the contemporary world try to act scientifically, or lead others utilizing techniques aimed at rationalizing the process of leadership, managers are driven more by artistic and charismatic dynamics than by science. Thus, this section will outline some of the paradoxes confronting managers of all bureaucratic organizations.

The next section of the chapter deals with the unique nature of police work. Several systemic dynamics common to police departments and sheriff's departments that are absent in other complex organizations will be explored, as well as the paradoxes that confront the individual police officers on the street.

After engaging these two sets of paradoxes, organizational leadership in general and police work in particular, we will proceed to outline several paradoxes relating to *police leadership* itself. The third section of this introductory chapter, "Some Police Leadership–Specific Paradoxes," will present an understanding of the third tier of paradoxes that color the police management/leadership reality. This section will emphasize that leading and managing police officers involves many paradoxes that operate to further complicate and confuse other paradoxes, in a sort of cyclical and ever-expanding way.

Chapter 1 then covers some principles of **organization theory**, the study of organizations to identify common themes for the purpose of solving problems, maximizing efficiency and productivity, and meeting the needs of stakeholders—this will be important to note throughout the text. While police work includes challenges and dynamics that are different from those that confront other organizations, there are any number of standard operational principles, studied for many years by organization theorists, that *do* speak to the police leader.

Finally, this introductory chapter will outline the flow of the entire text. If police management is indeed as complex and frustrating as we are suggesting it is, then even the organization of such a book takes time and reflection. Outlining all of the relevant topics in a systematized and rational order is aimed at giving the reader our method of attack for the discussion.

There are differences between leadership, management, and supervision. The words *leadership* and *management* are largely used interchangeably in the organizational world, and we will do so in this text as well. The definition of *to lead* is to guide, to conduct, or to direct; *to manage* is to control, to direct, or to guide. Thus, we will not work at making a differentiation here that is not necessary. However, there is a differentiation to be made between these two interchangeable concepts and supervision. *To supervise* is to oversee for direction, to superintend. Thus, supervision involves leading or managing while being present. Because of its very nature, there is obviously a great deal of leadership and management to be accomplished in police work. There is, however, little in the way of supervision. Because they work out on the street and not in close proximity to those who attempt to lead/manage them, the overwhelming majority of police officers are never supervised. This creates some unusual dynamics for the profession.

THE PARADOXES OF LEADERSHIP

Several paradoxes of leadership present difficulties to bureaucratic managers and organization leaders in general. They are not police-specific, but are the types of paradoxes that can frustrate managers in any complex organization, no matter what the appointed task involves.

Coping

In his book *The Age of Paradox*, Charles Handy enjoins all managers to focus on what the word *manage* means (Handy, 1995). He suggests that in contemporary times the process of organizational management has come to entail planning and control. But before it was purloined into meaning something else, the essence of management meant exactly what the word implies: **coping**, the process of managing taxing circumstances, expending effort to solve personal and interpersonal problems, and seeking to master, minimize, reduce, or tolerate stress or conflict. Management involves coping with the sorts of paradoxes that are involved in leading people and organizations. It often involves confronting paradoxes, accepting dilemmas, and tolerating ambiguity.

Furthermore, while we would like to think that leadership and management involve solving problems of all sorts, in actuality, many if not most organizational problems tend to persist. They are ongoing products of either organizational dynamics or results of the job that the organization is supposed to accomplish. What management entails, in lieu of solving problems, is managing, coping with, or tolerating (and working around) ongoing problems. The leader who cannot live with this reality is in for a frustrating experience in the professional world.

So we have our first paradox of leadership, true of managing any group of people in any complex organization, in that problem solving is often (perhaps usually) impossible. Leaders must continually strive to problem solve, to hone their problem-solving skills, and even to study problem solving in as scientific a way as possible. But often (again, usually) the best they can do is cope with and tolerate problems. Leadership involves working around problems and taking action that entails making what the great organization theorist Herbert Simon labeled as **satisficing** decisions (Simon, 1957). Satisficing is a decision-making strategy that attempts to meet criteria for adequacy, rather than to identify an optimal solution. Such decisions involve action that is only temporary and that provides transitory, band-aid type solutions. Simon's concept has made it into the mainstream of organization theory to the extent that it is used and reused to analyze organizational systems to this day.

Learning vs. Teaching

A second paradox of management is that leadership requires as much learning as it does teaching. Leaders are supposed to be teachers, involved in the ongoing task of imparting knowledge to subordinates that comes from a level of intelligence, education, and experience that is, presumably, not possessed by underlings. Paradoxically, it is sometimes, in fact, more important for the manager to listen and learn than it is to talk and teach. Leaders in **bureaucracies**, the administrative structure of a large or complex organization, must learn what their subordinates know about the practicalities of doing their jobs when interacting with the public. They must learn about pragmatic realities that have changed since they were subordinates. Only when leaders are in touch with the knowledge base of their subordinates can

BOX 1.2

SATISFICING

The word *satisficing* puts together the words *satisfactory* and *sufficing* into a concept familiar to most managers; the satisficing decision is one that works for the moment, and only for the moment, to cope with a situation, to pacify an outraged citizen, or to provide relief from a troublesome condition (Simon, 1957).

they work effectively to enhance it. But again, the paradox is that the leader is supposed to possess superior knowledge, information, and experience. To suggest that the effective manager needs to spend some substantial amount of time learning from subordinates appears to imply that the power, the authority, and the social status (not to mention the income) delegated to the manager are misplaced.

Furthermore, leaders must monitor the sort of "psychosociological reality" of their workers. How are people coping with frustration, confronting ambiguity, and dealing with the complex realities of the manager–subordinate relationship? All of these questions need to be answered by the effective manager/leader, and involve listening and learning as prerequisites to talking and teaching. This all might sound like platitudes—and to some extent it is—but that does not make it incorrect.

The Vulnerable Leader

Another paradox of leadership has to do with showing vulnerability. We often hear that managers and leaders are supposed to be strong, confident, and even imposing. They must possess a kind of certitude about the performance of their appointed mission. They need to exert the idea that they know what they are doing, that they have "seen it all before." They must be capable of dealing with the everyday problems of the organization, and confront change and unusual challenges with an answer ready at their fingertips. Leaders must possess enough charisma to accomplish their tasks. After all, if leaders do not possess these qualities, why are they in managerial positions in the first place?

All of this sounds fine—in theory. But in practice, there is a problem with exuding such certitude, strength, and power of knowledge. In interpersonal relationships, people usually develop the most effective influence when they show their human side and demonstrate, on occasion, vulnerability and uncertainty. Doing so invites empathy and openness from others. Given the importance of gathering information or intelligence in any organization, the human propensity to share information most readily with those who empathize creates this apparently contradictory reality: effective management is better served by leaders who sometimes exhibit vulnerability. This is exactly the opposite of what common sense appears to dictate.

This is a paradox that operates in all complex organizations, but it is amplified in police work due to the macho nature of the endeavor. Showing vulnerability in the midst of a group of individuals who are confronted with physical challenges to their toughness on a regular basis is awkward and troublesome, to say the least. But as is true in other organizations, the manager who can accomplish the complicated task of exhibiting at least a minimal level of vulnerability can be the most effective at accomplishing his or her charge in the long run.

Management as Politics

A fourth paradox relates to the fact that "management is politics." The very essence of management involves distributing, redistributing, and reinforcing power

BOX 1.3

EXAMPLE OF A PARADOX OF LEADERSHIP

In today's managerial world, everyone talks a great deal about **communication**, a process of transferring information from one entity to another. To be healthy, an organization needs to have open and accurate communication. In fact, entire textbooks are written in an effort to aid managers in becoming effective communicators (we have included such a chapter in this text). But there is a paradox involved in the area of management communications; while communication is a key element of successful management, so are distortion and deception. Located between line workers and executive leadership, supervisors must control the flow of information both up and down an organization's hierarchy. Sometimes this involves distorting data, soft-soaping reality, giving unrealistically positive (or negative) evaluations, motivating people to do the impossible, and so forth. In this way, "effective" communication cuts both in the direction of being open and honest and, at the same time, of being restrictive and fraudulent.

(Muir, 1977; Farson, 1996). This is politics, plain and simple. Because of this, the organizational leader exercises three basic forms of power over others: exhortation, reciprocity, and coercion. We will revisit the dynamics associated with these three types of power in greater length in Chapter 2. For now, suffice it to say that managers must exhort and reciprocate, utilizing positive forms of power, but must sometimes also threaten and cajole their subordinates. In doing so, they coerce. This is a form of behavior control that is resented, against which subordinates often resist and struggle. Furthermore, police officers understand the paradoxes of coercive power and that allows them a great deal of latitude within which to avoid being coerced by would-be police leaders.

Miscommunication

Box 1.3 gives an example of another paradox of management involving communication. It is a paradox that is experienced by managers in all complex organizations. In Chapter 6, we will see both sides of this important communications paradox. We will see that, while it is indeed important for the police leader to work at open and honest communication aimed at both subordinates and citizens, it is equally true that at times police leadership involves **obfuscation**, the concealment of intended meaning in communication, making communication confusing, intentionally ambiguous, and more difficult to interpret. This is our fifth paradox of management: leaders must work at communication and conscious **miscommunication**, an unclear or inadequate communication, with equal dexterity, sometimes attempting to accomplish both tasks at the same time.

Of course, as is the case elsewhere in the world of police management, the complexity of maintaining **symbiotic communication**, or mutual communication, is made problematic by the fact that police officers are themselves experts at deception. When they investigate, determine guilt or innocence on the street, or interview and interrogate citizens, police officers utilize deceptive tactics on a regular basis. Thus, the manipulative nature of controlling communications experienced by managers in general can be doubly troublesome in police managerial circles.

Managerial Incompetence

Amid all attempts to instill competence, effectiveness, and efficiency in complex organizations, management responsibility often falls to people who are inept, indecisive, and/or lethargic. Laurence J. Peter is most often given credit for noting this propensity in the Peter Principle, but others, including S. Adams and Lazear, have analyzed it in everything from serious studies of organizational ineffectiveness to comic treatments of the crazy nature of organizational incompetence (S. Adams, 2003; Lazear, 2004).

One way of explaining this organizational reality is to suggest that people rise to their level of incompetence. Moving up the hierarchy of a complex structure, competence is exhibited all along the way in order to ensure promotion. At some point, any given manager is promoted to a level that requires competence just beyond his or her abilities (Peter and Hull, 1969). Another conceptualization suggests that effective and successful practices or individuals will be utilized to approach progressively complex problems until they (the solutions and/or managers) are incapable of coping with difficulty. Finally, it has been suggested in a tongue-in-cheek manner that organizations "hide" their most incompetent operatives in positions where they will do the least harm (S. Adams, 2003). Often, then, leaders in complex organizations are simply unable to accomplish the tasks to which they are assigned. There are gaps. There are holes. There is a level of incompetence that is systemically created and that the individual leader can do little to influence in any positive direction.

Transcending Technique

Perhaps the most frustrating paradox of modern leadership involves the practical difficulties of attempting to manage in a scientific way. In its essence, and in the long run, leadership is unscientific. A central paradox for organizational leadership in general has to do with a longstanding attempt to make (or force) management into a genuine science. Since the turn of the 20th century and the invention of the concept of scientific management, researchers and educators have attempted to develop leadership into something that is logical, teachable, and learnable by anyone motivated to learn this "science." But it is not science. And, by translation,

REVIEW CHART 1.1

◉ SOME MAJOR PARADOXES OF LEADERSHIP

- Managing problems most often involves coping with and tolerating ongoing problems.
- Leadership involves as much learning as it does teaching.
- Effective leaders often create empathy for themselves by showing vulnerability, instead of infallibility.
- While leaders often attempt to eschew politicking, leadership *is* politics.
- For as much as they are often working on effective communication, leaders often miscommunicate on purpose.
- Quite often, leaders rise to their level of incompetence.

teaching it and learning how to manage it can be difficult at best and impossible at worst.

It has become evident over time that leadership involves dealing with insoluble dilemmas, tolerating confusing ambiguity, and coping with frustrating contradictions. Oddly enough, the study of organizational leadership involves attempting to learn certain theories, axioms, principles, shortcuts, and techniques—some of which are nothing more than pragmatic tricks of the trade—and then going into the real work of management and forgetting what one has learned in order to transcend technique. We will discuss this problem at length at several points in our discussions later. Suffice it to say that the approach to leadership that attempts to suggest that it can be done scientifically is rife with paradox and half-truths.

Having briefly outlined some paradoxes that visit every leader in any complex organization at one time or another—our first tier of the paradoxes of police management—we will now consider the nature of the police task and the paradoxes that are encountered by every police officer daily. This discussion covers the second tier of paradoxes confronting the police manager.

THE UNIQUE NATURE OF POLICE WORK

Police work is different from other occupations in several ways. It is full of paradoxes that confront the individual police officer on a daily basis. Because of this, police supervisors must attempt to deal not only with the general paradoxes of management and leadership previously outlined, but also with the paradoxical realities with which their subordinates are faced. There are many dynamics operating in the lives of police officers that work in opposition to how one might intuitively expect them to work. These paradoxes are so numerous and so important for the police manager to remember that we will take an entire chapter (Chapter 2) to review them. We will illustrate just a couple of these paradoxes here, before moving on to look at them more closely in the next chapter.

A Panoply of Paradoxes

The paradoxes of police work visited upon the individual police officer out on the street on a day-to-day (and sometimes minute-by-minute) basis are numerous and troublesome (Perez, 2010).

One example has to do with the overall function of the police. To the outside observer, it seems that the police ought to be well acquainted with their mission. It appears to be pretty simple. But a moment's worth of analysis of the three overall functions of the police (law enforcement, order maintenance, and service) shows that these functions can often conflict with each other. Enforcing the law "to the letter," for example, can create order maintenance problems, or disorder. So at the very beginning of any analysis of police systems, it is not absolutely clear what the police are supposed to do. Or, at the very least, it is not clear what they are supposed to prioritize. This conflict of functions leaves the police to decide what to emphasize, how to spend their time, and how to act toward citizens in millions of interactions daily. In turn, this makes police management difficult. In Chapter 3, we will analyze the conflict between multiple functions and goals; understanding it is critical to both police officers and police leaders.

Another paradox has to do with power. The police are very powerful individuals. They carry weapons, they wear uniforms and badges of authority, and they are empowered to use force. But the paradoxes of coercive power operate to diminish this power and create in the individual officer a feeling of impotence that is totally inexplicable to the non-police person. There are several sorts of regular interactions between police officers and American citizens that can make the police feel powerless. This feeling of powerlessness or frustration on the part of individual officers can inhibit a professional approach to police work and thwart supervisory attempts to infuse discipline and control.

Another example of the paradoxes of police work involves police stereotyping. Police officers are trained to hone their skills to quickly evaluate situations and people. Looking for potential trouble, and even assailants, the police must make quick decisions. Their training implants in them the idea that theirs is a dangerous occupation. While this is completely understandable and logical, it creates a propensity among police officers to stereotype individuals and situations as being violent when, in fact, most are not. The **vehicle stop** presents the quintessential example of this paradox. We show videos to academy cadets of police officers who have had their weapons taken from them and then are killed at what started out to be a normal car stop. This is meant to instill in the officer an attitude of caution at the vehicle stop. The purpose of this caution is to protect the police officer's safety.

But, of course, millions of vehicle stops are accomplished each year without incident. Statistically speaking, vehicle stops aren't particularly dangerous *at all*. Thus, a sort of artificially created paranoia about the danger of car stops produces unnecessary citizen–police antipathy and (seemingly) indefensible police **authoritarianism**. Put bluntly, when police officers treat vehicle stops as if they present dangerous situations, they are almost always wrong about this; car stops usually proceed without incident. This reality presents numerous troubles for the police leader, as they attempt to create positive police–citizen dynamics. This propensity to stereotype in the name of personal survival inhibits the creation of positive community relations.

Finally, one additional paradox of police work has to do with the machinations of the due process system. Because they wear uniforms, badges, carry firepower, and walk among the citizenry in public, police officers are the most obvious representatives of the criminal justice system. As such, one might expect that they would not only represent the system as emblems of justice, but that they would "buy into it" and stand for our due process legal system proudly. Unfortunately, this is quite often not the case. Because the police, by the very nature of what they do every day on the street, are concerned with factual guilt, they are often frustrated by the practical realities of the legal system. Often, factually guilty criminals are allowed to walk free on the streets of America due to legal technicalities. In other words, because some procedural rule has been transgressed, the factually guilty can go without punishment.

BOX 1.4

AN EXAMPLE OF A PARADOX OF POLICE WORK

For generations, police officers lived by a general rule of thumb when confronted with domestic violence. Because it made sense logically, the police tended to give abusive husbands lectures, but took no arrest-related action because such occurrences were "family business." This was because it *seemed* that if an abusive husband were to be arrested, he would later come back to his wife, madder than he had been in the first place, and would do more harm to her. This bit of intuition made sense, and it became part of "the way we do things" for the police in general.

But research into domestic violence has found that exactly the opposite is the case. In the long run, arresting a violent husband is actually the best thing to do for the health and safety of the wife. The paradox is that what made sense intuitively, and what had become standard operational procedure for a long time, turned out to be exactly wrong. In the real world, sometimes things work in the opposite way that they might seem to work.

This can frustrate the individual police officer and enhance the propensity for officers to misbehave. In the name of getting the job done, police officers will sometimes become involved in misconduct that is aimed at prosecuting criminals no matter how it gets accomplished. This is called "noble cause corruption," and we will revisit this problem numerous times in the text. This odd propensity of the due process system to (at times) *create* misconduct is profoundly troublesome for police leaders. They are caught between a rock and a hard place in some sense; they must understand the frustrations that lead to noble cause corruption—empathizing with the individual police officer on the street—and yet, at the same time, work to inhibit this very problematic dynamic. This presents us with the Dirty Harry problem, which we will define, analyze, and critique throughout the text. This type of misconduct presents particularly thorny issues to the contemporary police manager.

Licensed Violence

Another unique reality of the police experience involves the use of force. The police are empowered to use force in a free society. They can take away the freedom and even, under unusual circumstances, the lives of citizens. They can, and often do, use force against the very taxpayers who support them. American citizens are generally pro-police at a philosophical level. By and large, average Americans want to be good citizens, and they want to be supportive of those who risk their lives in the pursuit of enforcing the law, maintaining order, and providing service to their communities.

But there's an odd dynamic at work in America that comes from our Yankee, chip-on-the-shoulder attitude about governmental power and individual rights. While citizens on the street are supportive of the police in general, the minute they are confronted with the power of the police in their own personal lives, Americans will tend to rail against big government and complain about "big brother." The instant that the police enter the lives of individual citizens, when the blue lights go on in their rearview mirrors, American citizens often shift gears into a mood that is driven by a sort of anti-police way of behaving. This dynamic is the natural product of our country's most sacred, strongly held principles of individual freedom and of being left alone by their government. As such, it is totally understandable. But it makes the lives of police officers frustrating. And, in turn, it makes the job of managing police officers a difficult task that at times seems almost impossible. For no matter how circumspect police officers are with their application of force, American citizens will tend to think that just about any use of force is illegitimate. The police manager must understand this quintessential American philosophical reality: on the one hand, understanding the citizenry and their need to feel that governmental power is limited; on the other hand, teaching police officers to use force only when necessary, and to use it effectively and efficiently. They are caught in yet another paradox here: the need for the police to use force and, equally, to use as little force as is humanly possible. This is a difficult task for anyone to accomplish.

Organizational Discretion

A third, unique dynamic in police work has to do with how **discretion** flows through a police department's **organizational chart**. All complex organizations have formalized structures that approximate a **chain of command**. At the very top of the organizational pyramid sit the members of upper management. These people occupy positions that possess the most discretionary decision-making power. If an organization is producing, say, automobiles, those in upper management have the discretion to decide to stop the production of one line of cars, to increase the production (and marketing) of another line of cars, to discontinue production on any given line, to develop a completely new line, and so forth.

At the next level down in the pyramid, middle managers take the decisions made above and put them into operation. Sticking with the automobile manufacturing example, a decision might be made by upper management to "create a new SUV line to compete with the SUVs of Corporation X." Middle management then assigns marketing research about potential sales to other lower level operatives, assigns the development of the new product to engineers at still another lower level, assigns the design work necessary to prepare a production line to still other lower level experts, and so forth. Such middle managers also possess discretion, but not as much as those at the very top; discretion dissipates as one goes down the operational chart.

At the bottom of the pyramid in our automobile production example, and in virtually every organization in the world, sits the assembly line worker. This person has next-to-zero discretion. They stand in their place on the assembly line and do what they have been trained to do, mindlessly (to some extent) putting together the SUVs that those above them in the chain of command order them to produce. Discretion flows from the top down in virtually all organizations. This is the obvious, logical way to put together any organization, whether it operates as a public bureaucracy or in private industry.

Since police work operates in a paramilitary, chain-of-command driven way, it would appear that the flow of discretionary decision-making power from the top down would be even stronger in a police organization than it is when cars are being produced. But that's not the case. A unique thing happens at the very bottom of a police organizational chart; individual officers, operating at the very lowest level of the police food chain, go out into the street and make important decisions all alone, by themselves, without any immediate supervision. Immediate supervisors are usually not present when decisions are made to stop vehicles, to search, to arrest, to use force, and so on. These decisions profoundly impact the lives of individual citizens. From the person on the street's point of view, the individual police officer has a tremendous amount of discretionary decision-making power. In fact, unlike any other occupation, the men and women at the bottom in police work have the *most* discretion, relative to the lives of the citizens whom they police. This makes life extremely difficult for police leaders because the flow of discretion in the organizational chart is, seemingly, upside down. Police chains of command

REVIEW CHART 1.2

◉ THE UNIQUE NATURE OF THE POLICE FUNCTION

- Police work is driven by multiple paradoxes which frustrate police officers and police managers alike.
- The police are licensed to use violence in order to confront violence.
- Police discretion is greatest at the bottom of the organizational chart.
- The police subculture can operate to thwart attempts at logical, fair, and effective management.

operate as they do in most organizations to decrease discretion as one goes down the management chart *until* one comes to the bottom where, in a unique twist, discretion increases exponentially.

Subcultural Solidarity

The police subculture presents a fourth set of unique problems for police managers. Everyone in and around police work knows how powerful an influence the subculture has upon police behavior. Sociologists who study subcultures often point to the police subculture in particular as an example of how much **solidarity** and isolation can be created among co-workers, how an "us versus them" mentality can develop that inhibits the operation of external, societal, or organizational norms of conduct within a subcultural group (Thornton, 2005). How filled with irony then is the job of attempting to control the individuals who live and work within such a subculture? While chains of command apparently allow the police supervisor to order subordinates to do this or do that, in actuality, those who are being "controlled" are often "out of control." Surrounded by like-minded individuals who share a common experience and world view, the individual police officer can receive much in the way of sustenance from peers that can operate to support their *not* doing what supervisors command.

These dynamics make police management an extraordinarily difficult and challenging occupation. The uniqueness of police work necessitates that, as we discuss police personnel management, we keep in close contact with these realities. We must inform our discussion with a pragmatic, reality-based understanding of who it is police leaders are "controlling," and against what norms and values police managers must, at times, struggle.

We have considered the paradoxes of leadership in general. We have discussed the paradoxes of police work specifically. Now we must note several paradoxical dynamics that present the police leader with more trouble. In doing so, we overlay the police leadership role with our third and final tier of paradoxes.

SOME POLICE LEADERSHIP–SPECIFIC PARADOXES

What are some police management–specific paradoxes that do not confront the manager at, say, IBM? How does the uniqueness of the police officer charge combine with the paradoxes of management in general to create unusual, additional paradoxes for the police leader? The answers to these two questions create for us our third and final layer of police leadership–oriented paradoxes. Amplifying and enhancing each other, and thereby making police leadership so paradox-driven as to approach absurdity, these levels define the daily working reality within which all police leaders find themselves, whether out on the street or in the administrative structure.

Leading Leaders

In our discussion, we will be engaging several dozen paradoxes that haunt police leaders at every level. But perhaps *the* central, most important paradox involved in leading police officers is so important and ubiquitous that we should acknowledge its frustrating reality at the outset. Police officers are leaders, and to lead them involves leading leaders. It takes a number of talents and abilities to lead such leaders. Some of these talents are difficult, if not impossible, to teach or to transfer from one person to another. Though much time may be devoted to teaching the techniques of leadership and organizational management, some of these techniques involve charismatic abilities that are innate—natural gifts not possessed by everyone.

Police officers are leaders because when they arrive at the scene of any altercation, disaster, confrontation, accident, or suspicious circumstance they are immediately expected to be in charge. People naturally cede control over such events to the police. The public depends on police officers to make decisions, take effective action, and exercise authority. It is a dynamic that gives the police an important advantage if, and only if, they can utilize it in appropriate, logical, and effective ways. The police lead others by exercising power over them, depending on the legal position which they are granted by law, and even by utilizing charismatic authority, if they are able to do so. Because this is true, leading police officers is rife with paradox. Using techniques to control, motivate, and manipulate police officers can be totally ineffective, because those officers that the police supervisor attempts to control are themselves experts at controlling others.

One might be prone to say "so what" when confronted with this idea that leading police officers involves leading leaders. Why does this reality present the police leader with such a frustrating paradox?

The answer is that leadership involves controlling people's behavior in numerous ways, and sometimes this involves **coercing**. As we shall see in the next chapter, there are paradoxes involved in coercion that limit any coercer's ability to control the behavior of others. Most important is the fact that people who understand interpersonal power relationships can make themselves incoercible (uncontrollable) in several ways. Since police officers *do* understand coercive power

BOX 1.5

THE PARADOX OF LEADING LEADERS

One way that leaders maintain their control over their subordinates is by manipulating the rewards that are handed out in any given organization. But since police officers themselves are experienced at leading (they lead citizens), they understand well the dynamics involved. If they choose to do so, they can detach themselves from caring about certain rewards and, thus, avoid being led or controlled.

For example, one way that police leaders might control line officers is by rewarding them for good behavior with choice beat assignments. But, in many jurisdictions, every beat has its own particular attractiveness or charm. By convincing him- or herself (and others) that one beat is the same as another, that he or she does not care which beat they are assigned, the experienced officer can pull the rug out from underneath the control that a leader can exercise. If they don't care where they are assigned, they cannot be manipulated by assignments.

(and its limitations), they can often make themselves incoercible, if they so desire. The job of managing and leading the police can become complicated because officers will avoid being controlled by their own managers and leaders. This dynamic is operative in individual relationships between police leaders and police officers, of course, but it is also in evidence when the would-be leader interacts with officers in numbers. In other words, the police subculture is just as able to thwart being controlled as is the individual police officer.

Knowledge Is Power

Our second central paradox of police management involves one of the general paradoxes of management. Police supervisors must learn as often as they must teach. This is a dynamic that visits all managers in all complex organizations. But in police work, this problem is amplified to a substantial degree. In our current era of community-oriented policing (**COP**), where the modern, educated, individual officer is empowered to make decisions as an agent of change or a "criminologist in uniform," the line officer can possess a substantial amount of knowledge-based power over the police leader.

Many police supervisors are not out on the streets, working beats as they were when they were young street officers. Chiefs of police can often be far removed from the beat-working reality of their younger days. Middle managers, too—especially in medium-sized or large organizations—are aloof from the everyday realities of the street. This can even be true of sergeants. While in most police organizations, sergeants go out on the street in police vehicles, they do not work a beat the way they used to. They do not normally make traffic stops, do investigations, interrogate suspects, use force, make arrests, and so on. Because of these realities, the knowledge base of the police supervisor—at any level—is limited. They no longer experience and wrestle with the paradoxes of police work, ever present in the lives of street officers. But there is more here—more in the way of a sort of ignorance on the part of police leaders.

Not only are police managers limited in that they are no longer involved in the generalized, daily stress of the job, but they possess only a very limited amount of knowledge about what specifically is going on out on the streets. Who are the burglars on any given beat? Who are the "usual suspects" with regard to daily troublemaking? Where are the drug deals going down? Which young men (and, today, women) are the newest members of this or that **gang**? These and a thousand other facts are usually unknown to police supervisors. Their knowledge base is thus doubly limited, relative to the knowledge base of their subordinates.

A lack of such specific knowledge can be quite inhibiting to the supervisor. "Knowledge is power," as we often hear in our contemporary society, and the difference between the practical knowledge base of the supervisor and those whom he or she is supposed to control can be troublesome. How can one effectively allocate resources when one is ignorant of where the real problems (and, thus, priorities) of an organization might lie? How can one motivate others to do a professional job when those below in an organization are confronted with specific frustrations and pragmatic realities about which the would-be motivator is ignorant? How can assessment be fairly done if those doing the appraising are not directly involved in the realities where the organization is doing its minute-to-minute work? In other organizations, supervisors observe those beneath them doing the job on a regular basis. That is to say, leadership/management is immediate and constant. It is a hands-on reality in other complex organizations. But in police work, immediate supervisors do not supervise in an immediate, hands-on way. The essence of what the police officer attempts and accomplishes can largely be hidden from the view of the police manager. This inhibits leadership in profound ways, and it creates an oddly paradoxical differentiation between the power possessed by those in charge and those being managed.

Authority Paralleling Responsibility

In virtually all textbooks about the management of complex organizations, either public bureaucracies or private corporations, there is a discussion about how authority must parallel responsibility. That is, it is fair and just to hold a supervisor accountable for the job done by subordinates if and only if the supervisor possesses the authority to make decisions relative to those subordinates. If authority or decision-making power rests elsewhere in any organization, the supervisor cannot be fairly held responsible for the job being done by any subgroup in that organization.

This principle of organization theory is normally couched in a discussion about the unfairness, irrationality, and ineffectiveness of **micromanagement**. Managers are enjoined to let the supervisors operating beneath them do their jobs without interference. If important management decisions are being made by some-one elsewhere in an organization, taking authority away from the supervisor, it is neither intelligent nor just to hold the supervisor accountable when things go wrong. This makes perfectly good sense, and, again, it is an important managerial principle found in all studies of how to manage effectively.

But in modern day police work, with the current era of COP, this principle is, to some extent, eschewed. Modern police leaders operating under the princi-ples of COP are encouraged to be motivators, coaches, and resource people for their subordinates. They are supposed to do all they can to avoid old-fashioned, **command-and-control** management techniques. Police middle managers are sup-posed to acknowledge, embrace, and make effective use of the intelligence level of the average police officer today, with two or more years of college being the norm now. Police problem solving is supposed to be done "collegially" under COP, in a cooperative way, with managers leading and empowering groups of modern, edu-cated, well-trained, expert, on-the-beat police officers in developing solutions to problems on the street.

There is nothing wrong with this principle. In fact, it is an important change in the direction of genuine police professionalism, because it requires the police to problem solve as groups of other professionals (doctors, lawyers, teachers, engi-neers, and so forth) have always solved problems—led, not commanded, by their most experienced members. In our era of COP, group decision making of this type is being implemented around the nation.

The problem with police work in this regard is that when strategic plans are made in such a collegial way, middle managers are still held accountable in the long run for the effectiveness (or lack thereof) of a given strategy. Police middle managers no longer come up with strategies and implement them down the chain of command by issuing orders that are not to be questioned. But if and when things go wrong, police leaders are often chastised from above for developing ineffective and/or inappropriate strategic plans—plans which, in fact, they no longer create and implement themselves (or at least completely by them-selves). So, authority under COP does not necessarily parallel responsibility—a fact that is not lost on today's middle managers. They are caught in the change-over from the old style of command-and-control policing to the new style and new philosophy.

Never Apologize

Given the enmity which the average American can sometimes hold for the police, especially related to perceptions of the police physically abusing citizens, police supervision and leadership involves the attempt to create positive, supportive **police–community relations**. Supervisors must understand the frustrations experienced by beat officers, largely created by the paradoxes of police work, and strive to mollify the creation and maintenance of an "us against them" mentality among their charges. As rational as it is for police officers to have such a defensive subcultural mentality, it must be eschewed as much as possible. The business of police leadership is largely about helping officers avoid such cynical views about life and the citizenry they serve.

One simple and critical way to take the edge off of anti-police feelings among citizens is to encourage police officers, whenever possible, to communicate with citizens in logical, understandable, and reasonably deferential ways. There is nothing wrong with expecting police officers to make clear what it is that they are doing, what they are requesting of citizens, and why. There are almost never any secrets involved, and it is not necessary to keep secrets from the average honest, tax-paying citizen. A great deal of support and empathy for the police can be generated by explaining actions being taken.

Furthermore, when the police make mistakes, an almost magical dynamic can occur if they apologize to citizens who have been the victims of police error. People tend to react in a very positive way when the police acknowledge that they misunderstood a situation or the facts of an altercation. Again, there is nothing wrong with doing so, and a lot of good can come of it. Now, we are not suggesting that police officers make themselves vulnerable to lawsuits when they have made an arrest that might be questionable, or when they have used force in a marginally acceptable way. It might be foolish under such circumstances to issue some sort of apology on the street. But because they often listen to incomplete stories and make human errors, police officers can repair damage done, avoid citizens' complaints, and even create positive situations out of negative ones when they acknowledge error with a brief, simple apology.

BOX 1.6

NEVER APOLOGIZING

The great novelist Joseph Wambaugh, a former LAPD sergeant, wrote the best-selling novel *The New Centurions* in 1971. It was his first novel, and it was written about life in the Los Angeles Police Department in the early 1960s, when Wambaugh had worked there. In this novel, he illustrated our point about apologizing when he has his experienced officer, Kilvinsky, give a speech to a brand new rookie. Kilvinsky's Law, as the veteran puts it, includes this pearl of wisdom: "I treat everyone the same, white or black. I'm civil to all people, courteous to none. I think courtesy implies servility. Policemen don't have to be servile or apologize to anyone."

The macho nature of the police subculture tends to teach officers that to explain or to apologize is a sign of weakness, something an officer should never show to the public. Of course, intelligent, mature individuals know that an explanation or an apology is, in fact, something that indicates power and certitude in a person. If a person is willing to own up to error, that person is confident that errors are something of which they are seldom guilty. To take responsibility is to be honest, powerful, and self-assured. There is nothing esoteric or complex about this reality of interpersonal relations.

But because of police subcultural dynamics, this sort of maturity is difficult for officers to obtain, especially young officers who are plagued by doubt about the job they are doing and frustrated by the paradoxes of police work. Police leaders, whose job it is to motivate young officers to become responsible, accountable, and effective, and who do not get citizen's complaints, can often find it troublesome to attempt to motivate their young charges to accept this type of behavior as reasonable. The paradox here is that understanding the positive dynamics associated with an explanation or apology can mean that a young officer gets fewer complaints and develops a better, more positive future. However, young police officers tend to believe that exactly the opposite is true. They believe that to explain or to apologize is to indicate a *lack* of competence and understanding.

Of course, not all of the lessons learned in the study of organization theory are lost upon police work. Many of the concepts that business management and public administration textbooks and courses present to the student of management are relevant to the policing experience. Police work may be unique in several ways, but the police do live and function within a complex organization. They reside within a public bureaucracy. And much of what has been learned studying complex organizations and bureaucracies over the years is relevant to the police manager's charge.

Thus, we now turn toward a brief discussion of organization theory in general, once referred to as the field of "scientific management."

REVIEW CHART 1.3

◎ SOME POLICE LEADERSHIP–SPECIFIC PARADOXES

- Police leaders are involved in the difficult task of attempting to lead leaders.
- In police work, line officers possess a substantial amount of knowledge-related power over their leaders/supervisors.
- Under COP, a basic principle of management is often violated— authority does not always parallel responsibility.
- Even though explanations and apologies help create an easier workplace atmosphere, they are usually eschewed by police officers.

ORGANIZATION THEORY

For more than 100 years, people who called themselves organization theorists have analyzed, dissected, and critiqued complex organizations. Their initial efforts were aimed at streamlining businesses. To begin with, organization theorists were nothing more than **efficiency experts**, persons skilled in developing operations to improve the efficiency of an organization. They looked at assembly lines and organizational charts, and attempted to apply rational analysis to how things were done in the private sector workplace. Later, organization theory was applied to the newly created field of public administration, wherein governmental bureaucracies such as welfare organizations, unemployment departments, and agriculture bureaus were analyzed. Today, the efforts of such theorists to be analytical, logical, and critical of complex organizations is in evidence in every Business/Public Administration 101 textbook and class.

Our discussions in this text will build on some of the theories developed by such organization theorists, and will expand them to the administration of police systems and the supervision of police officers. Much of what organization theory has to say about complex organizations is not applicable to police systems, but some of it is. The police function may indeed be unique, making application to police systems and officers more complicated, intriguing, and frustrating than other bureaucracies. At the same time, police managers and leaders can learn a great deal from those who have been studying complex organizations for generations.

In this brief section, we will present a few of the classic principles outlined by organization theory.

Goals and Mission Statements

Theory in this field suggests that organizations should provide members with a complex pattern of communication that includes information, assumptions, goals, and attitudes that enter into decision making. This pattern also presents the individual with stable and understandable expectations. It provides a role system within which individuals can operate to further the organization's goals. A rationally organized system will also involve assessing individual and collective performance, and will provide for sanctions and **discipline** in the event of error and inefficiency. Theorists tell us that, in order to create such a rational, fair, understandable, effective, and efficient system, the complex organization must begin with an explicit consideration of the overall goals toward which it should aim its individual and collective efforts. In order to avoid confusion, the goals of any organization need to be enumerated and made clear.

Over the course of the past 30 years, **mission statements**, formal written statements of the purpose of a company or organization, have come into vogue in the field of organization theory in order to provide such explicit goals. To focus complicated and, at times, conflicting individual and subsystem goals on the specific goals of the organization, mission statements involve getting together administrative staff and workers to discuss overall goals. These statements tend to be vague and loosely worded at times (missing the point of making goals concrete and focused), but the logical reasons for mission statement creation are nevertheless sound.

Some people downplay and even ignore the mission statement creation process. This is often due to the process being abused in some organizations. Sometimes, bureaucrats decide to construct mission statements and then reconstruct them over and over again. This can make the entire endeavor appear to be a waste of time and, worse, can denigrate the importance of focusing on specific goals. Too much time spent **reinventing the wheel** can work against the interests of any complex organization.

But no matter what the downside might be of modern mission statement creation, attempting to be specific about otherwise vague goals and to prioritize between conflicting goals is an essential endeavor in police work. Organization theorists have emphasized for decades that large bureaucracies can suffer from goals that are, in the words of Aaron Wildavsky, "multiple, conflicting, and vague" (Wildavsky, 1987). This is a particularly thorny problem in police work, as we shall see in Chapter 3.

Structure

Aside from focusing on overall goals and mission, organization theory has always discussed organizational structure as a primary topic of concern. It is, of course, necessary to have some sort of organizational structure; attempting to operate without one is certainly irrational. Such a structure is a formal, intelligently constructed, systematized way of making decisions, considering and debating change, implementing policy, fixing responsibility, determining suborganizational goals, controlling communication, and assessing outcomes. These points about formal organizational structure are so obvious that some people consider organization theory to be nothing more than an artificially constructed, unnecessary field of study that states the obvious, over and over again.

But while some people in their field appear to expend too much time in stating the obvious, organization theorists have observed and pointed out several important dynamics about complex organizations that are not so obvious. One is that, over time, organizations develop informal systems through which information, control, and power flow. Such informal systems can develop a life of their own that is outside of the control of those who are *ostensibly* in control. Informal systems can not only work against the interests of the organization, but can foster cynicism among middle managers in particular, who notice that they are being held accountable for things over which they have no direct control. This is particularly troublesome given that organization theory has long noted authority must parallel responsibility or counterproductivity will develop.

Another theoretical point centers around **bureaupathology**, or "red tape syndrome," where the manifestations of exaggerated bureaucratic behavior include

BOX 1.7

BUREAUPATHOLOGY EXAMPLE

In a famous book about organization theory, Victor Thompson (1961) coined the term "bureaupathology" to explain the tendency for some suborganizations to develop goals that appear to be legitimate from their limited perspective, but that work against the goals of the overall organization. An example might relate to a division within an automobile manufacturing company that is in charge of building car frames. Suppose that, without consulting the organization's upper management, the frame-building division builds so many frames so fast that it eats up too many of the organization's resources, and the company ends up having to stockpile frames it cannot use. Thompson's point is that setting a record-breaking pace for frame building might make the frame-building division feel good about itself and about its ability to achieve its subgoals, but it might actually get in the way of the organization's overall goal of building complete cars. This would be counterproductive for the company, and it is a classic example of bureaupathology.

resistance to change and an obsessive reliance on rules and regulations. In any complex organization, suborganizations (divisions, departments, etc.) develop sub-goals. This is logical. The larger and more complex the task at hand, and the larger the organization, the more impossible it is for each subdivision to complete their subtasks without the creation of formal subsystem goals. But in creating such sub-goals (subdivision rules, subsystem policies, etc.), the overall mission of the organization can become lost. A subdivision can work to protect itself, its supervisors, and its workers by focusing on subdivision goals that inhibit the accomplishment of the overall organizational goal. When this happens, the subdivision has a sort of "illness" that one organization theorist, about 50 years ago, labeled bureaupathology.

Communications

Theoretical study in this field is full of critical analysis of how communication is supposed to flow within complex organizations, how it actually flows, and how its flow can be frustrated and thwarted. Reflection will draw the thoughtful analyst to an understanding of how important concise, authoritative, realistic communication is within any organization.

But in police work, and in any complex organization dealing with the public, communication has multifaceted dynamics. Effective communication by police supervisors is about both their ability to communicate with their subordinates (and to receive communication in return from their subordinates) and how their subordinates communicate with the citizenry. In other words, police supervisors need to communicate well, and they also need to teach others how to communicate well.

Organization theory will help clarify communication coverage with analysis of how supervisors need to communicate with each other, the pitfalls associated with communicating with subordinates, and how supervisors should be open to communication from below. Studies that model effective communication for police officers in particular, as opposed to other bureaucratic workers, will also enter into our analysis. Finally, how to put the two together and teach effective communication will be most important for our discussion in Chapter 5.

Motivation

One issue for managers of any organization involves treating their subordinates as if they are members of an athletic team. "Coaching" is often the term used in modern textbooks to explain how motivating and disciplining underlings should proceed. Courses, books, and seminars on motivation are forever present in the world of contemporary management, with entire careers built on the ability to teach motivational techniques. Former coaches and military personnel often recreate their professional lives after service, and go on to become motivational speakers or teachers.

This is all understandable, but the reality is that much of what constitutes great coaching and great motivation has to do with charismatic abilities possessed by individuals in leadership positions, particular to their personalities. Anyone who has spent time around coaching knows that some coaches obtain the best from their athletes by being cerebral, reflective, and intelligent. The quiet, calm, and analytical coach can be extraordinarily effective. However, other coaches are profoundly effective using force, fear, and screaming most of the time. The world of coaching has many examples of great and even legendary coaches of both types. There is no single best way to accomplish the coaching tasks of motivation and communication. Similarly, as we shall see in other chapters, there is no single best way to obtain accountability or to instill and maintain discipline.

Assessment

How is it possible to assess the performance of organizations, suborganizations, and individuals within organizations when the overall goals are multiple, conflicting, and vague? Can we assess organizational effectiveness and efficiency in the light of bureaupathology in complex organizations? How is possible to generate fair and equitable assessment tools in an environment where saboteurs and naysayers are ever present? Both classic organization theory and police-specific studies will enter into our consideration of **assessment i**n Chapter 7.

Theory suggests that it is critical to the integrity of an organization that assessment be done fairly, equitably, and with a focus that is clearly aimed at organizational goals and mission. Our discussion, true with the entire field of organization theory, will be complicated by considerations of how frustrating and counterproductive it can be to generate any assessment tools in the face of multiple, conflicting, and vague goals. Equally important, our discussion must take cognizance of police subculture–specific dynamics that appear to encourage cynicism, secrecy, and sabotage. As theory in the field of organizations meets practice in area of police work, some (seemingly) insurmountable problems develop for the police administrator empowered to assess the performance of subordinates.

Ethics and Accountability

Organization theory suggests that ethical frameworks should ideally be constructed "from the ground up" in rationally operated systems. **Ethics** represent a branch of philosophy dealing with values relating to human conduct, with respect to the rightness and wrongness of certain actions, and to the goodness and badness of the motives and ends of such actions. Organizational ethics should be built on a positive model, working their way from a baseline understanding of ethical imperatives to a consideration of how to handle specific ethical problems and dilemmas. Ethical frameworks should consider how to be a good, effective, loyal member of the organization, how to do the job efficiently, and how to develop general principles for accomplishing these tasks. These general principles are then applied to specific, ongoing, common problems encountered by members of an organization. This is what theorists mean when they suggest a positive approach.

Unfortunately for police administrators, police work is too often driven by a "how not to screw up" conceptualization of ethics. Both subcultural norms and formal police training tend to be driven by such negativity. Organization theory suggests that this propensity in police work is backwards; avoiding being sanctioned is inadequate as an operational norm. Put more simply, the idea that an ethically defensible performance on the job involves avoiding being a *bad* worker, instead of attempting to be a *good* worker, is destined to create animosity, diffidence, cynicism, and even sabotage among any population of subordinates.

In theory, **accountability** mechanisms need to be fair to employees in a judicial sense and also be pragmatically defensible. Police officers must be accountable to the law, but they must also be accountable to the public as civil servants. Especially in the age of COP, police officers are readily encouraged to elicit input from citizens and community leaders, and they must be held accountable for responding to that input. But police officers are also accountable to a multitude of police regulations and practical methods of getting the job done that are administrative in nature. Putting this all together, the sets of standards to which the police must be held accountable are multiple, conflicting, and vague; the police must answer to the law, the people, and administrative standards. Police accountability

BOX 1.8

MULTIPLE STANDARDS

There are multiple standards to which the police must be held accountable. Responding to a community's calls to emphasize disorderly conduct, a police department might make an extraordinary amount of arrests for that crime. In making those arrests, the police are responding to locally set community standards. Of course, when they are processing such arrests, the police must be held accountable to legal standards with regard to *Miranda* warnings, habeas corpus, and so forth. Finally, when arresting suspects, the police will cleave to administrative standards while frisking, handcuffing, and transporting suspects. In this way, a simple arrest for disorderly conduct responds to three separate sets of standards.

mechanisms must operate in a fair manner to hold officers accountable to these standards, but equally to keep an eye on practical, pragmatic, everyday methods of operation that officers develop to get the job done efficiently.

Theory in the area of administrative accountability suggests that review mechanisms are semi-judicialized systems which must afford workers the right to have their say, investigate all sides of questions of misconduct, generate morally defensible outcomes with regard to the guilt and innocence of accused workers, and keep an eye on the future implications of any individual decisions regarding accountability. An accountability mechanism must, therefore, take into consideration the fairness to the worker of an individual investigation and the perceived fairness of investigations in general (perception being just as important as reality in this regard), and make an effort to generate long-term learning and behavioral change in the errant worker.

Discipline

A great deal of work has been done by theorists in the area of nonpunitive, no-fault disciplinary systems. Discovering that negative sanctioning systems create diffidence and distrust in sanctioned workers, organization theorists have attempted to create disciplinary systems that are more prone to generate positive outcomes in the long term. In other words, such no-fault systems focus intently upon the future behavior of errant workers.

A police disciplinary system is, to some extent, a mini–criminal justice system. It receives accusations of misconduct, investigates them, makes decisions with regard to guilt or innocence, and then sanctions errant officers. Its overall functions are analogous to those of the criminal justice system. Both systems must get rid of the truly incorrigible worker/citizen by firing the officer guilty of egregious behavior or by putting the violent psychopath away in prison for life; exonerate those individuals that are investigated and found to be not guilty of misconduct/crime; and sanction, retrain, or rehabilitate those who have erred, but whose errors are less than fatal—not worthy of termination or life in prison.

In accomplishing the first two tasks, a disciplinary system must be judicious, fair to all, and create decisions that are legally defensible. In every sense of the word, it must be a courtroom-like operation. But in accomplishing the third task, a disciplinary system must be creative and, at times, ingenious as it attempts to mold the errant worker into a better worker in the future. Here, organization theory suggests that modern systems developed with this goal in mind can operate to make the sanctioning of misbehavior a positive thing in the long run. Such programs involve retraining processes, systems that erase the records of misconduct after an appropriate amount of time, and positive counseling, to name just a few examples of the operational dynamics of nonpunitive disciplinary systems.

Leadership

The importance of supervisorial leadership, motivation, or mentoring is another area of analysis for the organization theorist. Leadership is, to some extent, an art, not a science, and theory that analyzes the different types of authority (legal, traditional, and charismatic) was outlined by the original guru of organization theory, Max Weber, more than 100 years ago (Weber, ed. 1946). Theorists in the field analyze how administrators can manipulate, cajole, exhort, and coerce their subordinates into accomplishing various tasks utilizing these three forms of authority. Any supervisor has the organization's legal, structurally based authority working for them. Because of where they are on the organizational chart, and where their subordinates reside on that same chart, supervisors exercise legal authority when leading.

But organization theory points out that there is also a kind of traditional authority that can be of use to supervisors. In police work, the experience of supervisors, their age and wisdom, and their years within the police subculture can give supervisors far more power and authority over their subordinates than is afforded to them by the organizational chart. Even in police work, organized along paramilitaristic, chain-of-command lines, traditional authority can trump legal, rank-driven authority.

Finally, there is charismatic authority. Some leaders just have a certain way about them, an ability to command people with a personality structure that demands compliance from subordinates. Functioning as role models par excellence, the charismatic leader can motivate people to go above and beyond the normal call of duty: to do the extraordinary, in lieu of just doing the expected. The study of leadership in organizations is replete with examples and critical analysis of all three types of authority.

REVIEW CHART 1.4

IMPORTANT ELEMENTS OF ORGANIZATION THEORY

- Goal focus and mission statement creation
- Systemic structural integrity
- Internal and external communications
- Interpersonal motivation
- Job assessment and personnel evaluations
- Ethics and accountability
- Effective punishment and discipline
- Leadership, supervision, and management

THE ORGANIZATION OF THE BOOK

In Part One, "Organization," we will discuss how police systems are organized and how they *ought* to be organized. Important to this discussion, and indeed important to any person operating within the field of police work, will be Chapter 2's consideration of the paradoxes of police work. The experience of being out on the street as a police officer in America can be frustrating and confusing. Many dynamics engaged by police officers on the beat operate in exactly the opposite way as one might expect them to operate. The job is full of paradox, and the business of this chapter is to note how many of these paradoxes exist and to remind ourselves how they operate. Every person who dons a uniform and goes out on the street to police faces these paradoxes every day; those who lead them cannot even attempt to begin to be effective unless they understand the paradoxes involved in working a beat.

Chapter 3 discusses the importance in police administration of having definitive, specific, focused goals. Mission statements, in particular, will be discussed, and how important they can be in informing the ongoing operations of a police system. We will discuss the idea of justice on the street as a guiding principle, and begin to consider how contemporary police management systems and leaders can work to mold and motivate police officers to be modern professionals.

Chapter 4 is about structure. We will consider four different types of police organization, their strengths and weaknesses, and suggest some ways of creating police systems that produce an optimum amount of accountability while allowing for innovation and creativity. In this chapter, we will engage the philosophy of community-oriented policing (COP) and analyze the tremendous possibilities that it presents to the police of today and tomorrow. We will also critique this method of police organization and consider some pitfalls that are already appearing in what is a new way of thinking about policing.

Part Two, "Operating Principles," is about the daily grind of police management and leadership. In Chapter 5, we will discuss the critically important subject of communication. The importance of understanding the various dynamics of organizational communication is paramount in police work. Not only do police administrators have to communicate in a symbiotic way with their subordinates, but they must teach communication skills to subordinates who then, in turn, communicate with the public. In this way, police work involves a complex pattern of multiple points of communication, and, as a result, multiple *problems* in communicating. We will engage in discussions about "the social skills" idea and will draw into the debate several important conceptual frameworks developed in other professions. Particularly critical for police officers and police managers are studies done about confrontational skills.

Chapter 6 is about the sometimes amorphous, charisma-driven art of motivating police subordinates. A central paradox relates to this pragmatic reality: it is often impossible to quantify, teach, pass along, or learn some of the skills and qualities necessary to be a good coach and/or motivator. Much of this endeavor involves exercising personal attributes and characteristics that are endemic to individual personality; motivation and coaching often involve what makes a motivator tick, or how they are wired emotionally and intellectually. It is often not possible to teach or to learn how to accomplish this difficult task.

Chapter 7 will consider the always topical and frustrating difficulties that confront police managers with regard to evaluating the job done by subordinates. Beginning with a brief review of the importance of the problem of multiple, conflicting, and vague goals, mission statements, and the problems of bureaupathology, this chapter's discussion will consider the importance of saboteurs and negativity in police work. Modern assessment tools will be included, covering those that are currently operational and those that are theoretical. This discussion will give the police manager a number of options from which to choose when creating assessment tools.

Part Three, "Officer Behavior," is about police officer conduct and misconduct. It focuses on police behavior, good and bad, and what to do about accusations of misconduct, how to hold the police accountable, and what to do when officers are, in fact, guilty of misbehavior. In Chapter 8, we discuss police professional ethics from a positivist perspective, what it means to be a good officer, and how to encourage police managers to motivate their charges in positive ways. Attempting to avoid the negativity so often associated with police ethical frameworks—aimed, as they are, at "avoiding screwing up"—we will construct a positive view of police ethics that encourages ethical behavior by suggesting that police character is central to the entire endeavor of policing the streets of America.

Chapter 9 is about police review. We begin by reminding ourselves about the multiple sets of standards to which police officers must be held, and the many severe limitations that work to make holding the police accountable such a difficult task. From legal limitations to subcultural limitations, the job of police review is complicated in numerous ways. Internal review mechanisms (internal affairs) and external review (civilian review boards) are discussed, noting some interesting and nonintuitive strengths of external review.

Chapter 10 engages the topic of what to do about misconduct when it has been proven. Beginning with traditional, punitive disciplinary systems, coverage continues with some intellectually engaging ideas about no-fault discipline. Early warning systems and tracking procedures are discussed, as well as an overview of nontraditional discipline. Operational in many businesses today, and even in some police departments and correctional settings, no-fault discipline is certainly the wave of the future in our field. This chapter gives the reader an outline of the theory behind this movement, as well as practical examples of the policy in practice.

Part Four, "The Challenges of Leadership," brings all theory together in cohesive discussions about police leadership. Chapter 11 divides the topic of police leadership into sections about chiefs of police (and sheriffs), middle managers, and sergeants. While numerous students of police management have argued that each of these tiers of leadership is *the* most critical in police work, we will argue that they are all equally important. Modern police professionalism and effective leadership cannot be obtained in any police organization, no matter how logically constructed it might be in a systemic sense, unless all three of these levels of motivating, supervising, assessing, and disciplining police officers are operating in sync with each other and in conjunction with a logically based and pragmatically operational structure and organizational culture.

Chapter 12 brings our various topics together, reviews some of the most important principles of the work, and gives readers some additional thoughts upon which to reflect as they finish the book. This chapter includes both a summation and review of the topics previously treated, and a look toward the future.

As addendums to each chapter, we will include several additional elements aimed at fomenting classroom discussion and further clarifying our topics. First, there will be a set of discussion questions, which can be utilized in courses on police leadership and management to generate a dialogue between students and instructors. Second, we will include a set of practical scenarios, taken from the real-life experiences of the authors. Third, each chapter will include a list of definitions for key terms, which appear in bold when they occur in discussion in the text. Finally, there is a short bibliographical essay at the end of each chapter, suggesting additional reading for the reader interested in going further into any given topic.

DISCUSSION QUESTIONS

1. One author cited in the book suggests that management rarely occurs in the real world of bureaucracies. More often than not, leadership in complex organizations involves coping with or tolerating ongoing problems—problems that will never be solved because there are no solutions for them. What might an example be? What sorts of ongoing problems exist in organizations that can only be coped with or tolerated, but never solved?

2. Our book suggests that one paradox of management is that, for as much as we talk about leaders being effective at communicating, miscommunication—on

purpose—sometimes occurs. What is an example of this from the field of police work? When might the police leader be required to mislead his or her subordinates?

3. Review our brief discussion about bureaupathology. What is it? How does it work to engender counterproductivity in organizations? What might an example of bureaupathology be from the world of policing?

4. We suggest in this chapter that there are multiple standards to which the police must be held accountable. So what? Why is this important? What are some examples of how the three sets of standards conflict with each other? In particular, how do demands from the public often conflict with the law and, thus, the police roles of being "politicians" and "legal actors" collide with each other and require the police to ignore at least one of those roles?

KEY TERMS

Accountability: Defined as "A is accountable to B when A is obliged to inform B about A's (past or future) actions and decisions, to justify them, and to suffer punishment in the case of eventual misconduct."

Assessment: The process of documenting, usually in measurable terms, knowledge, skills, attitudes, and beliefs.

Authoritarianism: A political doctrine advocating the principle of absolute rule.

Bureaucracies: The administrative structure of a large or complex organization.

Bureaupathology (red tape syndrome): The manifestations of exaggerated bureaucratic behavior. They include resistance to change and an obsessive reliance on rules and regulations.

Chain of command: A system whereby authority passes down from the top through a series of executive positions or ranks in which each is accountable to the one directly superior.

Coercing: To force to act or think in a certain way by use of pressure, threats, or intimidation; to compel.

Command and control: The exercise of authority and direction by a properly designated commanding officer over assigned and attached forces in the accomplishment of the mission.

Communication: A process of transferring information from one entity to another.

COP: Acronym for community-oriented policing.

Coping: The process of managing taxing circumstances, expending effort to solve personal and interpersonal problems, and seeking to master, minimize, reduce, or tolerate stress or conflict.

Discipline: A rule or system of rules governing conduct or activity.

Discretion: The amount of allowed decision making by an organization in regard to the ability of individuals to make those decisions without supervisory permission.

Efficiency experts: Persons skilled in developing organizational operations to improve the efficiency of an organization.

Ethics: That branch of philosophy dealing with values relating to human conduct, with respect to the rightness and wrongness of certain actions and to the goodness and badness of the motives and ends of such actions.

Gang: A group of people who, through the organization, formation, and establishment of an assemblage, share a common identity.

Leadership: The capacity to lead and manage.

Management: Handling or directing with a degree of skill.

Micromanagement: A management style where a manager closely observes or controls the work of his or her subordinates or employees.

Miscommunication: An unclear or inadequate communication.

Mission statement: A formal written statement of the purpose of a company or organization.

Obfuscation: The concealment of intended meaning in communication, making communication confusing, intentionally ambiguous, and more difficult to interpret.

Organizational chart: A diagram that shows the structure of an organization and the relationships and relative ranks of its parts and positions/jobs.

Organization theory: The study of organizations for the benefit of identifying common themes for the purpose of solving problems, maximizing efficiency and productivity, and meeting the needs of stakeholders.

Police–community relations: The relationships developed between the police and the community, including both the negative and positive.

Reinventing the wheel: A statement frequently used to exemplify the need to continually review and reinvent ideas that have already been considered and implemented.

Satisficing: A decision-making strategy that attempts to meet criteria for adequacy, rather than to identify an optimal solution.

Solidarity: The show of total support (in any endeavor) from a subcultural group.

Subculture: A group of people with a culture (whether distinct or hidden) that differentiates them from the larger culture to which they belong.

Symbiotic communication: Mutual communication.

Vehicle stops: The act of conducting a car stop by a police officer using his/her emergency equipment (lights and/or siren).

ADDITIONAL READING

A complete discussion about the dozens of paradoxes that plague both the individual police officer and the police leader is included in *The Paradoxes of Police Work, 2nd Ed.*, by Douglas W. Perez (Cengage, 2010). With regard to our discussion about classical organization theory, the field was essentially invented on the heels of the work in the area of "scientific management," first opened up by Frederick Taylor in 1911 in his recently rereleased book *The Principles of Scientific Management* (Forgotten Books, 2008). The study of bureaucracy was first systematically approached by Max Weber in a work still read by organization theorists. Originally published in 1920, *The Theory of Social and Economic Organization* has been recently republished (Free Press, 1997). A contemporary updating of these ideas is included in *Taylorism Transformed: Scientific Management Theory Since 1945*, by Stephen P. Waring (University of North Carolina Press, 1994).

Herbert Simon, the first to coin the term "satisficing," did so in *Administrative Behavior* (Free Press, 1947). This work is a compilation of principles and insights that gives the reader an understanding of the first half-century of the study of complex organizations. Published a few years later, Victor Thompson's work *Modern Organization* (Knopf, 1961) was the first to present the idea of bureaupathology. The concept has been used, modified, and polished ever since, most recently by Brown et al. in "A Satisficing Alternative to Prospect Theory" (David B. Brown, Encino G. DeGiorgi, and Melvyn Sim, *Social Science Research Network*, November 23, 2009).

Regarding recent developments in the field, Charles Handy's *Understanding Organizations, 4th Ed.* (Penguin, 2005) provides extraordinary insight into the modern area of organization theory. *The Situational Leader*, by Paul Hersey (Center for Leadership Studies, 1997), is a short, eminently readable work that gives a quick overview of some contemporary thoughts in the field. *The Management of the Absurd,* by Richard Farson, is a sometimes comical, but insightful romp through some of the more paradoxical and inane realities of the world of organizations. Using practical examples and lacing them with humor, Farson engages the reader with a panoply of entertaining and realistic scenarios and case studies. A somewhat pedantic, but nevertheless synoptic, traditional approach to organization theory as applied to police work can be found in *Supervision of Police Personnel, 7th Ed.*, by Nathan F. Iannone, Marvin D. Iannone, and Jeff Bernstein (Prentice Hall, 2008).

And finally, the rather glib work by Laurence J. Peter and Raymond Hull, *The Peter Principle* (Bantam, 1969), treats the reader to the entertaining idea that in complex organizations people tend to rise to their level of incompetence. Universally acclaimed at the time, and adopted ever since, this work is hard to analyze, as it is meant to be humorous, but at the same time has a serious point to make about organization theory.

PART ONE

Organization

Part One engages the topics of organization and structure. First, we must acknowledge the part that paradox plays in the everyday life of all police officers, not just leaders. Chapter 2 will review a number of critically important paradoxes of police work and will illustrate why a consideration of the same is essential to the development of good police management. Chapter 3 will focus on mission statements and the paradoxical reality that, on a regular basis, police leaders have to work on defining and redefining what the police are doing in the first place. Finally, Chapter 4 will discuss several classic styles of police organization, and their strengths and weaknesses in today's policing world.

CHAPTER 2

The Paradoxes of Police Work

INTRODUCTION

To the experienced police leader, this chapter might provide little that is genuinely new. It is a review of what any manager already knows—or should know—about the individual police officer's experience. In America, virtually all police leaders have been police officers on the beat. This is unlike the European system, where the **police managerial class** goes through extensive academic training unknown to the street officer, and does not experience police work at its most basic level. American police leaders have firsthand experience with the paradox-driven realities of a beat cop. American **police managers** should remind themselves daily how frustrating and confusing it can be to face these ironies as a rookie with little street experience.

Any administrator knows that an inordinate amount of time is spent with those who are new to a job. It is important to remember how the rookie officer's world appears to him or her. Only after engaging in a discussion that reminds us how the isolation and frustration can color an officer's perceptions should we proceed to engage the topic of how to lead, manage, manipulate, mentor, and administer to police officers in general.

Police work is replete with paradoxes. On a regular basis, young police officers, in particular, are confronted by dynamics that work in the opposite way from how they might intuitively appear to work. No one who looks at police work from the outside can possibly understand how paradoxical it can be to attempt to do the job, how frustrated police officers can become, and how often they feel powerless in their jobs.

Police officers feel powerless? How can that be? Don't police officers carry all sorts of physical tools and legal powers with which they can accomplish their charge? Are they not surrounded by other police officers? Can't they call for cover and depend on a subcultural sense of duty and camaraderie? These feelings might seem paradoxical to begin with, but are a living, breathing reality that police officers must deal with on a daily basis. The competent police manager needs to be aware of both the individual paradoxes and the feelings of impotence that can haunt officers.

Let us consider the paradoxes of police work and remind ourselves how they can create feelings of isolation, and a necessity for the beat officer to cleave together with brother and sister officers, "the only people in the world who get it," to form a solid, unflinching subculture that can, unfortunately, work against effective police leadership.

THE NATURE OF PARADOXES

Everyone who experiences police work develops at least some level of frustration on the job relating to the **paradoxes** of that work. Policing is not what people expect it will be when they enter into the endeavor. Programmed by media imagery that is unrealistic, misled by a lifetime of observing only the tip of the iceberg of the policing experience, and driven by idealistic notions of what enforcing the law in a free society must be like, the average police recruit usually has some far-fetched ideas of what they are about to experience. It isn't that the police cadet believes the job will be easy. It is always made clear at the outset that the experience will be a difficult one. What is troublesome is that police recruits (and later rookies) believe their frustrations will come from an action-oriented, thrill-a-minute, dangerous, and exciting type of occupation. While perhaps feeling some trepidation, the average recruit braces himself or herself to deal with an adventure of sorts. Given that police work is often tedious and even boring, it is understandable that newcomers can be disappointed by the lack of adventure involved.

But the lack of action is merely a small source of dissatisfaction. Perceiving that being a police officer involves the application of force on a minute-by-minute basis and the ongoing exercise of a tremendous amount of legal power over citizens, rookie officers believe that to be a police officer is to be a profoundly powerful individual. Of course, nothing could be further from the truth. The recruit soon discovers that police work can be disconcerting precisely because, very often, the police *lack* the power to accomplish the basic charge of keeping people safe from harm. Thus, feelings of inadequacy in the rookie officer can develop not because of stress brought about by exercising too much power over others. The opposite is the case. Stress is most often brought about by possessing an *inadequate* amount of power over others.

The paradoxes of coercive power make up just one set in a larger set of paradoxes. Our discussion in this chapter will focus on these multiple paradoxes, and how young officers deal with feelings of impotence in both individual and collective ways. But before we move toward these paradoxes, we must briefly outline one paradox so critical that it forms the entire discussion in Chapter 3. This paradox has to do with the multiple goals and functions of police work.

At the outset, police work suffers from a confusing set of goals and functions. The police enforce the law; many people refer to police work as **law enforcement**. However, the police spend only a small amount of their time enforcing the law, approximately 8 to 12 percent (Perez, 2010). The other two major functions of the police are **order maintenance** and service, and these are arguably more important than law enforcement.

It is not just police supervisors and administrators who experience difficulties due to this multiple goal/function problem. The everyday police officer encounters this paradox; they don't always know what to prioritize and how to behave on the street. Beat cops get many signals from police subculture, coworkers, and administrators suggesting that enforcing the law, making arrests, and treating details in an officious manner make up the essence of the job. But they also get signals from today's **community-oriented policing** (COP) environment that suggest working a beat in a maximal way involves handling details while making as *few* arrests as possible. These signals come not only from community members, but from police administrators attempting to institute the new philosophy of COP.

How are modern police officers supposed to incorporate action-oriented decisions with discretionary power in appropriate ways? There is no one answer to this question. This mission confusion is so important that the next chapter will outline the multiple, conflicting, and vague nature of goals and functions in police work and discuss how to create and apply mission statements in contemporary police management and leadership.

PARADOXES ON THE BEAT

A number of central paradoxes face all police officers working on the beat. This list is not synoptic—that is, other paradoxes exist, and some of them are as important in their impact on individual police officers and on the police subculture as a whole (Perez, 2010). In fact, one of the most cogent reasons for the police subculture is that officers cleave together to form a tightly knit group precisely because only other officers understand the paradox-driven experience that plagues contemporary American police work.

Several paradoxical realities affect all police officers no matter where they work, whether inner city, suburb, or rural, and no matter what type of organization they inhabit in terms of size, history, and training. We begin with feelings of inadequacy that can arise from operating within the American due process–oriented legal system.

Due Process

The police are the most obvious, everyday representatives of the legal system. They walk among the citizenry in uniform as living emblems of the criminal justice system. In theory, they should be the proud representatives of the American **due process** system. They should be its first and foremost champions. They should be dedicated to the system's process. They should buy into the justice system's operations and exhibit a deep, abiding faith in its practical utility and moral efficacy.

But often they do not. Because of how the criminal justice system actually works, the police can be at odds with its due process principles. The fact that the police are often thwarted by due process and the system's organizational principles presents a profound central paradox for consideration. Some police officers are so inexorably opposed to the system's processes that they may break the law in order to accomplish what they believe to be their most important mission: protecting the citizenry by getting the bad guys off the street.

The American criminal justice system is the only system in the world that utilizes the **exclusionary rule** (Signorelli, 2010). Only in America do we "pretend" that evidence does not exist if it is obtained illegally. In England, for example, police officers who make illegal searches might be disciplined for misconduct by their equivalent of internal affairs, but the evidence they obtained is still accepted in court. The focus is on factual guilt in a way that makes more sense to officers on the street and is less prone to confuse and unsettle them.

BOX 2.1

THE DIRTY HARRY PROBLEM

A generation ago, the criminologist Carl Klockars defined the **Dirty Harry** problem for students of the police. He was referring, of course, to the movie *Dirty Harry* and the main character, Harry Callahan, played by Clint Eastwood. Harry cut corners. He tortured suspects to obtain information, ignored due process procedures, refused to obtain search warrants, and in general behaved in a cowboy-like, out-of-control manner.

His problem was his propensity to break the law in order to enforce the law. What Klockars meant by labeling this as a general problem for American policing is that some police officers become upset by how legal technicalities can allow factually guilty criminals to walk free. They can become so frustrated by this systemic reality that they will do anything to get the job done and get criminals off the streets. This type of police misconduct has been labeled **noble cause corruption** (Caldero and Crank, 2009) because it involves the police breaking the law to achieve a good, noble end. It is hard for leaders to fight this type of police deviance because it comes with its own rationalization. The Dirty Harry–type officer believes that he or she is doing the job of protecting the community (Klockars, 1980).

The modern police leader must understand their officers' propensity to behave like Dirty Harry. Equally, leaders must remember that the job of being a police officer is a real-life, nuts and bolts, no-nonsense type of experience. The police are enjoined to "find out who did it" in a factual sense. On the street, they must focus on substantive guilt. But because the system, after the fact, behaves in an entirely different way, the leader is caught between the logic and morality of the legal system, in theory and in practice. Put another way, the police leader is caught between the average officer and the law, as it operates within the American due process system.

The American legal system, driven by a fixation with procedural guilt, can appear to the police officer to be lost in a wilderness of **legal technicalities**. It often seems that the system is not interested in who is actually guilty of criminal behavior, but in playing a game that dances around factual guilt as if it is unimportant. The rules of the system seem to get in the way of finding the truth and making just decisions about citizen deviance.

This focus can frustrate police officers in a very personal way. When officers take the witness stand, the job of the defense is to impeach their credibility. This is how the game is played. By implying that an officer is lying, incompetent, bigoted, and/or unintelligent, the system can make the police officer on the stand feel attacked. In an effort to reach what the legal system considers to be the truth, through the give and take of one side struggling against the other, the system seems disrespectful to the individual officer and uninterested in the substance of what criminals have in fact done to victims.

So, an important paradox of the experience of police officers is that the system, which they *ought* to embrace and represent proudly, is rejected by a significant number of police officers because it seems to be against them. Some officers will be driven by the frustrations of this reality to behave in a Dirty Harry–like way; they will break the law and in doing so present to the police manager the most frustrating type of misconduct to deal with: noble cause corruption. In most jurisdictions at most times, inhibiting noble cause corruption is the most important ethics-oriented task of the contemporary police leader. In a police world that has largely done away with other forms of corruption, deterring Dirty Harry is of primary importance to today's police supervisor.

Of course, there are any number of rational arguments against the exclusionary rule. Both in legal and practical political circles, scholars and politicos have argued in favor of doing away with the rule (Long, 2006). The arguments involved are fascinating, and the modern police leader might want to understand the logic of this debate. But the immediate problem on the street today is that Dirty Harry exists and is encouraged by both the police subculture and, at times, the American citizenry, who are interested in results, not legal technicalities.

Stereotyping

When we hear the word **stereotyping**, we tend to interpret it in a negative way. Most of us are opposed to racial, religious, and sexual orientation stereotypes that are misused to discriminate unfairly against groups of people. But stereotyping, in

REVIEW CHART 2.1

EXAMPLES OF DIRTY HARRY'S NOBLE CAUSE IN ACTION

- *Testilying:* Falsifying testimony on the witness stand in order to obtain a conviction
- *Creative report writing:* Falsifying reports in order to obtain indictments or prosecutorial charges
- *Planting or dropsy:* Putting evidence (usually drugs) on suspects in order to frame them
- *Torturing or forced interrogation:* Obtaining desired information utilizing excessive force
- *Curbside justice:* Going around the system entirely in order to punish "bad actors"

and of itself, is an operational principle that everyone uses as a way to cope with life's complexities. It is natural and logical.

Psychologists tell us that everything we know is made up of nothing more than stereotyped notions of people, things, events, and language that are dropped into "diagnostic packages" stored in our brains (Schneider, 2005). When we see a blue shirt, for example, we determine it to be a shirt and the color is blue. In other cultures using other languages, the shirt would have other words and symbols attached to it, but in English-speaking America, we determine that the color of the "shirt" is "blue." We receive an external stimulus through our eyes, we perceive a type of article, we perceive a color, we compare this input to those boxes in our brain that have stored our understanding of things and colors, and we determine that it is a blue shirt. The label we attach to anything is nothing more than a stereotyped package stored as part of the grand scheme of information that makes up who we are and what we think we know about the world. Stereotyping makes life easier; there is nothing wrong with using stereotypes to navigate our way through contemporary life in America.

All people stereotype, but police officers tend to stereotype more readily than others. First, they live in a world driven, like all bureaucracies, by statistics and numbers. Police officers think in terms of **penal code** sections, vehicle code sections, and so on. They take the numbers associated with certain types of deviance and crime, and weave it into their on-the-street lexicon. A murderer becomes "a 187." An armed robber becomes "a 211 man." Police officers communicate efficiently with each other in their own subcultural language. This phenomenon is labeled by psychologists as a "perceptual shorthand" (Pinizzotto, Davis, and Miller, 2000). Police also stereotype by using organizational shortcuts such as radio codes for minute-by-minute communication.

Second, police officers, like others in the criminal justice system, tend to "normalize crime" (Sudnow, 1993). Since criminal behavior is by definition deviant, officers must drop all deviant behavior into diagnostic packages because of the dictates of **habeas corpus**. No matter how bizarre, disgusting, dishonest, horrific, or despicable human behavior might become, the police are driven to normalize it or attach a number to it. The police are forever asking themselves, "This behavior is disgusting, but what type of crime does it involve?" Police officers may joke in the locker room about how someone was arrested "for failing the attitude test," but, in truth, it is not possible to book someone for *any* type of abnormal behavior unless there is a code number attached to it. Deputies at the county jail's booking desk would not think it was funny if an officer showed up with someone in handcuffs but no specific charge to report. So the officer's job involves searching through stereotypical packages in their brain for categories, in order to label any deviant behavior.

Third, part of the craft of police work on the streets involves working the beat. Officers normalize how a beat looks, who belongs where, what the flow of traffic looks like, and when, where, and how daily life operates in a standard way. In doing so, they learn who belongs and, most importantly, who does not belong on their beats. It is part of their job to find out what is wrong on their beats. Once they know this, they have probable cause to deal with events and persons who do not belong, and can investigate whether unusual behavior is disruptive, malicious, and even criminal. Once again, this dynamic requires the police officer to regularly engage in stereotypes that deal with perceiving normal activity on their beat.

Under the ongoing threat of violence, the police are constantly looking for "symbolic assailants" (see Box 2.2). Police officers are taught to consider the possible danger posed to them by every person they see on the street (Skolnick, 1966). In order to help officers survive the police experience, managers amplify this tendency. In the contemporary police academy setting, cadets are shown video tapes of incidents where police officers have come under fire and even been murdered. Usually taken from cameras in cruisers, these tapes are meant to instill in the young officers an understanding of the danger involved in working on the street, especially with automobile stops. The message is that the individual police officer is vulnerable at a traffic stop. But the problem is that traffic stops rarely end up in violent confrontations, and they almost never end in injury or death for the officer. There are millions of traffic stops each year, and only a couple dozen end up developing into lethal confrontations. Attempting to prepare themselves for the worst, the police will treat a vehicle stop as being potentially dangerous. Officers will flood the stopped car with light, require the driver and passengers to keep their hands in plain sight, demand that the car's occupants remain inside the vehicle, and so forth. All of this is logical, but the behavior of the police under such circumstances *appears* to citizens to involve a sort of illogical paranoia aimed at perfectly harmless, ordinary people.

BOX 2.2

ENCOURAGING PARANOIA

Jerome Skolnick, a leading American scholar on policing, wrote that the police are forever looking for "symbolic assailants," or people who might pose a threat. Cadets are taught from day one in the academy to watch people's hands, never stand in front of a doorway, stand at arm's distance from any civilian, keep their own hands free and ready, and any number of other axioms aimed at protecting the officer from assault. But, in dealing with the public this way, the police are almost always wrong. What we mean is that citizens almost never pose any threat to the police. In a million daily interactions with the public, the police are confronted with citizens who may be upset and angry, but who are generally peaceful. By instilling a consistent, ongoing concern for officers' safety, police training creates an artificially negative perception in the minds of citizens that the police are paranoid, authoritarian, and irrational individuals.

There are several additional dynamics associated with stereotyping that exacerbate the paradoxical nature of the policing experience. These dynamics are troublesome for police–community relations, and, in turn, create difficulties for police leaders. These additional dynamics put more distance between officer and citizen than is already created by the powerful role of the police.

Police officers tend to see people as "cases," as do other professionals who deal with the public. Social workers, doctors, and public administrators are sometimes accused of losing their humanity because of this propensity. Paradoxically enough, keeping some distance from the population that they police, nurture, and administer is an absolute necessity in the world of the professional who deals with the public. Becoming too involved in individual lives and tragedies can cloud one's judgment, and can work against dealing with the public in a rational, effective, and fair manner. But it can also make the delivery of public services appear callous and uncaring. This is always true when people cease to be human beings in the minds of professionals and become cases. Police officers normalize crime for perfectly understandable reasons, but citizens resent this stereotypification for equally understandable reasons.

The police stereotype in a perfectly rational way, for completely defensible reasons, and in doing so, they end up creating a great deal of antipathy in the minds of the public. This is the most obvious paradox of police stereotyping. But the stereotyping involved in the police–community relationship goes both ways. The overwhelming majority of people hold stereotypes about the police. People generally only know one or two police officers at most; many know none. Almost always extrapolating from a very few, isolated experiences with the police, under the direst of circumstances, most people create negative stereotypes about the police that appear to be true. It is just human nature for people to behave this way.

But such stereotypes are most definitely not true. Police officers come in all shapes and sizes, with different life experiences, different levels of education and understanding, different political beliefs and opinions, and different strengths and weaknesses. They are not a monolithic set. They are as varied in their personality structures as the citizens they police. In recent years, studies about the intelligence and educational levels of police cadets entering the profession indicate that the police officer corps in the United States is becoming increasingly diverse in its demographic make-up and collective psychological profile (S. Walker, 2004).

All of this is lost on most people. Citizens choose to use stereotypes about police officers because they believe this will enable them to deal with the police effectively. When police officers—young ones in particular—are faced with such unfair stereotypes, they feel affronted and rebel. The more inexperienced the police officer, the more he or she tends to rail against the public's stereotypes. Police officers in this country are, after all, Americans; as Americans, they demand the right to be treated with dignity, respect, and without prejudice. They feel unjustly treated when they are massed together into irrationally driven cultural stereotypes, much as other Americans feel when they experience the same sort of treatment. Paradoxically enough, it is often the police who are perceived to treat citizens in such a prejudicial and discriminatory manner.

REVIEW CHART 2.2

◎ STEREOTYPED IMAGES OF THE POLICE

Police officers are:

- Overly aggressive, authoritarian types
- Racial and religious bigots
- Anti-gay and lesbian homophobes
- Not particularly intelligent or well educated
- Intolerant, rigid, and unresponsive to logic
- Uncaring and aloof from human suffering
- Politically archconservative

The police leader must understand this problem at its root; while it makes perfectly good sense for the police to stereotype in an effort to protect themselves and to get the job done efficiently, the dynamics of stereotyping create a great amount of antipathy for the police. How can the police accomplish both tasks at once? How can they protect themselves *and* consistently work the beat, searching for who is "wrong"? This problem presents a somewhat stifling conundrum for the supervisor. It takes creativity, inventiveness, and insight to lead young officers who are confronted with this paradoxical reality.

Discretion

For several hundred years of Anglo-American history—since the invention of western liberalism that ended the aristocratic tradition—we have fancied that we want to live in a world ruled by "laws and not men" (J. Adams, 1780). We adhere to the rule of law as a guiding principle for our system of government and law enforcement. The rule of law, not "the rule of cop," should be administered out on the street. As a people, Americans do not want to empower the more than 800,000 sworn individuals who are police officers in this country to operate with impudence. Americans don't want to acknowledge that there should be 800,000 different penal codes. One principle that drives any analysis of the police (or anyone who applies rules to other people) is that Americans want those who exercise the law's powers over others to cleave to the spirit of the law, not some personalized or subculturally created principles.

On the other hand, those familiar with police work understand that the world of the average officer has a great amount of discretionary decision-making power. The police are confronted every day by questions of whether they should intervene in what might appear to be private situations, whether they should arrest, whether they should use force, and what amount of force to use. Police work is all about such decisions. By applying their individual understandings of justice, the police put life into the law. In this sense, while we rail against the rule of cop, the actions of the police determine what the law really is. By using their discretion, the police define what conduct is acceptable and unacceptable.

Our innate sense of fairness suggests that the law should determine how the state deals with us as individual citizens. People want to think that the law is objective, not driven by whim or personal prejudice. But the law is inexact. No codified set of rules can completely and definitively determine how those applying the rules should act under all circumstances, in all situations. For example, there are times when arresting a young shoplifter or marijuana user would not be in the best interests of the community, the individual, or justice. Sometimes a lecture, a ride home, and a discussion with Mom and Dad makes more sense. In this way, holding back on the application of the law can be the best tack for the police to take. Doing nothing, doing less than what is legally required, or doing something genuinely creative and thoughtful is often the best course of action for the officer confronted with such situations.

There are times when the law doesn't dictate any specific course of action. Sometimes the police *want* to take action, and the law does not allow or demand it. By getting a would-be abusive husband to take a walk and calm down, urging a drunk at a bar to go home and sober up, or dispersing a group of teenagers with "if we have to come back, you won't like it," the police are doing their jobs. In these examples and countless others, they are clearly not involved in doing what is legally possible, but are infusing the law with common sense, maintaining order, and providing community service.

Police discretion is a critical element in the criminal justice system. But there is a problem hidden within this reality. When citizens see the police making discretionary decisions—when they understand that the police are, in fact, "making up their own minds" about whom to arrest—they are outraged. The law is supposed to be absolute, rational, and fair, not driven by the personal dictates of police officers in uniform. In the minds of the public, those who go to jail are supposed to deserve it; those who do not are supposed to be entitled to their freedom. In theory, the law is supposed to be above the fray of normal human feelings and motivations.

Today's police officers are, on average, more educated and better trained than their predecessors, and are empowered to make decisions in the interests of justice. None of this matters to the public. They see the police deciding to arrest someone, they compare this decision making to something they saw once before involving what they believe to be similar circumstances (a decision not to arrest), and they conclude that the police are unfairly empowered. Citizens may believe that "that cop arrested me because I'm gay," or "that cop disrespected me because I'm black," or "that cop just didn't like my tone." These feelings on the part of the public not only color police–community relations in a negative way, but develop long-term disrespect for the law in the minds of many.

BOX 2.3

MONITORING DISCRETION

The police leader occupies an awkward, paradoxical position vis-à-vis the exercise of officer discretion. Discretion not only exists as a practical dynamic, but it *has* to exist as an important element of the justice system. The police *must* use their minds (and hearts) to infuse reasonableness and fairness into the system. But discretion can be abused. In fact, the abuse of discretionary latitude is perhaps the single most important minute-by-minute form of misconduct in police work. The police leader must find a way to encourage the right kind of discretion and discourage the wrong kind. This is a tough proposition, given that police supervision is done in fits and starts, and from a distance.

As is true with stereotyping, the police leader must walk a fine line with regard to discretion. The manager must understand the importance of police discretionary decision making *and* acknowledge that citizens abhor it. In motivating officers to use their discretion wisely, the supervisor must instill a reasonable sense of proportion and a comprehension of the dictates of justice. They must be honest with their charges about how the public's perceptions about police discretion must be managed in a way that inhibits the development of animosity. In other words, the police have to "sell" their decisions. Often, they must take the extra time to explain the logic of what they are doing to the public. As we have already noted, police officers do not like to explain themselves, but they must be exhorted to do so. The police leader must instill an understanding in the officer that explaining things to citizens is not wasted and does not make the officer look weak. Such time can be important to the long-term relationship between police and the public.

Coercive Power

In 1977, William K. Muir, Jr., penned one of the most important books ever written about the police (*Police: Streetcorner Politicians*). His work involved an in-depth analysis of the paradoxes of **coercive power**, situations where the apparently powerful have trouble coercing the apparently powerless. He illustrated how often it is that the powerful, from presidents to parents, have substantial difficulty dealing with those who are supposed to have less power. In creating a profound comprehension of how these paradoxes work, he shed light on the idea often expressed by police officers that they feel powerless on the street.

Muir began by pointing out that there are three ways to influence the behavior of others and exert power over them. First, logic can be used to exert **exhortative power**. People can be urged to do the right thing, the rational thing, or the

Christian thing. By appealing to a person's previously internalized sense of right and wrong, a police officer can influence their behavior. Since this type of behavior control costs nothing (it only takes the time to explain the situation to someone) and it makes a person feel good to decide on their own to do the right thing, whenever possible it should be the first type of power utilized in attempting to influence others. The police do this every day, in a thousand different ways, when they urge citizens to behave themselves. Police leaders must understand how critical it is for their subordinates to engage exhortative power.

The second type of power is **reciprocal power**, or the power of trade or barter. A police officer can make a trade in an effort to obtain desired behavior. "You scratch my back and I'll scratch yours" is the operative notion. The police can do small favors for citizens in many ways and create a trade-off. While this type of power involves some cost to the person exerting reciprocal power, it is nevertheless still positive; the individual who is controlled decides that the trade makes sense and, as is true with exhortation, feels good about changing their course of action. When circumstances allow it (which is not always the case in police work), a person wishing to influence the behavior of others should always attempt exhortation first and reciprocity second. Both types of behavior control end up with the person who has been influenced feeling good about it.

The third type of power is coercive power. Coercion involves obtaining desired behavior from another by threatening to harm something of value to them, or what Muir calls a **hostage**. Examples of coercion could include phrases such as "calm down or you're going to jail," "if you come back here again, you and I are going to have a problem," "shut up and listen, or you'll get a citation." Unlike the positive aspects of exhortation and reciprocity, coercion is a negative type of behavior control. People do not like to be coerced because they do not like to be threatened. Powerful individuals should avoid coercion and use the other two forms of behavior control whenever possible.

Coercing others can be difficult or impossible due to what Muir labeled the four paradoxes of coercive power. First, it can be difficult to coerce those who are so disenfranchised that they have no hostages, or nothing of value to threaten. This is known as the paradox of dispossession. Muir discusses dealing with the homeless in this regard. In solving problems that involve the homeless, police officers are confronted with people who have nothing; they have no jobs, no status in society, no homes, and no reputation. They are dispossessed in a way that thwarts attempts to control them through coercion. The paradox of dispossession states that the less one has, the less one has to lose.

What if the police are confronted with people who *do* have hostages that can be threatened—jobs, families, homes, or social status—but they detach themselves from caring about them? This is the second paradox Muir discusses, known as the paradox of detachment. Muir uses the example of domestic disturbance to make the point that people who can consciously detach themselves from valuing their freedom can be difficult to coerce. As any experienced police officer knows, a wife can respond to the suggestion that if she doesn't calm down she (or her husband)

BOX 2.4

THE PARADOX OF DETACHMENT

The terrorists who attacked America on 9/11 illustrated the paradox of detachment. Driven by religious fervor, they were willing to die for their cause. They truly believed that dying on that day would allow them to go to heaven as a reward for their deaths in what they considered to be their *jihad*—a war against infidels or nonbelievers. These men had detached themselves from valuing their own lives. As a result of this paradox, they (and other terrorists targeted by America's war on terror) were incoercible. There is nothing with which they can be threatened that would dissuade them from continuing their destructive endeavors. In a real sense, they became uncontrollable by consciously deciding not to allow themselves to be coerced.

is going to be arrested by saying, "Go ahead and arrest the S.O.B." When this happens, the police are powerless to control the situation through coercion. The paradox of detachment suggests the less one values a hostage, the less effective is the coercer's threat.

As noted in Box 2.4, this paradox is applicable to America's current "war on terror" because it can be impossible to coerce people who are willing to die for their cause. Suicide bombers, like Kamikaze pilots during World War II, are impossible to coerce because they are willing to detach themselves from valuing what is arguably the most important hostage in the world: their own lives. Such individuals are, to a real extent, fearless. A person has to accept being coerced. If they say, "Go ahead and arrest me, I don't care," then the police are at a loss to obtain acceptable behavior from them.

The third paradox discussed by Muir has to do with the importance of making believable threats. Muir points out that if individual police officers or a police department as a whole have a reputation for being able to follow through on their threats (to arrest or to deal with individual citizens and groups with force), they can be extremely effective in coercing others. Especially when dealing with crowds, the police must show a tough face to the public. This is known as the paradox of face, which points out that the nastier one's reputation, the less nasty one has to be. Police officers know this intuitively; they are not often challenged, even when outnumbered, if they carry a "badass rep" with them.

On the other hand, this paradox suggests that when someone calls their bluff, a coercer must always follow through on their threats. Muir points out that, in dealing with crowds, the police must walk a fine line and take care not to make hollow threats ("you're all going to jail") since their bluff might be called. But if the police carefully manipulate their individual and collective reputations, then coercing even large groups can be done effectively and without often having to actually follow through on their threats. It is not often necessary to "kick ass and take names" if the reputation for being able to do so is preexisting.

Muir's final paradox of coercive power has two sides to it. The paradox of irrationality suggests that the crazier the victim of coercion, the less effective the threat. For example, juveniles often don't understand the situation that's presented to them; Muir says that anyone who doesn't get it can be difficult to coerce. Of course, juveniles are not the only citizens who, for one reason or another, don't understand what's being threatened, or that the police truly mean to go through with their threats. Drunk, stoned, frightened, old, crazy, or non–native speaking citizens form a long list of people who "don't get it." This group can be difficult to control.

While the first half of this paradox suggests that the crazier the victim of coercion, the *less* effective the threat, the second half of this paradox suggests that the crazier the coercer, the *more* effective the threat. In police work, this principle is best illustrated by the behavior control power exhibited by K-9 units. People are more afraid of dogs than police officers because dogs, in the mind of the public, are irrational. No matter how much a citizen thinks they understand how well dogs are trained and how effectively the police can control them, they are afraid of the threat of harm presented by a dog, an irrational, nonhuman antagonist. A dog isn't thinking about making sergeant some day or concerned about addressing citizens' complaints. A dog—no matter how well trained by its police partner—could be a nasty, angry, vicious animal, who presents a profound threat.

One of Muir's central points is that this list of people who can be difficult to coerce is not an obscure one, but a list of citizens with whom the police most often interact. The paradoxes suggest that it can be difficult for the police to coerce the homeless, people engaged in family disturbances, crowds, juveniles, the elderly, the drunk, the stoned, the frightened, and the insane. This is a veritable "who's who" of the people the police are expected to control. It makes no difference that it is relatively easy for the police to control average people who have jobs, houses, families, and valued reputations, and who are frightened of going to jail and being the objects of the police use of force. This group of citizens isn't often subject to the attention of the police, and their vulnerability to being coerced doesn't matter much. What matters, to the individual police officer and to those who attempt to lead officers, is how often the police feel constrained by the paradoxes of coercive power.

Muir points out these four paradoxes that limit the ability of police officers to coerce people, but there is more to his work. Not only do police officers suffer from the paradoxes of coercive power in the sense that they have trouble coercing others, but the opposite is also the case; the police can be coerced by citizens. Like most everyone else, police officers have many hostages for citizens to threaten, such as jobs, reputations, and mortgages that need to be paid.

Some citizens understand very well the citizen complaint process. They know that the average police officer doesn't want to be the recipient of such a complaint. Some homeless people learn that the police don't want to arrest them, and don't even want to put them in their police cars. Some people understand that police

REVIEW CHART 2.3

◉ MUIR'S PARADOXES OF COERCIVE POWER

- *The paradox of dispossession:* The less one has, the less one has to lose.
- *The paradox of detachment:* The less one values a hostage, the less coercible one is.
- *The paradox of face:* The nastier one's reputation, the less nasty one has to be.
- *The paradox of irrationality:* The crazier the victim, the less effective the threat. The crazier the coercer, the more effective the threat.

officers avoid making questionable arrests because they are concerned about moving up the chain of command (to make sergeant) in the future. Because of these realities, Muir suggests that the police can actually be coerced themselves; they can be cajoled out of taking actions that might otherwise be appropriate because they have hostages, they cannot detach themselves from the value of those hostages, and they cannot behave in a crazy and irrational manner.

Police managers must be cognizant of these paradoxes at all times, and remind themselves that young officers, in particular, can feel powerless. This feeling makes no sense to those outside of police work, who envision the police to be extremely powerful. But feelings of powerlessness are real for police officers on the street. The police supervisor must always be aware of the fact that police officers can behave in irrational and illegal ways at times because of the frustrations that can come from the paradoxes of coercive power.

Paramilitarism

It is said that the police are organized along **paramilitary** (or semi-militaristic) lines, because they have chains of command, uniforms that often exhibit military colors, and ranks that are analogous to those used by the military. Their rank insignia are the same as those of the military, with sergeants wearing three stripes and lieutenants wearing bars.

There are numerous reasons for this military focus. First, it makes the police visible. Citizens who desire the protection and support of the police can readily identify them. Second, it makes the police feel more accountable—police officers operating within a paramilitary structure are not prone to become involved in the types of misconduct that used to be rampant in American policing, especially the corruption of authority as peace officers. While police officers largely make their decisions and deal with citizens alone and without immediate supervision, membership in a paramilitary organization makes officers *believe* that they are under regular, intense scrutiny. This is true in all organizations run along paramilitaristic lines, not just police departments.

Third, paramilitarism instills a sense of duty to "the corps" of police officers. As is true in the military, the corps of officers exerts a pressure on individuals that motivates them to do their duty, even when they are outnumbered and in danger. This is a positive dynamic operating in police work that has always been the case in the military. This sense of duty makes the police behave in a more legally defensible way, making good, rational, and "correct" decisions in a legalistic sense. It generates a desire to look sharp, present a more no-nonsense carriage toward the public, and keep from misbehaving in any number of ways. It can motivate the officer to handle a hot detail without cover, if necessary, despite his or her fear of doing so.

These examples illustrate the positive side of taking a paramilitaristic focus, but there is a down side to paramilitarism. Studied a generation ago by Tony Jefferson in *The Case Against Paramilitary Policing*, there are tremendous drawbacks to this way of organizing the police, giving pause to anyone who is open-minded about the issue. Four important points can be drawn from Jefferson's work that illuminate the issue of paramilitary organization in police work.

First, going out into the world each day to fight a "war on crime" or a "war on drugs" (the idea of war being a necessary part of a militaristic focus) necessitates that the police operate as if they are struggling against an enemy in every sense of the word. Who is the enemy in such wars? Criminals, of course. Who are the criminals out there? Everyone who has broken the law, to be sure. Well, who is that? If we acknowledge that everyone who has drunk alcohol under the age of 21, driven a vehicle under the influence, smoked marijuana or used any other illegal drug (estimates place this number at about 70 million American citizens), and everyone who has broken any other law to be the enemy, then the police—under a paramilitaristic focus—are going to war every day against a huge population of American citizens. The enemy in any war on drugs includes a *majority* of citizens betweens the ages of 15 and 25. Millions of Americans are members of some sort of enemy camp in a war on crime. What's the problem here?

The problem for police leaders is this: what does the military do in order to prepare its charges to go into battle against an enemy? All militaries, throughout history, spend time dehumanizing the enemy so that killing is more acceptable to the citizen-soldier. If the enemy can be couched in less-than-human terms in the hearts and minds of soldiers, sailors, and marines, then it is easier to do violence to them. Military basic training has always included this type of dehumanization as a part of its indoctrination of young recruits. Basic training in the American military has included the dehumanization of "the Huns" during World War I, the "Krauts" and the "Japs" during World War II, and the "dinks" or the "slopes" during the Vietnam War. Such dehumanization is paralleled in the basic training of militaries elsewhere in the world. Today, veterans returning from America's two major ongoing wars (in Iraq and Afghanistan) discuss and write about this very same dynamic with regard to war (Glantz, 2008).

A paramilitaristic focus does the same for police officers; it dehumanizes the citizenry and works on a regular basis to create an "us versus them" focus. Citizens can become "assholes," "morons," and "losers." This is just a dynamic that develops naturally out of the war on drugs and/or war on crime metaphors. Nothing good comes from having the police consider themselves to be fighting *against* the citizenry; it's bad for the citizenry, the police, and the interests of justice.

Second, living and working within a chain-of-command structure, along military lines, tends to work against individual problem solving on the part of police officers. Following orders has always been about doing what you are told without question. The stronger the chain-of-command feeling is in any organization, the less prone its individuals are to think for themselves, try new ideas, avoid the propensity to believe that there is only one way to do things, and participate in the sort of "thinking outside the box" that we want to encourage in the modern, professional police officer. Under today's COP, our contemporary police officer corps—intelligent, educated, and well trained—is encouraged to become involved in the lives of citizens as agents of change, independent problem solvers, and "criminologists in uniform." That is how it should be. The continuation of paramilitaristic organizational principles in policing works directly against the development of these relatively new dynamics.

Third, the American public began railing against police "fascism" during the tumultuous era of the 1960s. At that time, we heard a great deal about how the police sometimes operate "like the Gestapo." People did not like the "man-with-no-eyes" sunglasses, the "occupying army" feel (of inner city policing in particular), and the fact that rotating beats had created a situation where people did not know their local police. Part of the call for the new philosophy of COP came as a result of these feelings on the part of the citizenry. Behaving in an aloof, detached, impersonal, paramilitaristic manner somehow made citizens distrust the police even more than they would otherwise.

Fourth, paramilitarism seems to have a fixation with police officer facades. "Haircuts and shoe-shines" are a big part of this. While there is certainly nothing wrong with police officers looking smart out on the street, having sergeants and lieutenants treat officers like children trivializes police work. Telling grown men and women, who are armed and licensed to use force against the public, to "get a haircut" or "shine your shoes" demeans the police endeavor. Focusing upon such trivialities is odd at best and debilitating at worst.

Numerous police organizations have done away with the "personal appearance" parts of their general orders. This change has had no deleterious effects on the police work. Left to their own devices, police officers present a civilized, respectful, and professional appearance to the public without being told to do so. The public is not offended in any way by allowing individual officers to, say, grow a beard if they see fit to do so. In today's America, no one considers that someone with a reasonably well-tailored beard, long sideburns, or an earring looks somehow "unprofessional." Why would they? Unfortunately, paramilitarism's operational norms work against such logical changes toward a more adult way of treating officers.

REVIEW CHART 2.4

THE DRAWBACKS OF PARAMILITARISM

A list of Jefferson's drawbacks of paramilitaristic policing include:
- It creates an "us versus them" feeling among both the police and the citizenry.
- It necessitates making citizens into the enemy in a warlike battle.
- It intimidates people unnecessarily.
- It focuses upon such trivialities as haircuts and shoe-shines.
- It works contrary to several of the principles of COP, especially those of collegial problem solving.

So paramilitarism presents us with still another paradox: while a paramilitary organization has a number of rational reasons for its implementation, it has an equally long list of reasons that one can use to argue against it. In an era when we are asking police officers to operate as problem solvers involved in working for change within their communities, paramilitaristic direction sometimes works against COP.

This first paradox of paramilitarism is accompanied by still another paradox. Even if we accept the arguments against it posed by such analysts as Jefferson, and understand that a lot of police–community antipathy can be created and amplified by its operations, paramilitarism is absolutely necessary under certain unusual circumstances. During riots, hostage situations, sniper-related events, and other circumstances where the police are involved in the degeneration of social norms and/or gun-related, life-threatening events, the police *must* behave like a military organization. When weapons are drawn and gunfire erupts, there must be a chain of command that fixes responsibility (who gave the order to fire, and what they knew when they did so). While paramilitarism might very well be deleterious to the development of good police–community relations on a day-to-day basis (99 percent of the time), it is a necessary part of the organization that the police must "morph into" at a moment's notice when such extraordinary events present themselves. In an era when COP is advancing and, at the same time, gang-related violence and gun possession on the street are on the increase, it is an important paradox for us to consider. For the remainder of our discussion, we will be exploring this problem: how to lead the police into an era where they eschew paramilitarism and, at the same time, are prepared for the genuinely violent confrontation.

Two separate paradoxes present themselves when we consider the ramifications of how paramilitarism impacts the police, the citizenry, and the relationship between the two. These paradoxes present a strange situation for the police manager. On the one hand, modern supervisors must attempt to instill an understanding in their officers that the public generally does not like paramilitarism and that citizens on the street are not the enemy. Young officers, in particular, need to be conscious of these potentially negative dynamics. On the other hand, the police have to be organized so that they can change into a military-type organization "at the drop of a hat" (when lethal or riotous situations present themselves) where chains of command operate to instill discipline, focus responsibility, and limit individual officer decision making.

The police leader is involved in creating and maintaining two organizations at once: a community-oriented system of problem-solving agents of change, and a militaristic system of people who do precisely what they are ordered to do. This presents the supervisor with two sets of problems and the need to develop two leadership styles: the COP style and the paramilitaristic, crisis-oriented style.

Media Imagery

In contemporary America, the media enjoy a rather strange, and sometimes strained, relationship with the police. With regard to the news media, there is an ongoing, symbiotic relationship that affords police news coverage that is generally favorable. Owned and operated by major corporations, and driven (in terms of content control) by advertising dollars that come from other major corporations, the news media, particularly television news, tend to be conservative and pro-police. However, in a paradoxical twist, if scandal surfaces, the media will turn on the police and cover it with an almost maniacal interest, seeking to profit from the scandalous and the unusual. The media can even exaggerate police wrongdoing if it "sells."

One issue that must be engaged by the contemporary police leader is that young officers need to be taught that the media are not the enemy. For some reason—perhaps due to the contemporary urban myth of the "liberal media"—police officers tend to think that the media are generally biased against them, if not overtly out to get them. This is not the case. On a day-to-day basis, the news media in America report exactly what the police say about virtually anything related to crime and the criminal justice system. Stories about criminals, gangs, drugs, and crime trends are printed or reported on the airwaves verbatim from police updates. Police leaders have to take the time to teach and persuade their subordinates to be positive and cooperate with the media. If the police do so, news coverage will continue to be almost universally positive and pro-police. If the police indicate an enmity toward members of the local media, a logical dynamic will develop, and the media *will* become negative.

With regard to the entertainment media, another set of dynamics is operable. Some totally unrealistic ideas are packaged and sold to the American public in movies and on television screens. These unrealistic ideas about police work can convince the average citizen that while the police on television or on the silver screen are competent and even heroic, their local police are the exact opposite—incompetent and ineffective. Since millions of Americans are inundated by the media with unrealistic ideas about how the pretend police solve crime, some people will believe their local real police are somehow unable to live up to "normal" police standards.

Several sets of unrealistic images are sold to the public by the media. First, there is RCMP syndrome. Named after the unofficial motto of the Royal Canadian Mounted Police ("A Mountie always gets his man"), this image drives people to expect the police to solve all crimes, even though actual clearance rates are far below such impossible ideals.

Second, as previously discussed, there is the Dirty Harry problem. Hollywood sells Harry as a hero who must break the law (procedural law) in order to enforce the law (substantive law). The entertainment media cheer this sort of noble cause corruption on a regular basis. In fact, so does the public. When police rough up the local bully, exercising Dirty Harry–type curbside justice, American citizens applaud. Such media-driven and community support for noble cause corruption makes dealing with Harry very difficult for contemporary police leaders.

Third, there is the idea of "cosmetized" violence. Coined by the ex-LAPD sergeant-turned-novelist Joseph Wambaugh, this term refers to making violence appear sexy and cool while transforming police officers into Superman-like heroes. As with RCMP syndrome, cosmetized violence makes local police seem incompetent to citizens who believe the images they see on the screen. In fact, as any experienced police leader knows, police work is often uneventful and even boring; police are often surprised by violence. It is one of the most difficult jobs of the police leader to help subordinates be aware of and alert to violence that *can* happen, without being too paranoid.

Fourth, there is an almost universal problem in America with *Miranda* warnings. The incorrect portrayal of *Miranda* warnings in television and movies shows viewers that arrestees are always Mirandized at the moment of arrest, which is, of course, incorrect. Again, this makes the local police appear to be incompetent. Even worse, it seems ethically inappropriate. Each year in this country, thousands of Americans believe they have seen police misconduct when they witness arrests that are not accompanied by *Miranda* warnings. Average citizens genuinely believe what they have learned on the screen.

REVIEW CHART 2.5

HOLLYWOOD'S UNREALISTIC POLICE IMAGERY

- The RCMP syndrome
- The Dirty Harry problem
- Cosmetized violence
- *Miranda* inaccuracies

The problem with such images is that they set up unrealistic expectations in the minds of the American public, expectations to which the real police cannot hope to accede. Paradoxically, while the media tend to be very pro-police on a regular basis, these types of unrealistic images tend to work against good police–community relations.

IMPACT

It is important to understand that all of these paradoxes come together to influence the attitudes and behavior of police officers, both as individuals and as a group. The job of the police leader is made doubly problematic; he or she must work with officers as individuals in an effort to mollify the multiple frustrations brought on by the job's paradoxes, while at the same time leveraging the positive power of group subculture and avoiding norms that are negative.

Anomie

As individuals, police officers can often suffer from what the great sociologist Emile Durkheim labeled **anomie** (Durkheim, 1997). This was Durkheim's term for the feeling of "normlessness" that many suicidal people suffer. These people feel that there is a disconnect between themselves and society. Their personal views of the world, how things function, and norms/values are out of sync with the feelings of the majority of people. For obvious reasons, the police officer who experiences citizen–police enmity out on the street, and feels the multiple frustrations of the job created by the paradoxes, can suffer from anomie on a regular basis. In fact, one can argue that police officers in general are the group of American professionals most often prone to suffer from anomic feelings and a consequent isolation from the public. Anomie is seen as so central to the police experience that a recent study focuses on how police leaders should effectively deal with it (Hays, Regoli, and Hewitt, 2007).

There are two important points to be made about anomie and police leadership. First, there are so many police officers who suffer from anomic feelings that it is perhaps the single most important reason for the creation of the police subculture. The police leader needs to understand this as a dynamic reality on the street. Second, a leader needs to be vigilant with regard to how lost, alone, and troubled some police officers will become. This is not to say that police officers in general are "in trouble." But it does mean that the competent leader had better be open-minded about the counterproductive dynamics and behaviors that might develop due to anomic feelings on the part of subordinates.

Subcultural Power and Solidarity

Sociologists tell us that a **subculture** is a "culture within a culture." It is comprised of people who, because of their unique work, hobby, or ethnic experiences, develop values that are at odds with those possessed by the society as a whole. A subcultural view of the world is such that members develop a perspective on life and operational norms that are unique and, to some extent, deviant as viewed from the perspectives of the average person and the larger **social order** (Gelder, 2007).

Any occupational group forms a subculture of sorts. But the police are known for having one of the most isolated from the public subcultures. Theirs is a subculture known for its solidarity, which is perfectly understandable. Given the frustrations and paradoxes of the policing experience, which they believe only other police officers understand, the police tend to cling to each other—not only to protect their physical safety, but also for the purpose of obtaining psychological sustenance. Only when surrounded by those who "get it" can the average officer maintain their sense of personal worth and feel safe in their professional world.

The police subculture guarantees, to some extent, that officers will have some interaction in life with those who understand their lot. Citizens, politicians, relatives, and friends seem to be unable to understand not only the paradoxes, but the reality that police work is a frustrating job that requires them to stand up for civility and the law, at their own peril. Working shifts around the clock, having days off in the middle of the week, being underpaid and unappreciated, the police officer may consider that only other officers have any idea of what's going on in their world.

Police officers usually have other officers for friends, go to police parties, take vacations with other police families, and join softball teams and flag football leagues with other police officers. They often go on hunting trips, play golf, or go to other social events with police officers. They isolate themselves in a way that is protective of their individual psyches. All of this is perfectly understandable. In being isolated from society at large and interacting almost exclusively with other officers, they develop norms that are driven by this experience. Some of these norms operate in a way that is counterproductive to the interests of justice and society, in general.

The police tend to believe in an "overkill" principle with the use of force. Because they are always outnumbered and they understand Muir's paradox of face, officers believe that developing a "badass rep" is necessary for their survival. In order to develop and maintain such a reputation, the police are driven by the idea that when physical violence erupts they have to "win and win big." They have to be undefeated when they get into fights with citizens. In the police locker room, this norm presents itself with comments like, "If one of us gets assaulted, the perp should end up in jail. If one of us gets *hurt*, the perp should end up in the hospital." In this way, the subculture rationalizes the excessive use of force, even when nothing truly dangerous or threatening to the safety of any officer has occurred.

Another police subcultural norm deals with investigations into allegations of misconduct. In former years, the "blue code of silence" prevailed, meaning that no police officer would (or should) aid in any investigation into the misconduct of other officers. Today, driven by modern notions of professionalism, this idea is not as powerful and controlling as it used to be. Contemporary police officers will often aid investigations into police corruption that involve selling the badge in exchange

BOX 2.5

Meat Eating and Grass Eating

Those who study police misconduct divide it into the categories of "meat eating" and "grass eating." Meat eaters are officers who look for opportunities to misuse their position and authority for their own personal gain. They actively seek out situations where they can "sell their badges" for money. Grass eaters are those officers who (1) take gratuities occasionally, but do not work at developing such personal rewards and (2) refuse to cooperate with investigations into meat eating. In the modern police subculture, there is less meat eating as time goes on. But grass eating of the second type can be rampant; police officers can refuse to cooperate with investigations into Dirty Harry–like behavior even if they themselves do not condone it directly. This presents the modern manager with a troublesome supervisory dynamic; instilling subcultural norms that operate to inhibit noble cause corruption is next to impossible in some police organizations.

for money (see "Corruption of Authority" in Chapter 8). Officer cooperation into misconduct investigations is no longer unheard of in American police work.

But when investigations enter into the arena of Dirty Harry–like behavior (noble cause corruption), even officers who would never consider becoming involved in such behavior will protect those who are (see Box 2.5). Police officers tend to believe that if some criminal is going to be let out of jail and a police officer is going to go to jail—because he or she lied on the witness stand, for example—they should not participate in helping that happen. Even otherwise honest police officers will resist (and work to thwart) investigations into noble cause corruption.

A subcultural norm that works directly against the development of COP has to do with the idea that "real" police work involves enforcing the law—and enforcing the law only. Officers who are committed to developing an ongoing relationship with members of the public—providing services other than law enforcement to their community such as mentoring teenagers, taking care of the elderly, and acting (as community-based policing demands) as agents of change—can often be labeled "social workers," an epithet among many members of the police subculture.

The paradox here is that, while the development of the police subculture is completely rational and understandable in many ways, it tends to create a set of problems that are bad for police–community relations and operate contrary to the interests of justice on the streets of America. A subculture known for is solidarity makes the job of leading the police arguably more difficult than the job of leading just about any other group of professionals.

REVIEW CHART 2.6

POLICE SUBCULTURAL DYNAMICS

- Solidarity within the group
- Police socializing: parties, vacations, and celebrations
- "Overkill" (support for excessive force)
- "The blue code of silence" (especially a tolerance for grass eating)
- Anti-COP diffidence (in some areas)

As is true with all of the paradoxes of police work, police managers must be constantly on guard with regard to this paradox. They must understand how important the subculture can appear to the individual officer, but be able to motivate officers to avoid too much entanglement with the subculture. While it might appear to be none of their business, police leaders should encourage officers to avoid the propensity to wrap themselves within the confines of the subculture in both their on-duty and off-duty lives.

 SUMMATION

In these and numerous other ways, the experience of being on the streets of America today can work to frustrate the individual officer, who may feel alone and isolated. Police officers tend to feel that only other officers understand their predicament. Replete with paradox, the police officer's experience can work to develop norms that operate directly at odds with what the police are supposed to accomplish.

The police leader must understand these challenging paradoxes and develop methods of supervising police officers that take it all into account. Nothing good can come from attempting to ignore the power of the police subculture and its norms, the frustrations experienced by the individual police officer, and the fact that creativity is required to control, motivate, manage, discipline, and mentor police officers engaged with the extraordinary experience of working a beat.

DISCUSSION QUESTIONS

1. Why is there a Dirty Harry problem in American policing? How does today's thoughtful police leader work against the acceptance of noble cause corruption in the minds of young, inexperienced officers?

2. Discuss the paradox of detachment. What is it, and how does it work? Discuss Muir's example of how people involved in domestic disturbances some-

times detach themselves from valuing their own freedom or even the sanctity of their own homes. Compare Kamikaze pilots, suicide bombers, and 9/11 terrorists.

3. The problems associated with paramilitarism bring some particularly troublesome debates to the world of everyday policing, as well as the field of police studies. This is because so many police officers are wedded to the paramilitaristic view. Why is this so? What are Jefferson's arguments against it? Which arguments are the most forceful, and which seem to be less convincing?

4. Discuss the unrealistic expectations about police officers and policing that Hollywood creates for American citizens. Why are these images important to police recruits? Why are they important to the average person?

5. In the text, we seem to be saying two things at once about the police subculture. On the one hand, we are suggesting that the existence of the police subculture is perfectly, logically understandable. On the other hand, we are saying that too much dependence on the subculture is a bad thing. Discuss this paradox and the dynamics of the subculture that are difficult for the police leader. How might a contemporary leader dissuade young officers from becoming too dependent on other police officers?

 KEY TERMS

Anomie: The feeling of normlessness sensed by people who feel out of sync with society.

Coercive power: Behavior control that involves getting a person to do what you want them to do by using threats to harm.

Community-oriented policing: A philosophy that encourages police officers to work in a cooperative way with all elements of the community (businesses, churches, homeowners' groups, schools, nonprofit organizations) to create a safer city/municipality.

Dirty Harry: Fictional movie character associated with the propensity for some police officers to become involved in noble cause corruption in an effort to "get the job done."

Due process: A legal process established to protect the rights of individual citizens.

Exclusionary rule: Procedural rule of law that holds that evidence obtained illegally is not permissible in a court of law.

Exhortative power: Appealing to another person's sense of logic in order to achieve a desired behavior.

Habeas corpus: The right of any citizen to be brought before a judge or court, in order to ascertain whether or not that person should be released from detention or restraint.

Hostages: Any things of value to a person that might be threatened in an effort to coerce.

Law enforcement: The enforcement of legal codes or legislation by officers appointed to enforce those codes (police officers); upholding the law through enforcement.

Legal technicalities: Procedural laws that enable or restrict the discretion of the court in handing down judgments.

Noble cause corruption: A mindset or subculture that fosters a belief that the end justifies the means regardless of legality or ethics; Dirty Harry–like behavior.

Order maintenance: Keeping order through legitimate and lawful means.

Paradox: A statement or circumstance that seems to conflict with common sense or contradict itself, but that may nevertheless be true.

Paramilitary: Organized in a semi-military pattern.

Penal code: A code of laws written and legislated for the maintenance of order and enforcement.

Police manager: A person of the rank of lieutenant or above in a police department or civilian person within a law enforcement agency designated as a manager (example: director of information management).

Police managerial class: Members of the administration of a police agency designated as police managers; upper level rank individuals.

Reciprocal power: The power of trade or barter.

Social order: A set of linked social norms, structures, institutions, and practices that conserve, maintain, and enforce "normal" ways of relating and behaving.

Stereotyping: Generalizations about people, places, or events.

Subculture: A cultural subgroup differentiated by race, profession, educational status, ethnic background, geographic residence, religion, or other factors that function to unify the group and (often) to isolate it.

EXAMPLE SCENARIOS

Disorderly Conduct?

An officer is issued a call for service from police dispatch that there is a man sitting parked in a vehicle at the parking lot of a neighborhood grocery. The complainant says the man is in a gray pickup truck, with a dog, and has been there for the last 20 minutes. The citizen reports she is concerned the man is "up to no good."

The officer responds, arrives at the scene, and notes a pickup truck with an older gentleman and a small poodle with a cap on its head. The vehicle is parked legally, and there appears to be no legal violation. The officer approaches the vehicle, and the man rolls his window down to talk with the officer. The officer asks what the man is doing in the parking lot. The man responds that he is waiting for his wife, who went into the store while he waited outside with their dog. He asks if he is violating any law. The officer advises the man to wait where he is and that he will return.

The officer goes into the store and returns to the truck after approximately five minutes. He tells the man he talked with the complainant, and she was embarrassed about calling the police, given the circumstance. The officer leaves the scene without incident.

This is an example of an instance where the police are called to check out a situation not known to be an illegal act, but nonetheless a situation that might be a threat to public safety. Not every call for service will involve a criminal act, in spite of how the situation initially appears or sounds.

Police are confronted with ensuring public safety while observing the rights of all citizens. This may require them to investigate situations that are not unlawful, but seem or appear suspicious. Did the officer's behavior and discretion allow this situation to be handled with diplomacy and professionalism?

Party

Police are called to a large party at a church. The complaint is that the partygoers are making a lot of noise. When a police officer arrives, he seeks out the party host to discuss the complaint. The officer notices no legal violations at the time, just a lot of people drinking, socializing, and dancing. The host is located and is intoxicated. He tells the officer that this is a wedding party and the cops have no business being there. The officer advises the host that the neighbors have complained and the party will have to be tempered, or he may be back and possibly have to shut it down. The host becomes more belligerent and tells the officer to get off the property; this is a church and he has no jurisdiction there. The officer, not wishing to create more problems, asks the host to step aside for a minute and asks for his ID. The host is still belligerent, but retrieves his ID and gives it to the officer. The officer runs a warrant check, and dispatch informs him the host has a $100 traffic warrant for his arrest. The host tells the officer to "shove it." The officer calls for backup and leaves the area to await the other officers. Eventually, the host is arrested, and the party is shut down without further incident.

What type of power did the arresting officer use? Could the officer have used another type of power? Discuss the types of paradoxes evident in this scenario.

Car Stop

An officer conducts a car stop on a vehicle he observes weaving from lane to lane late at night. There are four individuals in the vehicle. The officer has no backup, and he calls in the location of his stop, advising dispatch there are four people in the car. Upon stopping the car, he aims his spotlight directly into the back window. The light is bright and shines directly into the rearview mirror of the suspect car.

The officer exits his vehicle and approaches the stopped car very cautiously, with his flashlight in his left hand and his right hand on his pistol butt. There is no clear violation of law other than the slight weaving by the driver.

Can you identify the paradox in this situation? Discuss the possibilities surrounding this incident, including potential legal issues, if any. Is there any stereotyping in operation here?

ADDITIONAL READING

For an overview of the entire field of study of the paradoxes of police work, see Douglas W. Perez's *The Paradoxes of Police Work, 2nd Ed.* (Cengage, 2010). This work engages more than two dozen separate paradoxes associated with everything from the individual police officer's experience to the formation of the police subculture to the administration of police organizations. Tony Jefferson's important work on the subject is appropriately entitled *The Case Against Paramilitary Policing* (Open University Press, 1990).

Regarding coercive power and the paradoxes of coercive power, William K. Muir, Jr.'s *Police: Streetcorner Politicians* (University of Chicago Press, 1977) is the seminal work in the field. One of the most important pieces ever written about the police, this work engages not only the paradoxes, but makes important strides in our understanding of both police professionalism and the leadership roles of the sergeant and the chief of police (we will revisit Muir several times throughout the text).

With regard to the importance of potential violence and the search by police officers for "symbolic assailants," see Jerome Skolnick's *Justice Without Trial, 3rd Ed.* (Macmillan, 1994). Skolnick also investigates (and labels) the police officer's "working personality." Finally, this work is the first in the world of the social sciences to understand and to analyze the significance of the plea bargaining system in American criminal justice.

CHAPTER 3

Cleaving to the Mission

INTRODUCTION

In general, people do not begin journeys without deciding upon a destination. They do not begin to build a structure without a plan or template. They do not begin a painting or a sculpture without a vision. They do not create an institution without a substantive reason for doing so. Thoughtful planning, logical organization, and insightful analysis are at the heart of the creative process, the essence of how intelligent people accomplish difficult, worthy tasks. It is often said that "anything worth doing is worth doing well." Equally, to accomplish anything complicated, it is essential to plan and focus. Logic and planning can make up for a great deal in the way of logistical or fiscal limitations. Planning is a necessary requirement for the achievement of important goals. In other words, you cannot get there if you do not know where "there" is.

In this chapter, we will discuss the importance of focusing on organizational mission in the world of policing. It might seem axiomatic, but all organizations must have distinctive, rational, and realistic goals and, consequently, well-defined functions. For any **complex organization** to be effective or efficient at accomplishing anything, it must first decide on what it is supposed to achieve. Only after focusing on the end goals can a group of individuals collectively create a logical plan of attack for the fruition of those goals. Larger goals make the creation of subgoals possible. In turn, subgoal creation makes the creation of operational principles possible. Finally, such principles drive the creation of dozens of specific and sometimes pedantic rules and regulations. In police work, all of this involves working down from the process of imagining and creating mission statements through that of creating subgoals, and down to the preparation of what are often hundreds of pages of the specifics that are included in **general order manuals**.

This is all simple enough to understand. In fact, the reader might ask why we are wasting our time by stating the obvious. The reason is that for the police organization, as with many **public bureaucracies**, the long-term goals of the enterprise are far from clear. Unlike many corporations, clubs, and fraternal groups, there is great uncertainly about how to prioritize what the police department, social welfare bureau, unemployment insurance office, or school system should attempt to accomplish. Multiple sets of goals (and, consequently, functions) are assigned to such public organizations. Often, there is confusion and conflict between these multiple goals that make the administration of complex organizations an endeavor replete with paradox and frustration. At times, leadership in such bureaucracies is a next-to-impossible task.

The reader might say that while such confusion, conflict, and paradox might exist in other public organizations, the goals and functions of the police are specifically defined. It might indeed *appear* that no such conflict between goals and functions occurs in police work. Those who do not stop to think about it might say, "Well, the goal of the police is to enforce the law. That's why we call it 'law enforcement.' So why is this troublesome at all?" It would be nice for police leaders if this were the case—only one goal/one function to emphasize when hiring, training, disciplining, and managing police systems—but this is not the case. There is no one specific goal for the police, and no one specific function to emphasize. Thus, there is no one simplistic way to define the organizational mission.

Conflict and paradox abound for the police leader, and this is especially problematic where goals and functions are concerned. Conflict and paradox are not part-time, obscure dynamics in police work, but are constantly present, living, breathing realities for both police officers and police leaders. This chapter's focal point will be to zero in on the paradoxes presented to police leaders by the conflicts between goals and functions, and to suggest various ways of dealing with this central paradox of police leadership: that it is not certain what we want police *leaders* to do in the first place, because it is not certain what we want the police *organization* to accomplish.

 ## WHY MISSION STATEMENTS ARE IMPORTANT

There is a moment in the movie *The Color of Money* where the crusty mentor (played by Paul Newman) says to the talented, but unfocused, young pool player (played by Tom Cruise), "You gotta be yourself, kid … but on purpose." Newman's character is suggesting that, to be successful as a man in "a man's world" (or, indeed, as an adult in an adult world), one has to work on the constant project that is the creation of a human being's life. **Being yourself on purpose** is about focusing on that never-ending project (Perez and Moore, 2002). Conscious, intelligent adults know they cannot sit back and just let life flow over them. One must have purpose, direction, and focus to achieve anything worthwhile in life.

If this is true of life in general, then it becomes amplified by participation in certain professions that require committing to much more than just getting up and going to work each day. Some professions involve an ongoing commitment to accomplishing worthwhile goals while at work. And make no mistake about it: the life of a police officer involves consistently accomplishing something worthwhile. It is not just a job. It is not just a way to pay the bills.

It is no exaggeration to say that the endeavor of becoming a police officer involves a "quest" of sorts in life. Given the sacrifices, the psychic costs paid by the individual police officer, and the potential violence and danger involved, entering into police service is not a step to be taken lightly. Those who are interested in or committed to police work must understand the importance of developing a personal work ethic that centers on the pursuit of justice, and a pragmatic and effective working personality. If these things are indeed critical to the individual officer, then they are doubly important for the police leader.

All complex organizations require that the group be focused in order to avoid various pathological missteps (Thompson, 1961). A logically constructed, systemic approach is necessary. An organization must know what it is supposed to be accomplishing if it wants to have an effect and exercise influence in the world. What are the possible consequences of public institutions having no specific focus?

Not only is it possible for a great deal of time and money to be wasted under such circumstances, but a situation can develop where an organization actually works against its own best interests. A lack of focus on the overall mission of the organization can create odd patterns of behavior that are counterproductive. The social welfare system can actually begin to encourage poverty. The employment development department can actually begin to encourage unemployment. The military establishment can actually begin to encourage warfare. The criminal justice system can actually begin to encourage deviance. The police can actually begin to encourage crime and disorder. These are situations that define bureaupathology, outlined in Chapter 1, where a sort of disease overtakes an organization. Employees forget what they are supposed to be accomplishing and where they are going.

As odd as it might sound, the process of developing a specific understanding of what an organization is supposed to be doing can be difficult. Several decades ago, people began to embrace the idea of the organizational **mission statement** as a simplistic method for engineering systemic focus (Schnaubelt, 2007). For clubs, fraternities, private companies, and corporations, a mission statement is often easy to produce and might be summed up quickly and succinctly. For, say, the NCAA (National Collegiate Athletic Association) or a fraternal organization, such as the Lion's Club or the Elks Club, it might be simple to do such mission definition. The mission of a rugby team or a swimming club might be so obvious that specific definition is not necessary. In the business world, a corporate mission can be defined with a simple declaration: "Our mission here at General Motors Corporation is to make automobiles and to maximize profits while doing so." But for bureaucracies that provide services to citizens, it is not always easy to agree on the systemic mission (Goodsell, 2003).

Mission Confusion

Public bureaucracies are the types of organizations that are most prone to develop **mission confusion**. They are large and unwieldy. They are created and driven by politician-generated public policy decisions. At times, they have such vaguely defined charters that they may lose sight of the obvious. Because they are public institutions, they can lose and regain their budgets and charters regularly, depending on the political winds of change. The public can change its mind rapidly with regard to what tax expenditures it supports. When any organization has trouble defining its mission, it is guaranteed to create difficulty in administering its operations. Mission confusion within a public organization can generate chaos for top policymakers, middle management, those who deal directly with the public, and, by extension, for the public itself. In police work, not only can citizens and individual police officers be troubled by goal confusion, but police leaders can find themselves at sea in their efforts to instill direction in their charges.

During the **Great Depression**, a number of public bureaucracies were created to help millions of Americans deal with job loss and the inability to take care of their families. Among them were **unemployment insurance** organizations,

BOX 3.1

POLICE FUNCTIONAL CONFUSION

On the night that Barack Obama was elected president in 2008, hundreds of spontaneous demonstrations erupted across the nation. On college campuses in particular, there were impromptu parades that included thousands of students. They meandered their way across campuses and into adjacent towns. From the perspective of some people, these parades were loud and obnoxious events. Remember that this was a Tuesday night, a work night and a school night when most people want to go to sleep and stay asleep.

What should the police have done? Such noise and raucousness is disturbing the peace, plain and simple. The party was certainly not appreciated by thousands of citizens. But to enforce the law under such circumstances would have been next to impossible and might have created more disorder. Almost everywhere nationwide, the police decided to escort the parades, blocked off intersections to make walking revelers safer, and generally ignored the dictates of the law in favor of a pragmatic approach that emphasized common sense. Thus, the police eschewed being involved in law enforcement and became indirectly involved in disturbing the peace and quiet of hundreds of neighborhoods.

created on a state-by-state basis across the nation. The original idea was simple: employers that put people out of work would be taxed. The taxes would be paid into a fund used to help support laid-off workers—for brief periods of time—while they were out of work. It was all about short-term support and extending such support to people who were actively involved in looking for work.

New to America at that time, the unemployment insurance department's mission statement might have read: "To provide limited support on a temporary basis for people who are out of work, while they find a new job." This is a simple, straightforward statement, limited enough to help people within the bureaucracy focus their work efforts and accomplish their tasks. In other words, the mission statement might have helped convey the essence of their mission to members of the unemployment bureaucracy. It could be expected to generate reasonable sub-organizational goals for different departments. In addition, such a statement could help generate specific, minute-by-minute rules for everything in the organization, down to how the lines at unemployment offices should be manned.

Over time, things changed in America. Today's economic collapse has created a new problem for unemployment bureaucracies. Entire industries, manufacturing in particular, have been closed down. People are being laid off from jobs at American factories that will never operate again. Their jobs are being permanently outsourced to workers in other countries. These workers are losing the ability to utilize workplace skills developed over a lifetime. By the millions, they are being left without a job or a marketable skill. As these changes have come into play, the job of unemployment insurance departments has expanded. To begin with, the limit of 26 weeks' worth of payments that used to rule the world of unemployment benefits has been extended several times. Unemployment benefits have ceased to be a stopgap, short-term solution.

Other changes have ensued. Looking past the immediate crisis, the focus of American unemployment bureaucracies has changed. Their work now involves helping people obtain new training in new fields, and developing long-term, life-reorganizing strategies. Unemployment for millions of Americans is no longer a problem of limited duration, but a way of life. The bureaucracy once created to deal with unemployment over very limited periods of time is now an entirely different type of organization, with multiple goals and problems.

Thus, in today's America, the mission of unemployment bureaucracies is no longer straightforward or something that can be easily defined in one sentence. Unemployment insurance departments do still give people support for limited time frames. But now they also provide support for extended periods of time, so workers can relocate and find new positions. They are involved in helping people plan long-term strategies for obtaining new careers in fields that still provide jobs to American workers. They are involved in retraining, re-education, and a host of other endeavors aimed at reorganizing the American workforce. On a state-by-state basis, today's unemployment bureaucracies have decided, in some places, to morph into very different entities.

Today, there are several vaguely defined missions for unemployment bureaucracies to perform. Such multiple missions can be confusing for complex organizations. To make matters worse, sometimes these missions conflict with each other, and that confusion can make the operation of unemployment organizations frustrating and difficult to direct. Here is just one example of how the overall mission can twist lower level, day-to-day rules and regulations in a way that is challenging for the bureaucratic leader. The rules of unemployment insurance used to make a person ineligible for benefits if they were attending college or a trade school. This was because they would not be available to obtain full-time work, and should not be able to obtain benefits for being out of work, so the logic went.

But today, when going back to school is a necessity for millions of workers, what should the rule be? School still might make a person unavailable for full-time work, of course. The bureaucracy still doesn't want people to use school as an excuse to avoid working and "milk the system." But if a person is genuinely learning a new skill, wouldn't the system want him or her to continue with their education? Which is it to be? Should people who are in school obtain unemployment insurance or not? How should the overall mission of the organization steer such decisions?

It becomes even more difficult to agree on rules, goals, and priorities when faced with budget cuts in today's downward spiraling American economic sphere.

REVIEW CHART 3.1

SOME BUREAUCRACIES THAT HAVE MULTIPLE GOALS AND FUNCTIONS

Public schools

Conservation departments

Crisis intervention centers

Emergency management organizations

Battered women's shelters

Housing authorities

Parks and recreation departments

Human resource departments

Animal control departments

Juvenile courts

Alcohol and drug rehab centers

Probation departments

Health service providers

Public works departments

Water quality boards

Labor relations boards

Unemployment benefits have been extended for longer than their normal time frame of availability, and this has to be done by Congress. Millions of individuals (and hundreds of bureaucracies) have to wait, plan, and adapt to congressional action. As a result, unemployment insurance is now burdened with paradoxes, frustrations, and inconsistencies. Such difficulties in recent years have presented complex organizations with one of the central rationalizations for the development of the mission statement movement.

These problems are not limited to the field of unemployment insurance. Disability insurance bureaucracies, workmen's compensation departments, social welfare organizations, and a host of other public bureaucracies all suffer from the problem of specifically defining what they are supposed to do. The police belong on this list of public agencies and organizations with mission confusion, as well. They can also be frustrated by trying to define the mission—or missions.

Multiple, Conflicting, and Vague Goals

The reality that public organizations can lack a specific focus is commonplace in the world of bureaucracy, so much so that Aaron Wildavsky, a well-known political scientist and organization theorist from the University of California at Berkeley, coined a phrase to illustrate the problem for students of public administration. Wildavsky wrote that public bureaucracies suffer from goals that are **"multiple, conflicting, and vague"** (Wildavsky, 1987). This idea was the focal point for much of his writing and teaching, important not only to students, but also for practitioners in the field of public organizational administration. This work pointed out perhaps *the* most important paradox in the field.

Millions of people operate under the assumption that their governments understand what it is they are supposed to accomplish. To the average person, all public bureaucracies have specifically defined goals and functions. However, Wildavsky's central paradox proposed that this was almost never the case in reality. In any given bureaucracy, dozens (sometimes hundreds) of employees can hold completely different sets of priorities that can operate in ways that countermine and thwart each other.

Wildavsky took his original idea from the late 1960s and applied it to numerous public bureaucracies. He and his followers studied and wrote about an ever-expanding number of complex organizations over the next several decades. Bureaucracies of all shapes and sizes, at the local, state, and federal level, were subjected to analysis with regard to their confusion about goals and functions. This idea became an important part of organization theory, with inclusion in all textbooks as a general theoretical principle; particularized studies made it into the professional journals of the world. Finally, Wildavsky's idea has worked its way into the standard mode of analysis applied to all sorts of projects and systems at all levels for

BOX 3.2

THE DEBATE ABOUT AFGHANISTAN

The military history of the United States in the past several decades includes several interventions that began with one focus, and lasted long enough to develop a substantial national debate over whether the focus had become outdated. Discussions about the focal point of the war in Vietnam, in particular, were about the goals of that military intercession. As we have discussed, this can happen in any field of endeavor. But when it occurs with regard to military objectives, debate can be aggressive, divisive, and even violent. After many years of commitment, a national argument (first a discussion, then a debate, then a virulent argument) over America's goals in Vietnam politicized the war.

When the recent wars in Iraq and Afghanistan came about, early discussion focused on whether there was an appropriate **exit strategy**. The idea that a military intervention required an exit strategy in the first place came from the Vietnam experience, and from Wildavsky's idea. By the time the war in Afghanistan was six years old, a nationwide discussion about America's goals in Afghanistan ensued. This debate was about political realities, budgetary constraints, logistical troubles, and military strategies. But at its core it was about how an endeavor as important and costly as war should not be continued without specific, focused, agreed-upon goals.

more than two generations now. The multiple, conflicting, and vague paradox has become mainstream in the world of organization theory (Perez, 2010).

Wildavsky's idea expanded into the realm of corporate organizations—the private sector. What had been a public policy concern became a focus for those who studied large, complex businesses. People from different backgrounds analyzed large private corporations in exactly the same way as Wildavsky had analyzed public bureaucracies. **Chief executive officers** (CEOs) from General Motors, Coca-Cola, IBM, and others discussed the need to focus the efforts of everyone in their systems, top to bottom, on specifically defined missions. In doing so, the idea that significant amounts of time can and should be spent on defining the organization's mission was brought into vogue in American business, as well as in the world of public administration. By the 1970s and into the early 1980s, the mission statement had become the concern of everyone who operated within a large organization, no matter what form or function it took.

THE MISSION STATEMENT MOVEMENT

Beginning in the late 1970s, the movement to create mission statements for large organizations started in earnest. Several buzz phrases, including **values, vision, and purpose**, were passed around the corporate world and were considered of critical importance for inclusion in mission statements (Schnaubelt, 2007). Everyone—and we do mean *everyone*—in the world of complex organizations decided they needed mission statements. The corporate world is no different than any other; it can often be driven by fads that catch on like wildfire. Particularly in the competitive world of business, if some organization is obtaining an edge, others will follow its lead. The movement to create mission statements only had to be around for a short period of time before it became the latest thing in the business world, as well as in the bureaucratic world. It was in vogue and quickly became "all the rage" in America.

Going back about a century, in the era of massive industrialization in America, every attempt was made to make large organizations operate in logical and rational ways. The school of what was then entitled **scientific management** (briefly cited in Chapter 1) was born. Under the guidance of Frederick Taylor, an efficiency expert, scientific management quickly made its way into the halls of academia (Taylor, 1911). By the early 20th century, political science departments at colleges and universities began to include the subfield of public administration. Among other things, this field involves the study of organization theory as applied to public governmental bureaucracies. Today, entire schools within universities focus on this area of study. Very often, Taylor's work is the first substantive topic of study in the field, and the first thing a student of public policy is required to read. Wildavsky is engaged later on as a central element of what is gospel in organization theory.

While Wildavsky's publications and real-world teaching predated the movement by some years, this idea of multiple, conflicting, and vague problems with organizational focus eventuated in the creation of today's contemporary focus on the mission statement. For several decades now, the idea of the mission statement has become the modern day equivalent of Taylor's early call for making public organizational dynamics more logical and rational. Today, the overwhelming majority of public and private organizations all over the world have mission statements, easily obtainable on websites.

Missing the Point

For as much as the invention of the mission statement movement was logical and done with the best of intentions, all was not well. One problem with the movement was (and still is) that it could often waste substantial amounts of organizational time. Putting mission statements together involves spending time away from the day-to-day operations of the organization in order to focus on the overall. This is, metaphorically, a moment for focusing on the forest and not the trees. The trick with mission statements is for them to be generalized enough to make sense to everyone in an organization and focused enough that they do not end up being rambling, amorphous, or imprecise. The paradox here is, while the process of mission statement creation is something that has come to be an expected part of rational, effective, professional modern management, the mission statement process can backfire. Mission statements can be created in ways that make them inappropriate and useless.

Mission statements can work in exactly the wrong way, in the wrong direction, than they are supposed to work. They can end up being vague instead of focused, and so generalized that they are almost meaningless. The example in Box 3.3 is just such an example. This mission statement from the world of advertising is not useful to workers within the organization or to people outside of it. Furthermore, it discusses the field of advertising in general, and only relates to the specific organization involved at the end. It obfuscates rather than focuses. It confuses rather than educates.

BOX 3.3

A BAD MISSION STATEMENT

Here is the mission statement of an advertising agency, often cited as one of the worst examples of such statements:

Good advertising dramatizes the relevant user benefits of products and services in a novel way—rational in its information, emotional in its presentation. Good advertising distinguishes itself from the others in that it is better than they are. Good advertising is something you can expect from us—remarkably good (Chandiramani, 2009).

The misuse of the mission statement process can be problematic, not only in terms of what the statement entails in a substantive sense, but due to the process that is utilized in obtaining such a statement. If mission statements come from above and flow down the chain of command exclusively, they can easily be ignored by workers and subordinates. In police work in particular, where so much in the way of discretionary power rests in the hands of the individual worker, mission statements that are creations of those "on high" can be useless to the extreme. In an arena where traditional command-and-control styles of organization are changing into something new under the auspices of COP, mission statements miss the point entirely if they are merely constructed by upper level ranks and passed down the chain of command.

What Mission Statements Should Accomplish

An example of an excellent, police-specific mission statement is included in Box 3.4. The statement, from the Oakland (California) Police Department, is short in length, doesn't ramble, or become an elongated essay—a problem from which many mission statements suffer. It is focused in a way that is noncontroversial and mentions ethics up front as a critical element to what the OPD considers its priorities. Finally, it is understandable by everyone inside and outside the department, and is appropriately focused in a way that does not appear to make it the property of the police themselves, but of all the people of the city.

Mission statements tend to include declarations of values and principles, assertions of systemic visions, and pronouncements about organizational purpose. Some organizations use their mission statements as a publicity tool; others have internal use only mission statements that serve as a compass for leadership decisions, while still others publish their mission statements in annual reports meant to be read by investors and potential clients (Schnaubelt, 2007). There is no one overall purpose for mission statements.

BOX 3.4

EXAMPLE OF A GOOD MISSION STATEMENT

Here is the mission statement of the Oakland Police Department. It is an excellent one, being terse, focused, and understandable:

The mission of the Oakland Police Department is to provide competent, effective, public-safety services to all persons with the highest regard for human dignity through efficient, professional, and ethical law enforcement and crime prevention practices.

REVIEW CHART 3.2

THE ELEMENTS OF MISSION STATEMENTS

- *Purpose:* Sets the organization's current boundaries—what it does, who it is done for, and how and why it is done
- *Values:* Reflects the organization's core values; provides guidelines for choosing among competing priorities and resources
- *Vision:* Describes an ideal future; conveys organizational purpose in the largest sense—what impact does the organization want to have on society?

As mission statements take multiple forms and provide diverse utilitarian value, an interesting development has come to the movement in contemporary times. Today, young professionals are encouraged to create their own *personal* mission statements (Jones, 1998). As a part of the modern process of creating a résumé, today's professionals are supposed to have a mission statement that is framed around their own education, experiences, and expertise. The mission statement movement continues to expand and develop into additional areas of today's organizational world.

THE FUNCTIONS OF THE POLICE

As previously stated, the functions of the police are multiple, conflicting, and vague; it is not always clear what we are asking our officers to do out on the street. It has been several generations since those who study the police gathered the many different functions and split them into three main categories: **law enforcement**, **order maintenance**, and **service** (J. Q. Wilson, 1968). Each category is an equally important and defensible focal point for the police. They are multiple, to be sure, as there are three of them. They are vague—what exactly is a police officer doing when he or she makes an arrest for **disorderly conduct**? Is this strictly law enforcement? Does it involve being of service to the community, is it a matter of maintaining the social order, or is it all of the above? How about when the police check out a bar (a public assembly check, or PAC)? Is that law enforcement, order maintenance, or service? Which function is involved when giving teenagers a lecture about behaving themselves, handling a family disturbance, or getting homeless people to move out of a business area?

This can be an interesting discussion at the academic level, but it is not the multiplicity or vagueness of the police functions that cause paradoxical frustration. What's troublesome for police officers and leaders is that these three sets of functions can, and often do, conflict with each other. This conflict can present a daily, ongoing problem for the police. Conflicting goals and functions confront the police on a moment-by-moment basis on the street. Working out that conflict presents one of the most profound sets of paradoxes for all police, from the individual officer working on the street to the immediate supervisor (the sergeant), and all the way up to the chief of police or the sheriff. The conflict can come at the police from two different directions, as discussed in the following sections.

Enforcing the Law Can Create Disorder

The conflict between order maintenance and law enforcement cuts against efficient police operations in two distinctive ways. First, when the police enforce the law, they can create disorder. For example, making an arrest at a large party can create animosity and a larger problem than existed before, motivating a crowd to confront the police under such circumstances. Similarly, making a marijuana bust at a concert can create the same sort of animosity, and turn a previously docile gathering into an angry mob. Arrests made at domestic disturbances, in bars, when dealing with groups of teenagers, and so forth can all create disorder. In these and a hundred other ways, the pursuit of one police goal directly inhibits the accomplishment of another; the pursuit of one function frustrates the pursuit of another.

Being faced with conflict between law enforcement and order maintenance presents an ongoing problem for police officers, who often struggle with how far to push the letter of the law. In cities and college towns in particular, where the police are regularly confronted with large numbers of underage drinkers, marijuana smokers, and crowds, officers must consistently determine where to draw the line between what sort of drunkenness, rowdy behavior, and aggression is a threat to the social order and what is not. By using their own understanding of justice and sense of the limits of their abilities ("We can't arrest *everyone* who is drinking underage—we don't have enough time or jail cells for that"), the police limit the application of the law as it is written. Officers understand that they can go too far in applying the law and create problems for themselves and the community that are worse than those problems that already exist.

REVIEW CHART 3.3

THE GOALS AND FUNCTIONS OF THE POLICE

- *Law enforcement:* Acting as official representatives of the state and focusing on crime, the police apply laws and ordinances.
- *Order maintenance:* Acting as monitors or referees, and focusing on civility and tranquility, the police maintain community peace and quiet.
- *Service:* Acting as public servants, and emphasizing utility to the community, the police help, aid, and accommodate the citizenry.

For police leadership, this is an ongoing and important paradox. Leaders interact as role models, coaches, and mentors with young, impressionable officers on a regular basis, and need to embrace this paradox and discuss it proactively with their officers. Whenever possible, the realities of the law enforcement/order maintenance conflict should be discussed. It is the police leader's job to anticipate local problems that might present conflict on a regular basis. When an unanticipated conflict presents itself, police leaders should make the time to confront the experience and (to some extent) debrief the officers involved after specific details involving the law enforcement/order maintenance problem have been handled. Such discussions should focus on how things were handled, what was done well, and, finally, what might have been done differently. This might sound simplistic, but such a moment presents the police leader with the perfect opportunity to use the "sandwich technique" of coaching—critical comments sandwiched between two positive reflections (more about this in Chapter 6).

Such debriefings are often conducted out on the street, when sergeants meet with officers during their shifts. Quietly, over a cup of coffee or in squad cars, such

BOX 3.5

AN EXAMPLE OF CREATING DISORDER

This is a true story. A few years ago, at a huge concert held by the Grateful Dead rock group, a rookie police officer observed several individuals smoking pot in the midst of a crowd in excess of 60,000 people. The smokers were right in the front of the crowd, only a little way back from the stage. The rookie waded into the crowd in an effort to make an arrest. A small melee ensued that undoubtedly could have degenerated into a large, riotous situation. This is perhaps the most perfectly created example of how enforcing the law to the letter can actually create disorder. That is, in attempting to achieve one goal of the police (law enforcement), it can sometimes impact negatively on another goal (order maintenance). Furthermore, the Grateful Dead followers (known as "Deadheads") were a largely middle-aged, mature group—not the sort of crowd that one associates with rowdiness and disturbances. This action on the part of the young officer probably also negatively impacted the image of the police as being of service (a third goal) to their communities.

The rookie was guilty of gross misjudgment, of course. But was he guilty of misconduct in attempting such an arrest? No, he was not. No fairly operated police review system could find him guilty of misconduct, because smoking marijuana is illegal. The law is not "It is illegal unless it's done at a large concert."

communication and teaching can be as productive as any amount of formal training the young officer might receive. This sort of casual teaching opportunity often presents the good leader with an important moment where he or she can make the type of incremental difference in the life of a rookie officer that ends up being of critical importance.

The Limits of the Law

Enforcing the law can create disorder, but that is only one half of the equation presented by the conflicts between police goals and functions. Sometimes the police understand they need to take action, but the law—*as it is written literally*—does not provide the tools necessary to do so. This problem was first illustrated by criminologist Carl Klockars, who put together an axiom about police work. **Klockars's axiom** suggests a central, frustrating reality for police officers: "Situations which ought not to be happening . . . about which something ought to be done" (Klockars, 1985). Klockars was pointing out that some types of citizen misconduct "about which something ought to be done" are not illegal. The husband who is drunk in his own living room and destroying community property in his rage; the group of young toughs who are hanging around a convenience store, not drunk, not stealing anything (yet), but who are frightening the elderly night shift worker; the two crowds of gang members who are slowly gathering together in a parking lot in anticipation of a fight—these are only a few examples of situations that confront the police regularly, for which there is no legal action to be taken. No law has yet to be broken in these examples, but they all confront the police with situations that demand action. The type of action often taken is referred to as "semi-legal," "non-legal," and "quasi-legal" action by some students of the police. Again, this action is necessary because enforcing the letter of the law does not give the police the power to solve such situations.

So, we are confronted with a critical set of paradoxes. First, enforcing the law to the letter can create disorder. Second, maintaining order can require non-legal action. In this way, the conflict between law enforcement and order maintenance creates grand scheme questions for the police: What is it that we are doing out there? What do we prioritize? How do we choose between law enforcement

REVIEW CHART 3.4

KLOCKARS'S AXIOM

The police must attend to. . .
- Situations that ought not to be happening. . .
- about which something ought to be done. . .
- now!

and order maintenance, when each are equally defensible, rational functions of the police? This can present a profound problem for the police leader: how do they lead, motivate, and control a group of powerful individuals when it is not clear what we are asking them to do as their first priority?

CREATING MISSION STATEMENTS

Having discussed the reasons for the development of the mission statement movement and the utility of such statements in the organizational world, it is time to move toward a consideration of how such statements are created, how they *should* be created, and the substance they should include when created by and for the police (O'Halloran and O'Halloran, 2000).

The Process

Initially, when mission statements were new on the scene, they were usually created by administrative elites. Gathered together to evaluate the goals and values of the organization, administrators developed mission statements the same way they developed all internal organizational policy. It was only a short time before the endeavor of mission statement creation took a logical turn in the direction of getting away from the job site and the operations of the organization.

This development made perfectly good sense. After all, to create a statement about the long-term goals, values, and vision of an organization, it is necessary to put the minute-by-minute, pragmatic problems of daily operations to the side. Whoever is going to create a mission statement needs to push back from the mundane and focus on the overall or synoptic view of the organization. It is sometimes possible to accomplish this in the workplace, but as a rule it is not. Therefore, the idea was born of getting away from the daily workplace to make time for a retreat for mission statement creation. Moving the process away from the physical location of the organization's operation became so popular that consultants soon flooded organizations with competing offers to run retreats for the express purpose of mission creation.

But there was more to it than the idea of physically leaving the office. It was not long before people realized that if mission statements were to obtain all of their potential benefits, their creation should probably be accomplished in a more democratic way. Making acceptance of the statement universal throughout a company requires a buy-in on the part of everyone, from those at the bottom to those at the top. It makes good sense to have every level of an organizational hierarchy represented in such a creative endeavor. In addition, the types of retreats created for the purpose of mission statement production began to be enhanced by exercises aimed at the team-building metaphor, including having employees get together to solve physical problems, such as rope courses. It was here that the sometimes cynical nature of police officers began to work contrary to the intent of the endeavor.

Police officers tend to look at such artificially created experiences as a waste of time. This jadedness is something all of us in police work understand.

For small organizations, the logistics of mission statement creation do not present a major problem. As long as they are not organizations that must operate 24 hours a day, 7 days a week, it is possible to get everyone in one place for an extended period of time and have them collectively participate. To do this, it is necessary to shut down the office for a day. For larger organizations, representatives of different organizational levels (upper management, middle management, marketing, shipping and receiving, public relations, manufacturing, etc.) can come together for mission statement creation. Of course, how to choose who is "representative" of different organizational levels can become a controversial element of the mission statement process.

For all police organizations, mission statement creation attempted in such a democratic way—in the team-building mode—can be problematic, due to the simple logistics that require some officers to be on duty at all times. There is no doubt that getting buy-in from everyone is of critical importance, due to the powerful police subculture. Attempting to accomplish this can create a logistical nightmare. Even in the COP era, where the concept of policing as a team is in vogue, it can be difficult to get all levels of the team together.

COP comes into the discussion for two reasons. First, the emphasis of COP on lower level expertise and participation in organizational decision making plugs right into the need for mission statement creation to be done democratically. This policing philosophy demands that such participation come from all levels within the police bureaucracy. Second, the philosophy of COP encourages civilian participation in police policy development. COP includes, as one of its tenets, the idea that an ongoing citizen–police partnership should be developed in any given community. This partnership is supposed to infuse police decision making with citizen input because the police represent the citizenry; in a very real sense, the police work *for* the citizens. Neighborhood organizations, police policy boards, civilian review boards, and neighborhood watch groups are examples of how civilian input is supposed to be utilized in today's world of COP. Certainly, the mission statement creation process should involve citizen input as a critical element for its legitimacy.

Taking all of this into account, the creation of a contemporary police mission statement can be complicated. Civilian leaders, police leaders, interested individual citizens, and members of the police rank and file all need to be invited to attend whatever sort of forum is created for the process. Such invitations cannot be pro forma. They must be sincere, and those who participate must be genuinely welcomed into the process. Avenues must be made available for everyone to vent their ideas and participate openly. Small groups can be utilized to encourage input from citizens or police officers who might be reticent in a larger setting. Often, this process involves dividing into groups of 10 or 12 that include line officers, police leaders, civic leaders, and interested citizens. Of course, the number of interested citizens can sometimes overwhelm the number of other participants, but this must be allowed and encouraged, at least in the formative stages of mission statement development. Once small groups discuss their ideas, they come together into larger settings where ideas are reported and shared. Final mission statement configuration can be delegated to a small group, which reports to the whole later on, or can involve everyone. Of course, this can only occur if the number of people who stick with the process is a small enough number, about 30 to 50, to make it logistically possible.

The creation of such a group for merely the purposes of creating a mission statement is not logical or cost-effective, in terms of the time taken to work on such a project by everyone involved. But mission statement creation in contemporary America is often accomplished as part of the larger project of instituting COP. The development of COP, a partnership-oriented operational philosophy that often involves meetings between police officers, police leaders, citizens, and civic leaders, can delve into police policy with regard to recruitment, hiring, training, beat assignments, accountability, and administration. Thus, only a small part of the institutionalization of COP into any given police organization involves the collective creation of a mission statement.

There are, of course, numerous problems associated with such mission statement creation. First, there is the logistical problem involved in creating an atmosphere and physical space where everyone who should be included in the process can attend and participate openly and freely. Sometimes too many citizens respond to an open invitation to participate in local police policy development. Second, there is the opposite problem of so little citizen response that the civilian perspective is not represented in a realistic way. Civic leaders can overwhelm the more democratic representation of civilian perspectives that, once again, subverts the process.

Third, a scenario can develop where only civilian "rabble-rousers" and "troublemakers" attend such an event. This can not only skew information obtained, but it can cast a shadow over the process itself and call results into question. Open-mike public forums or town hall meetings can sometimes be captured by the loudest and most upset members of any community.

There is also the police officer side of the equation. Police officers can be a jaded group of individuals, and their perspective on mission statement development can be negative. If such a focal point is developed without rank-and-file approval, it can make the endeavor a waste of time. On the other hand, even if they are included in the definitional process, police officers can become cynical about mission statements over time (as can citizens), if—as is illustrated in Box 3.6—the process is repeated over and over. In time, no amount of sugar-coating can gloss over the loss of respect for the process and the statement itself if mission statement creation becomes an ongoing endeavor.

Thus, another paradox surfaces here. Sometimes, neither citizens nor police officers "stick with" the COP installation process as a whole or mutually created mission statements. When this occurs, mission statements can work in a counterproductive direction, becoming burdens to the organization, in lieu of facilitating positive relationships.

BOX 3.6

REINVENTING THE WHEEL

Mission statement creation can be time-consuming. Often, organizations take time off from their production schedules or workday endeavors to produce them, and it can be important for the entire organization to get together as a team to do so. But in some organizations, this process of mission statement creation has become a several-times-per-year event. When that occurs, the mission statement can become a joke within the organization, working against the very idea of making things more logical and focused. In writing and rewriting mission statements, some complex organizations end up sending out the message to members that focusing their endeavors is impossible to accomplish. This is, of course, exactly the wrong idea to formulate and advertise.

What Is Justice?

Before discussing what specifics should be included in police mission statements, we will focus on a crucial element of the police function. Whether or not it is specifically mentioned in a police mission statement, justice is a critical concept—not only for the community as a whole, but for the police in particular. It is, after all, called the criminal justice system. Even if that particular word is left out of a mission statement, the concept of justice underwrites, or should underwrite, everything the police do—everything done by individual officers, immediate supervisors, and leaders at any level, including the chief of police or sheriff.

Sometimes, even in the world of police work, people tend to tiptoe around the concept of justice. It behooves us here to discuss, definitively, what that is. If the efforts of the police and the criminal justice system are to be effectively focused and morally defensible, they must be driven by a concern for this sometimes amorphous concept. Police discretionary decision making *must* be directed and controlled by the ideal of justice in both the short and long terms. Furthermore, at several points in our discussion, this conceptualization of the meaning of justice will be apposite, especially with police ethics. Understanding classic philosophical definitions will be of substantial significance.

So, what *is* justice? If the system within which the police operate is indeed the criminal justice system, what is this system supposed to accomplish? What are its major tasks? For thousands of years, philosophers have debated what the essence of justice should be. For the purpose of our discussion, we will engage just two classic definitions of justice, with an eye toward developing an understanding of how the police must wrestle with still another paradox in their work. While people assume that the police have one definitive understanding of what justice means, there are two very different and competing ways of looking at it—and of prioritizing what the criminal justice system is supposed to accomplish (Perez and Moore, 2002).

One of the central principles of western liberalism, and one of the most important principles of American institutions, is that of equal treatment. In several places, our Constitution preserves for all citizens the right to **equal protection of the law**. Even the most casual student of American institutions is familiar with the clause's inclusion in the Fourteenth Amendment. This is a principle that guides much of American political and legal life. In fact, so central is equality to our thinking as Americans, it is credited around the world as being one of the basic American principles. It is no surprise, then, that one definition of justice often popular with Americans is **justice is equity**, or equal treatment (Pollock, 2008). To be equitable is to treat all people and situations alike, and be evenhanded when doing so.

One of the answers to the ancient problem of the unchecked, unlimited power of kings and lawgivers was the idea of the written rule. In lieu of a world where Khadi justice (absolute discretion exercised by the lawgiver) reigned supreme, the world of modern liberalism, ushered in during the Enlightenment, was driven by the concept of power being exercised equitably (Perez, 2010). No matter what a person's race, color, creed, ethnic identity, sexual orientation, or gender, our post-Enlightenment society is ruled by the idea that everyone has a natural "God-given" right to be treated equally. The reason for having rules in the first place is this modern desire for equity. Therefore, a perfectly understandable, acceptable, and morally defensible definition of justice is equity. Those who have been treated justly have been treated equally.

There are other definitions of justice that are just as powerful as equity. One such definition says that **justice is fairness** (Pollock, 2008). This is a common

BOX 3.7

DEFINITION OF KHADI JUSTICE

In the Muslim world, the Khadi was an ancient lawgiver. Both criminal and civil cases were brought to the Khadi for resolution. The Khadi had absolute power (and, thus, absolute discretion) to decide cases without accountability to any appeals process or any set of written rules. He had only to answer to his own conscience and whatever religious, political, or ethical concerns he considered to be fair. Thus, Khadi justice involved absolute discretion with no written rules. Furthermore, for the purpose of our discussion here, Khadi justice involved this lawgiver behaving in what he believed in his own heart and mind to be a fair way.

thread, drawn through many philosophical discourses and political treatises. To be fair is to be objective, honest, and unbiased, but it means something more as well. Fairness involves taking into account, without personal prejudice, all sides of a given situation before attempting any action or developing any potential solution. Fairness is the key concept in what is called **distributive justice**, which seeks to answer the question, "What is due to each person?"(Fleishacker, 2005). The difference between fairness and distributive justice may seem slight, but each can lead to very different outcomes when those who administer justice apply one or the other definition.

Suppose the police are confronted by three different shoplifters, all of them guilty of the same crime: pocketing CDs at a music store during Christmas week. One is a professional thief who sells such CDs for money at flea markets. The second is a sorority girl who shoplifts "for the fun of it." The third is a poor, unemployed, single mother who is shoplifting presents for her children at Christmas. If we were to consider our definition of justice to be equity, then the appropriate way for a police officer to handle these cases would be to treat each of the shoplifters in the very same way. Either they should all be taken to jail, they should all be cited, or they should all be let go with a warning. If justice is equity (and, again, that is a perfectly defensible principle), it would be unjust to treat the professional shoplifter, the spoiled sorority girl, and the single, unemployed mother in different ways.

On the other hand, if we were to define justice as fairness, then an analysis of the situation might end up with the attending police officer doing different things with these three different people. The professional thief might be taken to jail, with no questions asked. The sorority girl might be given the chance to reflect for a moment and come up with some sort of deferential and apologetic attitude. Then she might be cited and released. The single mother might find that the attending police officer intervenes on her behalf and convinces the store owner to drop the charges. If justice is fairness, then all of these actions are just; they are logically and ethically defensible. The fact that three thieves were treated in an *inequitable* manner does not matter because they were all treated *fairly*.

REVIEW CHART 3.5

TWO DEFINITIONS OF JUSTICE

- *Equality:* Justice requires equal treatment; people are considered to be precisely equal and therefore should receive exactly the same treatment.

- *Fairness:* Justice requires fairness; people are understood to be differently situated in life and therefore may receive different treatment according to what they are due or what they deserve.

This section's brief discussion may appear to be strictly an academic exercise, but it is not. The difference in these two conceptualizations of justice is important. Every day, police officers are confronted with situations that require them to wrestle with these two definitions and use their hearts and minds to employ the most "just" of the two. Of course, the paradox here is that *both* are morally and logically defensible. Because this is so, they present us with a classic ethical dilemma, where it is difficult to make a decision because both options are ethical in and of themselves. To treat people equitably is just, and to treat people fairly is just.

Here is a critical concern for the creative police leader. One of the most important characteristics of an intelligent person is the ability to tolerate ambiguity. Life is not painted in black and white, and the insightful person must understand the importance of nuance. The person with extraordinary problem-solving abilities is capable of keeping two concepts in mind at the same time and understanding that they are both true, even though they may be inconsistent with each other. This is the essence of dealing with paradoxes, at the heart of good policing. Especially when dealing with young officers, the effective police leader must illustrate that ethical dilemmas are troublesome, but understandable. The leader must support a young officer's attempts to wrestle with the nuance and inconsistency that he or she faces on the street. Here, with regard to these two different but equitable ideas about justice, the creative police leader must facilitate the young officer's tolerance of ambiguity and, at the same time, illustrate the utility of having two such definitions.

Police Mission Statements

Police officers see the worst in people on a regular basis. It is their job to engage in problem solving and solution development aimed at the most deviant and egregious of human behaviors. They must harden themselves, to some extent, against the development of too much empathy and sympathy for their fellow human beings. In fact, one of the most important paradoxes of police work has to do with a balancing act. On the one hand, police officers must remain in touch with their human emotions so they can be of use to their communities and engage the problems of people on the street. On the other hand, they must steel themselves against caring too much about the human tragedy they see on duty, or they may become unable to exercise intelligence and logic in their decision making, and cease to act as objective professionals.

It is perhaps the most important element of the police leader's job that he or she understand this paradox and do everything reasonable to help their charges deal with it. This is true whether officers are young rookies first experiencing the hard realities of life on the streets or experienced veterans who suffer from a cynicism that threatens to turn into genuine cynicism. Preparing them in advance whenever possible, and debriefing them after particularly difficult experiences, police leaders must act as fathers and mothers, brothers and sisters, mentors and coaches, priests, rabbis, and imams as they counsel their charges to go through the balancing act that is involved here.

We are making this point at this particular time because it relates to the stereotypification of police officers as jaded, if not cynical. There is no doubt that this stereotype has some truth to it. As we move to discuss the ideals that ought to be ensconced in police mission statements, we know that some police officers who read this will say we are dealing in platitudes. In fact, it is a common complaint of police officers that academic works are full of hackneyed and trite truisms. We will take the opportunity to acknowledge this truth (not only of this work but academic works about the police in general) and admit that we are indeed dealing in platitudes often in this book. Whether discussing mission statements, the concept of justice, or police ethics, we readily acknowledge this focus on platitudes. We are unapologetic. The time has come for police scholars and leaders to come together and encourage today's officers to do just this: think in terms of platitudes that expect the best from the police and encourage the development of genuine professionalism.

First, police mission statements should cleave to the general ideas exhibited by those who spawned the mission statement movement in the first place. That is, they should attempt to define and focus on the values, vision, and purpose of the organization. The idea is to spend some time focusing on the norms, mores, and values of the organization, then engage the organization's overall vision of where it is going and its ultimate purposes. The problem with mission statements is not that they avoid doing these things, but they spend so much time trying to include so much that the statement becomes a rambling, messy mini-essay.

Second, they should be realistic. While mission statements should encourage and expect the highest expectations from the police, they should also be practical. They should be written with an eye toward what utilitarian value they might create for the individual officer, as well as the public. For example, there is not much the police can do about the causes of crime. Even in today's world of COP, the police know they can have only minimal proactive impact on crime. Therefore, a police mission statement should tread lightly upon any propensity to suggest that the police will end (or even deter) crime in an effective manner. It would be ideal if the police can deter some crime, but it is impossible to deter all (or even much) crime. Mission statements should endeavor to steer clear of couching the police role as one that seeks to accomplish such a task.

Third, police mission statements should focus on the delivery of justice to the streets of America. Whether or not the word itself is actually mentioned, justice should be at the core of the police function at all times. "With an eye toward bringing about justice" is the type of phrase that might be utilized in this regard. Any attempt to further define justice—to differentiate between the two classic definitions previously discussed, for example—would be far too verbose to be useful.

A fourth point has to do with integrity. People sometimes misunderstand the definition of integrity. They believe it to be synonymous with honesty. But in actuality integrity is a certain *type* of honesty. People who possess integrity live their lives in such a way that their actions parallel their philosophy. What they do is congruent with what they say. People are not defined by what they say, what they think . . . or by what they say they think or what they think they have said. They are defined by their actions, and those actions should match what they say they stand for.

Our fifth point is so important that an entire chapter—Chapter 8: Ethics— is devoted to its discussion. Ethics cannot be detached from the idea of police competence. A police officer cannot be considered to be competent on the job unless he or she is an ethical professional. This marriage of ethics and competence is of such importance that police mission statements should mention ethics specifically.

Finally, working hand in hand with the new police philosophy of COP is the drive to create a genuine profession out of police work. Professionalism in police work, as with ethics, is such a major focus that we treat it in a number of chapters. The movement to professionalize the police includes the concepts of ethics, integrity, and justice. Police mission statements should include professionalism as an integral part of their focus.

IMPLEMENTATION

Several problematic areas can arise when instituting effective change in police organizations; it is not enough to merely create a mission statement. The police mission statement can aid police leaders in focusing both the short-term, day-to-day operations of the police department and the long-term planning that COP requires of today's police organization.

The Synoptic Plan

With the institutionalization of COP, it is essential that mission statements be read, accepted, and acted upon by everyone in the organization. The mission statement is meant to be a **synoptic plan** of attack to some extent, and it should encompass every individual and suborganization included in the overall organizational effort. Just as individual diffidence and subcultural obstinacy can inhibit progress toward genuine police professionalism in general and the goals of COP in particular, so too can they inhibit any meaningful application of the organization's message statement. Of course, it is unrealistic to expect everyone in an organization to accept every policy decision. There are always those who are naysayers, those who have a conservative approach toward change (meaning they are generally against it), and those who, because of disagreeable past experiences (real or imagined), are confrontational toward such platitude-driven endeavors as mission statements. In the police world in particular, such negative propensities tend to be exacerbated by dealing with life's seedier side on a regular basis.

But none of this changes the fact that mission statements can work in positive ways and be helpful in both the short and long run. Every effort must be made by police leadership to bring everyone on board with regard to mission statements and policies utilizing their focus.

BOX 3.8

An Example of Mission-Driven Decision Making

Suppose that a police organization's mission statement suggested that diversity was a high priority for the organization, due to the demographics of its community. In some jurisdictions, cultural and ethnic diversity create both enjoyable opportunities for citizens and troublesome dynamics for the police. Suppose that this organization operates within a jurisdiction that has decided to discontinue the once-required practice of utilizing affirmative action in public service selection processes. Under such circumstances, even though it is not necessary in a legalistic sense, the organization might very well decide to continue with affirmative action. This might be done so that, over time, police departmental demographics move in the direction of replicating the city demographics in general. Continuing affirmative action, even after it is no longer legally required, would be an example of mission statement–driven decision making.

All operations and decisions in a police organization should be made with reference to the mission statement. Selection and training—initial academy training and ongoing in-service training—should be underwritten by the mission. Discipline, too, must proceed in relation to the mission of the organization, as announced to all of its members. As Box 3.8 exemplifies, focus on a well-written and logically constructed mission statement can help everyone in a police department make decisions that are informed by the overall values and announced purposes of the organization.

Feedback Loops

A logically constructed organizational hierarchy and operational chart should include structurally supported **feedback loops**. Such loops are utilized to create data used to evaluate and re-evaluate, plan and re-plan, and problem solve in an intelligently run system. Feedback loops should be used to determine whether an existing mission statement is being utilized in an effective manner. Data obtained from such feedback presents an organization with "echoes" that can be used in re-evaluating and, eventually, rewriting the mission statement. As noted, this process should not become an ongoing, always changing endeavor, or organizations risk diffidence and counterproductivity. But, obtaining and making use of feedback can be an important method to ensure that an organization's operations are logically, legally, and morally defensible and, at the same time, responsive to community ideals and goals.

Be Aware of the "Good Ol' Boys"

There is a constant tension within today's American police culture created by a disparity between understanding contemporary change in the world, what it means to commit to police professionalism, and a lack of resolution to pursue the changes included within the COP movement. This disparity exists between modern, educated, far-sighted police officers/leaders and members of what is colloquially referred to as the **good ol' boys**. This presents a problem in implementing mission statements and, indeed, progress in the world of American policing. Stuck in an era gone by, the good ol' boys work against the logical and intelligent progress that mission statement creation and application attempt to bring about in the police world. Sometimes their impedance of progress is unintentional and created by a lack of understanding; sometimes it is a conscious effort to make sure that things remain as they are because this is, indeed, in the interests of the boys. Any modern organization and every contemporary police leader must take care to watch out for the boys and take steps to work around their naysaying efforts (more on the boys later in our discussions).

 SUMMATION

No organization can expect to be either effective or efficient unless it particularizes its mission with precise specificity. Public bureaucracies, in particular, tend to suffer from identity confusion because they have goals that are multiple, conflicting, and vague. Several decades ago, in an effort to make the best of the difficulties presented by this sort of confusion, the idea of the mission statement was born. In police organizations, the movement to specify values, vision, and purpose is embraced almost everywhere. Today, virtually all police organizations have publicized mission statements.

Some of these statements are of great utility, and some are not. But the fact that they *can* be useful is no longer debated by either scholars or police leaders. As long as care is taken to create meaningful and realistic mission statements, obtain acceptance for them throughout the police organization, and avoid the pitfalls of the good ol' boys, the mission statement can be an important tool for today's police. Every police officer, leader, and suborganization within a given police department can benefit from mission statements that help clarify and focus police goals in a way that effectively mollifies the limitations of police goal confusion.

DISCUSSION QUESTIONS

1. Discuss Wildavsky's idea of multiple, conflicting and vague goals. Most people are comfortable with the idea that enforcing the law can create disorder. However, focus on the obverse of that problem: the law *often* leaves police officers searching for semi-legal, non-legal, and quasi-legal methods to solve problems, because deviant behavior is quite often not "illegal."

2. Go online and search for mission statements. To illustrate the critical qualities of good, effective mission statements, come up with several examples of bad statements (this will not be difficult). Discuss what makes them bad in light of the points made in this chapter's discussion.

3. Compare and contrast our two concepts of justice: justice as equity and justice as fairness. See if you can come up with real-life examples of how specific police details might be handled differently, in light of these two distinctive ways of looking at justice.

4. Discuss the good ol' boys. Who are we talking about here? Where have you seen, experienced, or heard about such backward policing? In considering how deleterious for the future of policing such people can be, discuss how a good ol' boy subculture might negate the potentially positive impact of effective mission statement development and implementation.

KEY TERMS

Being yourself on purpose: The idea that a person must formulate a personal ethic and be who they are with purpose and conviction.

Chief executive officers (CEOs): The highest ranking officials in corporations or private businesses.

Complex organizations: Organizations, whether public or private, that are large enough to have suborganizations, chains of command, and organizational confusion.

Disorderly conduct: A section in most state penal codes that is vague and broadly focused, difficult to define and to question.

Distributive justice: A school of ethical thought that suggests justice involves giving to each "that which he deserves."

Equal protection of the law: Right guaranteed by the United States Constitution in several places, most importantly in the Fourteenth Amendment.

Exit strategy: An idea applied to military interventions involving planning to extricate the military from an incursion.

Feedback loops: Organizational processes utilized to obtain feedback about implemented policies so that re-planning and reorganization can occur in a logical way.

General order manuals: The specific, written operational rules and regulations of a police department, codified and put together into a book that is provided to all departmental employees.

Good ol' boys: Police officers who do not believe in the importance for the police of education, COP, and professionalism.

Great Depression: The worldwide economic downturn between 1929 and 1939 that saw unemployment reach 30 percent in some areas.

Justice is equity: The concept that to treat people justly is to treat them in exactly the same way.

Justice is fairness: The concept that to treat people justly is to treat them with regard to what they deserve, given their individual condition in life.

Klockars's axiom: The idea that the police must attend to things which ought not to be happening about which something ought to be done . . . NOW.

Law enforcement: One of the three main functions of the police; involves making arrests, serving warrants, and generally applying the law to human interactions on the street.

Mission confusion: The idea that in complex organizations there is often confusion about what the organization is supposed to accomplish.

Mission statement: A declaration of the values and purposes of an organization.

Multiple, conflicting, and vague goals: Wildavsky's idea that complex organizations suffer from inexact and even contradictory goals.

Order maintenance: One of the three main functions of the police; involves keeping the peace without necessarily utilizing the law as a tool.

Public bureaucracies: Complex organizations run by the local, state, or federal government that supply citizens with services.

Scientific management: The school of Frederick Taylor that spawned the field of organization theory around the end of the 19th century.

Service: One of the three main functions of the police; involves being of service to citizens without reference to the law.

Synoptic plan: A plan that looks at the overall and takes everything into account.

Unemployment insurance: Programs organized on a state-by-state basis operational since the Great Depression; provide temporary sustenance to people out of work through no fault of their own.

Values, vision, and purpose: Ideally, the elements that are included in a mission statement.

EXAMPLE SCENARIOS

A Mission Statement

Here's the mission statement of one southern police department: "The mission of the ____ Police Department is to serve with the ____ community to prevent crime and to promote the safety and well-being of all."

It is terse, to be sure. No one could accuse its creators of being long-winded. But it is odd, to say the least. The police plan to serve "with" the community, evidently. While we may understand the implications of this statement under COP, it seems strangely short, and it is quite expansive to suggest that the "well-being of all" is the main goal. Kind of like being in favor of world peace or motherhood and apple pie.

This is an example of a mission statement being too terse and limited. This statement is not utilitarian, in terms of creating community faith in the police, nor does it seem that it could be used as any sort of guideline for the purposes of aiding in police departmental decision making. Can you think of how such a brief statement might be improved (perhaps a great deal) without making it too verbose?

The Convenience Store

An elderly man is working the all-night shift at a convenience store. It is 3 a.m. and the place is deserted except for two car-loads' worth of teenagers who are "hanging around" the store—and have been doing so for several hours. They are not drunk. They are over 18 and, thus, are not violating curfew laws. They have not stolen anything (not yet). They have broken no laws. The clerk is becoming more and more concerned about the boys as the time of night gets later. The teens have come into and out of the store numerous times, but have purchased nothing.

The clerks calls the police, asking for an officer to "do something" about this "situation." Is this a reasonable call for service? What should the police do? If you agree that the police should take some action in this instance, what should they do—given that they cannot arrest or cite the teens? This is an example of how the law sometimes does not give the police the tools they need to handle situations which ought not to be happening, as Carl Klockars puts it.

Justice

It is late in the afternoon, and a police officer is sitting in her patrol car, catching up on paperwork. She is parked on a side street, on a winding, suburban road where people are known to speed far above the posted limit of 35 mph. She switches on her radar detector and turns her attention to reports that need to be finished. Occasionally, she sees someone drive by above 50 mph. When that speed shows up, she quickly puts her paperwork aside, moves out onto the road, gets up to speed, and stops the guilty driver.

Over the course of 45 minutes, the officer makes three vehicle stops. One driver is a local professional football player, who laughs out loud, jokes with his passenger (his lawyer), and suggests that whatever the fine is, it's nothing to him. A second driver is an 18-year-old college student, who seems quite upset at being stopped. He has a good attitude, explains that he has three different jobs—which he uses to pay his college expenses—and he's sorry to have been speeding between jobs. A final driver is a mother with a car full of kids who apologizes for losing track of her speed, because the kids were "just driving me crazy."

Are these circumstances the same? What would our "justice is equity" idea suggest the police officer do with these three people? What would our "justice is fairness" idea suggest the police officer do? What do you think the officer should do (and why)?

ADDITIONAL READING

For a look at contemporary ideas about the creation of mission statements for complex organizations, see *The Mission Primer: Four Steps to an Effective Mission Statement*, by Richard O'Hallaron and David O'Hallaron (Mission Inc., 2000). For a look at the somewhat recent development of personal mission statement creation, see Laurie Beth Jones's *The Path: Creating Your Mission Statement for Work and for Life* (Hyperion, 1998).

Regarding the idea of "being yourself on purpose," see Douglas W. Perez and J. Alan Moore's *Police Ethics: A Matter of Character* (Cengage, 2002). An excellent, concise discussion about our several methods of defining justice—and one that is related to the criminal justice field—is included in Joycelyn M. Pollock's *Ethics in Crime and Justice* (Wadsworth, 2004).

Aaron Wildavsky's work on multiple, conflicting, and vague goals has been published in numerous books and articles over the years. The most recent was in *Speaking Truth to Power: The Art and Craft of Policy Analysis* (Transaction Press, 1987). Carl Klockars's ideas about the things to which the police must respond comes from *The Idea of Police* (Sage, 1985).

Finally, to view and analyze contemporary police mission statements, one has only to go to the Internet and search for a short while. Mission statements, both good and bad, terse and elaborate, specific and vague are in evidence on the websites of virtually all contemporary police organizations. We will not suggest some bad ones here (in deference to professionals in the field), but they are easy enough to find.

CHAPTER 4

Structure

INTRODUCTION

In this chapter, we will discuss police department structural differentiations. We will not do so with an organizational, hierarchical chart in mind, but rather with the **organizational ethos** or "style" of administration as our focus. Of course, not every police leader is in a position to change organizational structure. Neither, for that matter, are they empowered to reflect on how a police or sheriff's department is put together and what is prioritized, with regard to law enforcement, order maintenance, or service. In this chapter, we will discuss the three common, classic styles of police work—the **legalistic, watchman, and service styles**—with an eye toward understanding that the majority of today's departments are organized around one of these three classical modes. We will also consider COP's impact on police organizational structure.

If it is true that a great majority of police leaders have nothing to do with overall organizational ethos creation, then why discuss this set of topics in such depth? First, no matter what is stated for public relations purposes, most police departments cleave to one of the three traditional styles of police work. While a large number of police departments are *espousing* the COP philosophy, they have not actually changed their focus. There is grant money and political support behind any effort to install COP or, at least, to publicize that this is what is occurring. So COP is what we hear about so often, but it is not what is occurring in American policing in most places. The three classic styles prevail, so all police leaders need to be conversant with them.

On the other hand, a large number of police departments *are* in fact reorganizing along the lines of the COP style. They are attempting to institute the change in philosophy to the new COP or professional era. Change happens slowly, due to subcultural reluctance and organizational momentum, but it is true that policing all across America is slowly moving in that direction. Because of this, every contemporary police leader needs to know the pros and cons of the COP movement.

The classic, threefold differentiation of styles of police organization was put together in the 1960s by James Q. Wilson, a public administration expert from UCLA. He did a nationwide study of different types of police departments, published in his now famous book, *Varieties of Police Behavior*. A brief consideration of Wilson's findings will help define and analyze COP.

 WILSON'S THREE TYPES OF POLICE ORGANIZATION

Wilson studied more than a dozen police departments around the country in his cross-subcultural study. He suggested a differentiation that has, since that time, become the standard for understanding organization in the field. Most departments exhibit some elements of each style. Any police leader who engages Wilson's typology will find parallels in his or her department. But overall, police organizations tend to adhere to one form or the other. Let us take a moment to review Wilson's threefold categorization (Peak, 2008).

The Watchman Style

Emphasizing the function of order maintenance has been emblematic of large northern police departments in America for more than 150 years. The priority of police organizations utilizing this particular style is to maintain order. The police operating under the watchman style answer calls for service, but do not tend to maintain a very proactive stance in a normative sense. This is a passive, reactive style. The watchman-type department is organized under the American governmental principle "that government governs best which governs least" (Adams, 1780). Translated into on-the-street policing, we have "that department that polices best polices least." The watchman-style officer stays out of the lives of citizens by being invisible in some sense and allowing the flow of life to go on without interference by police. The police are referees in the lives of citizens under such a style.

In some ways, the watchman style is like 19th century policing. Before police work was reformed, policing was not law enforcement oriented. There was no **War on Crime** mentality in American policing, and it was long before the **War on Drugs** would be "declared," first by President Nixon and then again by President Reagan. Nineteenth-century police operated long before the expectation developed during the progressive political era that government should have a proactive impact on the lives of the average American citizen. The police were America's one and only social welfare organization at that time, providing food and housing to indigent persons on occasion.

The watchman style of policing ignores many, if not most, minor violations. It especially downplays traffic offenses and juvenile transgressions. Given its focus on maintaining order, motorists and juveniles might be treated to warnings or moralizing speeches in lieu of citation and arrest. Motorists and juveniles are only subject to the power of the police if their behavior is considered to be genuinely dangerous. If no threat to the peace and quiet (the order) of the community is detected, the police back off. Under this style, the police are neither trained nor motivated in an ongoing way to enforce the law. They observe life on the street and, in essence, await citizen calls for service.

BOX 4.1

THE WATCHMAN AND CITIZEN FREEDOM

The watchman style of policing appears to many to be the best style in a country where we value individual freedom as Americans. Because this style makes so few arrests and, presumably, allows citizens the optimum amount of personal liberty to act in whatever way they wish, the watchman style appears to be ideal in terms of the degree of individual autonomy it provides for each and every American.

Under the watchman style, even a certain amount of vice-related crime is ignored. Gambling, in particular, tends to be considered by the police to be unimportant or a culture-specific tradition that is best left alone. Drinking is considered to be a part of everyday life. Even public drunkenness, if it doesn't involve any genuine threat to public peace and quiet, is disregarded. Certain types of prostitution—such as the "call girl" sort not evident on the street corner—are ignored. In general, nonviolent citizen disagreements are considered to be "personal" and not the business of the police. Watchman-style officers are prone to consider disputes between citizens to be private. In general, this is reactive policing to the extreme.

In watchman-style organizations, statistics are kept, but not focused on in important ways. Making lots of arrests does not help in officer promotion. Decisions regarding who deserves choice assignments or advancement are not predicated on a number of arrests. Other criteria, such as seniority and loyalty, tend to be emphasized when officer evaluations are conducted.

The watchman style neither acts in a proactive manner nor attempts to turn details into legal issues. It gives a tremendous amount of discretionary latitude to the police. Let us consider the positives and negatives of the style.

Advantages of the Watchman Style Watchman-style officers watch and wait. They eschew making arrests whenever possible and allow a great deal of individual liberty to citizens. These officers are not interested in interfering with the ongoing exercise of individual freedom. In America, a country that values the ideal of individual freedom, the watchman style can be seen to focus appropriately on allowing as much individual liberty as possible. This is a definite plus, perhaps the most important plus of the style.

Because of this general operational principle, and because they seldom upset citizens by making arrests, using force, or taking any action, watchman-style officers receive a limited number of citizen complaints. They receive far fewer complaints than the legalistic style; there is little to complain about. The potentially adversarial police–citizen relationship is mollified because the police follow the path of least resistance, which works to dampen the propensity toward citizen–police antipathy. Thus, under a watchman style, there are better police–community relations than often develop in contemporary times. The police are not often considered to be the enemy.

The amount of discretionary power entrusted to the police allows them *not* to take action as a part of their working personalities. In major cities, where there are large **ethnic enclaves**, this freedom of inaction can lead the police to have a great deal of sensitivity to cultural differences. This concept is called **cultural relativity** by sociologists and cultural anthropologists (Hunt, 2007). Black-on-black crime or Asian-on-Asian crime can be ignored as a "part of their culture." This leads, in turn, to fewer complaints about racism aimed at the police from ethnic minorities. The argument can be made that watchman-style policing allows for ethnic diversity in an extremely positive way.

Another advantage of the watchman style is when the police eschew making arrests, the taxpayers are saved a great deal of money. Arrests mean expenses for the criminal justice system. A type of policing that generates little in the way of arrest statistics also generates little in the way of expenses. Americans, being tax-conscious people, see this as a positive dynamic.

Finally, Dirty Harry–type noble cause corruption is discouraged by the watchman style. When no premium is placed on arresting citizens, certain types of crimes are allowed to go unsanctioned, and noble cause corruption is deterred. Nothing within the subcultural norms that develop under this style motivates police officers to take the job of ridding the streets of bad actors so seriously that they become Dirty Harry–like. The watchman-style officer does not tend to believe that taking aggressive police action is some sort of noble cause.

Drawbacks of the Watchman Style This style allows so much latitude to citizens that it almost encourages criminals. With regard to crime in general, this style emphasizes police inaction to such an extent that the police deterrence can be ineffectual. The propensity for the police "not to do their jobs" can be considered a "cause" of crime. This way of prioritizing police inactivity can encourage deviant behavior in general. It can embolden the individual criminal and even allow gangs to take over the streets of America.

Also, the amount of discretion involved in the watchman style is directly responsible for the construction of different sets of rules in different parts of a town or city. Unfettered by an organizational structure that might require the application of the law uniformly, the police can create as many different penal codes as there are police officers. In large, diverse cities, this can mean that there are different sets of rules, styles of policing, and lifestyles in different parts of the city. This differentiation of the law can lead to confusion, unfairness, and a cynicism about the law.

In exercising their discretionary decision-making powers, the police define the law on the streets. In doing so, they can create a better, more humane, and just legal system. The police can create a system that empathizes with individual citizens and allows for the development of justice in a fair manner. However, they might create a system that is driven by prejudice. Here, one of the positives of the watchman-style system becomes a weakness. Deferring to cultural differences can add to the misery and hopelessness of ethnic minority populations. This is a sort of bottom line argument; it does not matter *why* police inactivity occurs, it only matters that the police are not doing their jobs. The effect upon justice is clear.

Finally, while the watchman style encourages the police to exercise a great deal of discretion, it ignores a certain amount of crime—in particular, vice-related crime—and it places no premium on proactivity. Taken together, these realities encourage police corruption of the sort that is called **corruption of authority** (Perez and Moore, 2002). In fact, this type of police misconduct does tend to be present when watchman-style policing is in effect. This is because corruption of

REVIEW CHART 4.1

⊙ PROS AND CONS OF THE WATCHMAN STYLE

- Advantages
  - Fewest arrests of any style
  - Optimal individual liberty for civilians
  - Very few citizen complaints
  - Cultural sensitivity is encouraged
  - Tax expenditures are limited
  - Dirty Harry–type noble cause corruption is limited
- Drawbacks
  - Encourages criminal activity
  - Different sets of rules in different areas of town
  - Great amount of discretion encourages prejudice
  - Encourages corruption of authority

authority always accompanies **victimless crime** (O'Donnell, 2000). When there are no complaining parties, as is the case with victimless crimes, and the police are allowed the freedom of inaction that the watchman style provides, the system is almost "asking" for the police to become involved in taking payoffs from those who run illegal gambling operations, pimps, drug dealers, and so forth. The watchman style tends to manufacture police misconduct.

The next type of police organization to be discussed is a form of policing that is, in many ways, diametrically opposed to the watchman style.

The Legalistic Style

In the legalistic style, common situations are seen as law enforcement oriented; the general operational norm is that even minor altercations between citizens are couched in legal terms. Family fights, neighborhood spats, barking dogs, and loud parties are all considered to present legal issues. In fact, anything that does not present legal issues to the police tends to be ignored. Law enforcement is so highly prioritized that other functions (service to the community, for example) are only tended to when time permits. Non-legal functions are not considered to be substantial elements of the police function (Roberg et al., 2005). "Real" police work in the legalistic style involves the application of the law; everything else is secondary.

Legalistic-style officers make a lot of arrests and issue a lot of citations. This is true for felonious crimes, traffic violations, juvenile problems, and minor crimes, too. Motorists get tickets, juveniles go to Juvenile Hall, and petty criminals are arrested. Even such crimes as petty theft and vandalism, which do not threaten the peace and order of the community, are taken seriously. Drunks are taken to jail or to alcohol treatment centers, and are not allowed to remain on the streets. The homeless, though not often arrested, are considered to be "loiterers" and "indigent persons." Under the legalistic style, police discretion is limited. To be an officer is to fight crime and make arrests. Judges and juries decide what to do about suspects; the job of the police is to bring people before the bar. The legalistic officer enforces the law. Other police functions, considered "social work," are avoided.

In ethnic enclaves, the legalistic-style police do their jobs driven by the idea that there are no excuses relating to cultural relativism. The police operate with a constant, unabashed focus on being legal actors and utilizing the law as their primary tool. Non-legal, semi-legal, and quasi-legal methods of solving problems are eschewed. This is true everywhere, even in minority neighborhoods, where the watchman-style officer might avoid dealing with people's problems.

The legalistic style of policing is proactive and energetic. The police are aggressive, even-handed, and tenacious. When between specific details and on routine patrol, legalistic police officers consider their top priority to be "**fishing expeditions**" (Poteet and Poteet, 2000), looking for crime and criminals. The general operational procedure of the legalistic officer is to assert the power of the law and, equally, the police.

In legalistic-style police departments, numbers of arrests and citations are counted and categorized to ascertain whether the department (or even the individual officer) is doing the job. The priorities of the police are clear: the effective officer makes lots of arrests and issues a lot of citations. The best officer makes many felony arrests. In every way, the legalistic department operates so that making good arrests is rewarded. Clearly, one of the ways for a police officer to make it to the top is to create a reputation for aggressiveness.

Rather than being diverse and accommodating, the legalistic style is monolithic. It prioritizes law enforcement to the exclusion of all other functions. Citations and arrests are the principle implements of the police, instead of tools that are utilized only as a last resort (as with the watchman style). The focus is on making every citizen disagreement and every police detail into a legal issue of some kind.

Advantages of the Legalistic Style The legalistic style may seem to be rigid and overly aggressive in light of the passivity of the watchman style. But there are several important advantages to this style. First, aggressive policing is presumed to deter crime. Proactive efforts on the part of the police deter crowd- and gang-type activities, and maintain vigilance over any situation that is out of the ordinary. Such efforts are presumed to work to make lawful citizens feel safe and secure. The deterrent impact of legalistic policing is pronounced, and it is one of the style's greatest advantages.

A second strength of the legalistic style is that it creates one single legal standard everywhere. There is one set of universally applied rules for the citizenry because the exercise of discretion is limited. So there is **one standard of conduct** for the public and, equally, one standard of police conduct. Any given citizen meets the same sort of expectations from any given police officer. In some sense, this is a more just style of policing.

Since the decisions of the police under the legalistic style are uniform, they are more legally defensible or more legally "correct." The **"rule of cop"** is eschewed. This is good news for those who expect equity in the treatment that citizens experience from the police. The police are more often correct because they exercise so little in the way of discretion that their training takes over and controls their judgment.

Finally, the legalistic style inhibits corruption of authority; because it limits police discretion, the police are required to deal with all types of crime, even that associated with vice. When the police pursue victimless crimes aggressively and their system emphasizes making arrests, police corruption is limited.

Drawbacks of the Legalistic Style   No style of policing has all of the answers, and the legalistic style can be criticized like any other. First, the criminal justice system can be impacted with numerous cases under this style. The system is already clogged up; there are so many new convicts coming into the system, at such a rapid rate, that others have to be released. This is known as the revolving door problem, familiar to anyone in the system. Citations and arrests take up police time, jail cells, court time, and attorney time. The system spends more money supporting the legalistic style than it does on any other style. Furthermore, when the police arrest "everybody," time and money will be wasted on minor offenses. This can create a situation where there is not enough time and money to focus on violent, felonious crime.

Second, legalistic-style police officers are so overly aggressive that they can be perceived to be belligerent and even hostile toward citizens. This perception is a natural product of this style. This leads to citizen complaints—lots of them

BOX 4.2

◉ CITIZENS' COMPLAINTS ABOUT THE LEGALISTIC STYLE

One drawback to the legalistic style is that its operations tend to generate a great number of citizen complaints. This is because large numbers of arrests are made under this style and because ethnic minorities and juveniles, in particular, tend to be arrested at a relatively high rate. This gives rise to two types of complaints: those who feel the police are racist, and parents who feel the police are acting in an inappropriately brusque and harsh manner when dealing with children and teens.

REVIEW CHART 4.2

PROS AND CONS OF THE LEGALISTIC STYLE

- Advantages
  - Deters crime
  - One standard of conduct is applied everywhere
  - Police decisions are more legally "correct"
  - Inhibits corruption of authority
- Drawbacks
  - Large number of arrests/citations expends time and money
  - Police appear to be overly aggressive and even belligerent
  - More minority arrests lead to more complaints of police prejudice
  - Crime statistics increase
  - Encourages Dirty Harry–type noble cause corruption

(Perez, 1994). Legalistic officers cite drivers, arrest juveniles and adults for the most petty of offenses, and generally interact with citizens in an intrusive way. All of these propensities create large numbers of civilians who are unhappy with the police. Of all the styles of policing in America, the legalistic style obtains the most citizen complaints by a wide margin.

Third, police under the legalistic style make many arrests in ethnic minority areas, and an odd dynamic unfolds. The police under the watchman style are given so much latitude that they tend to eschew making arrests in minority areas. We could accuse the watchman style of encouraging racism by encouraging the police to normalize certain types of behavior, even criminal behavior, as being endemic to minority populations. The legalistic officer does the opposite, and emphasizes taking action in the inner city, where crime statistics tend to soar. The police make more arrests of minorities under this style, creating more citizen complaints. Also, the police are more often accused of racism under this style (see Box 4.3). This is odd because in the inner city the police are, in fact, doing their jobs in a more appropriate manner under legalistic policing.

The legalistic style is often given credit for minimizing corruption of authority. Fair enough. But the problem with this style of policing is that it tends to encourage noble cause corruption. If a police organization emphasizes arresting citizens, rewards aggressive behavior on the part of police officers, and generally motivates the police to get the job done by crime fighting in a proactive manner, then Dirty Harry–like behavior may very well develop over time.

BOX 4.3

EVERYBODY TALKS SERVICE

As we shall see shortly with regard to community-oriented policing (COP), virtually every police manager in America will suggest that their police department is a service-oriented department, no matter what type of philosophy *really* drives their department. Because it is politically appropriate to be so oriented, the service element of policing is the officially announced priority everywhere. Even in inner city areas, where the volume of calls is so great that the time necessary to employ the service style is not available, it is the style of choice for public relations people in police work everywhere.

The legalistic style might appear to be better than the watchman style on first glance. It appears to be more professional and seems to ask the police to do their *real* jobs in a more honest and straightforward manner. However, upon reflection, the legalistic style has significant drawbacks. It is different from the watchman style—substantially different—but it is not necessarily better.

The final style up for discussion is only found in areas where the police have enough time to prioritize service to their communities. In essence, the police need spare time to be genuinely service oriented, and that luxury does not present itself in urban areas and some suburban areas, where crime and gang activity have increased dramatically in recent years.

The Service Style

As noted in Box 4.3, the overwhelming majority of contemporary police leaders, not to mention local politicians, will suggest that their departments are service oriented. This is an effort to put a public relations spin on the public's perception of what is prioritized by the police. No matter what the reality, being service oriented is perceived among police administrators to be an absolute necessity in contemporary times.

Again, all police departments will suggest that they are service oriented—often putting the words "to protect and serve" on their patrol cars. But it is, in essence, impossible to accomplish a genuine service style of policing with the volume of calls that require a specific police response in cities. Urban policing simply involves too much activity for the police to have the time to prioritize providing service as their primary function.

In rural areas and most suburbs, the police usually have a "quiet" time of it, relative to the city. In such locales, there is a substantial amount of time available to the police between details. Sometimes there will be no calls for police assistance in an entire shift, so the police can execute the service style. Service-style police have the time to take all calls seriously—those involving legal issues, disruption of the social order, and requests for specific service. They have time to be involved with informal intervention, counseling, and protracted conflict resolution. Both order maintenance and law enforcement can be accomplished as parts of the job in the service style. Service-oriented police are far less prone to invoke the sanctions of the law than legalistic officers.

Policing in the suburbs and the country involves operating in homogenous areas, where a common definition of order prevails. This homogeneity makes police work easier because there is far less tension between people's various expectations for each other and the police. When any group enjoys a common definition of norms and values, there is a great deal of informal social control exercised by the group over the individuals in it. In the country, this means less need for policing.

When the police *are* called in rural areas, there is a common understanding of what the police ought to do. Little of the strain experienced by urban police is experienced by service-oriented officers. There is one uniform standard of conduct in operation, and police can treat just about anything with patience and understanding because they always have the time to do so. Under the service style, juvenile offenses are never ignored. No calls for police assistance of any kind are ignored, but teenagers tend to be treated informally. Motorists are always stopped for speeding because safety on the roadways is treated seriously, but they too will often receive a warning or a lecture rather than a citation.

Serious crime takes on a particular meaning in the service style because there is little crime to begin with. When the police are confronted with violence or felonious crime, they have the time to treat it as a major event. In the city, sometimes police officers have so many calls involving felonious crime that they cannot give it the attention it deserves. This is never the case in service-style rural or suburban areas.

Service-style policing is public relations oriented. Creating and maintaining a positive image is considered to be the job of everyone in police work. Rather than being reactive to problems that present themselves, the service police can operate in an outreach mode. They have time to be involved in public speaking to groups and schools, and become involved in teaching and education. The service style sees policing as a product, and the job of policing involves estimating the market and developing the product appropriately.

Finally, service-style police officers are hired and trained with an emphasis on accomplishing all of these tasks without receiving citizen complaints. Every member of a service organization is supposed to be an ambassador of the police department. While the requirement for college has expanded into every nook and cranny of modern police work, it was the service style that first acknowledged the need for such an education.

Advantages of the Service Style The service style is supported by the citizenry in the suburbs and rural areas. This style gets very few citizen complaints. Its public relations focus often makes for a positive and cooperative relationship between the police and the community. As we shall see in the next section, COP is an easy sell in police organizations and subcultures that were already service oriented.

Service-style officers are able to handle details informally because they have the time and latitude to do so. They can be aggressive if that is what is required. This seldom *is* required, but the alternative exists. They can respond to both community leaders and individual citizens. The luxury of the time the police have to work with makes this an almost idyllic type of policing. There are many advantages to it and few disadvantages. The problem is, of course, the wealth of time available and the homogeneous community factor cannot be replicated anywhere else.

Drawbacks of the Service Style   The drawbacks to service-style policing are few. Since the police are responsive to community concerns and values on a regular basis, the police enjoy an almost symbiotic relationship with the public. Officers tend to live in the areas where they police, and this makes for an implicit agreement about local values and what the police should prioritize. Equally, the police tend to be controlled locally—both formally and informally.

But there are drawbacks to the service style. The style lacks "action." It is one thing to expect veteran police officers to embrace the idea that not much happens on the beat where they police, but quite another to get young officers to accept such a reality. Rookie police officers come to police work with unrealistic media-created expectations about the job. Hollywood has taught them that police work

BOX 4.4

CRIME IN THE COUNTRY

How little can there be for the police to do in a rural area? How bored can a rural police officer become? Here are the FBI's crime statistics for 2005 in Grand Isle County, Vermont, population 7,600, located in five small villages:

Homicide/manslaughter	0
Rape	0
Robbery	0
Aggravated assault	2
Burglary	26
Larceny	38
Vehicular theft	0

Source: Uniform Crime Reports for Grand Isle County, 2005.

is action-packed. There is a certain romanticism about the idea that the police are involved in a "hero's quest" to fight wars on crime and drugs.

When service-style officers meet reality on the streets, they tend to be disappointed. They can be disillusioned, and they can get bored. There is nothing necessarily negative about boredom, say, on the graveyard shift. But boredom all of the time—consistent, overwhelming, debilitating boredom—can lead to trouble.

When young officers find out there is next to nothing to do out there, it can motivate them to act out in counterproductive ways. Young police officers with nothing to do tend to *make* something to do. Where there is little in the way of deviance and criminal behavior, harassing ordinary citizens can become the norm. Going on fishing expeditions in suburban areas can create disorder where there is none and can make the police into a local problem. Bored service-style police officers can present their police administration and community with unsettling situations, where solutions will need to be developed.

At the other end of the spectrum, there can be so little to do that veteran police officers can retreat into apathy. They might be found off their beats, sleeping on duty, having sex on the job, and even taking second jobs while on duty. Veteran service officers can degenerate into nonworking drags on the system, and service policing can develop problems involving both police officers with little and a great deal of experience.

REVIEW CHART 4.3

PROS AND CONS OF THE SERVICE STYLE

- Advantages
  - Fewest citizen complaints
  - Creates positive police–community relations
  - Informal conflict resolution is possible and encouraged
  - Police officers tend to live in the communities they police
  - Police respond to citizens and community leaders as consumers
  - Police have discretionary time to be proactive and community oriented
- Drawbacks
  - Young officers can become bored due to lack of action
  - This can cause them to go fishing for things to do
  - Experienced officers can become bored as well
  - This can cause them to become apathetic and counterproductive

Having outlined Wilson's three types of police organization, and the strengths and weaknesses of each, we will take a moment to talk about professionalism before discussing our last police style, the relatively new philosophy of COP.

A WORD ABOUT PROFESSIONALISM

For the purpose of our analysis, we will use the definition of profession that is accepted by most sociologists (Larson, 1979). In differentiating jobs, occupations, and vocations from the genuine professions, sociologists have come up with a number of definitive indicators. The genuine professions are medicine, law, architecture, teaching, engineering, and so forth. We will focus on six critical elements common to all professions. It is necessary for us to develop an understanding of the importance of COP, as well as the movement toward genuine professionalism in American policing.

The Definition of a Profession

First, the professions require their members to go through a prolonged and sophisticated academic experience (Roberg et al., 2005). They obtain an education at what Plato called the "academy." When we refer here to entering into academe, we are talking about obtaining a broadly based, generalized education at a university as a starting point. In most professions, there is additional, specific training that follows this generalized experience. That additional training takes substantial amounts of time; for example, medical school takes four years and law school takes three years. Many engineers, architects, and teachers obtain higher degrees than the bachelor's degree and have prolonged apprenticeships. It is only after high school and college that the professions obtain their specified training for the purposes of our sociological definition. We must be careful when talking about the police with regard to this specific training experience, because, while police academies constitute important elements in the overall police officer educational experience, they do not involve either the length of time or the breadth of knowledge necessary for obtaining a genuine education in academe.

The second characteristic common to all professions has to do with what the would-be professional obtains in their time at the academy. In academe, the professional comes into contact with a **systematized body of knowledge** that is unknown to those outside of professional circles, or laypersons (Freidson, 2000). The body of knowledge is substantial in both depth and breadth—that is, it is not easily obtainable in terms of time spent, and it is equally difficult to obtain in terms of the intellectual powers necessary to comprehend the knowledge base. Also, this body of knowledge is scientifically constructed (Geison, 1983). Outside of the profession, the specifics of this knowledge are so unknown that, as a society, we give great deference to the professions. They know something we do not know, and we grant them a great deal of latitude because of this.

A third characteristic has to do with the fact that problems are solved collegially within the professions. In most occupations, and especially in police work, decisions are made in a command-and-control manner. Decisions are made high up in the organizational structure and passed down the line of communication. This is true in businesses, factories, colleges, and so forth. There is an organizational chart in most complex organizations, and the fact that those in upper level management dictate policies and strategies to those below is almost universal.

In the professions, however, this is not the case. When difficulties present themselves, expert professionals from anywhere in the organization get together to troubleshoot and problem solve. Difficulties are not surmounted through a hierarchical process, but rather, professionals pool their intelligence and expertise, and attempt to create solutions that are, in essence, democratically constructed (Roberg et al., 2005). While there are professionals with more experience than others, younger professionals may have received cutting-edge professional training more recently than their more experienced colleagues; this moves decision making in the direction of a more collective mode.

A fourth characteristic directly links to points one and two: the professions are allowed to self-regulate. Standards for education, licensing, and behavior are determined by professional organizations, without outside interference (Carter and Wilson, 2009). As a society, we allow them to do this because we defer to their knowledge base. So deep is our collective respect for the academic experience and

BOX 4.5

RESPECT FOR PROFESSIONALS

A father's 3-year-old son has broken his leg. He rushes him to the hospital emergency room and tells the story to a nurse. The father is a medical student. He knows what has happened and exactly what needs to be done. The nurse takes the little boy away on a gurney and the father is asked to sit down and wait in the lobby.

What does the father, with his intelligence level and expertise, do? Does he protest and suggest that he wants to accompany his son into the ER? Does he argue that he won't be in the way and he just doesn't want to lose contact with his little boy? Or, despite his intelligence, education, and experience level, does he do what he is told, defer to the expertise of the professionals, sit down, and wait? This is based on a true story. The father sat down and waited; he did what he was told because he trusted the expertise of the professionals, even though those working in the ER were complete strangers to him and he was in the process of becoming a doctor himself.

the substantive knowledge held by professionals, society allows them to set up their own standards. All genuine professions have an absolute, unquestioned authority over their own endeavors. No one outside of any profession purports to have much to say about these things. On those rare occasions when laypeople suggest that they should have something to say about the regulation of a profession, such suggestions do not get very far.

Fifth, the professions are also allowed to self-discipline. Because of the same reasons listed under the fourth characteristic, the professions are considered to be capable of policing themselves. Accusations of misconduct made against professionals are handled by organizations populated by other members of the profession. Committees (or boards or commissions) of practitioners are responsible for looking into such allegations, and they are given great latitude in doing so. Even though members of the public who feel themselves to be aggrieved by professional incompetence, slothfulness, or dishonesty have the right to petition for redress of grievances, such petitions end up being considered by experienced professionals (Roberg et al., 2005).

The sixth and final characteristic shows that the genuine professional is known to possess an internalized ethical code. Along the way in their quest to obtain systematized knowledge, professionals obtain an ethical framework within which they pursue their craft. They are socialized into accepting this ethical framework, and then they operate in its shadow without any direct external interference (Pollock, 2008). The behavior of professionals is controlled by internalized values and norms that are socialized into their working personalities along the way through their professionalization process.

Analysis

This brief discussion of a complex topic has been necessary so we can engage two questions that are at the core of the development of police professionalism, as well as the center of the COP movement in American policing. They are perhaps *the* questions of the age in policing. Understanding the implications of these questions for the future of policing in this country is critical for all of today's police leaders. The first question is, are the police professionals? The second is, if they are not, what would it take to make them such? It is easy to anticipate the answer to the first question. Are the police genuine professionals? No, not yet. Or to be more accurate, the answer is, "No, not exactly . . . but almost."

Does modern American policing require an academic experience? The answer is, almost. Educational requirements are ever-expanding in today's world of policing. In many places, the requirement that police cadets have at least two years of college before they enter into the specified training of the police world (including the academy, FTO training, and in-service training) is already in place. In most jurisdictions, having any college experience is taken as a plus in the selection process. Within our lifetimes, it is extremely likely that police work will become a profession populated exclusively by college educated men and women. For now, this requirement is "on the way."

REVIEW CHART 4.4

THE ELEMENTS OF PROFESSIONALISM

- Shared academic experience
- Systematized body of knowledge unknown to laypeople
- Collegial problem solving
- Self-regulating
- Self-disciplining
- Self-created, internalized code of ethics

Does modern American policing require that officers plug into a systematized body of knowledge unknown to laypersons outside of the profession? The answer is yes. The combination of substantive topics over which the modern police officer should have command is unusually broad and deep. Police officers need to know about different types of law (substantive and procedural), physical tactics, forensics and weaponry, social skills and psychology, local history and culture, investigation and interrogation, and so on. An argument can be made that only modern, educated, accomplished police officers have expertise in this particularized, broadly based set of topics and skills.

Do modern police professionals solve problems collegially? The answer is that under traditional police management—command and control—the police do not behave like professionals. Decisions are made above and sent down the chain of command, as in the military. However, under COP, one of the critically important changes being instituted is that of policing in teams and making decisions utilizing the expertise of everyone on the team, from the most experienced ranking person on down to the least experienced beat officer. As the tenets of COP are institutionalized, this requirement of a genuine profession will be achieved.

Do the police self-regulate? Yes, pretty much. Generalized educational requirements, police academy curricula, and selection criteria are all controlled by experienced police professionals. This occurs not only on a department-by-department basis, but also in the form of Police Officer Standards and Training (POST) commissions. Such professionals also set a minimum educational requirement for specialized training, such as that for K-9 officers, forensics officers, and SWAT training.

Do the police self-discipline and possess an internalized ethic? No, not at all. It might appear at first glance that they do, because police-operated internal affairs (IA) bureaus look into allegations of police misconduct on a regular basis. But IA is not run by the police as a group of professionals. It is operated by police *departments*—those entities that hire the police. If police unions were to take part in police accountability, as serious professional organizations desiring to hold their own members accountable to internalized ethical standards, then self-disciplining and control over ethical conduct would be the case. If and when this type of professional ideal develops among the police as a group (and the professionalization movement is making progress in this regard in some places), then this element of the formula will reach fruition.

So, again, the answer to the question, "Are the police professionals?" is "Almost." The answer to this question has several parameters to it. If COP continues to develop collegial problem solving, if educational requirements continue to be expanded, and if the police rank and file, over time, become seriously interested in police accountability and ethical conduct, then the police will become professionals in every sense of the term. Those in charge of making the changes occur are, by and large, police leaders. At the highest levels of police organizations, managers are responsible for making systemic changes that can empower these developments. At middle management levels and among the critical sergeant corps in America today, interpersonal leadership will motivate and direct the police officer corps to work for and accept these changes. Finally, police leadership among the rank and file—in police union positions of authority, in particular—can provide essential guidance that brings to fruition the long sought after goal of police professionalism. With professionalism will come increased status, political power, responsibility, salaries and benefits, and acceptance into the world of the genuine professions.

 ## NEW PHILOSOPHY OF COP: MORE TALK THAN ACTION

It would strain credulity to suggest that there was a single police leader in this country who today had not heard of COP. But it is not true that police leaders—especially young leaders—are universally conversant with the history that brought the COP movement to the fore. So we will take just a moment to review that history.

COP's History: The Uniqueness of Planned Change

The unusual thing about COP is that it was the brain child of academics (not police officers or police leaders). Driven by the steep rise in crime of the 1960s, the findings of riot commissions indicated the police needed to change pronouncedly. The police were underpaid, undereducated, and undertrained. They were often guilty of excessive force and incompetence. They had handled student protests and inner city riots poorly. Police officers themselves had even rioted on occasion (a dynamic that was studied by Rodney Stark in the book *Police Riots*). People in the political world, the police world, and the academic world began to "think outside the box" with regard to crime and policing (Goldstein, 1990). What the police were doing was certainly not working. Crime had skyrocketed, and the police seemed not only to be ineffective in having any deterrent impact on the growing rate of crime, but to be a part of the problem in some ways. What should be done?

Ask criminologists to explain what causes crime, and they will answer that there are a litany of causes. Crime is caused by greed combined with opportunity, poverty and racism, economic stratification and a class structure, certain kinds of mental problems, and hopelessness. Of course, knowledgeable people knew that the police could not do much about most of these causes, in the grand scheme of things. On the other hand, there was probably *something* the police could do to affect some crime patterns on the street.

The idea of bringing the police closer to their communities came to the fore slowly over the course of the 1960s and 1970s, but COP did not take off as an idea that might be institutionalized until the 1980s. Largely given credit for its invention were George Kelling and James Wilson (see Box 4.6). In the early 1980s, they wrote a famous article entitled **"Broken Windows"** that set COP in motion. They argued that crime in the inner city, in particular, was largely produced by residents feeling a profound disengagement from their neighborhoods (Wilson and Kelling, 1982). When a community degenerates and there is evidence of physical neglect and social disorder on the street, the citizenry can begin to become apathetic. They can think that things have gone past some imaginary point of no return, where there is no hope for their community. They can think that caring about their local neighborhood is a waste of time and cooperating with the police is equally a waste of time. In short, citizens can give up on being engaged in community life (Miller et al., 2010).

BOX 4.6

BROKEN WINDOWS

The "broken windows" theory of Wilson and Kelling posits that one broken window can quickly lead to a building full of broken windows. A building full of broken windows can lead to blocks full of broken windows. Blocks full of broken windows can impact the feelings of safety held by members of the public, as can other signs of physical dilapidation and neglect. Broken windows, burned-out cars, uncollected garbage, streetlights that do not work, uncut lawns ... these and other signs of indifference and disintegration can affect the quality of life felt by people in their community. Furthermore, social disintegration can lead to such feelings, as well. Public drunkenness, street prostitution, loitering, disorderly conduct, and other problems can also create a feeling of hopelessness, a lack of connection to the community, and a fear of crime in a neighborhood where such signs of indifference are in evidence. The initial concept behind COP was nothing more than the idea that the police should pay attention to these signs of degeneration and should require that others do so as well (Wilson and Kelling, 1982).

This realization led to several conclusions. First, fixing broken windows in a neighborhood (picking up the garbage, cutting the lawns, fixing broken street-lamps, and similar endeavors) could make people who have given up begin to be reconnected with their communities. Second, when citizens interacted with police officers who were on foot patrol, as opposed to in police cars, people felt safer. They sensed that their streets were safer. Foot patrol—more importantly, the direct, face-to-face, person-to-person contact that it represents—was important, if only in a psychological sense. Third, the police *could* impact crime. There were any number of programs and practices that the police could utilize to influence people to become more engaged in their communities and deter crime by improving the quality of life in a given neighborhood.

The new philosophy was debated by academics, picked up by politicos and police leaders, and instituted in a dozen places to begin. Picking up momentum quickly, COP expanded during the 1980s and became the "new philosophy of American policing" (at least in theory) by the 1990s. There are as many explanations of COP as there are criminologists who study it and police leaders who attempt to implement it. In fact, one of the criticisms of COP is that it is not clearly defined. Definitions are vague, overlapping, and at times contradictory. We will attempt to steer a center path here and give the reader a general idea without getting into the debate about which definition of COP is best. In the following sections, we will outline several of the major elements of COP that are agreed upon by most experts (Friedman, 1992; Kelling and Coles, 1998; Skogan, 1990).

Police–Community Partnership

As the label implies, COP's philosophy is community based. One of its central themes is the idea that the police should interact with the community on a regular basis, rather than being aloof as in recent decades. The idea here is that community input is essential. Of course, members of the community, even elected representatives and community leaders, do not directly manage police departments. But the taxpayers of a city, town, or county have ideas about what the police should prioritize, and the police should be responsive to those ideas. Furthermore, the police are so few in number that they cannot fight crime, deterioration, and disorder on their own. An ongoing, interactive, mutually supportive relationship between police and community is essential. When the philosophy of COP came along, this type of relationship had not existed in most places in America for several generations.

A Broader Definition of the Police Function

Another element of COP is the idea that the police function should be more broadly defined. Emphasis should be placed on law enforcement, order maintenance, *and* service—all at the same time. Furthermore, under COP, the service element expands to include a number of tasks that have been foreign to the police in recent years—since as long ago as the 19th century. The police need to work together with communities to identify ongoing problems and troubleshoot for solutions. They must consider themselves to be in the business of deterring crime before it occurs. As agents of change, the modern police should utilize strategies they never attempted in the past. They should be counselors for potentially troubled youth, serve the elderly, interact with schools to deal with vandalism and drug use on campus, and deal with street people in a way that inhibits the development of disorder before it becomes a problem. In these and numerous other ways, the police under COP are supposed to be proactive and engaged in their communities.

Personalized Police Service

Face-to-face interactions with the public are prioritized to include some long eschewed practices, such as foot patrol, bike patrol, and even horse patrol. Officers who work in patrol cars are encouraged to leave their vehicles whenever possible and interact with the people. Officers are assigned to beats on a semi-permanent basis so they can develop a service orientation toward the public. The police should take the time to meet with local small business owners and get to know them. Having police who are considered anonymous officers in uniform by the community is counterproductive and illogical. As has always been the case with the service style of policing, COP demands that the police consider their work to be a business of sorts. They should package and market it to the community.

Proactive Crime Prevention

COP involves ongoing problem solving that (again) includes members of the community whenever possible. Members of the honest, hard-working, law-abiding public must take part in the maintenance of order. This does not imply that citizens become involved in vigilante justice, but that people need to trust and cooperate with the police, and feel free to ask for help. This philosophy suggests a comfort zone needs to be created that does away with the coldness for which the police had become known under earlier paramilitaristic approaches. The police need to take a more serious approach to the sort of minor violations and disorderly conduct that impact quality of life. Reactive policing is only a small part of the police function. The police need to engage in overt, ongoing, proactive order maintenance activities.

Decentralization

Police work under COP needs to become more decentralized. Discretion is expanded at all levels, and lower level expertise is utilized. The fact that today's police officers are more intelligent, better educated, and better trained than ever before needs to be acknowledged. Today's officers can be "criminologists in uniform." The expertise that they obtain out on the beat, combined with their extended educational backgrounds, should be utilized. The old-fashioned command-and-control way of doing things is eschewed in favor of team-oriented problem solving. Led by more experienced and perhaps higher ranking officers, the police who patrol the streets are encouraged to develop anti-crime strategies as a team. Such strategies are a product of their individual and collective expertise.

The idea is to have a more democratic problem solving system in place, more effective because it takes advantage of the expertise of those officers who are out on the street. In addition, this philosophy attempts to make use of input from citizens. The local high school principal, the leader of a **neighborhood watch** group, and/or the members of a **neighborhood block organization** (Peak, 2008) are all community people with something to contribute. In this way, lower level expertise is plumbed and utilized, police decision making is decentralized, and the entire process becomes a collective endeavor.

Department-Wide Acceptance

COP is a new philosophy and, in some sense, it changes everything in police work. It calls for the employment of a new kind of officer, and it changes training, management, and leadership, and how the police are held accountable. Furthermore, COP attempts to employ volunteers from the community. Neighborhood organizations can be created, advisory boards can be developed, civilian review of the police can be instituted, and citizens can even participate in ad hoc ways. The idea of partnership between police and citizens is a powerful concept that must be drawn throughout the organization.

All of this is revolutionary. It impacts who the police are and what they do. To change police work in such a profound way, it is essential for everyone in a police organization to be on board. This cannot be a band-aid attempt at image polishing. It must be seen by everyone, from top to bottom, as an important change to which they are committed. Any feeling that COP is something that "some of us" do, while others revert to "normal" police work, is counterproductive and must be resisted by police leadership at all levels.

BOX 4.7

COMMUNITY ORIENTED POLICING SERVICES (COPS)

The Office of Community Oriented Policing Services within the Department of Justice is an agency that has supported this new type of policing since 1995. It has invested more than $12.4 billion in aid to encourage the effort. Over 13,000 state, local, and tribal agencies have been assisted with monies used to pay for officers, training materials, and a host of publications (CDs and DVDs included) that expand knowledge in the field (www.cops.usdoj.gov).

REVIEW CHART 4.5

ELEMENTS OF THE PHILOSOPHY OF COMMUNITY-ORIENTED POLICING

- Logical, planned change
- The "broken windows" theory of crime causation
- Police–community partnership
- Broader definition of the police function
- Personalized police service
- Proactive crime prevention
- Decentralization, with emphasis on lower level expertise
- Department-wide acceptance

There are dozens of books about COP and, as noted in Box 4.7, an entire federal office within the Department of Justice is dedicated to the concept. We have only highlighted an endeavor that is much more far-reaching. For as much as it is critical for the modern police leader to understand the history and philosophical underpinnings of COP, it is equally important to understand some criticisms of the movement. It is toward those criticisms that we now turn.

 ## COP CRITIQUE

While acceptance of COP by academics and most police leaders is unquestioned, there are several philosophical difficulties with the idea. There are also pragmatic problems with its application. COP has become so popular as a goal in police circles, with so much emphasis placed upon it, that it has become difficult to analyze. It has come to be defined in too many different ways and utilized to describe too many different programs. Some have questioned whether COP is real or just a new form of rhetoric (Greene and Mastrofski, 1988). Here are a few typical criticisms.

Lack of Rank-and-File Acceptance

Everyone agrees that COP is a philosophical change of direction for police work. As such, it requires acceptance everywhere within any police organization that attempts it. The implication is that this new style cannot work without the power of both the administration and the subculture behind it. Unfortunately, this is exactly what has been found to be the case in some locations. COP has been opposed by the entrenched establishment of rank-and-file police officers in enough places that the lack of universal commitment is regularly observed in some departments. Since COP is meant to be a complete change of attitude, strategy, and administration, it can be thwarted by naysaying at any level. As can be the case with any form of change in police work, the power of subcultural tradition can be controlling.

COP is not something that can involve a few officers being serious about it when a majority of officers consider it to be an unwanted nuisance that operates on the side. In some departments, police administrators have amplified this problem by creating "COP units" that operate independently, outside of the dominant administrative model. This is exactly the wrong thing to do. When this occurs, the chance for changing the entire police culture and police management style is nonexistent. COP has to be considered "real police work" by everyone.

Middle Management Resistance

While some difficulty for COP is created by rank-and-file officers railing against it, some middle managers also rebel against its operational realities. Under COP in operation, authority sometimes does not parallel responsibility. COP can be defeated by middle managers just as easily as it can be defeated by the rank and file.

The principle that authority must parallel responsibility in complex organizations is a basic idea, found in just about every introductory textbook in the fields of both public administration and business administration. It suggests that if they are to be held accountable for the effectiveness of subordinates, supervisors should be given authority over subordinates. If an administrator does not have authority to command and control what is done by his or her subordinates, then how can the poor performance of those subordinates be held against the administrator?

This principle is often violated in the administrative world. This occurs when a supervisor complains about **micromanagement** (Chambers, 2004). Micromanagement is the propensity of someone from higher up in an organization's structure to come into a suborganization to make changes and later hold the supervisor accountable for the fact that the changes did not work. The supervisor's authority over the group has been violated, and therefore he or she can rightfully complain that it is not fair to hold them accountable for the group's performance.

This is a practical problem that has occurred in some police jurisdictions attempting COP. While the new philosophy has created a collegial way of problem solving, the middle manager still tends to be held accountable if things do not go well. Having lost the ability to command and control that they possessed under the old system, middle managers under COP are sometimes still held responsible for the lack of success of a strategy when it fails. When this happens, COP appears to be unfair to middle managers. Add this sort of resistance to that of lower level officers in many organizations and we have a recipe for disaster.

Evaluations

Americans expect accountability where their tax dollars are concerned. COP represents a huge change in how the police do *everything*, including how they spend money. People are naturally driven to know if it is effective or not. Arguably, if

COP is effective, crime should go down. According to the theory of "broken windows" that is behind the philosophy, the partnership between community and police should work to decrease crime in the long run. Its effectiveness should show up in the hard numbers that make up crime statistics.

But what if crime goes up under COP? Would that prove that COP is ineffective? The paradox is that this would not necessarily be true. If a greater degree of trust were to develop between the public and the police—as is supposed to be the case under COP—people would turn to the police for help and aid in investigations more often. More community support for police investigations would mean more crimes would be solved, but more crimes would be reported, as well. As a result, crime statistics would increase. Paradoxically, this increase in crime may occur because COP is working well.

In fact, this is the case. In some places, COP has produced comforting statistics because crime has gone down; in other places, crime has gone up under COP (Roberg et al., 2005: 96–98). That does not necessarily mean that COP is not working. Normal crime statistics are by no means definitive as gauges of police effectiveness under COP. If this is true, how *can* COP be effectively evaluated?

Under COP, a large number of schemes have been created in an attempt to evaluate the performance of individual officers, teams of officers, and police organizations. Such schemes often seek to evaluate the quality of life or the feelings of safety on the street in the minds of the citizenry. The logic is that if the quality of life goes up and/or the feeling of safety increases, then COP is working. This is presumed to be true regardless of whether crime numbers change.

Individual assessment tools have also been developed to determine the competence of police officers under COP. The assessment measures involved are often long, complicated, protracted research tools that are different in virtually every location (Roberg et al., 2005: 97). Their substantive effectiveness at developing any realistic picture of the professionalism of officers is debated just about everywhere they are attempted. The reputed jadedness of police officers contributes to this debate.

Both of these types of assessments are complicated, vague, and sometimes difficult to understand. Evaluating the "quality of life" for citizens is difficult at best. Evaluating the "job done" by individual police officers or groups of officers is equally difficult. We will examine just how difficult this can be in Chapter 7. For now, it is enough to note that the evaluation of COP is problematic; millions of dollars can be spent without any way of proving they have been spent wisely.

Reinventing Past Problems

Even the most ardent supporters of COP acknowledge that it is somewhat like 19th century policing. It involves such tactics as foot patrol, semi-permanent beat assignments, and an ongoing, personal relationship between individual police officers and citizens. COP also involves a redefinition of the police that harkens back to an era when they were more oriented toward social welfare. All of this is being done with the best intentions.

BOX 4.9

OLD WINE IN NEW BOTTLES

The metaphor "old wine in new bottles" is often used to discuss the framing of old ideas in a different way. Several critics of COP have suggested that this "new" philosophy is merely a way of going back to the 19th century—undoubtedly, a bad idea. Among them, Samuel Walker (a police historian) suggests COP enthusiasts misunderstand the history of 19th century policing, painting a flowery, unrealistic picture of an era that was actually rife with corruption, incompetence, and "curbside justice." Walker finds that going back to the "good old days" might not be a very good strategy (Walker, 1984).

We must take the assertion "COP is like 19th century policing" and ask ourselves what 19th century policing was really like (Walker, 1997). To be sure, the police were closer to the community and remained on their beats for extended periods of time. But, police officers in that era used these dynamics to create ongoing payoff schemes that bilked local businesses, intimidated individual citizens, and controlled communities in undemocratic ways. The police had much more discretion then and used it to convolute the law; they made it work for the police and against the interests of justice. The 19th century police took a minute-by-minute interest in the maintenance of order on the streets. They were on foot and directly engaged those who were drunk, those who sold illegal substances, those who were involved in prostitution, and so forth. They utilized this reality to further their own corrupt interests and apply excessive force so often that they were known for prosecuting "curbside justice" on a regular basis.

If COP is anything like 19th century policing, we should be very leery of its propensity to recreate such practices. Of course, we do not have the same type of uneducated and unprofessional officers on the street today as were on the street back then, but are we in fact asking for such problems to recur if we go back to that era? Unfortunately, the answer is, "Who knows?"

Problematic Assumptions

The COP philosophy is based on several assumptions that, in some places, have proven to be false (Roberg et al., 2005: 95–99). It assumes that citizens will participate actively and consistently as partners with the police. As it turns out, sometimes citizen interest and participation—great when COP arrives—wanes over time. People lose interest and want the police to do it all because "that's what they are paid for." Police interest and commitment can also fade over time. The police can revert to form and deal with crime-related problems among themselves (as has been the case for generations) without reference to community input.

Furthermore, COP assumes the communal development of strategies will eventuate in the implementation of tactics that mirror those strategies. It assumes that the process will possess a certain level of integrity. In practice, however, police officers will sometimes revert to solving problems utilizing their own personal philosophies and experiences, rather than utilizing tactics developed for COP. The movement has spawned a different type of police training, and it is assumed that this training will have a long-term effect on police behavior. While some research indicates the police who experience community-oriented training leave with a solid understanding of its principles, other research shows that when they go out on the street, traditional subcultural values tend to take over and drive police decision making.

Finally, the philosophy of COP suggests an ongoing reevaluation of strategies, tactics, and assessment tools will be a consistent part of the process. It is assumed that constant reevaluation will keep strategies fresh and responsive to new community developments. But it turns out that the bureaucratic propensity to institutionalize a single way of doing things tends to inhibit this type of ongoing creativity.

Several of the assumptions that underwrite the philosophy may not hold up over time; how COP really operates in practice can be problematic. The nexus between theory and reality is not yet set in stone in America, as the police almost everywhere wrestle with what COP will eventually look like. COP is just too new to know how effective it will be in the long run.

This list of criticisms is disconcerting, but must be taken seriously. Efforts must be made to answer such "standard" criticisms of COP in action. As we progress over time, it is important to remember the good news: the police officers of today are not those of the 19th century. In terms of intelligence, education, training, and subcultural commitment to integrity and competence, contemporary officers are not likely to become mired in the problems of the past.

REVIEW CHART 4.6

CRITICISMS OF COMMUNITY-ORIENTED POLICING

- Lack of rank-and-file acceptance in some places
- Middle management resistance: authority does not parallel responsibility
- The impossibility of definitive evaluation
- Reinvention of past problems
- Problematic assumptions
- Police subcultural resistance

BOX 4.10

SUBCULTURAL NAYSAYING

Instituting COP is particularly difficult due to the power of the ubiquitous police subculture. As noted by numerous authors over time, police work is a profession that tends to include more than its share of naysayers. Because they see the worst in people, as a consequence of the job they do, police officers tend to be a very jaded, if not cynical, group of people. That pessimism can be aimed at change—any sort of change—in the police world. This is particularly important when we view the revolutionary nature of the changes COP is attempting to bring about in American policing.

Criticism should not be read to imply that COP is not an important idea or that it will not work in the long run. COP is critical to the future development of the professional police in America. It is an idea, or set of ideas, whose time has come. Nothing is more important to the police in America than this drive toward the achievement, finally, of professionalism.

SUMMATION

It can appear that COP is either in place or being put into place everywhere in American policing. But this is not the case. The rhetoric is there—virtually all across the nation—but a large number of police departments actually maintain one of the three classic styles of policing differentiated by Wilson back in the late 1960s. In those departments, the move toward the new philosophy is progressing slowly due to police subcultural opposition, pragmatic problems associated with any change, and troublesome assumptions about COP in operation. Given that such a new philosophy requires everyone in the department to absorb the change wholeheartedly, it will be some time before COP becomes the norm across America.

It is critical for police leaders to understand these facts. They must know their police culture, of course, but also know their local history, the history of COP, and whether, in their jurisdiction, the move toward COP is occurring in reality or is an empty public relations ruse. This knowledge is of vital importance to the police leader because it is upon their shoulders that the future of American policing—of professionalism—rests.

There are several central paradoxes involved here. One is that, while instituting COP, we are at once encouraging innovation and discouraging micromanagement. For police leaders, this creates a fine line to walk when motivating and assessing their charges. Furthermore, while COP is the wave of the future, dealing with Wilson's three classical styles is today's reality. Encouraging the evolution of

COP is a central part of the police leadership role, to be sure. On the other hand, realistic goals and pragmatic realities present leaders with the requirement to be both in tune with the *ideals* of the movement and conversant with real-life exigencies. For while COP ostensibly creates new organizational structures and communications models, in fact, informal systems are how things are always accomplished anyway!

DISCUSSION QUESTIONS

1. Many people (and police officers) believe that the watchman style is the best style of policing. Usually, this is because they appreciate the laid-back and noninvasive nature of this mode of policing. Discuss the strengths of the style, but equally discuss the substantial drawbacks to this form. Why is it considered to be an old-fashioned, outdated, and even unprofessional style by so many people?

2. Some people consider the legalistic style to be the optimum form of policing, largely because they see so much of it on television and/or because they have military backgrounds. Discuss how the legalistic style discourages old-style corruption of authority, but also encourages Dirty Harry–style policing.

3. Discuss how boredom, either for rookies or more experienced officers, creates what are pretty much the only drawbacks to service-style policing.

4. Consider the sociological definition of professionalism discussed in the text and our analysis of it. Discuss whether or not you believe that American policing is moving in the direction of becoming a genuine profession. What will it take for this to come to pass?

5. In police work today, we are all hearing about COP on a regular basis. What are its drawbacks? Aside from those that you have read in the text, can you think of any additional problems with the theory of and/or implementation of COP as you understand it?

KEY TERMS

Broken windows: A theory or parable cited by criminologists James Q. Wilson and George Kelling in 1982 that suggests if windows in old houses or buildings are not repaired the condition of the structure will continue to deteriorate. This condition continues until crime begins to occur and expand.

Corruption of authority: Overextending or underutilization of the authority given to a peace officer through improper use of discretion. Example: Making a fabricated/false arrest.

Cultural relativity: An individual's beliefs and activities as understood in terms of his or her own culture.

Decentralization: The delegation of power from a central organizational authority to suborganizations or bureaus.

Department-wide acceptance: Ideology or philosophy accepted by all entities and levels of an organization.

Ethnic enclaves: A neighborhood, district, or suburb that retains some cultural distinction from a larger, surrounding area.

Fishing expeditions: A non-specific search for information, especially incriminating information. Example: An officer goes out on his own and seeks information about a person or group to see if he can find out anything incriminating without any initial factual basis for doing so.

Legalistic style: The style of policing that operates by the standards set by law.

Micromanagement: A management style where a manager closely observes or controls the work of his or her subordinates or employees.

Neighborhood watch (neighborhood block organization): An organized group of citizens devoted to crime and vandalism prevention within a neighborhood.

One standard of conduct: A specific standard of conduct based upon specific rules, policies, or laws. In the context of legalistic style of policing, the one standard of conduct is the law.

Organizational ethos: The moral character of an organization.

Planned change: An effort, planned organization-wide and managed from the top, to increase organization effectiveness through interventions in the organization's processes, using behavioral-science knowledge.

Police–community partnerships: A partnership formed between the police, community, schools, churches, and businesses to support the mission and goals of the enforcement of laws and performance of service in the community.

Proactive crime prevention: Checking the crime activities in the community and developing plans on how to prevent the same crimes from occurring in the future using modern methods of data collection, preventive crime techniques, and organizational resources.

Rule of cop: When a police officer makes a decision based upon arbitrary judgment against rules, policies, or laws.

Service style: The style of law enforcement predicated upon the notion that the police are available to the community to perform a service rather than just enforcement of the law.

Systemized body of knowledge: Knowledge in an area (such as science, medicine, police work) where each component of that area is set up in a systematic order for reference and definition.

Victimless crime: Refers to infractions of criminal law without any identifiable evidence of an individual who has suffered damage in the infraction.

War on Crime: Generally known to have been an established agenda by President Richard Nixon based upon recommendations from a committee (Commission on Law Enforcement and Criminal Justice) assigned to research crime in America and ways to stop it and to help fund state and local law enforcement agencies in their effort against criminal activity in their areas and communities.

War on Drugs: A prohibition campaign undertaken by the United States government, with the assistance of participating countries, intended to both define and reduce the illegal drug trade.

Watchman style: A law enforcement style of operation based more upon passive, reactive enforcement than an active and proactive style of enforcement. Officers working under this style of law enforcement basically wait for calls for service rather than seeking violations of the law.

EXAMPLE SCENARIOS

Officer Jones Confronts a Suspect

Officer Jones's chief espouses the theory that his officers should be available to citizens only when requested. In the community, they should be invisible. If a need for service is sought by the citizens, then they respond. Otherwise they sit back, make rounds in the community, and act on situations only when they observe a significant violation of the law. This method of policing does not really satisfy Officer Jones, as he believes he should be out seeking law breakers and catching "bad guys."

One day he spots a juvenile whom he suspects of committing burglaries on his beat. He stops the boy and conducts a "field interrogation." The juvenile's parents complain to the police chief, and Officer Jones is summoned to the chief's office to receive counseling for acting outside the philosophy of the department.

What style of police work did Officer Jones portray in this example? What style did his chief want him to follow? Did Officer Jones actually do anything wrong in this scenario?

What could Officer Jones have done differently to address his concern that the juvenile he confronted was actually committing burglaries in the neighborhood? How might he have acted in concert with the chief's wishes?

As an additional exercise, think about (discuss) how each of our different styles of policing would approach this one simple interaction. What would be different? Furthermore, what would be the strengths and weaknesses of each style?

Officer Jones Again

Officer Jones decides to change departments and is hired by a nearby department as an experienced officer. His new chief believes in the philosophy of making your presence known at every opportunity. Every officer has a "take home" patrol vehicle. The chief believes this enhances the presence of police in the community and also gives the department an edge in an emergency call; all vehicles are ready to roll at the time of contact and are ready for immediate service.

Officer Jones has received a commendation for "making" a juvenile on two burglaries in his beat. He accomplished this by conducting regular "field interrogations" and making other street contacts and forwarding the information to the detective division. While on calls for service to burglary victims' residences and businesses, he dusted the points of entry for fingerprints and submitted the print cards to the crime lab for possible future use.

Officer Jones's activity was rewarded when a detective discovered that the juvenile with whom Officer Jones had made a field contact had burglarized a residence on Officer Jones's beat. The detective got "hits" on the prints, and the juvenile was arrested for the burglary of two houses.

What type of law enforcement style does Officer Jones's new chief promote? Can you argue that he might, in fact, be portraying one of several different styles? Which ones?

ADDITIONAL READING

This chapter's discussion about the three styles of police organization are based upon James Q. Wilson's classic work *Varieties of Police Behavior* (Harvard University Press, 1968). Other excellent studies of differences in police organizational styles are *Styles of Urban Policing: Organization, Environment, and Police Styles in Selected American Cities* (NYU Press, 1988), by Jeffrey Slovak, and "The Influence of Environmental and Organizational Factors on Police Style in Urban and Rural Environments" (*Journal of Research in Crime and Delinquency* 27[2], 1990), by Cohn P. Crank. Unlike Wilson, who studies only urban and suburban departments of large and intermediate size, Crank takes the time to study and to reflect upon rural policing styles as well.

In *Organizational Structure in American Police Agencies: Context, Complexity, and Control* (SUNY Press, 2003), Edward R. Maguire finds that there is great resistance to the stylistic change from traditional forms toward COP. We included in this chapter a reference to the Community Oriented Policing Services office of the U.S. Department of Justice. The website for COPS is found at www.cops.usdoj .gov, where the student can find almost unlimited information about the subject.

In our consideration of the lead-up to the COP era, we discussed *The Wickersham Commission on Law Observance and Law Enforcement* (U.S. Government Printing Office, 1931). Also important is *Police Riots* (Wadsworth, 1972), by Rodney Stark. This work is essential to any understanding of why so much pressure was brought to bear regarding changing the philosophy of policing nationwide.

The classic piece in the field of community policing, of course, was George Kelling and James Q. Wilson's article in *The Atlantic* from March 1982 entitled "Broken Windows." *Problem Oriented Policing* (McGraw-Hill, 1990), by Herman Goldstein, also ended up being considered a classic in this field. Since that time, there have been dozens of works about COP, including *Fixing Broken Windows: Restoring Order and Reducing Crime in Our Communities* (Free Press, 1998), which was written by George L. Kelling, the original co-author of the broken windows theory, and Catherine M. Coles.

Now that the movement toward COP is more than two decades old and there is a wealth of research in the field, the student may wish to consider more contemporary books such as *Community Police: Partnerships for Problem Solving* (Wadsworth, 2007), by Linda S. Miller and Karen M. Hess, *Community Police and Problem Solving, 5th Ed.* (Prentice Hall, 2007), by Kenneth J. Peak and Ronald W. Glensor, and *Community Oriented Policing: A Systematic Approach to Policing, 4th Ed.* (Prentice Hall, 2007), by Willard M. Oliver. Finally, it is interesting to note that the COP movement has become international. *Community Policing: National and International Models and Approaches* (Willan Publishing, 2005) is a work by Preeti Nijhar and Mike Brogden that informs the reader of international experiences in the field.

PART TWO

Operating Principles

In Part Two, we will move away from theoretical discussions toward more pragmatic considerations about how police supervision and leadership is accomplished. Chapter 5 examines a central role of the police leader—that of teaching communication skills to his or her subordinates. Chapter 6 is about motivation, suggesting that the police leader is very much like a coach, and police leadership involves many of the pitfalls of coaching. Chapter 7 is about the always troublesome problem of assessing the performance of police officers. How does the supervisor fairly assess the performance of subordinates while at the same time motivating them to take chances and attempt to accomplish their multiple tasks in creative and innovative ways?

CHAPTER 5

Teaching Communication

INTRODUCTION

Communication between professionals and citizens is important in all helping professions, where workers deal with the public. But in police work, as opposed to social work or the medical field, *everything* about professional effectiveness hangs on communication. Meaningful communication can make or break the achievement of the major goals of the police, and determines how efficient the police are at accomplishing their main functions. Communication travels both up and down the chain of command. Communication between officers out on the street is critical, but so is internal communication within the police organization. And everything—all that the police can and do accomplish—is predicated upon how well police officers communicate with the citizenry they serve.

Therefore, a vital role for the police leader is teaching **communication skills** and monitoring the use of them by subordinate officers. So important is this function that we have begun our set of chapters about the more pragmatic roles played by the supervisor with this topic up front. Aside from being aware of the dynamics visited upon police officers by the paradoxes of police work and understanding police organizational dynamics discussed in the above chapters, the role of police leader is most defined by the ability of the supervisor to instill communication skills.

In past eras, conventional wisdom held that effective police–citizen communication could not be taught. Just as there were those individuals who were "born leaders," there were those who were "born communicators." It was as if interpersonal communication was something that was accomplished through the use of special **charismatic skills**, with which people were or were not naturally endowed (Mumford, 2006). Today, we know better; we know how to teach effective communication. In this chapter, we will engage the reader with several sets of ideas unknown to police administrators until very recently. In doing so, we begin with a central theme in the world of communications study: a focus on the difference between academic intelligence and social (or emotional) intelligence. Understanding this differentiation—one that has been made only recently in the field of organization theory—is important because it is changing what we think about individual communications skills, personnel assessment, and how and why individuals operating in the people-oriented professionals become effective.

SOCIAL INTELLIGENCE

In America, we are accustomed to hearing about people's intelligence quotient, or **IQ**. The IQ is a calculated percentage that relates any individual's native intelligence (not their level of education) to the average person's level of native intelligence. When we talk about this type of intelligence, we are discussing an academic intelligence. People take intelligence tests and their scores are compared to those of others their age. The number that is thus developed—the quotient—is actually a percentage that indicates where the individual belongs on an imaginary

BOX 5.1

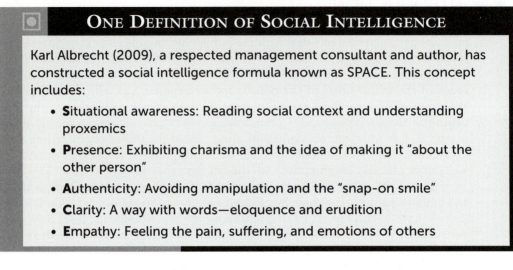

ONE DEFINITION OF SOCIAL INTELLIGENCE

Karl Albrecht (2009), a respected management consultant and author, has constructed a social intelligence formula known as SPACE. This concept includes:

- **S**ituational awareness: Reading social context and understanding proxemics
- **P**resence: Exhibiting charisma and the idea of making it "about the other person"
- **A**uthenticity: Avoiding manipulation and the "snap-on smile"
- **C**larity: A way with words—eloquence and erudition
- **E**mpathy: Feeling the pain, suffering, and emotions of others

continuum that stretches between the most intelligent and the least intelligent people. The individual's test score is divided by the average score of people their age, and that creates the number about which we have heard so much.

An IQ of 100 indicates an average IQ. Those with higher IQs are smarter; the average police recruit's is above average (Guller and Guller, 2003). A person whose IQ approaches 140 is considered to be a genius or near genius. At the other end of the spectrum, a person whose IQ is between 70 and 80 is "borderline deficient." People who are between 50 and 69 are morons, between 20 and 49 are imbeciles, and below 20 are idiots (Wechsler, 1944). It is interesting that all of these words have made their way into the American vernacular as similar terms, connoting some level of intellectual incompetence. In the world of clinical psychology, they have specific meanings.

A person with a high IQ is capable of doing well in the world of formal education or professional training; he or she is considered to be capable of ingesting great amounts of information and investigating complex concepts. The IQ is a measure of *intellectual potential*. As such, it is of great importance in the organizational world of the police, but is not the only important indicator of officer brain capacity.

Today, when we study interpersonal relationships in the bureaucratic world, we are concerned with IQ at the selection level. When hiring bureaucrats, we are concerned that those who are hired to interact with the public have a basic intelligence level high enough to be trained to perform necessary skills. Since modern-day hiring requirements are so protracted and sophisticated, this level of basic intelligence is possessed by every candidate who is hired to work in any public bureaucracy. Having a sufficiently high IQ is, in other words, seldom a problem for today's public servant.

Much more important than a person's IQ is their SQ, or **social intelligence** quotient (Carkhuff, 1973; Goleman, 2006). This is because a high SQ is often wanting in bureaucracy (especially police work) today. As implied from the definition in Box 5.1, the socially intelligent person can benefit the police organization in numerous ways. High SQ people interact well with the public, criminal suspects, superiors within the police organizational structure, and subordinates. While IQ is important in the modern police officer, it is not something that should overly concern police leadership. In today's police world, it is SQ that is sometimes in short supply.

The police must respond to domestic scenes, calls for service involving irrational people, and crowd scenes where potential violence hangs in the air. They must help distraught and fearful individuals, and handle many situations that require a steady hand. All of society's ills are visited upon police officers on the beat every day. The best officers are the ones able to handle the **vagaries** of daily encounters with people who are at their worst. Not only must officers deal with irrational people, but they must be able to handle their own emotions through difficult circumstances. Furthermore, responding to these types of stress-laden situations is something that goes on throughout the entire professional lifetime of police officers. It never lightens up or gets easier. One reason for police officers leaving the profession is that some of them cannot handle this reality.

Officers with "social smarts" are usually the ones who can work through daily situations, go home, and **decompress**. They have learned to grant themselves enough time to work off the continuing stresses of responding to difficult incidents and dealing with people who are at their worst. For many years, we called the socially skilled officers who could balance their emotions "unique," "special," or "super professionals." As it turns out, these people are socially smart. They are able to get through daily high energy situations with little physical effort. They rarely get into altercations. They infrequently receive citizen complaints. They don't often draw their weapon or use force unnecessarily. In general, they are more personally self-aware and centered; professionally, they tend to move up the chain of command rapidly, due to these positive characteristics.

Such officers have always appeared to possess some kind of special quality that is difficult to pinpoint. Something in their backgrounds or personal psyches has usually been credited with allowing them to behave in psychologically healthy ways. Something quirky or even charismatic has always been considered to be the cause of their superiority. But today, we have clearer explanations of the qualities these individuals possess. Furthermore, those qualities can be described, modeled, and taught. Lumped together generally, these qualities are called interpersonal communication (IPC) skills, **social skills**, or emotional skills.

Good interpersonal skills have always been a staple of those officers working the street who are most successful in their work and personal lives. Coupled with common sense, being interpersonally competent can make an officer's life easier and less complicated.

BOX 5.2

EMOTIONAL INTELLIGENCE

In making the point that being concerned with IQ is often of limited value in the organizational world, some authors have discussed social intelligence (SQ) and **emotional intelligence** (EQ) as alternative constructs. In our discussion, we will not take the time to differentiate between the two. This is because SQ and EQ overlap to a great extent, and both are alternatives to the historical fixation with IQ. Without getting into the specifics too deeply, it could be argued that EQ is a critical part of SQ and vice versa.

Social Intelligence in Action

Officers Jane and Tom are on patrol. They receive a call for service to respond to a domestic violence situation. Dispatch advises them that a child says her mother and father are fighting and she is afraid her dad will seriously hurt her mom. Dispatch advises the unit to respond immediately. Upon arrival, both officers exit the patrol car and rush to the open front door of the residence. They hear loud voices and a noise sounding like breaking glass. They enter the house and see a man and woman arguing (but not physically fighting) with each other. Neither person appears bruised or injured. The situation is tense, and it is clear that things might quickly turn into a fight or physical confrontation.

The officers separate the couple to calm the scene and determine the problem. The couple's energy levels are very high. While Tom talks to the woman and attempts to calm her down, Jane moves the man away from the woman into another room. The man appears far more hostile. Jane, in a very even voice, encourages the man to calm down so they can get the information necessary to keep the situation from becoming a full-fledged domestic dispute. Both officers wish to keep things from developing into the sort of altercation where someone ends up going to jail or getting hurt. Jane's even level of behavior and tone of voice seem to have an effect on the husband, and his energy level begins to come down some. He is still very agitated, animated, and loud, but Jane senses he is no longer so upset that he wants to fight.

Sizing the man up, Jane tells him to sit down and that she wants him to help her understand the problem. The man's energy dissipates a little more, and he moves to sit in a chair. Jane continues to closely observe the man to determine if he has a weapon or is working himself up for another round of yelling. Jane stays several feet away from the man and faces him, keeping direct eye contact. While the man is sitting, it appears as though Jane's posture and position are no threat to the man, but it is clear that Jane is in control of herself and the situation. Using an even tone of voice, Jane gets the man to calm down and to tell her what the problem is.

Tom has more of a problem with the woman. She seems relieved that the police appeared in the first place, and she readily submits to being separated. She sits down on the living room couch, but she remains on edge and uncomfortable. With some difficulty, Tom obtains the woman's side of the story. In the end, Jane manages to determine there was no physical contact between the couple. She even gets the man to volunteer to leave for the evening, understanding that he should not return until both parties calm down enough to talk. An arrest is alleviated.

Upon leaving the scene, Tom asks Jane, "How did you do that?" "Do what?" Jane responds. "Get the guy to calm down and not get worse. If I had tried to do that with the guy, we would have been in a fight." Jane says, "I don't know, I guess I just b---s----ed him."

This brief scenario exhibits the type of detail with which all police officers are familiar. It presents the police leader with an example of the type of communication skills we are discussing. In the following sections, we will keep this brief scenario in mind when talking generally about interpersonal social skills. In particular, we will talk about the training model taught to police officers by Stephen Sampson, a conflict resolution and interpersonal skills specialist.

THE SOCIAL SKILLS MODEL

In recent years, police agencies have been exploring various training models that might help improve officer communication skills and might enhance their ability to manage people and situations. In the early 1970s, police agencies began to develop specially trained officers who were experts in managing domestic violence situations. Whenever possible, these domestic dispute teams were assigned to every family disturbance or ongoing neighborhood problem. In its day, this was a radical idea. The accepted notion was to temper and defuse domestic situations, and take as little action as possible. This was because such altercations were considered by the police to be civil violations. Unless either party was injured, domestic disturbances were "none of our business," as far as the police were concerned. Officers working in these specialized domestic violence units received training in dealing with family violence. Most of the training at the time was scenario-oriented, asking officers to act out (and work out) examples, such as the one posited above.

Similarly, in the late 1960s, professional psychologist Robert Carkhuff developed a helping skills training model for counselors (Carkhuff, 1973). This model was created to help people in the social welfare professions deal with individuals who needed guidance and counseling to overcome social and emotional problems. Derived from very closely observed and monitored research into the human communication process, the behaviors of good communicators were broken down into nonverbal and verbal components that supported the specific characteristics of highly interpersonally skilled individuals. This model required special training; communication was taught as a skill, not just an amorphous conception. The model was taught successfully to working professionals in the helping sciences.

Then John D. Blakeman and associates restructured the counseling model to make it relevant to those interpersonal skills that are utilized in management (Blakeman et al., 1977). This model allowed a person to develop the skills necessary to manage human behavior rather than counsel people through emotional problems. Blakeman and his colleagues were able to use the Carkhuff model (again, this model was developed to help counselors with their interpersonal skill sets) in prison settings by teaching behavioral management skills to correctional officers. The idea was to teach those officers how to more easily manage inmates (and themselves) by using an interpersonal skill set that good communicators use. As one might imagine, managing inmates is a difficult task even if someone possesses good interpersonal skills. Prisons provided a fertile proving ground for the type of interpersonal communication training that we can offer today to contemporary police officers.

Blakeman and his colleagues then decided to research the effects of their efforts in a longitudinal study. After training correctional staff with the interpersonal communication (IPC) skills model, Blakeman and his colleagues examined pre-training and post-training data. They noted that six months after receiving training, the officers who went through the program had improved their work environment in several ways. Sick leave use decreased, complaints against officers dropped, and inmate assaults against staff were down from the pre-training period. Furthermore, there were fewer officer injuries on the job, and the use of vacation leave decreased. Overall, the trained group of officers improved their on-the-job performance, while a comparison (or control) group did not.

As a result, this model was adopted by the **National Institute of Corrections**, and has been successfully taught throughout the country to other correctional and detention agencies. Over time, other agencies confirmed similar, positive results. For example, at the Broward County (Florida) Sheriff's Office's Detention Division, the deputies were trained in 2003 by one of the authors, using this model. Positive results included fewer incidents of violent confrontation and less vacation and sick leave time taken off. We can conclude that interpersonal skills have been noted to be a cornerstone of good people management, and these skills can be taught and learned. This was a genuine breakthrough in the world of socially interactive professions. As one can envision, it has now made its way into police work.

More recently, there has been a body of research conducted regarding social and emotional skills, and their impact in the business environment. Daniel Goleman, an internationally known psychologist, completed studies in the realms of social and emotional intelligence (Goleman, 1998; 2006) and noted that managers who possessed specific emotional competencies (self-awareness, self-management, **social awareness**, and/or social skill) were most likely to be the most successful salespersons (highest percentage of profits), the most successful leaders (the best employee retention rate with the highest performance per unit), and most likely to succeed (get results).

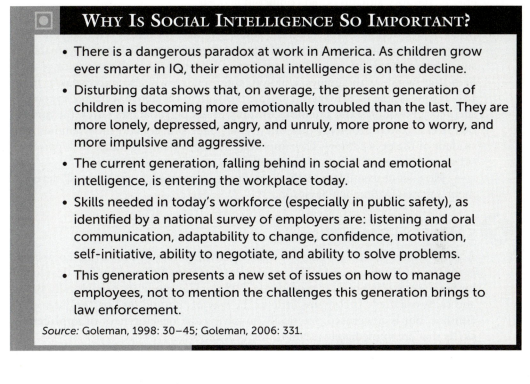

BOX 5.3

WHY IS SOCIAL INTELLIGENCE SO IMPORTANT?

- There is a dangerous paradox at work in America. As children grow ever smarter in IQ, their emotional intelligence is on the decline.

- Disturbing data shows that, on average, the present generation of children is becoming more emotionally troubled than the last. They are more lonely, depressed, angry, and unruly, more prone to worry, and more impulsive and aggressive.

- The current generation, falling behind in social and emotional intelligence, is entering the workplace today.

- Skills needed in today's workforce (especially in public safety), as identified by a national survey of employers are: listening and oral communication, adaptability to change, confidence, motivation, self-initiative, ability to negotiate, and ability to solve problems.

- This generation presents a new set of issues on how to manage employees, not to mention the challenges this generation brings to law enforcement.

Source: Goleman, 1998: 30–45; Goleman, 2006: 331.

Robert J. Sternberg, of Yale University, suggests that studying social intelligence may be a better predictor of a person's success in life than the standard academic intelligence surveying method. He posits that IQ testing focuses "more intently on 'inert' knowledge, thereby excluding a whole range of intellectual abilities" (Sternberg, 1997: 11–13). While we will not go any further into the specific debate over IQ versus SQ in this discussion, we will simply note that being socially and emotionally competent is of critical importance for workaday police officers out on the street. Again, it is arguably even more important than native intelligence.

In the domestic scene presented earlier in the chapter, Tom asked Jane how she managed to get the arguing husband to calm down, and Jane replied that she really didn't know, but that she just BS'ed the guy. This might indeed appear to have been the case. However, all of the behaviors demonstrated by Jane show a competent, emotionally and socially mature officer. In the following sections, the specific skills that Jane demonstrated will be illustrated and discussed. It is important to note that while these skills are usually—historically—acquired through trial and error, they can be taught to anybody. If the recipient of this type of training applies these skills consciously, there will be an improvement in interpersonal competence resulting in the ability to become more proficient at dealing with high energy, negative situations and conflict in general.

We have suggested that by improving these competencies (**social skills**), the performance of police officers on the street will improve. However, that is not the only positive dynamic associated with this sort of training. It is equally tenable to suggest that the ability of individual police officers to cope with the strains of their lives after work—with families, children, and friends—will also improve over time. Just as Jane is able to manage the hostile husband in the above scenario, so too can she manage troublesome situations off duty in her personal life. Given the numerous stress-related problems that often visit police officers and their families, any student of the police knows how important it would be to inculcate such personal, off-duty skills into the lives of police officers.

Now let us examine directly the police training model for social skill development, created by Stephen Sampson.

SAMPSON'S MODEL

A good model for the purposes of training officers how to be socially competent is the Social Intelligence Skills for Law Enforcement Officers model, developed by Stephen Sampson (Sampson et al., 2006). The model is behaviorally based and skills oriented. It contains little in the way of "should do" or "ought to do" content, but is structured practically, involving the development of **application skills** that are immediately useful to the beat officer.

The learning plan is designed to replicate the manner in which highly interpersonally skilled officers communicate. There are three modes of skills presented to the participants. The first, **sizing up** the situation, involves the elements of positioning, posturing, observing, and listening. This mode represents the beginning of the communication process during a one-on-one or one-on-many situation. The second mode, communicating, engages the verbal exchange portion of what highly skilled officers do when they communicate effectively with others. The last mode is called the application. This mode blends the nonverbal sizing-up skills and the verbal communicating skills to enhance the officer's ability to manage behavior in succinct ways.

The IPC model begins with a consideration of the logical and intuitively obvious skill of sizing up individuals and situations.

Sizing Up

Generations of police officers have learned how to size up situations in an informal but practical, almost casual way. Sampson and colleagues have brought together some of the subcultural wisdom involved in this endeavor and melded it with information gleaned through psychological study to come up with a pragmatic, teachable formula for sizing up situations on the street. Previously considered to be something developed out of the individual police officer's "sixth sense," sizing up, as it turns out, is eminently teachable and transferable—from experienced communicators to those who are neophytes.

Positioning Positioning consists of three components: distancing, looking directly, and facing off. Again, these are commonsense rules of thumb that psychologists have distilled down into teachable parts.

Distancing Distancing is known as **proxemics**, involving the skill of placing oneself at the correct distance from another person, given the circumstances of a specific interaction. This is a critical skill for the police. It involves being close enough to communicate, but far enough away for the officer to be safe.

Looking Directly Looking directly is the ability to be able to see (observe) all of the other person and their body language. By looking directly at the person with whom one is communicating, all facial expressions and body movement can be observed. This helps the communication process because the officer can observe nonverbal language, which gives him/her the ability to accurately assess the situation. All too often, police officers involved in stressful interactions tend to take an aloof and reserved posture. Because they are both worried about potential violence and concerned about being too "involved" in a situation, they fail to focus appropriately on the people with whom they are interacting.

Facing Off Facing off squarely while communicating gives an officer the appearance of paying attention to the person or persons he/she is confronting. While the looking directly skill involves taking in all that is happening in a substantive sense, facing off squarely is about the process that is going on; it is about how police officers appear in the eyes of citizens.

BOX 5.4

THE "ARM'S LENGTH" PARADOX

Standard police training attempts to keep officers safe in numerous ways. One axiom taught to rookies is, "Keep citizens at least an arm's length away from you at all times." To allow a person closer than arm's length can give them an unfair advantage over an officer when combined with the element of surprise.

Yet, paradoxically, the level of trust between two people can be elevated substantially if they position themselves closer. Standing in a bit closer indicates both openness and an invitation to share information. Officers going through this training are forced to deal with the paradox of approximating exactly how close is close enough for safety *and* for effective communication.

Thus, good positioning involves a set of skills that allow an officer to be close enough to communicate, but far enough away to be safe, observe all the body language and expressions the person is demonstrating, and begin the process of accurately sizing up the situation.

Posturing While it might appear to be redundant, the skills involved in police officer posturing are different, albeit still critical, from those discussed directly above.

Standing Erect By standing erect, an officer projects an aura of competence and presence. It implies professionalism and seriousness. This may be very important when communicating with witnesses and victims as well as with suspects. Again, we are focusing on process at this juncture, not substance. The *appearance* of knowing what you are doing establishes a dynamic of attention on the part of both participants in any interaction. An officer can also use this dynamic to help keep his or her own attention level high.

Eliminating Distractive Behaviors This principle of effective communication is possibly one of the most often violated in social interactions between people. Allowing distractions to compromise communication can be the death knell of effective give and take. Common distractions include activities such as cell phones ringing, jingling change in pockets, clicking a pen, smoking a cigarette, or just looking away while someone is speaking. The message sent when such ancillary activities are allowed to proceed interferes with the communication process in both substantive and procedural ways. Not only might an officer miss something critical that is said or done, but he or she appears to be unfocused or uncaring. When a person is not paying attention to another, it is insulting and rude. This kind of behavior can be a significant cause for the misinterpretation of messages. Distractive behavior can be cause for a lapse in careful observation during high energy situations.

Inclining Slightly Forward When an officer can do so, inclining slightly forward can indicate that the officer is focusing on the person with whom he or she is engaged. This nonverbal behavior is powerful because it indicates that an officer is serious and committed to taking in what the other person is doing or saying. Of course, this element of the posturing formula is similar to that of distancing. That is, there is a fine line—a balance of sorts—that must be observed when leaning in. To lean too far forward violates what is called an individual's **personal space**, and can be taken to be a form of intimidation. When a citizen interprets an officer's actions to indicate a desire to be intimidating, rather than responsive and open, leaning forward can create exactly the opposite effect than it is designed to obtain.

Effective posturing coupled with good positioning can create a promising beginning to positive communication between parties. These are skills that officers with good social skills demonstrate unconsciously. Further, these skills help keep the officer safe from any aggressive actions on the part of the person with whom he/she is communicating.

Observing Sizing up also involves a set of skills that are specifically focused on the citizen or suspect.

Looking Carefully Keeping a close eye on citizens and suspects—and their behaviors—has been axiomatic for officers since the invention of the uniformed police more than 200 years ago. It is obvious that, when looking for potential violence or people who might assault the police, nonverbal clues should be investigated. What is perhaps not so obvious is that such clues are important to everything—all forms of information—that police officers are required to obtain. The police must always look for body language, facial expressions, and changes in expected normal behavior so they can gain insight into a potential problem. All of this observation comes together and assists the officer in supporting the next component, which is inferring.

Inferring This component is a skill that good communicators acquire on the street as they move from being rookies into more experienced veteran officers. An amalgamation of bits and pieces of knowledge about the law, how people react to the police, and the pragmatics of highly stressed situations comes together over time to create the ability to infer from nonverbal behaviors of the person with whom they are communicating. The veteran officer notes the person's feelings, energy level, and so forth to help them tell if the behavior suggests one of a number of alternative behaviors. This helps the officer in determining the next two components in this sizing-up formula: deciding whether situations or individuals are normal or abnormal, and threatening or nonthreatening. In making such an inference, a police officer utilizes a stereotyping dynamic, discussed in Chapter 2. As a part of their working personalities, police officers apply common sense and observational powers to behavior on the street (Skolnick, 1966). They consistently make a pattern or picture in their minds of what the beat looks like under normal circumstances. The construction of this pattern involves taking note of traffic flow, commuting realities, the shifts of local manufacturing plants, the startup and finish times of schools, and so forth. Once the construction of a normal picture has been accomplished, it is easy for a police officer to determine that which is abnormal or does not fit the pattern. This is the essence of working a beat as a modern American police officer.

Deciding Normal/Abnormal In determining whether things are normal or abnormal for a given situation, an officer will need to consider the person he/she is communicating with and the circumstances. If the person is acting strangely (talking to himself or moving in a manner that signals danger), that person may be considered to be acting abnormally and the officer may believe trouble could be brewing. Over time, as an officer develops experience in the field, the definition of what an officer is looking for—what might constitute something abnormal—expands. Police officers look for people who are nervous, frightened, excited, depressed, elated, and/or driven by a host of other emotions. They look for small things, such as people wearing coats on hot days or people who exaggerate their "non-interest" in the police, trying too hard to fit in. Put succinctly, the obverse of the abnormal is the normal, and it is the job of the police to confront the negative of the photograph painted under normal circumstances.

Deciding Trouble/No Trouble   In many instances, the officer who possesses good communication skills can tell by the behavior of the person or persons with whom he/she is dealing, whether to be ready for potential trouble or not. An officer may note the person is agitated or edgy, and that behavior may raise the level of awareness of the officer for potential trouble. The officer may still want to keep himself/herself in a safe position and posture to be ready to react, just in case the situation turns the other way. Similar to the search for the abnormal, the search for danger is, to some extent, more important; it involves not merely constructing a list of people with whom the police need to interact, but searching for people who might assault police officers. Searching for the abnormal involves looking for probable cause; searching for trouble involves life and death.

The skills of observation are crucial to any officer's ability to be safe and to know what is going on around him or her. This is especially true when the officer is confronted with a threatening situation. Looking carefully at the environment, number of people, body language, facial expressions, and so forth can give clues about what the officer may need to be careful of. Skolnick (1966) called this searching for "symbolic assailants."

Listening   The final element to the sizing-up formula, listening, involves suspending judgment, picking out key words, identifying intensity levels, and reflecting upon the mood.

Suspending Judgment   For just about anyone under just about any circumstances, suspending judgment—waiting to hear all sides of an issue "until the facts are in"—is difficult to accomplish. For police officers, it is doubly difficult because they are so

BOX 5.5

THE PARADOX OF NORMALIZING CRIME

By definition, all criminal behavior is deviant, because it deviates from norms written down in penal codes. But to the bureaucrats working within the criminal justice system, all such deviant behavior must be codified or given a number. For a person to be arrested and placed into the legal system, a specifically determined legal code section must have been transgressed. Thus, the people who operate the legal system need to normalize crime in order to do their jobs. They must normalize the abnormal (Sudnow, 1993).

often moved to make judgments quickly in order to protect themselves from harm. It requires officers to concentrate on what is actually being demonstrated and match the observed behavior with what is being said. Perhaps an example is in order.

An officer can observe a person with a low energy level, a body language showing dropped shoulders, and the facial expression of being sad or confused. When the officer asks the person, "How are you doing?" the person responds, "Fine." The nonverbal cues do not signify the person being fine. There is a disconnect between what's being said and what the officer is observing. So the officer may heighten his or her level of attention in order to adequately handle a situation that might arise.

Picking Out Key Words Officers who are very good communicators have the capacity to pick out words or phrases that are key to the message they are receiving. They know how to look for those words in order to better understand any given situation that is at hand. Any key word can give a clue to the possibility of a problem or no problem. An example might be when a man refers to his ex-wife as his wife. Just that simple slip of the tongue can give an observant officer a key with which a domestic altercation might be handled.

Identifying Intensity Listening to the intensity of what a person is saying can give clues to underlying feelings. Officers who listen for the volume, pitch, and tone of the speech of the person with whom they are dealing can get an idea if the person is angry, scared, confused, sad, and so on. A person may dislike another, but not to such an extent that they hate them. A person may be upset by an altercation, but not hysterical or irrational about it. Plumbing a person's intensity of feeling can be of critical importance in understanding a situation and, concomitantly, in determining how to handle it.

Reflecting on Mood Considering the mood of the situation (based on the person or persons with whom the officer is dealing) means thinking about whether the mood is positive, negative, or neutral. This helps the officer in making a more accurate decision about how to handle the situation.

Understanding the above skills, polishing them, and being able to blend them into one's personality allows socially skilled officers to be effective. They are able to **position**, **posture**, **observe**, and **listen** closely and accurately to determine what is going on. These four basic skills give the officer the ability to be safe, accurate, and alert for any endeavor. Officers utilizing these four skills set the stage for the next set of skills necessary to better determine how to manage the situations and persons placed before them.

Communication

We now move to consider how an officer might respond to the input experienced from interactions with citizens. Communication includes responding, as well as asking relevant questions.

REVIEW CHART 5.1

SIZING-UP SKILLS

- Positioning
  - Distancing (proxemics)
  - Looking directly (observing body language)
  - Facing off (squarely)
- Posturing
  - Standing erect
  - Eliminating distractive behaviors
  - Inclining slightly forward
- Observing
  - Looking carefully
  - Inferring
  - Deciding normal/abnormal
  - Deciding trouble/no trouble
- Listening
  - Suspending judgment
  - Picking out key words
  - Identifying intensity
  - Reflecting on mood

Responding   Responding consists of three components: responding to content, responding to feeling, and responding to meaning.

Responding to Content   Socially skilled officers and investigators understand, when talking to victims, witnesses, or suspects, that getting the facts is crucial to their decision making in managing the situation. When we say that good officers can "respond to content," we mean they can listen to the person talking and then respond to their statements by paraphrasing them. For example, a suspect tells an investigator that he was only driving the getaway car when the robbery happened, but he didn't know the passenger robbed the convenience store where he dropped him off. The driver thought that the passenger only stopped to buy some cigarettes. The socially skilled investigator might respond by paraphrasing, "So what you're saying is you didn't know the other guy actually robbed the store when you let him out to buy cigarettes." This response helps the investigator make sure what he heard is accurate. Perhaps the suspect is not telling the truth, but the investigator repeats what he believes the suspect is claiming anyway. This allows and potentially encourages the suspect to continue to talk. As any police officer knows, the more a suspect talks, the greater the opportunity to determine the facts. Thus, the more the suspect talks, the more accurate are the decisions made.

Highly competent socially skilled officers know how to use paraphrasing as a way to manage energy levels, confirm what they heard as accurate, and ensure that the person talking to them knows the officer is really listening. All of these tasks are accomplished by this one, simple, easy way of responding to content.

Responding to Feeling Socially competent officers understand that empathy with victims, witnesses, and suspects helps them get to the bottom of problems quickly. They are able to establish rapport with whomever they are talking to. This rapport, in many instances, encourages more communication and elicits the discovery of more facts. Responding to feelings is the act of stating the feelings of the person the officer is questioning. By expressing the inferred feeling back to the citizen, the officer is able to let the person know he/she clearly understands their predicament. This also encourages more communication.

In the practical example presented previously, Jane might have said to the angry husband, "I understand you are angry right now. Just sit down, and let's get to the bottom of it." This lets the husband know the officer is there to solve a problem and understands his predicament. It allows the husband to know that the officer is willing to talk and hear his side of the story. It also helps lower energy levels; this is important in highly volatile situations.

Interpersonally skilled officers know the value of empathy. They are able to accurately identify a person's feelings and express those feelings back to them. This not only encourages more communication with the person, but helps the rapport between the two increase. Good rapport usually brings more critical information into the ongoing communication process.

BOX 5.6

EMPATHY

It behooves us for just a moment here to talk about empathy. The act of empathizing involves projecting one's consciousness into another or taking the part of another to imagine what it must be like to be them. Empathy is not the same as sympathy, which involves feeling sorry for another person. Everyone is capable of empathy, but it is critical that the propensity for police officers to become jaded and even cynical about people never completely negate this ability.

Responding to Meaning The highest level of responding is being able to identify not only the feeling being generated, but the reason for the feeling. Socially skilled officers attempt to seek out the reason for the problem confronting them. One way to continue and expand the communication process is to repeat the feeling being presented by the citizen and give feedback by echoing the inferred reason for the feeling.

For example, a witness states, "There was a big argument and one of the men was yelling at the other one, saying something about his car being keyed by the guy he was yelling at, and that he was gonna get even." The officer responds by saying, "The one guy, the suspect, was angry because the victim keyed his car and that's why he shot him?" If the witness acknowledges the officer's statement as correct, the officer has confirmed the expressed feeling and the reason for it. This will be helpful in making his or her case against the suspect. Skilled officers know the importance of finding the feelings behind criminal acts and the reason for those feelings. This kind of communication can help determine the motive of the act perpetrated by the suspect.

Officers who know how to **respond to feeling and meaning** possess a high social skill level. When people believe an officer really understands them and appreciates the situation, they have a tendency to open up and give more information. The officer is connecting feeling with meaning, such as "You're angry" (feeling) with "because they keyed your car" (reason). This skill is useful in all communication endeavors whether on the job, dealing with family members, or any situation where communication is required to solve problems or make accurate decisions.

Asking Relevant Questions A second critical communications skill involves asking relevant questions.

Using the 5WH Method All officers are taught the basic techniques for asking questions and interviewing suspects or witnesses. Asking who, what, where, why, when, and how allows the full of range of questions to be presented. This lets the socially skilled officer really "dig down" into a situation and get the facts. As is true with newspaper reporting, an officer should work on asking every one of these questions at every detail.

The interpersonally skilled officer knows how to use the 5WH method beyond just asking who, what, where, why, when, and how. He or she understands the need to reflect upon the answers to these questions and move to the next step of the process.

Reflecting Upon Relevant Answers There is an old adage that the right question will generate the right answer. The answer given to a relevant question will also give the socially skilled officer information about whether the person they are communicating with is being up-front, hiding something, or being purposely vague. After reflecting on the answer, the officer will ask another question or use one of the **responding skills**.

Here is an example. In our earlier scenario, Jane calms the husband down, he sits in a chair, and opens up to her: "I can't ever win with this bitch. She continuously takes everything I say or do negatively and it really infuriates me!" Jane asks a relevant question, "Is that what she did this evening?" The husband says, "Yeah, when I came home from going to the store like she asked me to do earlier today, she started in by saying, 'You always make up some excuse for going to the store just to get away from here.' That isn't why I went to the store. I went there because she asked me to."

Jane responds to feeling and meaning by saying, "So you're upset because she keeps on hassling you over going to the store and then accuses you of going there for reasons other than because she asked you to go?" The husband says, "That's exactly right, I gotta get outta here!" Jane responded to the husband by asking a question and followed up by using a responding skill. It settled the husband down and allowed him to vent, to some degree.

Socially competent officers know how to **recycle** their communication skills. Ask a relevant question, then respond to the answer by using a responding skill, as demonstrated above. The ability to use skills in this format increases the ability of the officer to be multifaceted in his/her investigative capabilities. This set of skills allows for gathering more accurate information, which leads to making better decisions.

Once the socially competent officer uses his or her sizing-up skills (position, posture, observation, and listening) and supports those skills with good verbal communication (responding and asking relevant questions), he or she sets the stage for the next set of skills as a competent socially skilled professional. These are called the **application skills**.

Applications

A substantial part of the police officer's day involves dealing with people. While people sometimes think the police are constantly involved in law enforcement, perhaps 90 percent of what a police officer does involves **handling requests** and

REVIEW CHART 5.2

COMMUNICATION SKILLS

- Responding
  - Responding to content
  - Responding to feeling
  - Responding to meaning
- Asking relevant questions
  - Using the 5WH method
  - Reflecting upon relevant answers

making requests. Police work is about answering questions regarding everything from citizens' rights to directions to locations. Every detail involves—at the very least—ascertaining basic information for the purposes of report writing. Furthermore, the police are constantly engaged in trying to get people to do what they want them to do. It stands to reason it would be good for them to train, teach, and learn the best methods of how to apply those skills. The last set of skills in the IPC training model involve managing behavior.

All of the above skill sets are combined by the expert officer to accomplish the multiple tasks of handling requests from citizens, making requests of citizens, and reinforcing appropriate citizen behavior.

Handling Requests   Handling requests involves two steps: checking out the situation, using the 5WH method, and responding with a reason (such as "Yes, because . . ." or "No, because . . .).

Checking Out the Situation   Handling requests requires officers to use sizing-up skills and verbal communication skills to manage whatever requests come their way. One way that may be done is by asking a proper question to determine the best answer and an accurate solution.

Here is an example of handling a request by asking a relevant question using the 5WHs. A narcotics officer has requested a meeting with her division chief. At the meeting she states, "Chief, I'm having some problems with the officer I am working with, and I want to change my assignment and work with another officer." The chief replies by asking a question relevant to handling her request, "Why do you want to change?" The officer says, "Well, when we work together he makes innuendo about issues of sexual content, reading porn books while we are on surveillance, and suggests we should get together. I just don't want to endure his attitude and behavior."

The chief goes on to say, "So you're saying he's actually harassing you." Here the chief is responding to verbal content to make sure he understands her concern. The officer says, "Yes, sir, and I have constantly told him I do not like his advances, but he just blows me off." The chief asks another relevant question, "Have you reported this to your supervisor?" The officer says, "Yes, sir, but he has basically ignored the situation." The chief asks, "What you want is a change of partner, not a transfer out of the unit?" This is another relevant question, this time with an opportunity to handle her request properly. The officer says, "Yes, sir, that's all I want."

Responding with a Reason   Continuing with our scenario, the Chief then says, "I will have this situation investigated more closely and give you a response about your partner as soon as I find out more. In the meantime, I will see to it that you will not work with this officer for the time being because of the situation. Your unit status will depend on the outcome of the inquiry." The chief has handled the officer's request with relevant questions, and based on the information the officer provided, will check out the situation.

BOX 5.7

THE POWER OF EXPLANATION

Many, if not most, police officers tend to believe that explanations should never be made to citizens. They consider it a sign of weakness to explain their actions to the public. The modern police leader needs to work against this false understanding and teach young police officers that the person who explains their actions actually indicates a power of personality. Such a person knows that they are fallible, but also knows that most often they are correct. Furthermore, not only does a brief explanation of actions being taken indicate this type of personal power, but in an age of COP, explaining to the public what "we" are doing is a part of the new philosophy of American policing.

As you can see, using the 5WH method of questions with the officer allowed the chief to hone in on the problem with accuracy. This step also allowed the officer to get the best possible response. Further, when adding a response and a reason, it ensures the problem is accurately addressed, with no confusion about the outcome.

Making Requests Now we will briefly discuss the obverse situation of handling requests: making requests.

Checking Things Out Before an officer makes a request of someone, the first thing he/she should do is check things out. Is the person ready to complete the request? Is the person able to complete the request? Is the officer making a reasonable and legal request? The officer will use the same skills in checking things out for making a request as he/she did in handling a request.

Taking Action One very important thing to remember about making requests is there are different sorts of requests in complex organizations. Sometimes, requests may come as "soft requests." Such a request is more of a suggestion. At other times, requests are more firm, calling for immediate action or resolution. Finally, some requests are, in fact, orders or directives. While sizing up a situation, an officer must consider which style to use, asking or directing the person in question to do what he/she wants done.

A soft approach may be all that is needed to get the issue taken care of. For example, the officer may want a citizen to move out of the way of traffic. She asks the citizen, "Ma'am, would you please move to the sidewalk and let the vehicle through?" This soft request may be the best method for this situation. A stronger approach may be needed in the same situation where the citizen ignores or doesn't respond to the soft request. The officer may then say, "Ma'am, please move to the sidewalk," gesturing with her hands for more emphasized effect. If that technique does not work, then giving a direct order is obviously needed: "Ma'am, move to the sidewalk now," using animated body language and hand gestures to make the point.

We are now at the point where using the sizing-up skills (position, posture, observation, and listening) along with the verbal communication skills (responding and asking questions) are readily mixed together and applied with handling requests and making requests. The officer is getting close to the end portion of a complete interaction involving reinforcing behavior (getting someone to comply or do what one wants them to do in the most efficient way possible). In other words, they are managing behavior.

The last of the IPC skills involves **reinforcing behavior**. This ensures what the officer wants done is done in the best interpersonal way, given the circumstances as they are accurately sized up by an officer who is socially skilled and emotionally mature.

Reinforcing Behavior Reinforcing behavior means attaching or withdrawing something pleasant associated with a behavior. Punishment means associating unpleasant consequences with a behavior. There are two types of reinforcement, nonverbal and verbal. The three steps of reinforcing behavior are reinforcing positively, reinforcing negatively, and punishing.

Reinforcing Positively Nonverbal positive reinforcement might be demonstrated by an officer nodding his head and smiling when noticing a person who moves his vehicle to provide more space for better pedestrian movement. Verbal positive reinforcement might be demonstrated when a sergeant expresses something positive toward one of her subordinates by saying, "Bob, thanks for always being prompt with your reports. It really makes my job easier."

Reinforcing Negatively Nonverbal negative reinforcement might be demonstrated by an officer observing a person cutting into a line at a sporting event. He shakes his head and frowns at the person trying to cut into the space. Verbal negative reinforcement may come in the form of the officer in the same situation adding a verbal statement: "Cutting in this line is not allowed. Move to the back of the line."

Punishing An officer notices a person is parking in a handicapped zone without a handicapped license sticker or license plate. The officer shakes her head and frowns disapproval to the person, who parks there anyway. The officer approaches the person and advises him that he cannot park in that space unless he has a handicapped sticker and/or license. The person refuses to move. The officer writes a citation for the person for violation of the parking infraction (punishment and unpleasant consequence as a result of a behavior).

In this section, we have seen all the interpersonal skill sets applied. In each situation, an officer must be positioned, postured, observant, and listening to engage in the next level of the communication process, which is to verbally communicate by responding to nonverbal or verbal questions and/or asking questions. Finally, the officers utilized the last set of interpersonal skills, which is to manage behavior by handling requests, making requests, taking action, reinforcing behavior (either positively or negatively), and/or reinforcing through the act of punishment.

What this model represents is the actual behavior socially competent officers demonstrate when communicating and dealing with others. They naturally size up situations. They know how to position themselves in a way that makes them safe, yet able to adequately communicate. They know how to posture so they are in control and are demonstrating attentiveness to the person or persons with whom they are dealing. They carefully observe the nonverbal gestures presented by the person or persons with whom they are engaged. This allows them to determine if the situation presents a problem. They listen closely to what is said so they can be accurate in their response to the situation.

Socially competent officers use the sizing-up skills to make an accurate assessment of what they will do next. The second skills set they automatically use is communicating: responding to nonverbal or verbal behaviors and asking questions. Last, after sizing up the situation and communicating with the person or persons, they move forward to take some sort of action by either handling a request, making a request (includes giving an order or direction), or providing a punishment.

REVIEW CHART 5.3

APPLICATION SKILLS

- Handling requests
  - Checking out the situation
  - Responding with a reason
- Making requests
  - Checking things out
  - Taking action
- Reinforcing behavior
  - Reinforcing positively
  - Reinforcing negatively
  - Punishing

It is this model that most closely resembles the chronological behavior of interpersonally competent people. The model is simple, easy to learn and apply, and good for officers to emulate. It has been researched and applied within numerous agencies throughout the country with significant success.

This communication model is only one of many models that may work for anyone who wishes to improve their social and emotional ability. One thing is very clear: communication is the most important skill an officer can possess. It is a skill that requires frequent examination and review if one wishes to become better at managing themselves, situations, and others.

In the earlier scenario, it is clear that Jane is a skilled communicator. She was able to take charge of the situation and get the husband to calm down and talk. This effort caused a volatile situation to be tempered for a skillfully managed outcome. Jane, through trial and error, became good at her ability to manage herself and situations emotionally and socially. This is good news for Jane and those citizens who encounter her and her expertise. But it is not a good thing that relatively little effort is made in most police arenas to promote better officer interpersonal communications capabilities. Often, the only efforts taken along these lines involve instituting coercive methods of compliance, such as ordering, threatening, or using force.

SUMMATION

Social competence and interpersonal skills are arguably the most desired characteristics by police executives, in relation to what they want out of their staff. Perhaps the paradox associated with this prized quality is that most police agencies spend the least amount of time training their staff in how to communicate. Little is done in developing specific skills to manage conflict, negotiate issues, get people to lower energy levels, observe and listen closely, read nonverbal cues, and develop relationships. Those skills are talked about, encouraged, and even supported, but relatively little "how to" training in communication is presented to police officers.

It has long been known that these skills are critical to all elements of police work. Investigators—the really good ones—are usually highly competent interpersonally. They have the skills necessary to gain a person's trust, engage in conversation, negotiate, and get the information necessary to close a case. They bring a very high level of interpersonal competency to their endeavors with witnesses, victims, and suspects. Communicating well allows them to solve cases that less interpersonally skilled officers would not be able to.

This is true for all effective officers working in the field. Where the skill is perhaps the most critical is in leadership positions, where getting officers and staff to do their jobs requires significant people skills. The higher up the organizational ladder one goes, the greater the need for the focal leader(s) to be interpersonally skilled. The paradox of police communication is that skilled communicators are highly regarded, but the amount of energy given to teaching, training, and role modeling those skills is wanting.

DISCUSSION QUESTIONS

1. Discuss the idea of social intelligence. Differentiate it from academic intelligence. In other words, what does IQ mean and what does SQ mean? How does the idea of SQ relate to the always-present police subcultural idea of "street smarts"?

2. Consider our briefly described example of a domestic disturbance. What are some similar examples of domestic disturbances from your own street experience? Discuss an example of how one was handled well and an example of how one was handled poorly.

3. The idea of proxemics suggests that police officers need to observe an optimum physical distance from civilians. They cannot be too close (as discussed in Box 5.4) and they should not be too far away, as discussed in our consideration of IPC. Discuss what you feel this optimum distance is and why.

4. Discuss the idea of normalizing crime, first suggested by David Sudnow and cited in our text. Consider how police officers must deal with all sorts of strange, deviant, and even disgusting behavior, and how they must consistently work to place such behavior into categories. For the purposes of discussion, consider some odd occurrences from your own on-the-street experience and discuss how they were categorized/numbered/labeled by police officers.

5. Our discussion in this chapter includes suggesting that police leaders should "respond with reasons" when taking action involving subordinates. How does this fly in the face of the police subcultural value that one should "never apologize, never explain"? Discuss how an effective leader might pass on to subordinates the idea that this value is inappropriate in modern, professional, COP policing.

KEY TERMS

Application skills: The third tier of interpersonal skills in the IPC model, also known as behavioral management skills.

Charismatic skills: Influencing through charm, magnetism, and persuasion.

Communication skills: The second tier of interpersonal skills in the IPC model.

Decompress: To undergo release from pressure, especially emotional pressure.

Emotional intelligence: The ability to know oneself in order to cope, self-regulate, empathize, and self-initiate.

Handling requests: The act of handling a question or request for help or service.

Interpersonal competence: Having confidence in oneself when dealing with others; being skilled in all aspects of interpersonal communication.

IQ: The intelligence quotient is a score derived from one of several different tests designed to assess people's intelligence relative to the general population.

Listen: Absorbing of the meanings of words and sentences that leads to understanding facts and ideas.

Making requests: Asking someone for help or service.

National Institute of Corrections: A federal agency set up to assist correctional agencies who request their services to solve problems or assist in development of services.

Observe: The ability to see and infer, or make an accurate conclusion from what is observed.

Personal space: The region surrounding a person that affects them psychologically, in terms of it being their domain or territory, or about which they feel uncomfortable if entered by another.

Position: The way a person places themselves (in relation to distance, facing squarely, and making eye contact) when dealing another person or group.

Posture: A term for body language. The manner in which a person stands or sits (upright, inclined slightly forward, slumped, relaxed).

Proxemics: A set measurable distance between people as they interact.

Recycle: In the context of interpersonal communications skills, the ability to rotate between using the responding skills and asking questions while verbally communicating with others. Example: Ask a question, then use a responding skill ("What you're saying is....") to respond to the answer.

Reinforcing behavior: Initiating a negative (punishment) or positive (reward) action to ensure a desired behavior does not or does continue.

Responding skills: A set of skills in the second tier of the IPC model that require the person communicating to reinforce. Example: Paraphrasing a statement from another person to ensure what they said was understood.

Responding to feeling and meaning: A set of skills in the second tier of the IPC model that require the person communicating to reflect the emotion they see and hear, as well as the reason for the feeling from another person. Example: "You're feeling sad because your father passed away."

Sizing up: Checking out one's surroundings and environment by observation and listening.

Social awareness: An awareness of social activities and actions.

Social intelligence: Somewhat synonymous with emotional intelligence; deals with how a person gets along with others, works together, and interacts with others in a positive manner.

Social skills: Any skill facilitating interaction and communication with others.

Vagaries: An unpredictable or erratic action, occurrence, course, or instance.

EXAMPLE SCENARIOS

Handling a Request

An officer has requested time to meet with his captain to discuss some concerns he has about the last promotional process. The officer comes to the captain's office on time as agreed and knocks on the door. The captain invites him in. The captain is occupied on the telephone and engaged in using his computer. The officer stands next to the captain's desk, waiting for an invitation to sit down. The captain continues to talk on the phone and use his computer, discussing some issues he is referencing on the PC. He briefly looks up while still talking on the phone and says to the officer, "What's up?" then returns to his conversation on the phone, ignoring the officer and his question. The officer tries to respond, but when he does, the captain continues, distracted, on the phone.

The captain then looks at the officer and says, "What do you want, man?" The officer again begins to respond and the captain ignores him, continuing the conversation on the phone. Discouraged, the officer leaves without getting his request considered.

What were the specific interpersonal barriers the captain demonstrated that caused this situation to not be properly handled? What should the captain have done to make the officer's meeting with him better?

Sergeant's Evaluation

A lieutenant has set up a meeting to go over an evaluation of an incident with one of his shift sergeants. Before the meeting begins, the lieutenant sets up his conference table with two chairs to conduct the review. The sergeant comes into the office, and the lieutenant offers her a seat and sits down next to her. He introduces the topic and tells the sergeant she is there to be debriefed on a domestic violence incident that occurred the day before, where she and two of her subordinate officers made an arrest.

As the lieutenant reviews the case, he tells the sergeant he likes how she wrote her report and how the incident was handled. There is one small area he advises her to consider next time she and her officers respond to a domestic violence situation: to ensure the combatants are separated before interviewing them. He asks for her input: Was there any lesson learned from this situation she could take back and share, so another officer could learn from the incident? The sergeant responds that she learned the first thing she would do in the future during a domestic incident would be to ensure the couples were separated, and to move the children to another area while conducting the investigation.

Both supervisor and subordinate discussed the incident without interference or interruption. When the meeting ended, the sergeant left the debriefing feeling confident and relieved that she received good advice and reinforcement for doing a good job. What specific interpersonal skills were used in this scenario? Do you believe the lieutenant gave up any power or authority because of the individual, empathetic attention he gave to the sergeant? If so, why? If not, why not?

Field Interrogation

A street officer observes a suspicious person walking near a place where a lot of known drug deals are conducted. As he watches, the man trips once, stumbles, and is unsteady on his feet. Concerned the person may be high on drugs or intoxicated, the officer pulls up and exits his police vehicle. He does not advise dispatch of his location or intentions.

The officer approaches the man and in an authoritative voice says, "What the hell is wrong with you? Are you too loaded to know what you're doing?" The officer grabs the man, spins him around, and starts a pat search, looking for ID, a possible weapon, or drugs. The man half stumbles, quickly turns around, and hits the officer in the face with his elbow. The officer falls to the ground, stunned and unable to quickly recover.

The officer is not seriously injured, but is shaken by the incident. The man runs and gets away without being found. What do you believe the officer learned from this encounter? What interpersonal dynamics did the officer fail to demonstrate? Are there times when an officer should encounter suspects or individuals without proper assistance or backup?

ADDITIONAL READING

Robert R. Carkhuff broke open this field of study in 1973 with his historical work entitled *The Art of Helping* (HRD Press, 1973). It was read everywhere in the corporate world for more than a decade and still presents an excellent standard introduction to the ideas in the field. As is often the case with organization theory, Carkhuff's work became in vogue and thus translated into all sorts of applications in both the world of business and the public sector.

The reader who is interested in social and emotional intelligence may want to examine Goldman and Boyatsis's work entitled "Social Intelligence and the Biology of Leadership," *Harvard Business Review*, September 2008. Goleman wrote about emotional intelligence in 1998 (*Working with Emotional Intelligence*, Bantam) and about social intelligence in 2006 (*The New Science of Human Relationships*, Bantam). Even more recent is Karl Albrecht's *Social Intelligence: The New Science of Success* (Hoboken, NJ: Pfeiffer, 2009). As was the case a generation ago with respect to Carkhuff, Albrecht is often cited and utilized. His ideas have been expanded and morphed into "how to" works, used in both the public and private sectors.

The Handbook of Interpersonal Communication, 3rd Ed., by Mark Knapp and John A. Daly, is a collection of research essays on the art and science of interpersonal communication. More specifically focused toward discussions about police work is *Social Intelligence Skills for Law Enforcement Officers*, a workbook on how to develop interpersonal skills in police work by Stephen S. Sampson.

CHAPTER 6

Motivation: Coaching and Closing Gaps

INTRODUCTION

Our discussion in this chapter will focus on something to which we have alluded several times already. It is the idea that much of what the good leader does is rather esoteric. It is more art than science. It is driven by **charisma**, rather than logic. The great leader, and even the good leader, is often the sort of person who has a certain "something" that is hard to quantify. The job of being a police leader requires more than just a wide-ranging skill set, required of every person who attempts to be an effective police officer. A leader needs to be imaginative and resourceful. Simply learning how something "is always done" is not appropriate as there is no one way to accomplish the many various roles of the police. Therefore, to lead police officers is to acknowledge their differences and innovative abilities when possible while, at the same time, controlling their behavior directly when necessary.

The police leader must take the complex and distill it down into palatable portions for younger, less experienced officers. As they feel their way in the police world, rookie officers need to be guided and motivated in a way that does justice to the job they must accomplish and does not short-change the citizenry. At the same time, the leader must make room for imagination, as well as error, on the part of officers who are learning and growing in their roles. In other words, when dealing with younger officers, the police leader must be forgiving as well as tough—when each is required—and deal with subordinates in a realistic way.

On the other end of the spectrum, when dealing with veteran officers, the police leader needs to be less demonstrative in terms of teaching and coaching, but more creative. Experienced, **salty officers** can be knowledgeable and skilled enough to need little in the way of guidance. But they can also be so solidly entrenched in both the subculture and counterproductive habits that they require an innovative approach if the leader is to have any impact on their behavior.

In this chapter, while discussing the police leader as teacher, coach, and motivational expert, we will begin by describing what motivation is and how it might be accomplished. We will then analyze the coaching element in police leadership and deal with a number of gaps that exist in police work—gaps between rules and regulations, police work as it is taught in academies, and the pragmatic realities of police work on the street.

MOTIVATION

There is a rather entertaining quote from Supreme Court Justice Potter Stewart that is famous in the world of constitutional law studies. He and the Court were having a difficult time wrestling with their desire to differentiate between something called "art" and something called "pornography." What was the difference? Both *Hustler* magazine and the ceiling of the Sistine Chapel have pictures of naked people. How could a community prohibit one and at the same time encourage the other? The difference was debated over time, not only in practical terms, but in legal terms and in various famous cases about pornography. Finally, in the case of

Jacobellis v. Ohio (1964), Stewart wrote that while he was having trouble constructing a definition of pornography that was acceptable, "I know it when I see it." This statement—included in a Supreme Court opinion—has been a joke in the world of legal studies for two generations now.

What Is Effective Motivation?

We hope that the point here is obvious: some things are hard to define with the sort of specificity we would like, but we know them when we see them. So it is with motivation. The coach, teacher, parent, president, or sergeant who is able to motivate others exerts a certain type of aura and influence over people that is often hard to define. To be able to motivate people successfully is an art form. Of course, what constitutes motivation is perhaps the central question in a book about police leadership. But when we attempt to define it, we might very well take a page from Stewart's book and remind ourselves that we shouldn't worry too much if we are unsuccessful in creating such a definition. We know what it is when we see it. We know a great leader when we see one, and we know exemplary leadership when we see it or experience it.

Of course, the police spend a great deal of time motivating citizens. They motivate members of the public to behave themselves. Theirs is a role that involves behavior control, something at which they are supposed to become expert. They exert power over others and can suffer from the paradoxes of coercive power,

BOX 6.1

"EVERYBODY OVER THE HILL . . . NOBODY LIVES FOREVER!"

There are those individuals who command the attention, respect, and even devotion of others. They are the natural born leaders who can demand incredible sacrifices of their troops. They are the men who can get others to charge into gunfire by shouting to everyone that they should get up out of the foxhole and go over the hill . . . and that they should do so because nobody lives forever. They are the women who can lead firefighters into a burning building. They are the types of people who motivated others to charge up the stairways into the World Trade Center on 9/11.

The question for us to engage is this: How much, if any, natural born leadership is teachable and learnable? How much can someone, just because they have passed a sergeant's exam, be taught about leading? If they are not naturally gifted with charisma, is it still possible to be an effective leader?

illustrated and analyzed by Muir (Chapter 2). Since this is true of the rank-and-file police officer, it certainly must be center stage in the role of police leaders. They must possess an understanding and an ongoing awareness of the paradoxes.

Our discussions about the paradoxes of coercive power were extensive enough that we will only recall the overall ideas here. The police will utilize exhortation, reciprocity, and coercion in their efforts to control citizens on the street. Here, we will merely remind ourselves of the formula and take just a moment to lament, to some extent, the difficulty that police leaders will face on a regular basis if they attempt to influence the behavior of their subordinates by coercion. We will then consider what sociologists have declared to be the definitive discussion of authority for more than a century. Police leaders possess authority over their subordinates, and a discussion of both of these sets of dynamics—those associated with power and those associated with authority—is apposite here.

Power Revisited

In Chapter 2, when discussing the paradoxes that plague everyone in American policing, we confronted the paradoxes of coercive power. We talked about how frustrating it can be to police the streets when a substantial number of citizens are incoercible. At this point, we revisit power and the police, but focus on the exercise of power by police leaders aimed at the police officer corps.

In our discussion about the powers that are available to the police officer attempting to control citizens, we agreed with Muir that exhortation, reciprocity, and coercion should be tried whenever possible. Whether it involves police officers controlling citizens or police leaders controlling subordinates, the three types of power should be attempted in that specific sequence. Exhortation is a positive form of behavior control that costs the exhorter nothing; it should be attempted first. Reciprocity is an equally positive form of control, although it does cost the recip-rocator something; it should be attempted second. Finally, coercion is a negative form of control that is resented, and should be attempted last. Here, we will briefly consider these three forms of behavior control in reverse order of priority.

To use a rather trite phrase from the 1970s, when coercing one's children, one is involved in the exercise of "tough love." All of the books about parenting talk about how avoiding coercion should be a priority, but that the intelligent parent should never be loathe to utilize coercion, if necessary. So it is with police leadership. When the control of police behavior is essential—not when control is merely about making some irrelevant statement about "who's in charge here"—then coercion might be required. The paradoxes of coercive power come into play here, of course, and the intelligent leader should be aware of them and the tremendous limitations they bring to the formula.

Here is a reality that cannot be stated too often: police officers themselves are experts at coercing others. Whether or not they have read Muir and his academic analysis of the paradoxes of coercive power, the police intuitively understand these paradoxes. When police leaders try to coerce police officers, they (the officers) are expert at avoiding being coerced. This is just a reality of life on the street for the police leader. In particular, officers can inoculate themselves from being coerced—utilizing the paradox of detachment to their own advantage—or, equally, they can call a supervisor's bluff and use the paradox of face in their favor. The police supervisor must be circumspect about attempting this type of behavior control.

We have talked a great deal already about how important it is for police leaders to be creative. We will continue to do so. It is a topic of such import that it cannot be overdone. Sometimes, such a discussion has to remain rather vague, because genuine creativity is just that—it is creative. It involves looking at existing situations and coming up with alternatives. It involves engaging standard operational procedures and inventing new ones. In the incident case, it involves looking at different ways of controlling the behavior of police officers and creating reciprocal power relationships that are innovative. We suggest that a leader can and should work to invent positive, reciprocal power-oriented ways of motivating officers. In other words, the creative leader looks to reward good behavior rather than punishing misbehavior.

What can be utilized to create incentives, as opposed to using threats? Box 6.2 presents a very bad example, but there are numerous good ones. Officers can be given choice assignments, positive evaluations, and recommendations to obtain preferred duties. In the long run, officers can be championed at higher levels by immediate supervisors in a way that aids career path development. Reciprocity is, to be sure, an excellent way of controlling behavior. It brings out the best in police leaders, as they use their imaginations to motivate.

BOX 6.2

LEADER CREATIVITY: A BAD EXAMPLE

In a suburban California sheriff's department, a sergeant once attempted to motivate his officers to become more active on the street. He suggested at a lineup that he would shoulder the expense for a fifth of bourbon, which would go to "the first person to make a good bust tonight." While this was a laudable attempt to use reciprocity in lieu of coercion—rewards rather than punishment—to control police behavior, it was an extraordinarily poor example of judgment. This little reward scheme implied two things at once. First, it suggested that good police work involves making arrests. This is an ancient principle that is, hopefully, going by the wayside in our current era of COP. Second, it placed officers in a "race" of sorts ("the first one who . . .") that might very well have encouraged them to make marginally legal arrests. The whisky went to the officer who made the first arrest, not to the officer making an arrest of someone who genuinely *deserved* to be arrested.

And then, of course, we come to exhortation. We have made the point else-where that when police officers confront civilians they wish to control, they should attempt to utilize exhortative power whenever possible. The rationalization for this particular police officer–citizen behavior control is that when citizens decide to do something because it is the right thing, the logical thing, or the Christian thing, they (the citizens) feel totally comfortable with the decision. It is their decision, in every sense, and this makes people feel good about themselves. They feel good about the police officers who couched things in terms that allowed them to make the positive decision.

The same logic is true with respect to police leaders controlling the behavior of their charges. When exhortation is used, it results in decisions that leave police officers with a good feeling about themselves and their supervisors. Since it costs nothing but the time taken to verbalize the chooser's rationalization, this type of behavior control is always preferable to the other two alternatives.

But there is more. Police leadership is largely about helping to create and main-tain long-term modes of insightful thinking, creative problem solving, and specific skill development that accept and further the goals of COP. Thus, exhortation is not just about motivating officers to handle individual details with intelligence and dispatch or handling the job in the short run with empathy and understanding. It is about the long-term philosophy that every single officer possesses. It is about encouraging modes of thinking that are professional. It is about promoting the idea that a new blue line is being put into place on the streets of America.

The creative leader uses his or her intelligence and ingenuity to craft individual situations and specific details into learning opportunities. He or she encourages long-term, professional approaches to problem solving in general. He or she manipulates even critical events and crisis conditions into teaching examples. In these and many other ways, police leadership is all about creativity where the exercise of behavior control is involved. Exhorting police officers to "be all that they can be" is what this is about.

Is this discussion filled with platitudes? Yes, it is, to be sure. But that does not lessen its importance. Focusing on ideals—goals that push the edge of the envelope—is one of the requirements of the job today. Being a police leader in an era of such profound and pronounced change, as we are now experiencing in American police work, *is* about focusing on the sorts of idealistic, long-term goals that are redefining who the police are today and what they will be doing in the future.

Weber's Authority

Among other things, the great sociological theorist Max Weber was famous for his conceptualization of the three kinds of authority that work to regulate people in the world (Weber, 1946). Clearly relevant to our consideration of how to lead and control police officers, Weber's work is apposite for us here because it defines authority as a particularized form of power that relates to the position of the police leader. Authority, as Weber saw it, is the right to command or the right to exercise power. Power is relational in that it involves one person controlling another. Authority is not relational in that it is a form of behavior control that a person grants to another (in one of three ways, as we shall see below).

People of all sorts can exercise power over each other; it is a regular element of interpersonal relationships of all kinds. We exhort our children to become good (or better) people. We use reciprocity to control subordinates all the time. Giving people a paycheck involves nothing less than using reciprocal power to get them to come to work and to do things that they normally would not do (operate a machine press for eight hours a day, for example). We coerce our significant others sometimes with threats (to pack up and leave, to withhold sex, and so on).

But the exercise of authority is something different. It involves a very particularized type of power. In modern societies, there is a hierarchy of command to which everyone must adhere. This command structure is created and maintained as authority. Weber's analysis of authority is perfectly on point for our entire set of discussions in this book. All police leaders possess authority; some possess more of it—and more types—than others.

Weber suggested that there are three different sources of authority: legal or rational authority, traditional authority, and charismatic authority. We will discuss all three but will focus—here and later on in our considerations about leading the police—on charismatic authority with special emphasis. That is because Weber brought specific meaning to something with which we have been wrestling all along: the fact that so much of what people consider to be excellent leadership is determined by a rather amorphous dynamic. Some leaders "have it," and others do not seem to. Thus, charismatic authority must be analyzed and understood by anyone involved in police leadership.

Rational-Legal Authority This is the sort of authority created for individuals as members of a hierarchical structure. In a bureaucracy, Weber suggested that the rules of the organization and the patterns of standard conduct create roles, or ranks and positions, which are populated by individuals who inherit their authority because of where they are placed into the structure. That is, their authority is given to them by the structure itself and is not transferable to others. When a person leaves a position where they possessed **rational-legal authority**, they lose that authority. Whether they move up in an organization, and obtain a different type, form, or amount of authority, or move down (or leave), their original authority is gone. They are placed into their positions in the first place due to qualifications; this is an authority limited by a time frame and the particular position they temporarily occupy.

The police supervisor most definitely possesses rational-legal authority. The moment that someone makes sergeant, for example, they accept the position, embrace the title, put chevrons on their uniform, and immediately exert an influence over others within the organization that they did not possess beforehand. The transition is seamless. Whether or not those around him or her are happy about it, the new sergeant has an immediate level of authority. New sergeants behave differently toward others; others, in turn, behave differently around them. The type of authority present in such a scenario is given to the newly appointed supervisor by the organization's rational and legal right to do so. So powerful is this sort of authority that we seldom even stop to think about it. Someone "made sergeant" is all we need to hear, and we place that person into a different category in our minds. A newly minted higher ranking person has a different sort of aura than the very same person previously.

Weber tells us this is not only logical, but an important effect of the bureaucratic way of doing things. A hundred years ago, he was the original champion of the logic of bureaucracy. Weber lived during an era when the change was being made from old style, corrupt ways of administering the state into an era of civil service–type organizations. Theses changes were driven by the ideals of competence and objectivity. He suggested that bureaucrats, given their positions due to their individual competence and experience, would behave in a more emotionless, objective, prejudice-free, and, thus, just way than their corrupt predecessors. Today, we are used to people railing against the dynamics Weber favored: bureaucratic coldness and lack of concern about the individual citizen's particularized story. This, Weber wrote, was the way that bureaucrats were *supposed* to behave, as it took personalities and biases out of the citizen–state equation.

So, modern police administrators possess the type of rational-legal authority that Weber favored. Their exercise of this authority is almost universally unquestioned. In fact, paradoxically, when such authority is questioned it is done so from the perspective that the *individual* exercising the authority is incompetent. The authority itself—coming from the structure and legitimacy of the organization as a whole—is never questioned. A bureaucrat might be incompetent or biased, but a bureaucracy never is.

Traditional Authority Weber's **traditional authority** is a type where the legitimacy of the person exercising the authority is based on custom or tradition. A certain group of individuals—the dominant group of the tribe, clan, or family—is granted authority in perpetuity. Often, this comes from religious or spiritual roots. Thus, the priest, rabbi, shaman, or imam is such an authority figure, as is the chief, lord, or queen. Throughout human history, this type of authority has been utilized to maintain inequality and hierarchical structures that we in America have difficulty understanding. Sometimes, the hold such authority has over people in traditional societies is hard for us as Americans to imagine. Because this type of authority is no longer relevant in American society, it certainly has nothing to do with today's police.

Charismatic Authority For the purposes of our incident discussion and the rest of our travels through the world of police leadership, Weber's third type of authority is the most important. His definitions and analysis of charismatic authority are important to everyone who wishes to understand how someone who has accepted the mantle of "leader" from a rational, legal system might move to become a "great leader." To create and maintain charismatic authority is to extend one's influence beyond rational-legal authority.

BOX 6.3

CHARISMATIC AUTHORITY

This form of leadership is not considered to be transferable, teachable, or learnable. It is based solely on recognition (or acceptance) by followers to the claims of leadership of the charismatic person. Charismatic authority is not only troublesome because it cannot be transferred—a sort of administrative woe—but because it can degenerate into a situation where those immediately around the charismatic ruler inherit authority. When (or if) this happens, charismatic authority turns into traditional authority, which can be supported by myths or sacred ideas (or ideals). This is the sort of power exercised by, for example, a dictator.

Charismatic authority is based on individualized, personal characteristics, such as perceived courage, intelligence, dignity, or integrity. Charismatic leaders are followed because of a personal bond people feel toward them. Such leaders in history include Alexander the Great, Julius Caesar, Adolph Hitler, Mao Zedong, and Mahatma Gandhi. In today's world, Osama Bin Laden and Barack Obama can realistically be considered charismatic leaders. All important leaders possess charisma to one extent or another, and those who are able to mesmerize large crowds with their rhetorical skills are said to be charismatic.

Charisma is not transferable, as we have noted. The dynamics involved in the maintenance of charismatic authority are ongoing—that is, the charismatic leader needs to continually reaffirm this form of authority. Such a leader needs to continue to lead on a regular basis—to exhibit the type of special qualities that created his or her authority in the first place. This is one difficulty with this form of influence.

REVIEW CHART 6.1

WEBER'S TYPES OF AUTHORITY

- *Rational-legal:* Formalized belief in law (legal) or natural law (rational); obedience to a set of principles.
- *Traditional:* Inherited rule; conservative perpetuation of the status quo; feudal or clan or tribal based.
- *Charismatic:* Belief in the vision and extraordinary, specific gifts of a particular individual.

With this understanding in place, we will now move to consider the traditional command-and-control method of police leadership. We will examine its logic and its strengths and weaknesses. Then we will discuss other methods of controlling police officers, driven by the concept of charismatic authority just defined.

COMMAND AND CONTROL

The traditional police organization includes the installation and maintenance of the **command-and-control** model of military leadership. For generations now, as a paramilitaristic organization, the police have taken it as gospel that the way to create and maintain discipline, effective communication, and accountability is to utilize a military-like chain of command. As is often the case in the field of human endeavor, it is difficult for those hired, trained, and experienced within this model of leadership and administration to envision any other way of doing things. Thinking that occurs "outside the box" is a rare occurrence. This is true in any complex organization because of the power of tradition and momentum, but even more true in police organization, due to the conservatism and solidarity of the subculture.

Utility of Command and Control

The traditional command-and-control system of police leadership is based on the military model (Seddon, 2005). As analysts have often noted in recent years, this model is outdated and inappropriate for police work *almost* all of the time. It is, to some extent, a troublesome reality that many police organizations stick to some form of command and control management, even though it is antithetical to logic, the philosophy of COP, and the development of professionalism. The model persists because of a sometimes present paradox: no matter what its drawbacks, there are circumstances under which the command-and-control model must be in place and operate effectively to limit discretion, control the exercise of police power, and fix responsibility. Such circumstances involve prolonged confrontations, usually involving gunfire (discussed below).

The logic behind the command-and-control model of management suggests that leadership involves simple tasks. Managers decide what is to be done and communicate their decisions down the chain of command. Leaders then monitor the actions of their subordinates and exercise control over them. In this way, discretion is limited and the command structure is in control all of the time. The classic explanation of how this is supposed to work in the field of police administration is discussed in a book by O.W. Wilson first published over 50 years ago. Later republished with a co-author, this work was considered for many years to be the police leader's "bible" (Wilson and McLaren, 1977).

Command and control makes perfectly good sense in the military. To begin with, boot camps instill both a fear of commanders and a propensity to follow orders in a thoughtless manner. Second, in the military, subordinates are almost universally under the immediate supervision and control of their superiors. While soldiers, sailors, or marines in the military are exhorted to **adapt and overcome** (discussed later) when they are without supervision, this is rare. Usually, commanders are with their troops in direct control of them, right next to them in the field. Because of the movement toward paramilitarism that occurred during the **reform era of American policing**, this military-type model has been followed in police work for generations.

Fixing Responsibility In discussing the dynamics associated with the command-and-control model, we are engaging the similar pros and cons associated with police paramilitarism. The arguments in favor of this form of leadership include the rather obvious point that it fixes responsibility. This is true in general of hierarchies, but it is a specific strength in the military. Under circumstances where this type of leadership is exercised, everyone knows who gave the order to do what and when. Furthermore, when real accountability is sought—especially when something has gone wrong or people have been injured or killed—it is possible to discuss and analyze what was known at the time a given order was issued. Experienced police leaders know, though Hollywood imagery suggests otherwise, that police work is not a particularly dangerous occupation. But on occasion, the police use force and even lethal force. The American public demands accountability when this happens. The command-and-control model creates a forum where this sort of accountability is possible.

CYA As is true in the military, people in police work sometimes talk about the principle of **CYA** ("cover your ass"). The idea, of course, is to make sure, when you take action, you are "covered" from accusations that you misbehaved. One can CYA by double-checking with a supervisor about an order or getting something on paper or e-mail, so it can be saved. Simple. Obvious. What might not be obvious is that CYA works both ways. It covers whomever has been issued an order or a

BOX 6.4

FIXING RESPONSIBILITY: WHEN COMMAND AND CONTROL IS NECESSARY

Especially in our current era of COP, when the drawbacks of paramilitary policing are well understood, we sometimes lose sight of the fact that command and control is necessary under certain, specific circumstances. When faced with snipers, hostage situations, riots, or protracted firefights, the police must instantly morph from a community-friendly, service-oriented group of individual agents into a well disciplined, hierarchically controlled, army type of group. When guns are out and lethal force is likely to be used, chains of command must be used to fix responsibility and ensure a measured and controlled approach to the use of violence by the police.

go-ahead and, equally, holds the authority figure accountable. As is true with rule application in general (rules always cut both ways), this principle works to protect people on both sides of a decision or action taken. No one needs to work very hard at CYA when the command-and-control model is in operation.

Organizational Rationality   Then there is the problem of **organizational rationality**. We have made the point in several places that complex organizations can suffer from bureaupathology when the operations of subgroups, divisions, or departments within an organization work for their own interests. They can follow rules created at the microscopic level and lose sight of the overall goals of the organization. Sometimes, day-to-day operations can forget or ignore the mission. In theory, one way to avoid such bureaupathology is to have an inflexible accountability mechanism. Command and control is supposed to work to ensure that discretion is limited and supervision is immediate. When this happens—again, in theory—the organizational mission is respected. The operations of the organization are rationally, logically focused on the mission in a way that does justice to the idea of mission statement creation in the first place.

Unusual, Violent Confrontations   Finally, command and control works in a militaristic way to ensure that the police are ready for unusual, violent confrontations such as riots, hostage situations, and shootouts. One of the problems with COP—one of its paradoxes—is that its civilian-friendly approach to policing eschews the military model as a basic tenet of operation, but it then can leave the police unprepared for such violence. In the name of being open and receptive to the public, the COP philosophy accepts as gospel the idea that paramilitarism is inappropriate almost all of the time. It seeks to avoid the type of distancing that paramilitarism creates between the police and the citizenry. But when it does so, it ignores the fact that when guns come out and shots are being fired, the demand for accountability heightens. Even though this happens on a very limited basis, it is a valid criticism of COP to point out this accountability problem. Under command and control, chains of command are operative at all points in time and, thus, the police do not tend to be caught off guard by violent confrontations.

These are several substantial arguments in favor of the traditional, military-like machinations of command and control. Add them together with the power of subcultural conservatism and organizational reluctance to change, and we find a pronounced propensity in the police world to want to stay with this particular form of management. Yet the police world is in fact moving away from command and control. Why? What is the impetus behind change in this arena? What are the substantial arguments against this style?

Critiquing Command and Control

The command-and-control model does not fit well into the type of police administration being constructed all over the country under the auspices of COP. This is for several reasons (Meese and Ortmeier, 2003).

REVIEW CHART 6.2

THE UTILITY OF COMMAND AND CONTROL

- Creates uniformity, and logic to operations
- Develops accountability for actions
- Fixes personal responsibility
- Protects those who follow orders and "behave themselves"
- Delivers military-type leadership for violent, gun-related events

General Drawbacks First, command and control involves controlling people exclusively through coercion. As we pointed out in Chapter 2, as well as in this chapter, people do not like to be coerced. They tend to rail against it. In the case of police officers, who coerce others on a regular basis, being the objects of such absolute power is not well accepted. And, as experts in power manipulation, if they are motivated to do so, police officers can behave in any number of ways that work to limit the impact of command-and-control leadership. Command and control does not suffer from this type of problem in the military world, as the average soldier, sailor, or marine is not an expert at coercing others.

Second, command and control requires immediate supervision. It does not work well if supervisors issue orders and then only occasionally monitor the impact of those orders. In police work, immediate supervision is almost never possible. Sergeants who are supposed to "control" line officers see them at the beginning of their shifts and at the end. In the middle of a standard shift, a sergeant will move around from beat to beat, checking in with his or her subordinates. If it is logistically possible, sergeants will show up at numerous details in order to monitor their officers. But in the grand scheme of things, minute-by-minute supervision is rare. The discretionary decisions made by police officers—to make or not to make vehicle stops, to invoke or not to invoke the dictates of the law, to use force or not to use force—are almost universally made alone and without supervision. There is no realistic way for police leaders to control most of what happens out on the street.

Third, because of the amount of information and expertise obtained by today's COP officers out on patrol, the ability of supervisors to know what to do in the first place is limited. Throughout the history of policing, beat officers have always possessed substantial specific knowledge about their beats unknown to their managers. But in today's world of COP, where a great amount of discretionary power is afforded to officers on the street, it is doubly difficult for police leaders to issue orders that are meaningful in any sense. Supervisors today are at a disadvantage; they know far less than those they are supposed to control.

Fourth, in the command-and-control model, supervisors are sometimes supposed to be "**swift and ruthless**" about misconduct. In the military, this makes perfectly good sense; any break in the chain of command can cost soldiers, sailors, or marines their lives. But in police work, being swift and ruthless is almost never appropriate (Glenn, 2003). Exactly the opposite is usually called for in police work. When an officer has erred, the police leader needs to be measured and empathetic. Sanctioning, when it is relevant, needs to be done in a thoughtful and cool-headed manner.

Fifth, and without deprecating the intelligence and abilities of police leaders, the lack of substantive expertise on the part of police elites can be viewed from below as more than ignorance; it can be seen as incompetence. As we noted when discussing the Peter Principle in Chapter 1, some of those who move up the chain of command in any organization can end up in positions where they are working beyond their capacities to be effective. As the Peter Principle points out, they rise to their level of incompetence. Add to this their lack of particularized knowledge about crime-related patterns and individual perpetrators, and there is a propensity for police leaders to have only a minimum level of impact upon specific strategies on the street today. Again, this is not to be disparaging about police leadership. It is merely to note some facts about contemporary police work.

So, despite its logic, the command-and-control model presents numerous drawbacks, and these drawbacks have been noted with regard to nonmilitary organizations for quite some time. One can observe in the literature about police administration a growing discomfort with command and control that goes back more than a generation. The limitations of treating the police mission as if it were a military one have not just recently come to the fore. However, with the advent of COP in the past two decades, new arguments against command and control have emerged.

COP-Specific Drawbacks Command and control operates in a way that is diametrically opposed to the type of innovation that is encouraged by COP. When commands are issued and passed down the chain, the entire operation works to inhibit individual creativity. In fact, that is command and control's purpose; the model is aimed at ensuring that decisions made high up are respected and implemented without question and independent of any propensity to be creative on the part of subordinates. In the military, this is essential, but in modern police work, it is not. The philosophy of COP attempts to utilize the intelligence and education of today's modern officers by considering the individual beat cop to be an innovator or an agent of change. The philosophy behind command and control works in exactly the opposite direction.

The same idea in a different direction has perhaps an even more direct impact upon police leadership on the streets. Command and control inhibits taking chances. If the modern leader is supposed to allow his or her young officers to try different ways of problem solving, develop their own way of operating on the street, and create their own working personality, command and control is in essence the enemy. In a bygone era, when the average police officer possessed an average intelligence, no formal education beyond high school, and next to nothing in the way of effective training, command and control was instituted in an effort to mitigate propensities for police officers to be incompetent and corrupt. And

BOX 6.5

TAKING CHANCES

Over the years, several important analysts have pointed out that it is important for the creative leader to allow his or her subordinates to experiment with different ways of handing problems so they do not fall into the trap of thinking there is one and only one way to do something (Bruner et al., 1956). For this dynamic to produce creativity and progress in the individual police officer, as well as the officer corps, it is necessary that the police leader allow not only for taking chances when things work out well, but for making mistakes when they do not (Muir, 1977).

it worked. This form of control ended the corruption of the 19th century police force almost everywhere.

Today, we are not dealing with the types of police officers who require command and control. The average police officer has a higher intelligence level than the average citizen. The average police cadet entering into the officer corps today has two years of college behind him or her. Police academies, FTO experiences, and in-service training systems provide the contemporary officer with a sophisticated and synoptic level of training that used to be unknown. All of this makes cleaving to command and control a dated, futile, and even counterproductive endeavor.

Furthermore, COP requires a new sort of problem solving. Taking advantage of the developments noted above, this philosophy seeks to utilize lower level expertise by flattening the chain of command and encouraging collegial problem solving. This particular element of professionalism is critical to the development of modern policing because, instead of ignoring reality, it takes advantage of the sophistication and education of the contemporary officer. To be sure, collegial problem solving can work to make things more complicated for the police leader. In the "good ol' days," it was easier to issue commands than work to monitor and control their implementation. Today, the police leader is more of a mentor/facilitator and therefore must work to take advantage of expertise at lower levels. But for as much as this requires creativity, the police leader should never shirk from the requirement to do so.

Command and control works to limit the progress being made toward the institution of the new philosophy of COP, and can amplify the roadblocks that stand in the way of the development of police professionalism in general. Command and control is the exact antithesis of what is required to further these important and laudable goals.

So, the command-and-control model of police leadership is considered to be almost completely irrelevant to today's police organizations. But the key word here is "almost." This is because—as noted when we discussed the drawbacks of

REVIEW CHART 6.3

DRAWBACKS TO COMMAND AND CONTROL

- Coercion is negative and replete with paradoxes
- Requires immediate supervision, which is rare in police work
- Fails to take advantage of modern police officer lower level expertise
- Requires "swift and ruthless" leadership, which is counterproductive
- Discourages creativity in individual problem solving
- Inhibits officers from taking chances
- Limits the development of modern police professionalism

paramilitarism—there are situations under which command and control becomes necessary. When hostages are taken, when riots occur, or when guns are drawn, it is necessary to issue commands and to control the forces of the police. This is a central paradox of police leadership.

For all of the reasons listed above, in some places—where the limitations of command and control are appreciated and analyzed—the world of police management has been searching for alternative methods of supervision for a generation. Modern analysts suggest that police leaders are more like coaches or teachers than commanders (Couper and Lobitz, 1991; Muir, 1977).

UTILIZING CHARISMATIC AUTHORITY

The role of a police leader can be like that of a sports coach, given Weber's definition of charismatic authority. The implementation of a successful coaching model is predicated upon the coach possessing at least a modicum of charisma. Not everything in coaching is learnable and transferable, as is the case in the world of police leadership.

The police leader as coach is often a good analogy, but it is not perfect. So, to begin with, we have to consider how the coaching metaphor is not *exactly* relevant to the police leadership role.

Coaching

One central paradox of supervising police officers relates to the **coaching** metaphor. Being a police leader is like being the coach of a team in many ways. The rhetoric of COP in particular suggests that modern police leaders should be like coaches (Cordner, 2005). The team analogy may often seem perfect. The police dress in uniforms, they go out into the street to work together in unison, they are outnumbered, and they are involved in a "contact sport." They need to coordinate their efforts, possess discipline, and have an appropriate esprit de corps. Looking at the policing endeavor as a team enterprise seems to be perfectly logical and utilitarian. So, if the police are a team, then police leaders are coaches—some of the time.

As has been pointed out in our discussion about the limitations of police subcultural norms, the police can fall into any number of counterproductive propensities if they focus too much on "us against them." This conceptualization is central to the sports team ideal. With regard to paramilitarism, the police only need to be a team some of the time; behaving like a team all of the time is not a good idea. Since so many decisions are made by individual police officers, alone and without "coaches" or "teammates" present, the analogy can be a flawed one.

Leading police officers involves the same dynamics as being an athletic coach and entails utilizing the same skill sets (Gardner, 2008). Football coaching, in particular, seems to present us with a good analogy. There is danger on the football field. People get hurt, sometimes badly, and—on rare occasions—players even die. The danger factor is similar to police work, and the need to work together in a disciplined fashion is appropriate. The leadership mechanism is also similar; the head coach is like the chief, offensive and defensive coordinators are like middle managers, and the team captains—who play out on the field with other players—are like sergeants.

There are several lessons to be learned by police managers that are analogous to those of a football coach. First, a football coach learns that the rules for the team must be set up and administered equitably. Everyone must be treated in the same way, or the integrity of the coaching staff will suffer in the minds of the players. To have favorites or make excuses for players is antithetical to good coaching, as with supervising police officers.

However, the paradox here is that everyone's situation is not the same in life. Everyone is different. They live in different family situations. They have different levels of experience, intelligence, and maturity. They have differing capabilities and expectations. They have different histories on the field or on the job. In order to be a good coach or police leader, one has to understand this. In administering subordinates, this central paradox is often in evidence: you must treat everyone the same way, and yet you cannot treat everyone the same way. A good police leader has to understand and live with this sort of paradox.

This leads to another coaching axiom: unless it is completely unavoidable, it is not appropriate to discipline an athlete in front of the team. Doing so can create a level of animosity in the erring player that makes him diffident and even an enemy of sorts. Even if he does not quit the team literally, a coach can "lose" an athlete by embarrassing him in this way. So, even if a football player knows that he has messed up, the coaching job of chastising him needs to be done quietly and on the side. An errant police officer needs to be dealt with in this same way. Anything and everything that is said to an erring officer should be done quietly and in private. This rule should never be broken *unless* a player has messed up often enough that to discipline him has become something the leader wants to do in order to make a point to others. So it is with football, and so it is with policing.

BOX 6.6

COACHING EXAMPLE

The strange and even perplexing nature of what it takes to be a leader is illustrated by a dynamic from the world of coaching. The successful coaches of the world are divided into two groups, or two distinctively different types of coaches. There are the coaches who were champions as athletes, who understand and love their sport, and who stick with the sport as they get older. These people participated at the highest levels and know the championship experience in an up-front and personal way. They usually refer to themselves jokingly as the "has-beens."

Then there are the coaches who were never really that good at their sport, but were absolutely fascinated by it and by the pursuit of excellence. They study, analyze, and attempt to empathize with the championship experience. These people usually refer to themselves jokingly as the "never-wases." One can find both sorts of coaches in any given sport, being successful at any number of levels.

There are two odd things about this dynamic. The first is that there are about two of the "never-wases" type of coaches for every one of the "has-beens." The second is that there are (definitely) more coaches at the most productive, successful, championship level from the "never-wases" group than there are from the "has-beens" group. No one knows exactly why this is so. But it indicates that coaching is indeed an eclectic and esoteric endeavor that can't be easily pigeonholed or categorized. There just is no one correct or even most appropriate way to do it well.

Still another coaching point that is critical in police work has to do with giving positive feedback when someone has erred. In coaching, they talk about the **sandwich technique**, and this, too, is relevant in police work. The sandwich metaphor relates to engineering a conference with an errant subordinate in a three-tiered way. First, the coach/supervisor says something positive about the athlete/officer. Second, the bad news is delivered (about whatever misconduct has occurred). Third, the coach/supervisor ends with something positive. As simplistic as this might appear, it works. When supervisors have negative news to present, this little technique can often make the impact of the experience end up being positive.

An additional coaching point has to do with having a generally positive attitude, whenever possible. This, too, might sound simplistic, but in police work it is all-important. Because of the multiple, overlapping frustrations faced by police officers on a regular basis, they can become jaded and even cynical—about people, the job, and life in general. No amount of sugar coating can change the fact that police officers see the absolute worst in people. Even in upper middle class areas, where many people assume that life is good and little trauma exists, the police are called on to deal with the kind of domestic violence (as just one example) that most people know nothing about. Nothing impacts more positively on this propensity more than having an ongoing, positive, "you can do it" attitude on the part of the supervisor.

Oddly enough, even this reality presents us with a paradox. In the coaching world, it has long been known that there is no singular successful way of motivating athletes. There are successful coaches who are "**screamers**," known for regularly ranting and raving at their players as a means of motivating them. At the other end of the spectrum, there are the coaches who are cerebral and measured—who never seem to "lose it" and scream. Strangely enough, both techniques can be effective. Coaches learn over time that there are those individuals who respond to negativity and those who only react well to positive stimuli. Furthermore, sticking to one type of motivation does not always work. Something that many athletes never figure out is that coaches who are naturally prone to one sort of motivational technique or the other will sometimes plan to go out of character. The calm coach will—as a tactic— go into an unusual rave in an effort to get athletes to "straighten up and fly right." The "screamer" can make a big impression by giving a cool and calm motivational speech.

It might not appear that this set of dynamics is important for the police leader. Screaming at police officers is never an appropriate mode of motivation and communication. However, the idea that some people respond to positive stimuli and some respond well to negative stimuli is useful. This is just an individual personality-driven dynamic in life. Because of their upbringing and the make-up of their psyche, any person might be more or less prone to respond to negativity. If done quietly, and on the side, a negative approach can be effective.

We will discuss one more coaching-related dynamic here—a dynamic that provides the police leader with an excellent opportunity for creative thinking. While coaches learn that the **negative sanctioning** of an athlete should be avoided in general, unless an individual has messed up so often that a point must be made to everyone on the team, the positive example can and should be used publicly. Police officers always notice when administration tends to be done in a negative direction. The citizen complaint is taken very seriously, but the positive feedback that some-times comes into an organization is not communicated. Locker room naysayers are known to point this out, and it is an unfortunate reality that in many police depart-ments they are correct; positive feedback from the community is held in abeyance, while negative feedback is treated openly in front of the police officer corps.

The effective police leader, like the effective coach, should endeavor to make positive points in public. Noting that an officer has made a good arrest or that a creative solution was found to solve a particularly thorny problem are things that should be celebrated in front of everyone. It is not enough to mention such posi-tive examples to people on a one-on-one basis. It is much more important to take

BOX 6.7

THE CENTRAL PARADOX OF COACHING

The coach of a high school football team sets out a rule: "We have had too many players missing practices, and I have had it. From now on, you will not play on Friday night unless you attend every practice, all week long." The coach makes it clear that there will be no excuses; this policy applies to everyone equally—it is understandable and fair. It is in the team's best interests.

Then, on a Thursday afternoon, the starting tailback has to leave school to take care of his younger brothers and sisters while his mother goes to the hospital emergency room with the flu. He misses practice. The kid is being a good son and brother. He is living up to the idea that family comes first in life. He is not missing practice due to any capricious or silly reason. He's being dependable.

What will the coach do on Friday night, when this tailback—the kid that the team cannot win without—is ineligible to play because of the attendance rule? Does the coach bend the rule because this was an unusual circumstance? Or does the coach stick by the rule—and thus lose the game—because to break it would be to lose integrity?

The central paradox of coaching is this: A coach must treat every player in the same way or the integrity of the team will suffer. But every player is different, with different lives, strengths, and weaknesses. Therefore, the coach cannot always treat everyone in the same way.

advantage of the arena that the daily (or nightly) lineup presents, in order to give positive feedback to creative officers in front of the group. Nothing but good things can happen because of this, and the negativity of the naysayers can be momentarily thwarted when a leader chooses to use this type of opportunity in such a way.

Leaders must possess integrity—that is, the behavior of a leader must be in concert with his or her personal belief system. This is philosophical integrity. But the police leader must also possess practical integrity. He or she must behave in the same way demanded of their charges. Thus, the police leader must be a role model.

The Role Model Ideal

Charisma refers to a type of aura that surrounds a person to which others respond with respect, admiration, loyalty, or a sense of duty. Its manifestation at an individualized, personal level is in the ideal of the role model. The hero, dictator, champion athlete, or religious leader all have charisma of a macroscopic sort, of course.

But anyone can have charisma of a more microscopic, individualized type. This has to do with being a role model.

When we hear the term "role model," several different images come to mind. Some role models are individuals who have had direct impacts upon our lives. They are the great teacher, outstanding coach, successful uncle, or boss who has been particularly influential in our development. Others can be role models for us without our even having had any direct interaction with them. They can be great writers or actors, performers or politicians, or professionals in our field. We only know them from a distance or, in other words, we know *of* them. These people are what Aristotle called "exemplars," whose lives represent paradigms in our world, for one reason or another (more about Aristotle's exemplars in Chapter 8's discussion about character).

It might sound odd to some, but the excellent police leader must be prepared to be a role model. This involves teaching by doing, of course. More than we might assume, younger officers, in particular, will watch and learn from such exemplars. In police work, this has to do with even simple things, such as personal carriage and demeanor. There are many different ways of handling interactions with the public, some of which are not obvious possibilities to the rookie officer. For example, police officers can often use humor to disarm situations and individuals. If an officer has the personality to carry this off, being humorous and "non-police-like" can work to the distinct advantage of the officer on the beat.

Most citizens do not expect a jovial interaction with the police. Equally, they do not expect that the police will behave in a particularly cerebral way, with a great deal of empathy, or with a genuine interest in, say, a person's job or hobby. Approaching people in any of these ways flies in the face of stereotypes that people hold about police officers. Such approaches can help to disarm members of the public and give officers an edge. Again, if the experienced officer is comfortable with that sort of approach, it can be beneficial to teach the younger officer how useful such a tactic can be.

Teaching rookie officers that it is all right to do the unexpected, as long it is comfortable, can make all the difference in a leader's effectiveness in influencing a particular subordinate. But it is in another direction that the role model idea can often cut. As is true of the chief of police—upon whom we will focus in Chapter 11—the **spotless lifestyle** is absolutely critical in developing and maintaining the personal integrity factor. The leader must only drink in moderation, only sleep with his or her own significant other, pay bills on time, and otherwise behave like a responsible member of society when off duty. This might sound like a recipe for boredom, but it is all part of the mantle that one accepts when one becomes a leader. Particularly in a profession where so much in the way of binge drinking and frivolity can be emblematic of off-duty behavior, the police leader has to be prepared to avoid excesses (as Aristotle would put it) and remember that he or she is not a member of "the gang" anymore.

Finally, having a personal ethic is so critical that we will spend much of Chapter 8 discussing this important concept. As we shall see then, encouraging the development of a personal ethic by every police officer is an important part of the role of the police leader. If this is true, it is imperative that the effective police leader have his or her own personal ethic in place and in evidence on the street. Police leaders cannot demand the creation of a personal ethic on the part of their charges until they have done so.

Can You Teach/Learn Charisma?

It sounds odd to suggest that charisma cannot be taught. If it is so important to police leadership and cannot be taught, then why have we spent so much time discussing it? The reason is twofold. First, it is important for the thoughtful and effective leader to understand as much as he or she can about leadership. Since charismatic authority can be of monumental importance in motivating people, whether or not a particular supervisor has a gift in this regard, he or she should acknowledge and understand as much about it as possible.

Second, it is in such a discussion that charismatic authority meets the role model concept. That is, being a role model most assuredly *is* something that anyone can accomplish. Without too much effort, and a little bit of focus and energy, anyone can create in themselves a role model for their subordinates to follow. There is nothing particularly esoteric about it. Therefore, if the leader observes and acknowledges in himself or herself a lack of natural charisma, our discussion about the role model idea can be very important. A leader who finds that he does not engender a following in a natural way can consciously work to develop in himself an important and even impressive persona as role model. Being thoughtful, disciplined, measured, and behaving with integrity are all characteristics that anyone can practice and enhance.

BOX 6.8

THE ROLE MODEL IDEAL

There are several definitions of the word "integrity," one of which will be the focal point of our discussion about character in Chapter 8. For the purpose of this discussion, integrity refers to the congruence between a person's philosophy and their behavior. That is, a person has integrity if they live a life that mirrors their belief system. They lack integrity (they are hypocritical) if they say one thing and do another.

This concept is crucial to the ideal of the role model. No one in any leadership role—anywhere, at any time, under any circumstances—can be effective if they do not live up to the rules of conduct they espouse for others.

So, we are suggesting that there is good news with regard to learning how to be a leader. Can a person learn to be a charismatic leader? Probably not. But—and this is the good news—can a person learn to be an excellent leader? Without a doubt.

CLOSING GAPS

Once we have spent the requisite time to define an organization's mission, we then must work on putting into place several levels of operational norms that bring the mission into specific relief and aid members in its pursuit. The overarching mission is more completely illustrated by the general working principles that are often created and maintained by suborganizations of divisions. Then these norms are even further distilled down into the specific, minute-by-minute rules of daily practice for the rank and file. In every organization ever put together, there are gaps; gaps between policies and ideals as announced and practices and rules of thumb on the street.

There are other sorts of gaps, as well. There are the gaps between members of the apparently solid and strongly bonded police subculture. Membership in various suborganizations, such as the patrol division and the traffic bureau, creates gaps due to differences in daily duties and perspectives. There are the gaps that exist between supervisorial staff and line officers. Even though every supervisor in American police work comes to their leadership role with line officer experience (which is not the case in Europe), they still develop a distance from those with whom they used to possess a bond, known in sociology as perhaps the most significant subcultural bond in the organizational world.

Also, there are gaps between the philosophy of COP and the goals of modern police professionalism and the operations norms and systemic realities of the officer on the street. Some of these gaps have been briefly investigated before in our discussions, but now is the appropriate time to make clear how critical these several realities are.

Between Mission and Pragmatics

We begin by revisiting our discussion about mission statements. The very essence of the mission statement—the reason for its existence—is to focus everyone in an organization in a way that ensures everything is accomplished in congruence with long-term interests, from the insignificant detail of organizational process to major policy decision. But there is sometimes a substantial gap between mission statement and pragmatic operational reality. The larger the organization, the more complex its goals and dynamics, the more troublesome is mission focus.

Almost everything ever written about mission statements suggests that an organization cannot have just some of its people or subgroups focused on its mission. The ideal, and indeed the target of the mission statement, is to have every policy and norm, from top to bottom, focused on and driven by the overall mission. Hiring, training, discipline, administration, and day-to-day leadership all need to be mission-driven. The role of police leader, at every level, must include a conscious, proactive, and aggressive effort to focus on mission and make sure that any gaps that appear between mission and pragmatic operational norms be closed. The leader does not want to sound like the proverbial broken record, but every single decision needs to be made with reference to mission.

Between Supervisors and Line

A second gap exists between supervisorial behavior and line officer behavior. This gap persists in all organizations to one extent or another. In fact, it is the most important reason for immediate supervision in the first place. Why do we have sergeants? Because without them, police discretion might lead to as many different penal codes and general order manuals as there are police officers. Put simply, the reason—*the* reason—for supervision is to keep the gap between announced law, police regulations, training and police practice to a minimum. A congruence problem (gap problem) between mission and behavior can then be paralleled by a congruence problem between specific police policies (not to mention the law) and lower level behavior. These are similar, albeit substantively different concerns.

Between Professional Ideals and Operations

A third gap exists between the ideals of professionalism and COP and police daily operations. Several parts of the COP philosophy and elements of professionalism need to be monitored in this regard. First, collegial problem solving is a critical change that is in progress today, and there is an ongoing propensity in many police organizations to inhibit this evolution and go back to hierarchical decision making. Second, in some jurisdictions, there is a propensity to move backwards in time with regard to police accountability (which we will consider in great depth in Chapters 8, 9, and 10) to a situation where the monitoring of police behavior is kept more secretive instead of becoming more open and above board. Third, partially driven by the creation of the **Department of Homeland Security**, police paramilitarism is expanding in some places as it ebbs and recedes in others. This is a particularly disconcerting development to those who understand and support the idea of the police in America becoming genuine professionals.

Each of these various gaps are troublesome and, to some extent, issues of import to all police leaders. Of course, strategic decisions are the business of police leaders at middle and upper levels. Such decisions should be made with an eye toward understanding these developments. The daily and immediate supervision of the street sergeant must also be conducted in an effort to exert pressure in the direction of closing these gaps, aimed at the development of integrity in American police administration.

BOX 6.9

COLLEGIAL PROBLEM SOLVING CANNOT BE LED

One paradox of police leadership is that if we are to achieve one of the most important goals of the COP movement—that of eschewing the old-fashioned command-and-control model of leading and moving in the direction of collegial problem solving—police leaders have to "get out of the way." That is, while collegial problem solving can be heartily encouraged, it cannot be led. If decisions are made collectively, in a more democratic fashion than is historically the case, the leader needs to be self-aware enough to move aside and allow younger and perhaps even less intelligent officers to take their turn at the helm of decision-making responsibility.

 ## A TO-DO LIST

How does all that we have discussed come together into a coherent whole in the modern leader's arsenal of skills? Some of this chapter can be frustrating for those who consider themselves to be **"charisma challenged"** in life. But theirs is not an impossible situation. Police leaders can always work on several key areas of their own personal repertoire while at the same time being aware of their limitations. Here is a sort of to-do list, upon which the police leader might focus in attempting to respond to the ideas presented in this chapter's discussions:

- Be realistic about limitations. Know your own and recognize those of the police organization within which you operate. Furthermore, remind yourself on a regular basis about how powerful the subculture is and, therefore, what can and cannot be accomplished by the individual leader.

- Try your best to avoid the command-and-control mode. No matter how long you have been in police work, and no matter what the mode of operation is in your particular organization or suborganization, work on more subordinate-friendly methods of control. Motivate, teach, and coach—make that your mantra.

- Remember what constitutes charisma and acknowledge it; what elements do you possess? If you draw a blank here, just be aware of the power of charisma in others so you might operate around it and even utilize it in others to accomplish your own goals. A subordinate who has charisma and is in your "court" can be quite valuable. Put such a person on your team.

- Work on being a coach. Don't just stop at the limited list that we have shared here, but—especially if you are charisma-challenged—do some reading and research on the principles of successful coaching. Are we suggesting that you "study" coaching? Absolutely.

- Work on becoming a role model. While it might be impossible to create charisma, it is definitely possible to work consciously on one's role model potential. Make this an ongoing project that becomes a part of who you are. Recall Paul Newman's "You gotta be yourself, kid . . . but on purpose."

- While attempting to accomplish any and all of the above, keep the philosophy of COP and the goals of police professionalism in mind. As if those principles constituted your very own mission statement, focus on them as your primary "quest" in police work. As you do so, work consistently on closing the gaps that we have illustrated above.

 ## SUMMATION

One of the paradoxical realities of leadership is that effective, insightful, future-looking leadership is absolutely crucial in police organizations and, yet, only some elements of it are transferable. Whether a police department is following one of the traditional three styles of Wilson or making a serious effort to install COP in the name of generating professionalism, any police organization must focus on its mission at all times. From top to bottom, leading must involve such an ongoing mode of operating.

In the long run, effective leading is largely about making yourself into a genuine professional. Leadership in today's police work is about committing yourself to the goal of changing yourself, your subordinates, and your organization in the direction of the future of the new blue line. You must do so as if you were a member of a genuine profession, so you avoid falling into the pitfalls that have plagued police work until very recently (historically speaking), when to be a police officer meant merely being a blue collar worker with a limited education and vision.

DISCUSSION QUESTIONS

1. Perhaps *the* most important question with regard to charismatic authority is this: Can charisma be taught (or transferred)? Reflecting upon this chapter, discuss this question, positing both sides in turn—that is, discuss the idea that charisma is not teachable (and why) and, concomitantly, how it might be transferred.

2. Although virtually all people in police work today are familiar with the command-and-control concept, what are the arguments—the pronounced drawbacks—against this type of police organization?

3. After discussing Question 2 and making arguments critical of command-and-control leadership, turn the debate on its head; discuss those circumstances under which command-and-control organizational principles are absolutely crucial (in other words, engage the central paradox here).

4. What is the "sandwich technique" for giving subordinates negative feedback? Construct several examples and then discuss examples invented by others.

5. What does the text mean when it suggests that police leaders must have spotless private lives? Think of as many examples as you can of how the responsibility of being a leader in today's police world requires police managers to behave in ways that are circumspect, with regard to the images they portray in their private lives.

KEY TERMS

Adapt and overcome: A term and mantra credited to the U.S. Marine Corps of being able to adjust to an occurring adversity, adapt to the circumstances, and then overcoming the adversity, whatever it might be.

Charisma: A trait found in persons whose personalities are characterized by a personal charm and magnetism (attractiveness), along with innate and powerfully sophisticated abilities of interpersonal communication and persuasion.

Charisma challenged: A person lacking the traits of charisma but trying to overcome that characteristic.

Charismatic authority: The sociologist Max Weber defined charismatic authority as "resting on devotion to the exceptional sanctity, heroism or exemplary character of an individual person, and of the normative patterns or order revealed or ordained by him." Charismatic authority is one of three authorities defined by Weber.

Closing gaps: Creating a bridge between policy and working reality. Example: If a policy describes a method or procedure to accomplish a goal and the policy cannot be met by the procedure developed, an officer may have to "close the gap" between policy and achieving the goal by another creative avenue.

Coaching: A method of directing, instructing, and training a person or group of people, with the aim to achieve some goal or develop specific skills.

Command and control: The exercise of authority and direction by a properly designated commanding officer over assigned and attached forces or units in the accomplishment of a goal or mission; a method of operation for many police departments in America where the organization functions by a strict chain of command.

CYA: "Cover your ass." This phrase is commonly used in police work to describe an activity that allows an officer to justify his/her actions.

Department of Homeland Security: A cabinet department of the United States federal government with the primary responsibilities of protecting the territory of the U.S. from terrorist attacks and responding to natural disasters.

Fixing responsibility: Attaching responsibility to a specific endeavor, entity, or agency for the completion of a goal or the outcome of an event.

Negative sanction: A corrective and/or disciplinary action taken against an officer that is a punishment to correct behavior.

Organizational rationality: An experience that occurs when personnel in an organization lose sight of the overall goals and mission of the organization and act outside those goals and mission.

Professional ideals: An established set of virtues that exemplify a particular profession. Examples: Empathy, conscientiousness, objectivity, collegiality.

Rational-legal authority: A form of leadership in which the authority of an organization or a ruling regime is largely tied to legal rationality, legal legitimacy, and bureaucracy; authority given by structure.

Reform era of American policing: In the early 1900s, a professionalization movement sought to reform the inefficient and corrupt police agencies that had developed during the 19th century. During this reform era, there was a total restructuring of police departments and a redefinition of the police role, due to the perceived failure of police to enforce the law.

Role model ideal: A set of virtues demonstrated by a leader to his/her followers through actions and behavior. Examples: Good listener, honest, trustworthy, courageous.

Salty officers: A tenured officer with a contemptuous attitude toward the organization and others who do not believe in his/her outlook.

Sandwich technique: A method of managing subordinates where the focal leader uses a three-tiered approach to dealing with the follower whom he/she is taking corrective action against: (1) present something positive, (2) present the negative issue (corrective reminder, written or verbal), (3) follow up with a positive issue.

Screamers: Leaders who yell at their followers when presenting them with directives or corrective actions.

Spotless lifestyle: A person who possesses no negative activity or demonstrated negative behaviors in their background (criminal, economic, professional, or personal).

Swift and ruthless: A method of employee corrective action or discipline utilized by some leaders where they swiftly and ruthlessly administer their punishment or corrective action(s) to demonstrate a no-nonsense approach.

Teaching leadership: A concept that suggests leadership is not a genetic gift but can be taught through education, training, and example.

Traditional authority: Authority based upon custom, lineage, or tradition. Examples: King, queen, imam, chief of a tribe.

Weber's authority: Sociologist Max Weber's concepts of his described three types of authority: legal, traditional, and charismatic.

EXAMPLE SCENARIOS

Soft Leadership

Sergeant Jim Rassmussen is an investigative sergeant in charge of a burglary/narcotics three-man team. The purpose of his unit is to work burglary and theft cases and any narcotics activity at the street level. His team has a theft specialist and undercover narcotics specialist working together. The basic mission of the team is to decrease property crimes in area 6 of their community. The notion is that burglars commit theft and burglary to support their drug habits, and drug addicts are thieves and burglars.

Rassmussen has two very strong personalities in his subordinates. Neither of them are "wallflowers." Rassmussen has been a supervisor for only three months and is relatively new to focal leadership. He has been trying to use a soft approach with subordinates, deferring to their expertise and letting them make their own decisions about how to serve search warrants and work their cases.

To begin with, the experiment of soft leadership worked pretty well. But one night, the sergeant tells his team not to serve a search warrant on a certain suspect because the location of the house to be searched was not well delineated in the search warrant. They served the warrant anyway, without his approval. Coincidently, they served it on the wrong residence. There were no injuries or damage to the residence, but the residents were extremely upset and reported their dissatisfaction and anger to the chief of police. Rassmussen is in hot water. He now must take corrective action with his subordinates and will likely receive some himself.

What should Rassmussen do, given the style he has been presenting to his officers? Even though he is upset, doesn't he need to be consistent with his tone and approach in order to be fair? Should he change his leadership style with the team, if he is allowed to continue as team leader?

Hard Leadership

Captain Carol Brown has been transferred to the records division of her department. This occurred because the records division has been performing poorly for the last six months and Brown is known for her no-nonsense style of leadership. She is generally a command-and-control type of leader. Her philosophy is for her subordinates to, "Do as I say and follow the rules. Do not veer from those tenets and you'll be okay."

Her predecessor's leadership style was more charismatic. Everybody liked Captain John Pendergrass. He was humorous, level headed, always smiling, and had the habit of covering for his followers.

Brown now has some work cut out for her. The staff at records are slow to respond to requests for reports from the detectives and street officers, not to mention citizens. When reports do get to their intended party, there are often missing pages and coffee stains or smudges on the documents. The records division has hampered other divisions in the department because they operate by a different standard. Obviously, they do not consider themselves an integral part of the organizational mission. This is evident by the performance and attitudes of the staff.

Captain Brown has decided she will call a meeting of her supervisors before she does anything else and set a clear line of expectations. Shape up or ship out!

How does Brown begin to change the method of operation of the records division in a fair way? Knowing that a different form of leadership existed previously, she wants to start changing things, but understands that the previous regime had different expectations. What does she do? Why?

Team Leadership

Commander Steve Samuels just left the chief's office and he doesn't like what he heard. The chief just informed him that his command will be increased to include two new beats to be absorbed from the north side of his area. This set of beats is the most active and has the highest crime rates in the entire community. He already does not have enough staff to manage the area for which he is currently responsible. This addition will increase his overtime and stretch his officers beyond what is bearable.

He does not like the new edict, but decides he will meet with his lieutenants to inform them of the new assignments and get their input. During the meeting, Lieutenant Sherry Ward states she doesn't know how they are going to handle this new area without resources. Her feeling is that they always get dumped on anyway and this isn't anything new. She is against the addition and thinks the commander should go back to the chief and tell him so.

Lieutenant Chad Worthington disagrees and says, "Commander, my folks and I will do whatever we need to do to make this work. You can count on us."

Lieutenant John Gray says, "Worthington, you have always been a suck-up, and that will never change. How do you think you'll do this without the resources?"

Lieutenant Sheryl Fong says, "I don't care what they or we do. It just doesn't matter."

Commander Samuels has a dilemma on his hands. What does he do under such circumstances? He has everything under the sun among his subordinates: unrealistically upbeat support, negativity with an attitude, and hopelessness that is palpable. How does the creative commander engage such disparate attitudes, future expectations, and analyses of the situation?

ADDITIONAL READING

Weber's world-famous discussions—not only about the nature of charismatic authority, but also the rationalizations for bureaucracy as the best way to systematize a public organization—are included in *From Max Weber: Essays in Sociology*, edited and translated by H. Gerth and C. Wright Mills (Oxford University Press, 1946).

Our discussion here began with references to the command-and-control model of police management. Two excellent works that analyze and issue critiques of this antiquated method of supervision are *Freedom from Command and Control* (Productivity Press, 2005), by John Seddon, and *Training the 21sth Century Police Officer* (Rand, 2003), by Russell W. Glenn. Glenn focuses in particular upon how the command-and-control model must give way to methods of supervision that are commensurate with COP.

In *Supervising Police Personnel: The Fifteen Responsibilities, 6th Ed.* (Prentice Hall, 2006), Paul M. Whisenand suggests a list-like approach to police supervision that, while a bit on the dry side, is nevertheless indicative of a more traditional approach to the topic. Counter to this traditional focus is *Leadership, Ethics, and Policing: Challenges for the 21st Century* (Prentice Hall, 2003), by Edwin Meese and P. J. Ortmeier, which suggests that such an "old style" approach will not work and that, indeed, the new philosophy of more collegial problem solving is the appropriate approach for the future of policing. With regard to the ever-expanding field of alternatives to traditional police supervision, the idea of practicing "upward discipline" is embraced by Nathan F. Iannone, Marvin D. Iannone, and Jeff Berstein in *Supervision of Police Personnel, 7th Ed.* (Prentice Hall, 2008).

Two fine works on coaching are James Flaherty's *Coaching, 2nd Ed.: Evoking Excellence in Others* (Butterworth–Hermann, 2005), and Thomas G. Crane and Lerissa Nancy Patrick's *The Heart of Coaching: Using Transformational Coaching to Create a High-Performance Coaching Culture, 3rd Ed.* (FTQ Press, 2007).

CHAPTER 7

Assessment

INTRODUCTION

Every organization seeks to quantify the productivity of its operations. There are numerous types of **assessment tools** used to determine the output and productivity of organizations in general. Then there are tools and programs used in police work in particular. Organizational assessment is an area of police operations that has many not-so-obvious facets and presents us with several unfortunate paradoxes. Modern standard assessment tools are numerous. Statistical reviews, data reviews, output assessments, organization evaluations, **roundtable** reviews, and **CompStat** initiatives are all examples. Furthermore, there are unique tools or systems developed within individual police organizations that are also utilized to help police leadership determine if it is effectively and efficiently accomplishing its purposes. We will discuss each of these assessment tools. Along the way, we will visit several paradoxes that make police **assessment** more difficult and inexact than it might appear to be at first glance.

The use of assessment tools is a way for an organization to determine where it's been, where it is now, and where it wants to be. In both private enterprise and public administration, most organizations now base their assessment systems on specifically delineated mission statements, particularized organizational goals, and definitive objectives of sub-organizations. The idea is to have a basic, strong, clear foundation for the purpose of organizational focus and then effectively determine how the mission is going to be accomplished via more pragmatic and specifically focused rules and regulations.

This is done by examining what direction leadership is currently aiming toward and where they want to go for the foreseeable future. Leaders need to create a roadmap of sorts to determine how best to get there. This is accomplished by determining what goals (**subgoals** are absolutely critical here) are needed to fulfill the mission and how to develop systems that allow for the assessment of organizational standing and progress.

As we took some time to point out in Chapter 3, no logically organized (and run) bureaucratic organization can achieve its goals without a clear mission statement. In this chapter, we will not be examining again how to develop a mission statement but, rather, how important it is for people to understand the subgoals and sub-missions that underscore day-to-day, minute-by-minute operations in the workplace. We will examine the issue of an organization as a total system, made up of individuals and subgroups, leadership, and sub-organizations. The basic notion of this chapter is to determine how the substantive impact of the mission of a police organization can be assessed for its effectiveness and efficiency. We will examine some tools that are used to assess mission accomplishment and compare and contrast some traditional modes of assessment with new and progressive tools that are being created in the name of COP.

We start at the beginning—with the mission statement—as promised earlier in our discussion.

THE MISSION: AGAIN

It is important to remind ourselves that the mission of the organization is the "linchpin" which works to hold together the overall rationale for the existence of the organization in the first place. Without a clear purpose, an organization is doomed to follow no clear path to operational success. Again, we have spent enough time focusing on that specific topic. At issue in our discussion here is the fact that it is of critical import that various divisions and units within an organization possess overlapping sub-mission statements that act as guides for the activity of that division or unit, and are congruent with the organization's mission. In other words, divisions and units must have their own goals and objectives commensurate with the organization mission in order for their success to be achieved.

There is a joke shared in public administration circles that comes from, of all places, *Alice's Adventures in Wonderland*, by Lewis Carroll. It has to do with the importance of mission statements and the specificity of focus necessary for organizations to be effective and efficient. It's a conversation that occurs when Alice meets the Cheshire Cat. Alice says, "Would you tell me, please, which way I ought to go from here?" The Cat says, "That depends a good deal on where you want to get to." Alice replies, "I don't much care where . . ." And the Cat interrupts, "Then it doesn't matter which way you go." The point this story makes is, "How can we

BOX 7.1

MISSION SUCCESS, THEN A VOID

In a Southern police department, a charismatic leader provided a clear mission for the staff to follow. He made sure they all had a basic idea of their purpose. Training and subgoals were clear and focused. In the short term, the goals of the organization were fulfilled, improvements occurred, and productivity and morale increased. Unfortunately, when this specific leader left the organization to become an executive elsewhere, the new leader had all of the mission statements removed from public view. Believing mission statements to be a redundant waste of time, he pressed on without their focus. There was no clear mission afterward, and the operation continued to function, but without a clear unified purpose. Productivity and morale both plummeted. In the long run, the clear and unqualified focus on organizational mission was merely the product of individual charisma. It was not an integral part of how the organization itself worked. When one particular person left, the mission was lost and confusion ensued.

get to where we want to go if we do not have the right map to get there?" Without a clear direction, no organization can be successful in creating what it is trying to produce or in providing the service it is attempting to administer.

"A mission statement acts as an invisible hand that guides the people in an organization" (Hansen, 2006). This means that the mission statement cannot be just another piece of paper gathering dust in the executive's office. It needs to be a living, breathing part of the organization's life. It is absolutely essential that an ongoing part of the organization's focus is the creation and regular recreation of subgoals and operational principles that are used to reach their fruition.

Subgoals Should Be Tied to the Mission

For the organization to be effective, successful, and productive, the mission statement must be ingrained in the minds of the people working there. It must be shared, and leaders must require that everyone be familiar with its contents. Developing familiarity with the mission can be achieved in various ways, some of which are quite simple. The mission statement can be posted where it can be publicly seen. It can be read at the beginning of every training session. It can be taught to supervisors and mid-managers, as well as required for use in every proposal made to improve the organization. In fact, one logical reason for the creation of a terse mission statement is that the more precise and focused it is, the more places it can be utilized. Some organizations have terse enough statements that they can even publish them on their stationery.

As we noted in Chapter 3, a mission statement cannot be treated as if it is some sort of secret. Since they have both internal and external functions, mission statements are meant to be shared—within and without. Tom Peters, in his book *A Passion for Excellence*, suggests that attention, symbols, and drama are what get people in an organization primed for its mission (Peters, 1985). It makes the organization ready for productivity.

Unfortunately, the first paradox in the incident chapter is that this does not happen in most police agencies. In all too many departments, when mission statements are shared, it appears as though they are shared through shallow means. The missions might be posted in the lobbies of agencies so visitors can see them. They may be hidden in documents, such as proposals for improvements or in budget requests. Sometimes mission statements will be shared in participant manuals at in-service training sessions. But it is a rare agency that operates with a focus on the mission of the organization in relation to the line staff having a clear idea of the purpose of that organization. That is to say, the process of mission statement creation and mission statement maintenance is a completely public relations–oriented endeavor. Nothing of substance is achieved or even attempted in such departments. One thing is very clear about mission statements: leadership must "walk the walk" and "talk the talk" if they expect the mission of their organization to be fulfilled. The integrity factor is absolutely critical here. To proclaim a mission and then show

BOX 7.2

EFFECTIVE MISSION STATEMENT INTEGRITY

A rural chief of police was encountering difficulties in his agency. The staff was having difficulty getting along. His operation was working well, and his staff were performing their duties admirably, but there was an undercurrent of disconnection between the senior staff and the junior staff. One group operated one way, and the other group operated the other way. To neutralize these tendencies, the chief decided to set up a training program aimed at every officer and civilian in the organization. He collaborated with the International Chiefs of Police to incorporate their Leadership in Police Organizations training (West Point Military Leadership Training) with all of his staff, including himself and the command staff. The "linchpin" of the training is the mission of the organization and how to close the gap between the line staff and the executive staff. The training is being conducted in regular sessions every year. Mission statements, operational examples, constant communication up the chain of command and down are laced with the verbiage and symbols of the Police Leadership Model. As of this writing, he is seeing at least anecdotal evidence of positive change.

that it is not taken seriously by leadership is to encourage a general cynicism among the police officer corps.

Goals are a projected state of affairs a person or group plans to achieve. Goals for any organization must be set based upon and tied to the mission of the organization. They must be concise and specific. This will set a clear understanding of whether or not the organization is achieving its mission during any assessment sessions. If goals are not achieved, changes can be implemented and/or new goals determined. The goals of the organization can and should be fluid. This is because leadership can change, community goals and sentiment can change, and even the situation on the street can change. Organizational mission needs to be able to conform to such variability.

It is important for leaders to ensure that goals they set for the organization are specific and can be tied to **quantifiable data**. This way, the goals can be observed as successful or not depending on the outcome of the data collected. For example, a police agency may develop a goal of zeroing out the number of burglaries in its community. It can then set up a database that tracks how many burglaries occur and a data track of the clearances of those burglaries that did occur. Both of these databases can help the agency identify where and how burglaries occur, and data can show how close the organization has come to fulfilling its goal.

BOX 7.3

EXAMPLE OF A SUBGOAL

Within the goal of zero burglaries in a community during a month, the subgoal of how the prevention of burglaries will occur might state, "Investigators will promote a neighborhood watch process in their areas of responsibility. Those groups will be encouraged to report suspicious activity and any burglaries they may witness." Data on the number of neighborhood watch tips provided can be developed as well as the number of tips that brought about a clearance of a burglary or an arrest of a suspect.

Organizational Structure

The subgoals of an organization should also be driven by the overall mission of the organization. A subgoal is a part or smaller component of a goal. It operates to refocus an overall goal, so it puts into practice some particularized operational utility. Let us take a specific example to illustrate several points.

The mission of Continental Machinery and Support Services Inc. is to "utilize the extensive expertise of management and staff to provide high quality equipment, professional support services, and competitive pricing for our global equipment customers to meet the particular unique needs of each client and project, and to provide ongoing support to assure total customer satisfaction" (www.continentalmach.com). This is a real company, but our extrapolations—from here on—are intuitively driven. It is a heavy machinery company. One of its sub-units is its logging division. When a potential job comes into the division, it must evaluate that job. For this purpose, it might send out an assessment team composed of an engineer, a machinery expert, an accountant, and a public interest lawyer.

The team analyzes the delivery, setup, operation, and take-down costs of any given job. In parallel, the lawyer does research into any environmental factors, lawsuits, or regulations that are apposite. The accountant puts it all together into an estimate. Standard operational norms and procedures are in place that regulate the job of this subgroup, including everything from its travel costs (per diems and so forth) on down to the format they must use to show their report to "corporate." Once on the job, another group—the operations section of the logging division—takes over. This subgroup is divided into the heavy equipment group, the product hauling group, the loggers unit, and so forth. Each unit has its own operational rules and budgetary restrictions. Everything that can be planned for in advance is taken into account, down to how much communications will cost between the office and the customer.

We've taken a moment here to walk through this exercise in order to point out that the mission is translated into rules and procedures for potential job assessment, budgetary development, logistical support, travel, on-site operations, and so on. Each subgroup has its rules and goals. The hauling group, for example, has rules about how many hours any given trucker can drive in a week (much like those applicable to airline pilots), how far they can drive, and how the organization plans to meet all of the relevant regulations of the several federal organizations that administer interstate trucking. The overall mission is distilled all the way down to specific rules about how long drivers may take for their meals on the road.

The police are not involved in delivering a construction-oriented product, so there are some differences, but in general, there are analogies to all of these units and operations. There are police divisions that plan, produce budgets, develop specific strategies, and divide up the division of labor on the street. The investigative division, for example, has rules that are specifically focused on clearance. Clearance is something that is not of the slightest interest to anyone in, say, the patrol division. But clearance is so important in investigations that there must be specific rules about how cases are handed out, how they are cleared, and when they must be reported as such. Furthermore, a particular type of accountability is in place so that abuses of the system do not occur in the misguided effort by some investigators to appear to be more effective and/or more efficient with their time. All of this is accomplished with the mission of the organization in mind, but—equally—with no particular relationship to other sub-organizations.

One important issue here has to do with including staff in the development of operational norms, goals, and rules. This can be an important way of obtaining a buy-in from those who are subject to them. Direct participation in at least some subgoal definition can expand this buy-in. This is a (sort of) entry-level strategy. Another strategy aimed at such an acceptance involves ensuring that everybody is somehow included in the celebration of organizational success when that is relevant. When success is being achieved—as determined by the information collected from assessment tools aimed at the goals set for the success of the mission—citing efforts, contributions, and achievements of everyone can be important. This might sound trite and even obvious, but tying individual subordinates into organizational mission accomplishment in this way is a good way to cement the relationship of each person's role in the accomplishment of the mission.

One concept that is a staple in the world of organizational theory has to do with maintaining the boundaries of sub-organizations. Organizations are administered by dividing them up into sub-organizations, of course, and this is done with logical rationalizations. But when sub-organizations begin to take on lives of their own, they can create (metaphorically) hard shells around them in order to protect them from outside interference. When this is done, the sub-organization tends to create "boundary spanning" devices in order to lessen the uncertainly they face from without. So, for example, detectives from the burglary division will create and maintain informal relationships with members of the patrol division, even though interactions with uniformed officers are almost never necessary. This is done in an

REVIEW CHART 7.1

Three Tiers: Mission, Subgoals, Rules

- *Mission statements:* Entire organization
- *Subgoals/objectives:* Divisions, departments
- *Rules/regulations:* Individual workers, crews

effort to maintain some sort of informal and indirect control over clearance—by anticipating new incoming case loads and by learning in advance what the near-future potential might be of clearing a substantial number of cases due to the arrest of the local professional burglar by the patrol division.

Getting staff to buy in to sub-missions is also a means of ensuring that they know the boundaries of their roles, and any effort on the part of staff to sabotage the mission will not be met with good will or tolerance. Knowledge and creativity on the part of the immediate leadership within the organization is critical in creating a group of people willing to support the organizational mission. Below, we will visit the types of followers who can "make or break" organizational efforts at success and outline ways to attempt to co-opt them into the organizational mission.

A word about the idea of **co-opting** is in order. Philip Selznick wrote a book that is famous in the organizational theory field about the Tennessee Valley Authority during the Great Depression. *TVA and the Grass Roots* was an in-depth study of the agency that was put together to administer the dozens of dams, hundreds of bridges, and thousands of miles of roads that were built by federal dollars in an effort to help bring the country out of disastrous economic times. These various projects brought electricity and indoor plumbing to millions of people in the poor rural South during the 1930s. The projects were successful in both an engineering and a political/sociological sense.

The administration of the gigantic bureaucracy that was invented for these purposes was a rousing success. So successful was the TVA that it became a famous example of bureaucratic and governmental effectiveness. How had the people in charge put together a multimillion dollar organization that spanned a dozen states, required cooperation to develop between local, state, and federal officials, and succeeded in creating jobs for hundreds of thousands of the unemployed? What those in charge did was then a brand new, untested strategy. The administrators involved at the federal level looked at existing bureaucracies, from the city and county levels up to the state and federal levels, and put together an overarching, logically constructed bureaucratic hierarchy that utilized current employees in its power structure. They appointed existing officials to federal positions that maintained and even increased their individual income and status. This worked to inhibit natural tendencies for local pride and power to mitigate progress. This is how local people—at all levels in hundreds of cities and counties and a dozen states—ended up being coaxed into buying into the projects. Selznick, in his study of the TVA, deemed the process "co-optation"—a combination of the words "cooperation" and "cooperative"—and his term stuck. Today, it is a part of the American vernacular. But it is apposite here. It refers in our incident discussion to obtaining cooperation from the rank and file by allowing them to participate in the creation of subgoals and, on some occasions, subprocedures.

Avoiding Bureaupathology

To review, bureaupathology is the propensity for the development of elaborate rules and regulations such that followers are expected to abide by those rules and regulations even if they are contrary to the mission of the organization or the productivity of the staff. Victor A. Thompson, the term's inventor, noted that many people in bureaucratic organizations developed feelings of alienation, loss of identity, separation between public and private life, and even an absence of meaningful work (Thompson, 1961). As a result of this general alienation, people can become lost in a morass of bureaupathology.

This syndrome is often found in police agencies in America. Many American police departments operate with more reference to their operations manuals than basic purposes or missions. Sub-organizational rules and regulations sometimes become more important than the purpose or mission of the organization, and any new or suggested improvements for the fulfillment of the mission are blocked by rules that govern the operation of the sub-organization. Of course, as we have noted, there is a need for rules and regulations in any bureaucracy. Rules help set up guidelines and, sometimes, boundaries of expected action or behavior. However, rules and regulations should not be used as reasons for not completing duties or taking actions that would significantly help fulfill the mission of the organization.

We have examined the mission statement and goals aspect of the organization, and fundamentally concluded that the mission is the "linchpin" of the organization's success. We noted that any agency should include overlapping mission statements from each division/unit of operation and they should be tailored to the primary mission. We identified that goals, specific and quantifiable, along with well developed subgoals, are important to help determine the success or lack thereof of divisions/units toward the accomplishment of the primary goal. We have discussed that organizations need to be careful about succumbing to being "bureaupathologic" in their efforts to fulfill their mission. Executive leaders would be well advised to keep their organizations out of the bureaupathic syndrome.

Now is the time to examine the characteristics of the people we want to co-opt for the fulfillment of the mission of the organization. Some officers may never be brought "into the fold," so to speak. But the effective leader must have knowledge of the characteristic behaviors of certain counterproductive officers. Knowledge of such officer types—archetypal officers, if you will—and what they might try to do can save the executive and immediate supervisors a lot of time and wasted energy. Put another way, knowing in advance about saboteurs of various kinds can help greatly in leading organizations logically and effectively.

BOX 7.4

AN EXAMPLE OF BUREAUPATHOLOGY

A commander of the Crimes vs. Property unit of a police agency decided that his investigators were not adequately performing their duties. He noted some investigators were clearing cases without making enough contacts with potential witnesses of local residential burglaries. As a result, he issued a new investigative manual rule and shared it with his detectives. The rule was written as, "Every investigator will make personal contact with each residence on each side of the victim's residence and the three residences across the street during their hours of duty. The hours of investigative operations will be Monday through Friday, from 8 A.M. to 4 P.M." This rule created a situation where the detectives had difficulty making day contacts with residents because the local residents mostly worked the same hours as the detectives and were not available for contact until after 5 P.M.

Residential burglary cases were kept open for longer periods of time due to the edict. Detectives found ways to "kiss off" potentially good cases with evidence that could possibly lead to a suspect by suspending the cases due to lack of information. Suspended residential burglary cases increased significantly, and cleared cases dipped. Residential burglary rates increased. When queried about the increases in burglaries, the detectives cited that rules and regulations kept them from doing their work effectively. They felt as though their jobs had become mired in futile activity due to the absence of meaningful investigation and too much bureaucratic red tape.

NEGATIVITY

It is well known that police work is basically a negative experience, due to the nature of what the police see and do. They mostly see and react to the worst in people, violent behavior, crises, death, and emergencies. Officers see man's inhumanity to man perhaps more often than members of any other profession. Even in the police academy, cadets are bombarded with examples of the negative aspects of the job (Cook, 2003). They are told stories about officers being sued or becoming alcoholics, drug users, and wife beaters. They are told that police officers suffer high rates of suicide, get injured on the job, and must be very careful to protect themselves from harm. They are also made aware that there is significant liability involved in the profession. Sure enough, when officers reach the street, all of these negative things seem to occur.

The result of experiencing this type of input, day in and day out, eventually has an effect on an officer's psyche. This is not to say that all officers come out of their long-term tenure worse off for the experience, but a substantial number do.

There is a tendency for the negativity encountered on the street to creep into and become part of the nature of some officer's personalities. They become **naysayers**, and their influence can have a chilling effect on the organization. This can happen despite the fact that their numbers (those of the naysayers) tend to be quite low. Only about 15 to 25 percent are naysayers, one researcher suggests (Kelley, 1992), but they possess an inordinate amount of organizational power. Let us take a moment to look at several types of naysayers—sometimes known as **saboteurs**—and examine their behavioral characteristics.

Types of Saboteurs

This section is presented because the authors believe that how leaders (executive and immediate) deal with negative employees will certainly make a difference in the "climate" of an organization. This is as important for students of police work as it is for focal leaders in the profession. Knowledge of the types of negative employees can give leaders the ability to easily identify those behaviors and take action to correct or neutralize them when needed, especially since we know these individuals can easily disrupt the mission of the organization.

The Snitch Police officers despise a **snitch**. Unfortunately, every agency has some. They are the employee who works hard to be in everyone's business and is quick to report anything that can be capitalized on for personal gain. Their goal is usually to ingratiate themselves with the person to whom they are reporting their "findings." They are always aware of what will impact them personally and have an agenda aimed at making others look bad. Such persons can be spotted at every police gathering place: the water cooler, break and dining areas, the staff lounge, and the local police hangout. They are engaging and interpersonally skilled. Perhaps a good title for these saboteurs is "interpersonal predators." There is no boundary they will not try to subvert. In many instances, these people are formerly exemplary employees who were marginalized or possibly came close to termination. They take out their anger and frustration on others in the form of being a "tattletale" or by "sucking up to the boss." These employees are obviously toxic to the workplace.

The Gossip One truism in police work (or any other business) is, "You're never going to erase **gossip** altogether." But it is important to know the differences between gossip, rumor, and innuendo because of the destructive nature of these kinds of activities. The workplace gossip can have a strongly negative influence on the morale of the organization. Gossip can be "energy-sucking, time-wasting, and debilitating for morale" (Richardson, 2009). The organizational gossip can be observed meandering about the organization telling others, "You know what I heard?" or asking questions about sensitive or personal issues such as, "I just talked to Sally and she says our supervisor just made a pass at her." These behaviors obviously have a great impact on workplace dynamics. Talking about potential upcoming concerns like job redesign, budget cuts, or promotions in an inquisitive manner cannot be considered gossip. But when a person begins by accusatory types of statements, there may be a problem. Generally, these employees seek acceptance and want to be liked and known as knowledgeable within their working environment. Unfortunately, they see the workplace as a sort of social club.

The Backstabber Leaders tend to deplore anyone who exemplifies a **backstabber**. Backstabbing in police work is the fastest route to ostracism. Nonetheless, there may be more of these types of employees in police work than leaders want to admit. The backstabber behaves by "clearing a way to claw their way to the top" (Mayzer, 1999). They are known for such acts as passing on information (blind copy e-mails, social networking systems), withholding information, and spreading rumors. Nonetheless, according to Karen Stephenson of UCLA's Anderson School, backstabbing "tends to happen in organizations with limited or no accountability regardless of the size or type of company." Law enforcement cannot be excluded.

The Crybaby Crybabies are employees who whine about everything, from the minimal raise they received and the poor equipment with which they were provided, to the partner they work with. Their behavior is incessant. While police officers also deplore crybabies, there is evidence that there are plenty of those types in police work. These are the "**slugs**," the "call dodgers," and the "case dumpers" (Glennon, 2009). These workers may complain about one negative comment on an evaluation, but are completely clueless about their competence as an officer. The crybaby officers are the ones who create an absolute nightmare for their supervisors, who may have to spend as much as 90 percent of their time managing these employees. Their very nature sucks the life out of an organization.

REVIEW CHART 7.2

SABOTEUR ARCHETYPES

- *The snitch:* The informer who deflects attention from himself or herself by consistently focusing upon others
- *The gossip:* Attempts to be "in" and important by passing along anything and everything said about others
- *The backstabber:* Duplicitous subordinate or coworker who attempts to expand his or her own value by denigrating that of others
- *The crybaby:* The whiner who finds fault with everything and everyone in order to mask his or her own inadequacies
- *The CYA guy:* Self-serving "cover" is consistently created in order to avoid responsibility for error and to limit work assignments

The CYA Guy This is the officer who justifies all behavior (negative or positive) by claiming that he or she has **"got your back**." This employee is one who has usually not been involved in any real police activity and does not self-initiate, but backs everybody up when they need it. These employees will say anything to make their police officer constituents believe they are the sole supporter of their fellow officers. Actually, when a real problem arises and there is a need for another officer to have genuine support and substantiate the appropriateness of an action taken, this type of officer will tend to say, "I was there, but I really didn't see anything." The CYA guy is worth watching—carefully—because what is said or done in the presence of such officers can be turned against the police leader.

The 20/60/20 Rule

The **20/60/20** rule is a "rule of thumb" method used by leaders to make a field assessment of the strengths and weaknesses of his or her followers. A review of the performance of practically any group of employees will allow a leader to divide the group into three categories.

The top 20 percent of any complex organization is comprised of strong performers. These individuals present little in the way of trouble for the leader. They do not require motivation or much in the way of supervision. They do not present accountability mechanisms any sort of difficulties and, indeed, tend to get the overwhelming majority of the work done in any police department. They are, as the label implies, the top performers. They reside in every corner of the organization and are the best in each area of the workforce. They do their jobs well and understand what results are required of them. They possess the skills required to deliver on the jobs to which they become assigned. If they lack the requisite skills, they are the sort of people who will go out and obtain them.

These are the officers who possess integrity. They are honest and hard working. They are respected by coworkers and customers, or in police work, the citizenry. These are self-motivated types who accomplish their work whether their superior is around or not. Given how little immediate supervision there is in police work, the long-term goal of COP and police professionalism is to populate the profession with as many top-20 percenters as possible. Another way to put it is this: as time goes on, one goal of modern professionalism is to make the 20 percenters into 30 percenters and then into 40 percenters. They make up the group from which the leaders of the future will come.

The middle 60 percent is comprised of average performers. In the roles of motivator, coach, and teacher, the police leader finds that this is where their efforts are aimed, under normal circumstances—that is, motivating and leading this middle group involves much of what the job entails. When there is no crisis or trouble, this is where the teaching is aimed in any organization. It is where, to some extent, police leaders can obtain a great deal of satisfaction in the long run. As role models in particular, it is here that substantial progress can be made. While most of the 60 percenters are not particularly motivated to work hard in most organizations

REVIEW CHART 7.3

THE 20/60/20 RULE

- The top 20 percent are strong performers.
- The middle 60 percent are average performers.
- The bottom 20 percent are weak performers.

Note: The key issue is, of course, where does the police leader focus his or her time?

("soldiering" is what they do best), they *can* be motivated and *can* be moved, in the long run, to enter into the ranks of those who accomplish good works.

The middle 60 percenters, the average performers, are "pretty good" at accomplishing their jobs. Most of the time, under most circumstances, they do most of what they are supposed to do. These are nice people who are basically good employees. Again, as noted above, they can be motivated—by the right kind of leadership—to move up and become members of the upper percentages. They can even become leaders in the long run.

The bottom 20 percent of any organization is comprised of weak performers. Not only can these people be troublesome because they get little of the work done, but they can be the group that morphs into the worst sort of saboteurs and counterproductive naysayers. These workers are not productive. They come in late and waste time. They sandbag most of the activities in which they become engaged. They need constant supervision and constant monitoring. In other sorts of organizations, they can be watched. But in police work, the bottom 20 percent cannot be monitored all of the time because of how often police officers do their jobs—spend entire shifts—without supervision, essentially alone on the street. They are alone with the opportunity to do nothing, to do counterproductive things, to engage in corrupt practices, or to be saboteurs. Because of this, police work's bottom 20 percent are more troublesome than those same percenters in any other occupation or profession.

So what the 20/60/20 rule suggests is that while the leaders are managing the top 20 percent and 60 percent without difficulty, they are obviously having to spend time managing the 20 percent of the nonperformers, and spend an inordinate amount of time doing so, to the detriment of the other 80 percent.

Anti-Sabotage Strategies

What to do? What to do about the saboteurs? In a profession where there are so many roadblocks placed in the way of controls that could be used with saboteurs in other occupations, what can be accomplished? When saboteurs cannot be physically isolated, and when they depend on so much in the way of subcultural solidarity and support, what strategies can creative police leaders utilize in order to make headway against this group?

Co-optation For the purposes of our discussion here about dealing with saboteurs, co-optation is almost synonymous with assimilation. In businesses (private enterprise), as well as in public organizations, leaders often co-opt with workers to solve problems, address concerns, or help engage in fulfilling a mission. One method police leaders can use to encourage marginal performers is to co-opt their efforts with the employees who are most resistant to change or who do not perform to a level or standard required for current operation. Co-optation requires a good deal of skill on the part of focal leaders. The employees or officers not fulfilling their obligation to the mission of the organization may best be managed through co-optation, especially if the leaders believe that the less-than-optimal performers have the ability to perform to a predetermined standard.

Co-opting can be accomplished in numerous ways. One way is to meet with the persons, outline the reason for the meeting, determine the willingness of the employee to accept the challenge of meeting certain standards toward a mission, determine an acceptable measurement of the performance, and take action on initiating the plan. The final act is to evaluate the outcome of the effort—that is, to assess the activity of the group or organization and determine if success occurred or not. This effort could be a one-time project or a long-term condition. Co-opting *can* work in police agencies. The most difficult agencies within which to co-opt are those with strong, adversarial unions or officer associations, or those with a tradition of hands-off treatment of marginal employees.

Neutralization Another method of managing saboteurs is that of neutralizing their activities. The best focal leaders are skilled in identifying the individual likes and dislikes of their followers. They know their subordinates and what makes each one tick. When they really engage the art of supervision, these leaders are adept at neutralizing the naysayers. They should be able to identify the **malcontents** and apply their substantial leadership and supervisory skills. Basically, they can and often do intervene in the naysayer's activity and temper their toxic behavior through direct confrontation. Leaders can explain their reason for doing so and the consequences of the naysayer's behavior. In many instances, this action may only temper the naysayer. But if the supervisor sticks to his or her guns, the naysaying activity can be neutralized.

But there are many other ways to minimize naysayers and malcontents. A short list might include:

- *Setting expectations:* A good leader should present a clear and equal expectation of the behavior and actions of their subordinates and set goals to achieve those expectations. When followers have clear expectations and goals established through their leader, they are motivated to perform better (IACP, 2002). The key to this method is follow-up and evaluation of the individuals.

- *Motivation through consequences:* E. L. Thorndike, an early 20th century American psychologist, asserted that "when behavior in a particular situation is followed by satisfaction, the satisfaction will become associated with that situation. When that situation reoccurs, the behavior is also likely to reappear. By contrast, any behavior that produces discomfort in a particular situation is less likely to occur when the situation reoccurs" (Thorndike, 1905: 202). Good focal leaders know how to utilize MTC (motivation through consequences). Those who do can also help neutralize naysayer behavior.

- *Job redesign and evaluation:* This is the art of moving an employee into a position best suited for his/her skill sets and psychological strengths and setting expectations followed by evaluation. This sort of focal leadership can help neutralize an employee not satisfied in his/her current work setting. Sometimes just a change in jobs can motivate employees in positive ways.

Neutralizing naysayers is difficult to do. But agencies that set out the best practices in employee management can make great headway in treating their employees as though they are an important, integral part of the organization. Doing so usually gets more positive results than not managing them at all.

The paradox to the described methods of neutralization is that sometimes leaders often misapply the methods. This misapplication only causes the rank and file to become more convinced that their leaders are not competent. The followers then begin to lose respect for the focal leaders and only become more moved than before to be naysayers. As noted in Box 7.5, in a cyclical fashion, attempts to neutralize sabotage can create even more attempts at sabotage.

Feeling good that he had the "guts" to be direct with these officers, he waits to see the fruits of his labor. Instead of the MTC working as he had hoped, the situation gets worse. The remaining officers begin to dismiss him. When he comes into their presence, they are silent, offer no commentary, and basically avoid him. Unbeknownst to him, the troublesome officers had gone to their fellow team members and told them that they were singled out for no reason. They suggested that not only was Sergeant Jones an incompetent supervisor, he was unfair in his dealing with them. The troublemakers suggested to the other officers that "if he did this to us, he'll certainly do it to you." Sergeant Jones now has a bigger problem on his plate. He has to take action to recover from his first action.

Elimination It is important to note that this portion of the chapter is in no way presented as a legal guide to employment law. This section only addresses the potential possibilities of employee behavior and actions, and what a focal leader may do or recommend when an employee is not performing to a required standard. Progressive discipline, counseling, reminding, rewards and punishments, management through consequences, job redesign, expectations, and goal setting are all methods that should be utilized before considering elimination.

But elimination must be (briefly) examined. No agency in today's modern work environment will take a direct approach at eliminating an officer from his

BOX 7.5

EXAMPLE OF MISAPPLICATION OF A NEUTRALIZATION METHOD

Sergeant Jones is in charge of a 12-person burglary suppression unit. The burglary suppression team's objectives are to respond to and suppress burglaries in identified neighborhoods or business areas where burglary activity has increased. He has a great crew of well skilled, highly motivated officers. His problem is he has two officers who, while doing great work, are affiliated with several officers from another unit who are departmental malcontents. He notices their behavior and sees that it is affecting his other officers.

Sergeant Jones decides that he must take a strong approach with these officers. He knows both are tenured, with strong personalities and close links to higher command leaders. He decides he will address the issue in what he rationalizes is a "just and fair" way. Having learned some new leadership approaches from recent in-service training, he separates the officers from the others and sits them down to set out some motivation through consequences. He outlines specific actions and behaviors he expects from them and the consequences they can expect as a result. His goal is to neutralize their gossiping and rumor-mongering within the unit.

or her job without clear and evident cause. Current employment laws, unions, police activity leagues, political issues, and department rules and regulations usually approach the management of officer behavior from a progressive view. As we shall see shortly in Part Three of our book, there are tremendous limitations placed upon the potential of eliminating employees. This is true unless, of course, an officer is clearly guilty of violating a major administrative rule (sexual harassment, bringing discredit to the agency, receiving gifts, etc.) or violating criminal law. So it is important to note that eliminating a malcontent from an organization is a difficult, energy consuming, and time intensive effort. It is not advised as a single approach to the management of malcontents. However, it should not be ruled out if the evidence is present to dismiss the offender.

Perhaps the reason malcontents are allowed to have a continued presence in some agencies is that the agency leadership is weak. The focal leaders may not want to expend the energy or time necessary to focus on these employees and take positive action to correct their behavior. Perhaps they do not possess the emotional ability to deal with the malcontent's interpersonal skills. In some instances, they may actually agree with the sentiments or actions of the malcontent. Nonetheless, managing the malcontent or naysayer is the responsibility of the focal leadership. Arming focal leaders with the best training and exposure to good leadership skills will be paramount to tempering and perhaps eliminating malcontent behavior in the future.

ASSESSMENT TOOLS

Obviously, there must be some form, device, or mechanism by which focal leaders can measure the performance of their followers and units. Equally, there is the need for the overall police organization to do the same. In this section, we will examine both individual and group assessment methods. These methods are important for any modern police agency if it desires to be accountable and demonstrate that accountability to its citizens. Assessment and evaluation allow the focal leaders to see the fruits of their labor, determine what did not work well, and evaluate what did work well in relation to the outcomes of their mission and goals. These mechanisms give the agency a channel for continual quality improvement.

Such ongoing assessment keeps the agency and its followers on track and focused toward the mission and current goals of the organization. Over time, these mechanisms can be extremely useful when additional staff or funds for capital improvement are needed. In today's world of tough economics, funding shortages, and the public demand for transparent operations, it is imperative that police agencies develop sophisticated assessment and evaluation processes to keep up with the agency's direction and the public's need to know how the agency is doing.

In the following section, we will examine basic methods of individual evaluation and assessment and then follow up by examining the paradoxes to those methods. We will also check out some modern mechanisms utilized by police agencies to manage their organizational operations and discuss the potential of those methods in achieving the organizational mission.

Standard Measurements

Most police agencies in the modern era have initiated performance evaluation mechanisms for evaluating individual staff performance. These processes vary in style. The processes allow supervisors to conduct a review (evaluation of performance) of the officers under their command on a yearly basis. In some instances, agencies utilize a performance evaluation process that offers individual employees "pay for performance." Additionally, many agencies in America also utilize performance evaluation mechanisms with their new employees called field training programs. There are agencies that only track the performance of employees and followers by basic data accumulation—how many arrests are made, how many calls handled, how many traffic citations are written, how many clearances are made by the investigators, and so on.

In the modern era, community policing advocates the evaluation of officers not on traditional indicators of performance, such as calls handled and arrests made, but on problem-solving efforts. Yet agencies have been slow to change their appraisal systems to more creative systems. Most assessments still call for traditional, quantifiable performance indicators that are irrelevant at best and contradictory with the community policing paradigm at worst (Patterson, 2009).

Arrests and Citations As mentioned above, changing to measurements that are true indicators of employee performance has been a slowly evolving process. Utilizing response to calls for service, arrests made, and traffic citations initiated only tells an encapsulated version of the police officer's activity. In the modern policing era, officers conduct far more activities than those mentioned during a day on the beat. They devote considerable time to patrolling and surveying their areas for any unusual activity or signs of criminal behavior. In our era of COP, it is increasingly true that officers independently and creatively plan solutions to problems in their beats, make contacts with business owners, conduct frequent public assembly checks, interact socially with their communities, and make extensive personal contacts inside and outside the agency.

Utilizing only basic standard measurements of an officer's activity, such as arrests made and citations initiated, are indices that are easily quantifiable but do not tell much about the real activity of the officer and employees of the department. Perhaps the paradox here is that simple measurements are quantifiable—that is why there is an almost universal propensity to utilize them—and they are easy to accumulate. They paint *a* picture, but they do not clearly show *the* total, overall picture. They omit the overwhelming majority of the time and effort expended by most police officers on most shifts in most departments, operating in any one of four styles of policing (watchman, legalistic, service, or COP). Furthermore, they bear no relationship to the performance of the officers on the street or the non-uniformed employees in the "shadows," those employees who act as a support mechanism for the beat officers (records unit employees, communications employees, emergency response employees, etc.). In fact, it is easy to see why, several decades ago, the police in America began to attempt the development of other, more sophisticated assessment tools.

Blake also made several close associations with local business owners. She encouraged them to report any activity that looked suspicious or any criminal activity they observed. The detectives from the robbery unit credit Blake's frequent socialization with the businesses as a factor in the decline of robberies in the beat.

Reports/Details Handled The first, most "primitive" alternatives to the long-standard assessment method of simply counting up citations, arrests (felony and misdemeanor differentiated, of course), and property and violent crime have been fairly obvious. Details handled and then details handled per hour have been calculated in some places. The first computerized programs instituted three decades ago calculated how much time was spent on all different sorts of details and then how much "routine patrol" time was left in a shift. That time, in turn, was divided by a computer into calculations about how officers—individual officers—utilized their "spare time."

BOX 7.6

WHO'S THE BEST OFFICER?

Officer Bowes works in what his agency considers the toughest, highest crime rate area in the city. He has been in this assignment for approximately four years. He is very active in his effort to minimize criminal behavior in the area. He serves existing warrants as a specialty of his personal brand of crime fighting. He also makes as many felony arrests per month as he can find. He prides himself on being the tough cop, a guy who gets things done. Recently, he served 30 arrest warrants and conducted 12 felony arrests in his beat, a personal record.

Officer Blake also works in the same beat area. The agency determined that at least two officers need to work this crime-ridden area in order to manage the frequent calls for service and the constant criminal activity that seems to permeate the zone. During the same month that Officer Bowes made his record arrests and warrant services, Blake was involved in the following activity. She answered a call for service on a domestic violence case where she had to arrest the wife and husband and make sure their 1-year-old child was placed in a safe location, pending the parents' release from custody. She broke up a major gang problem when she intervened in what looked like nothing more than a gathering of youth in the neighborhood park. According to gang activity detectives, her presence and gathering of names from the group helped them place several gang members in the area where a homicide occurred and tied them to the death of a rival gang member.

These first calculations were done in response to the then-revolutionary idea that the best police officers might not be the ones who make the most arrests. By the early 1970s, the idea had crept into police circles that maybe the best officers were the ones who could handle the greatest number of details—especially potentially volatile ones, such as domestic disturbances or crowd confrontations—*without* making arrests. Thus, police work flirted for the first time with ideas that have become rather commonplace today. The calculations made in an effort to assess the job done by the police, while primitive by today's ever-expanding standards, were honest efforts to bring some modern sophistication into the assessment process.

Contemporary Tools

As a result of the limited information standard measurements presented, modern agencies are developing more comprehensive indices to give a broader picture of the individual and collective performances of their agencies. The goal is to show

REVIEW CHART 7.4

STANDARD ASSESSMENT TOOLS

- Details handled
- Arrests made/citations issued
- Clearance rate(s)
- Major reports written (accidents, DWIs, deaths, etc.)
- Miscellaneous (sick leave taken, vacation days taken, tardiness, etc.)

what really occurs in the agency and how the agency is fulfilling its mission. Now we will take a moment to discuss the sorts of assessment tools that are, to some extent, cutting edge in the police world.

Accountability Initiatives In 1994, around the time of the implementation of the Community Oriented Policing Services (COPS) program, police agencies began to seek improved assessment methods to evaluate their efforts. The COPS initiative helped foster a clear need on the part of the agencies receiving grant monies that they needed to address the outcomes and outputs of their efforts. The outcomes and outputs would have to come from other types of indices than the standard numbers of arrests made and traffic citations issued.

How much overtime did officers accrue? When did they accrue it? Was it over an extended period of time or a compressed time frame? What about sick leave usage? How much? Again, over what period of time? Was sick leave being used to create "normal weekends" or "normal vacations" by officers who wished to do all that they could to avoid the shift work that is endemic to policing? How about citizens' complaints, especially those involving excessive force? How about lawsuits? This is an area that used to be unusual in American policing, but was increasing in its significance as CompStat came into being. Whether they found officers to be culpable or not, it was perfectly logical to follow the trail of complaints and lawsuits.

CompStat CompStat, perhaps the first and certainly the most widely used of the modern era accountability initiatives, began with the New York City Police Department (NYPD) in 1994. After a year of implementation, the program was credited with bringing down crime 60 percent. This program, or process, has been copied and implemented in a variety of different agencies in America (Los Angeles, Baltimore, Atlanta, etc.), as well as in England and Canada.

The CompStat process is based on identifying and analyzing crime problems, patterns, and trends to engage department personnel at all levels in developing creative strategies and tactical responses to identified problems (NYPD/Chief of Department, 2002). The NYPD CompStat process is based upon five principles, shown in Review Chart 7.5.

REVIEW CHART 7.5

CompStat Principles

- Accurate and timely intelligence
- Effective tactics
- Rapid deployment of personnel and resources
- Relentless follow-up
- Assessment

Basically, the CompStat process was designed to deal with crime data, citizen input, disorder-specific problems, organizational leadership, and actions taken to solve identified problems. All leaders were required to be present for weekly briefings regarding their area of responsibility. The attendance was mandatory. The process obviously utilized more than just general arrest and citation data; it utilized very objective, specific data to determine if the efforts toward solving a problem were effective.

CompStat received its name from a program developed by Jack Maple, a New York City Transit Police officer. The method tracked crime through pins stuck in maps and was first called Charts of the Future. CompStat was a variation on that model, computer-based, with overlaying portions of the process interfaced with other processes (problem solving, leadership, planning, etc.). Also among the areas tracked under the CompStat process were such issues as cost of operations (use of sick leave, unit vacancy rate, overtime use, etc.), complaints against the department (internal and external), and potential liability issues.

The effectiveness of the CompStat style process is still controversial. In some agencies, the process is rigorous and commanders are subjected to weekly sessions where they receive very demanding briefings with stiff penalties for not succeeding at their endeavors. In other agencies, the process is demanding but is done as a learning exercise where failure is sometimes seen as a "lesson learned," and those lessons are converted into better problem-solving efforts with different approaches. In other words, there is more tolerance for potential failure than in the NYPD model.

One thing is certain about the CompStat-style accountability initiative: it is currently the most comprehensive of the accountability processes. The feature that seems to lend itself to the success of the process is "relentless follow-up." This feature ensures that if a commander brings a solution to the CompStat session and the chief is not satisfied with the effort, the commander is given the directive to follow up on the issue because it will appear again during the next session.

BOX 7.7

EFFICIENCY AND PRODUCTIVITY ASSESSMENTS MAY *NOT* BE RELATED TO MORALE AND SATISFACTION

Perhaps the central problem relating to our discussions about assessment has to do with the lack of a nexus between what have traditionally been the elements sought after by assessment tools—efficiency and productivity— and what conventional wisdom suggests is of critical importance in the workplace—morale and job satisfaction. It might be that these things are not as interrelated as we have believed them to be for generations in the world of complex organizations.

Return Loops Accountability processes help agencies develop **goal redefinition** when it is clear that the goals set were perhaps not the right ones. The accountability process is designed to be timely in nature and able to respond to data in the field. As a result, the system has to be flexible in order to maintain its effectiveness. Trends are more effectively dealt with in real time than they are several weeks after the agency discovers them. A trend is supposed to generate a new policy or approach. In this way, the "return loop" process generates useful information for the organization. This is a positive feature of CompStat. We discuss some common "return loop" processes below.

Command Staff Roundtable A more benign accountability initiative style is the **command staff roundtable**. This process is similar to CompStat in that the information reviewed and discussed is digested and acted upon by the executive commanders in weekly or biweekly sessions. Not as demanding on the area commanders because it is not as public in nature, it is nonetheless sometimes just as effective. Usually the chief, deputy, and assistant chief and division commanders gather data on issues, problems, concerns, and situations, and review the data gathered to identify any trends or patterns of criminal activity in their community. The commanders discuss the issues they see, take their problems to their subordinates, and foster methods and activities to manage the identified issues. They then meet the following week to review their plans and outcomes, and continue the process each session.

This process is no less potent than CompStat. It does not put pressure on the division or unit commanders in the same manner as the CompStat process, but perhaps that is the point. The chief of the agencies utilizing this process may wish to employ a softer approach to crime fighting, and does so between him/herself and the upper command staff. The same "maps and pins" data collection is used in these styles of accountability processes.

Middle Management/Team Roundtables Some agencies utilizing the command staff roundtable method also experience their middle managers mirroring the command process. They often establish their own "mini-roundtable" processes so they can work together to help their commanders solve problems and act on crime patterns and trends as soon as possible. In this system, there is clear team effort exercised. The results can be impressive, and the likelihood of the teams becoming more bonded improves because everyone is involved in the effort of solving the problems presented.

Efficiency/Productivity Assessments Police **efficiency and productivity assessments** are intended to measure, compare, and assess the performance of police forces in an effective, fair, and transparent way. Some key performance areas that can be assessed in a police agency are reducing crime, investigating crime, promoting safety, providing assistance, resource use, local policing, and citizen focus.

Efficiency/productivity assessments can be conducted in several ways. The agency can conduct its own assessment, an outside entity can conduct an assessment, or an external government agency can be tasked to conduct an assessment. These assessments can be very useful to a police agency, but they can also pose a problem. If an agency is working well, its operations are following well-established standards, and it competently assesses its progress in mission and goal achievement through a comprehensive accountability process, it can probably profit from a comprehensive assessment. If an agency is not operating within clear and well-established standards of operation and standards of assessment, it may experience a negative evaluation from a comprehensive efficiency/productivity assessment. But of course that can still work to create a better organization in the long run.

A feature of the individual and organizational assessment processes not previously discussed is what in those processes determines the overall organizational moral and satisfaction. It can be safely said that an agency can utilize its assessment processes to accomplish much good. The numbers can be telling, and they can help an agency present its operation to the community, citizen groups, the news media, and other governmental agencies to shed light on the agency's achievements. There is no question that data can be helpful in supporting an organization's cause or purpose.

But data alone does not tell the whole story of any agency. An agency can tout their operations through data that can sometimes be skewed. Numbers can be "played with" in order to help promote established outcomes required by executives. A case in point is the accusation in the *Atlanta Journal Constitution* ("Crimes, Goals, and the Next Chief," November 29, 2009) that commanders working in New Orleans in 1996 were under so much pressure to cut crime rates that their accountability initiative did so by "routinely downgrading crimes to lesser offenses."

These kinds of actions on the part of employees to try to fulfill goals that may be difficult or impossible to fulfill mean that workers may take any action deemed necessary just to keep their jobs. This kind of activity can create major morale problems for a police department. Certainly, the satisfaction levels of the

BOX 7.8

PUBLIC SENTIMENT TOWARD POLICE DEPARTMENTS WITHOUT DATA

A member of a midtown homeowner's association was so livid about repeated carjackings, home invasions, and burglaries in his neighborhood he sent angry e-mails to politicians with the heading, "Chief ___, where are you?" Even though the chief accepted an opportunity to meet with the homeowner's group, they were unimpressed. The use of a CompStat program was touted as the best device ever used to bring crime under control. Citizens who were not advocates of the accountability program said they would rather see police than statistics because their perception was that crime had not receded. The citizens of this community perceived that, to the police, data appeared to be taken more seriously than visibility and responding to calls for service.

employees working for commanders who are themselves under pressure to perform can be problematic if they are subjected to "fudging" numbers. While declassifying crimes to lesser violations may not be illegal, given the guidelines of the proper manner crimes can be reclassified, the process of making adjustments to data can be very troublesome.

So, while assessment processes and productivity reviews are important to the accomplishment of the mission of any modern police agency, how those processes are set up, operated, and evaluated is always important to the credibility of those organizations. It is important to note that citizens do not just want to see numbers and statistics about their police departments. They want to know that the police are available. They want to believe they are safe in their communities. They want to be familiar with the police officers who represent and protect them. Consequently, the morale and satisfaction of the officers who work for an agency are important because their attitudes and feelings will be transmitted to the community and citizens will know how their department is really operating.

SUMMATION

Organizational malcontents can create havoc in a police agency, lower morale, and contribute to dissatisfaction. Because these negative tendencies show up in almost every modern police agency, those agencies must develop mechanisms to neutralize the negative behaviors of the few—the saboteurs. As a result, modern police departments can establish accountability, evaluation, and assessment processes for both the individual officer and the agency as a whole.

Therefore, good supervisors and the agency leaders they work for will develop possible anti-sabotage strategies, such as co-optation, neutralization, and potential elimination if necessary. In the case of agency accountability mechanisms, the use of standard measurements such as numbers of arrests and/or citations issued has been overridden by modern police agencies in favor of accountability initiatives that seek to accomplish much more in terms of fighting crime, promoting community safety, and providing assistance to the community at large.

CompStat attempts to ensure that all things flow from the mission, and therefore personnel evaluations and organizational assessments must be tied to the mission. While accountability and assessment processes are important in the tracking of crime trends, crime patterns, and community police problems, data and numbers in and of themselves are not enough to make an agency effective and productive. Officer and community morale and satisfaction are often more directly tied to intangibles, such as visibility, police presence, and personal experiences with police–citizen interactions. In other words, morale and acceptance can—unfortunately—be driven by idiosyncratic, particularized events.

 ## DISCUSSION QUESTIONS

1. Virtually all complex organizations have mission statements today. What is the mission statement of your police organization? (If you are not an in-service police officer, find the mission statement of your university.) How might you critique it? Is it too vague or too specific? Finally, does organizational behavior actually cleave to the mission?

2. Without getting into specific individuals (people that you or those in your discussion group actually know), discuss examples of each of the archetypes of saboteurs from the text. Which are the most dangerous to organizational health, in your estimation?

3. Discuss creative ways for police leaders to motivate and coach those 60 percent of employees who are "soldiering" through their professional careers.

4. What do you think of the standard assessment tools utilized in most police organizations? Discuss how you might critique such tools, since they do not necessarily measure what today's police leaders want to measure with respect to police productivity.

5. Does your police organization utilize any of the contemporary assessment tools mentioned in the text? If so, critique what you know about them in operation. If not, which ones might work at your department?

KEY TERMS

Accountability initiatives: Programs or processes that evaluate the outcomes of goals set for the mission of an organization. This process is usually conducted in a open forum with a committee of executive staff (chief of police, assistant chief, deputy chief) presenting questions to commanders (majors, captains, commanders) regarding their areas of responsibility. Example: NYPD CompStat.

Anti-sabotage strategies: Strategies developed by superiors/supervisors of an agency to neutralize or inhibit the negative activity or behaviors toward employees or the agency by malcontent staff. Example: A sergeant takes corrective action against an officer spreading malicious rumors about other officers.

Assessment: A review of an operation and outcome based upon and validated against a set of predetermined standards.

Assessment tools: A set of standards (questions, standards, evaluations) used to guide the review of an activity, unit operation, or accomplishment of a set of goals.

Backstabber: A person or "friend" who says positive things in front of another but condemns or criticizes them behind their back.

Command staff roundtables: Formal meetings of executive officers (chiefs, assistant chiefs, deputy chiefs).

CompStat: An accountability program developed for use by NYPD by Chief William Bratton utilizing computer programs to help determine trends and patterns of criminal activity in the city. Commanders are subsequently queried periodically about the gathered data to help strategize where crime is occurring, and send resources to those areas to address the problems.

Co-opting: Assimilating employees into the philosophy of the organization and its goals; a method of management that encourages those who are more resistant to organizational philosophy to join with superiors to achieve the goals of the organization.

Efficiency/productivity assessments: A program designed to measure, compare, and assess the overall performance of police forces in an effective, fair, and transparent way.

Goal redefinition: The act of redefining a set goal for a person or system to achieve. Sometimes done when the original goal or expectation for achievement was not fulfilled or an inaccurate goal was set.

Gossip: Idle talk or rumor, especially about the personal or private affairs of others.

Got your back: A statement used to let others know the person making the statement can be trusted to support them when needed.

Malcontent: Someone who is peevish or disgruntled.

Middle management team/roundtables: Formal meetings of midlevel police superiors (captains, lieutenants).

Naysayers: Disgruntled people within the organization who make negative statements about other people, their superiors, or the organization; also known as malcontents.

Neutralization: To counterbalance or counteract the effect of; render ineffective.

Quantifiable data: Information or data expressible as a quantity or relating to measurement.

Roundtable: A meeting of police agents where discussion of trends and patterns of criminal activity can be reviewed and discussed, and plans can be made to address any concerns emanating from the data.

Saboteurs: A subversive group or individual that supports anything contrary to the mission of the organization and engages in efforts to defeat the mission.

Slugs: Employees who "sandbag" the efforts of the organization to accomplish its mission; ditherers.

Snitch: An informer who breaks the "blue code of silence" and whistleblows.

Subgoals: A subsection of an original goal that describes what success would look like when the objective is reached.

20/60/20 rule: A leadership model that states 20 percent of the workforce work diligently for the organization and well with others, 60 percent of the workforce come to work every day and do their jobs, and 20 percent are malcontents, barely produce, and cause supervisors to spend more time trying to manage them than the remaining 80 percent of the workforce.

EXAMPLE SCENARIOS

Supervision of Naysayers

Sergeant Jamison has been placed in charge of the northeast area command of his department. Jamison is known for his no-nonsense approach to leadership. He is a tenured, time-tested supervisory veteran. He will need to be his best in this new assignment. The northeast area is known to have more malcontent officers than the other areas of the agency.

On his first day as supervisor, he encounters Officer James Brooks, a long-term officer who has a sketchy record of service. Brooks has been before the police disciplinary board at least three times during the last year and beat a termination recommendation due to a technicality. Upon meeting Brooks, Jamison hears a statement that causes him concern. Brooks introduces a new female officer who just arrived from the training program. His statement to Jamison is, "Check this out, Sarge, fresh meat for the troops."

Jamison is chagrined, to say the least. He takes Brooks to the side and dresses him down curtly about his statement, and suggests his behavior, at least, borders on hostility and, at most, is harassment toward a female officer. Jamison is pondering what corrective action he will take. Given Brooks's past behavior, he has a lot to work on.

What might this sergeant do that would be positive and learning oriented? Given the experience level of the errant officer, what are the limits placed upon making any progress at all? Is Brooks a lost cause? How might some genuine creativity be exhibited here?

Followership

Jackie Bell may be one of the most talented officers in the department. She comes to work early every day. She reads the briefing board faithfully. She has worked the west side night shift as a patrol officer for the past three years and has a high activity rate. Officer Bell recently read that three white male youths were active in street robberies on older citizens. On her own, she examined the logs and field interrogation information and noted that the greatest number of their acts of robbery occurred at the city's "5 Points" business area around 6:30 P.M. to 8:30 P.M.

She decides to conduct a personal stakeout in her police vehicle near the sites of the most criminal activity. One evening, she observes three suspects matching the descriptions of the suspects in the collected data. She notes there are several older citizens coming and going from the area grocery store and other close convenience shops.

At 7:10 P.M., she sees the people she is surveying move into positions of advantage as they eyeball a likely target (an older woman with a purse and bag full of groceries). Officer Bell calls for support from her fellow beat officer and, at just the right moment, bursts on the scene of the three suspects grabbing the old woman's purse while she fights to keep it from being wrestled away.

Bell and her partner capture two of the suspects in an "on view felony arrest," one of the most difficult types of arrests to make. She and her partner receive a commendation for their effort. Bell is obviously one of the type of followers all supervisors wish they had under their command. She thinks on her own, strategizes, self-initiates, acts without being told what to do, and is an exemplary officer in every fashion.

Here we have an exemplar, or role model, for other officers. She seems to have all of the bases covered. How might a creative leader work to improve even this type of officer? What might be done to create not only a better officer, but someone who might be able to move up the chain of command and be a leader?

CompStat

Captain Bartlett is the zone commander of the downtown area of the city. There have been spikes of burglary activity and grand theft three months in a row in his command. Burglary and grand theft clearance rates for those crimes have gone down. He must be prepared to account for the spikes in those Part I crimes at the next CompStat session, and he is concerned that the numbers will cause him some significant problems with executive command.

As he prepares for the CompStat session, he takes a closer look at other types of crimes in his zone. Carjacking is down 30 percent, and clearances for that crime are up 50 percent. Robbery is almost nonexistent, with only three occurring during the last three months. Assaults are down 50 percent, primarily due to a strong anti-gang activity effort initiated by his patrol officers and investigators. Homicide is also down 50 percent from last year.

As he ponders the negatives, he also ponders how to exploit—neutralize— the negatives in a CompStat session and amplify the positives noted with other Part I crimes. Furthermore, the captain has developed an action plan for how to bring the burglary and grand theft rate down. Hopefully, he can appease his executive commanders.

What might be an appropriate strategy for this captain with regard to approaching the meeting? How might he mollify criticism by creating an overall façade of progress? How does he avoid appearing to be "playing departmental politics" with such a strategy?

ADDITIONAL READING

In this chapter, we once again discussed the idea of bureaupathology. This is the brain child of Victor Thompson, first exhibited in co-optation—a concept that made it all the way from academia to American street vernacular—and envisioned in the extensive study of the Tennessee Valley Authority, undertaken by Philip Selznick in *TVA and the Grass Roots* (Harper Torchbook, 1966). Tom Peters draws together several of these concepts and some of our discussions about different styles of leadership in *A Passion for Excellence*, which ended up being a bestseller (Random House, 1985).

CompStat—first "invented" at the New York City Police Department—is explained in *The Turnaround: How America's Top Cop Reversed the Crime Epidemic*, by William Bratton (former NYPD commissioner) and Peter Knobler (Random House, 1998). The concept, of course, has been around for more than 15 years and has been instituted in many places, tested, and evaluated in arenas other than the police world. An excellent book that brings together some of the ideas of the current practice of CompStat and some examples of non-police CompStat usage is *The CompStat Paradigm: Management Accountability in Policing, Business and the Public Sector*, by Vincent E. Henry (Looseleaf Publications, 2002).

Unfortunately, there has yet to be a definitive study of early warning systems; the only reading published in the field can be found in several police textbooks, most notably Samuel Walker and Charles M. Katz's *The Police in America, 4th Ed.* (McGraw-Hill, 2002), and Roy Roberg, Kenneth Novack, and Gary Cordner's *Police and Society, 3rd Ed.* (Roxbury, 2005).

PART THREE

Officer Behavior

In Part Three, we will engage in an analysis of police behavior. Chapter 8 discusses police ethics from a positivist perspective, suggesting for contemporary police officers an "ethic to live by." Chapter 9 engages the classic debate about who should attempt to hold the police accountable for their actions, civilian or internal review systems. Chapter 10 discusses what to do about police discipline in the reality that traditional, punitive systems do not work, but modern, no-fault systems are new and untested.

CHAPTER 8

Ethics

INTRODUCTION

As much as police leaders today tend to be open to discussions about police **ethics**, the rank and file can still be guilty of taking a tongue-in-cheek approach to the subject. For large numbers of officers, there is still a disconnect between the idea of being ethical and the idea of being competent at their jobs, as if the two are not inexorably linked together. Many police officers consider that while learning the skills and academic subjects necessary to perform their craft in a competent manner—in the academy, while patrolling with an FTO, or when obtaining in-service training— they are somehow not involved in learning anything about ethics. Put another way, officers often think ethics is the title of one briefly considered topic at the police academy, and nothing more. When discussing those subjects and skills that are critical to the making of an excellent police officer, nothing could be further from their minds than the topic of ethics.

In this chapter, we will argue that competence and ethical behavior are not only linked in some way, they are critical to the entire endeavor of policing. A person simply cannot be a good police officer unless he or she is an ethical officer. Beginning with this principle, we will discuss the concept of character and how it impinges upon the choices that police officers must make on the street. We will discuss schools of thought that have confronted philosophers for several thousand years. At the end of that discussion, we will suggest something that we will call "an ethic to live by" for the consideration of the reader.

Next, the critical nature of the role of the police leader will be discussed in a similar manner—that is, we will argue that a person cannot be a good police leader without being an ethical police leader. The two, again, are inexorably linked together, and one role the contemporary leader must play in today's police world is encouraging the development among their charges of a personal ethic that informs their working personalities out on the street.

We begin with a discussion about how ethics have, and have not, been approached historically in the world of police work.

THE HISTORICAL TREATMENT OF POLICE ETHICS

Young police officers might find it difficult to understand how and why a dialogue about ethics is central to any discussion about police competence. This is to be forgiven in light of the short shrift traditionally given to ethics in the police world. The good news is that rookie police officers, possessing more than two years of college education on average, are thoroughly capable of engaging the sometimes esoteric topic of ethics. Unlike police officers from just two decades ago, today's officers have all been in the college classroom long enough that a discussion about ethics—straight out of Philosophy 101—is something they have already experienced. Today's recruit is neither intimidated nor intellectually confused by a discussion about the philosophical underpinnings of ethics.

This is good news for everyone involved in contemporary police work, or at least it should be. As we have suggested in several chapters along the way, the systematized knowledge base obtained by the professional when matriculating through their academic experience includes, as a critical element, the discussion and development of a personal ethic. This ethic is a part of the police officer's working personality, and it is impossible to be a genuine professional without it. Police officers engaged in the pursuit of professionalism must analyze and embrace ethics as a critically important element of their working experience. And, by translation, the role of modern police leader must involve encouraging the development of a solidly based personal ethic in the mind of every police officer on the street today.

We are making a procedural point here: the modern police officer is intelligent and educated enough to understand a discussion about philosophy and ethics. But there is more. Expanding our consideration of ethics is of substantial import to the individual officer, the police leader, and the profession as a whole.

In the past, the unsophisticated approach taken by many in policing toward ethics had to do with the roots of American policing. Historically, police officers were not a particularly educated lot, and when they (understandably) were guilty of misconduct, a sort of **"boys will be boys"** attitude prevailed. Until the 1960s, police work was universally considered to be a blue collar job. Educational requirements were limited—a high school education or GED was sufficient—and in many places there was next to nothing in the way of training. The conceptualization of police work was limited to a combination of being a bouncer at a bar and a referee at a boxing match. As we have previously discussed, this conceptualization has changed; police work has come to mean something entirely different.

BOX 8.1

THE STANDARD ACADEMY LECTURE ABOUT ETHICS

It is an unfortunate but almost universal reality in American policing that police academy discussions about ethics are conducted in a rather negative way. Since so little time is allotted to discussions about ethics in policing, academies tend to bring in speakers from internal affairs departments who present brief lectures focusing on "how not to mess up." Instead of discussing what it means to be a good, competent, and professional police officer—approaching ethics from the positive side—these discussions focus on what it means to avoid being a poor officer. Thus, as it is engaged in most police academies, the topic of police ethics involves the implicit suggestion that *to be a good officer involves nothing more sophisticated than attempting to avoid being a bad one.*

Labeled by some as **"the new blue line,"** police work has been completely reinvented (Skolnick and Bayley, 1988). Along with this redefinition have come several developments relating to ethics. Since at least some college is now required to be hired into what is now being called "the profession," the criminal justice major—unheard of just 45 years ago—has become the fastest growing major on American college campuses. With its growth has come a concern for criminal justice ethics at the college level. Slowly increasing in its sophistication, this study in ethics is inculcating into most police cadets today an understanding for both philosophy in general and ethics in particular. Ethics has made its way into the curriculum at many police academies, too. But here, several problems have surfaced with regard to the amount of training in ethics and the sort of training made available.

To begin with, not every academy in contemporary America even includes ethics as a part of its curriculum. In-service training is even worse. A survey done by the **International Association of Chiefs of Police** found that 17 percent of all police departments provide zero in the way of ethics training. Furthermore, 35 percent provide no ethics training for supervisors (IACP, 1998).

A second concern has to do with how little time is spent on ethics in police training. In a separate nationwide survey, it was discovered that the average police academy in America includes 3.5 hours of discussion about police ethics (Das, 1986: 70). That is 3.5 hours out of 600 to 700 hours of academy training. Only 17 percent of American police academies provide 8 hours or more ethics training (IACP, 1998). This is woefully inadequate. Spending so little time on such a subject implies to cadets that the topic is of little importance. This also implies that ethics is one subject, only one subject, and a marginal subject at that.

Still another problem relates to the *type* of training that is done with regard to ethics. As Box 8.1 suggests, academy training in ethics involves discussing ethics "backwards." That is, such training almost universally consists of lectures about how "not to screw up." Looking at ethics from this negative perspective is more than just inappropriate; it is exactly wrong. If the goal is to instill a personal ethic in police officers that approaches police work from the perspective of what good officers *ought* to do—which, undoubtedly, such training should entail—then the existing perspective comes at ethics from the wrong end of things.

Constructing a **personal ethic** should include building an understanding of the positive requirements of ethical behavior up from a baseline discussion of what it would mean to be a good person and a good police officer (Perez and Moore, 2002). Today's academy cadet is intelligent and educated enough to be able to do this—to understand some basic philosophical principles relating to being ethical and doing good works in life. So it would appear essential that cadets should be taught with an eye toward taking advantage of their intelligence and education levels. Instead, academy training almost universally ignores the intellect of today's "new" cadets and treats them with the outdated approach of a "thou shalt not" type of message.

BOX 8.2

CORRUPTION "SAVES TAXPAYER DOLLARS!"

While few police jurisdictions today experience the type of corruption that was once commonplace, there *are* those places where payoffs are a part of normal police operations, and local politicians have a rather bizarre approach to such corruption. As was once said out loud and in public generations ago, in places where payoffs are commonplace, police salaries can be kept to a minimum, at embarrassingly low levels, because of the tacit understanding that graft will "make up the difference" between what the police are paid officially and how much they "really" make (Lane, 1967).

For example, one classic topic in the field of police ethics has to do with the free cup of coffee. Giving free coffee to police officers is a time-honored tradition in America. Waitresses and coffeehouse managers like to do it because when the police are around citizens behave themselves, they pay their tabs, and they certainly do not rob the place. In some locations today, the police will eschew obtaining free coffee, but in many places it is still a piece of Americana. However, some citizens do not like this. They resent seeing the police being treated to such "**freebies**." This topic is often engaged when ethics are discussed in the academy. In the past, the academy lecture on ethics included a brief suggestion that taking a free cup of coffee "is the same as taking money from drug dealers." Neither the internal affairs officer giving the lecture nor the cadets listening believe this. Thus, when they go out on the street, rookie officers ignore the lecture.

But today's college educated young cadets can be treated to a very different discussion. They are fully capable of engaging in a debate that treats them as being capable of understanding the philosophical issues. Today's officer can be engaged with the idea that when people give the police free coffee there can be a **quid pro quo** involved, which implies they will be treated differently than other citizens if they are, for example, stopped by the police. The tacit understanding is that free coffee "purchases" a degree of latitude from the police for the waitresses and coffee house managers who provide the coffee. Thus, it should be avoided due to the possible ethical problem for the officer. This is a more logical and sophisticated way of engaging a touchy issue.

PROFESSIONALISM REVISITED

In Chapter 4, we took a significant amount of time to discuss the sociological definition of what constitutes a profession. That discussion considered the importance of the academic experience, substantive body of knowledge, collegial problem solving, self-regulation and disciplining, and internalized ethic that constitute the elements of the genuine professions. It was a definition based upon a collectivity of individuals. That is, it considered police officers as a group and sought to consider if they were, in fact, a group of professionals.

Now we will discuss a fascinating idea of Muir's. He suggested that to be a professional a police officer needed to possess several specific world views. Muir's thesis was an individualistic definition of professionalism. He did years of research that involved riding along with several dozen officers. He watched them and witnessed their achievements and limitations, strengths and weaknesses, and successes and defeats. In the end, he categorized them along several lines and came up with four distinctive officer types. One of these types, critical for our consideration, was the professional. The questions he asked in making his four-part table had to do with what he labeled "passion and perspective" (Muir, 1977: 50).

Passion

Muir began with a discussion suggesting that there were two different types of **passion** within the personality structures of the officers he observed. He was focusing on the use of coercive power which, as seen earlier in our discussions, was central to his studies of the police. In observing police officers in the line of duty, Muir suggested they displayed one of two types of approaches to the use of coercion. Officers were either comfortable with coercing others or they were not. This differentiation was critical, in his estimation.

Some officers had integrated into their working personalities the ability to coerce comfortably. That is, they had no trouble with the reality that a person who coerces is, to a real extent, a bully. Getting people to behave the way you want them to by threatening to do harm to them or to something that they value is bullying, plain and simple. Some officers were comfortable in playing this role and some were not. Muir did not take issue with those who could bully comfortably. He did not see bullying to be a bad thing. In fact, he suggested that without the ability to rationalize bullying, an officer could not be effective on the street.

The point here was that **principled violence** (Muir, 1977: 50) was what coercive power *should* be all about. When exhortation and reciprocity fail, the effective police officer knows that coercion is the next and last resort. There was nothing wrong with this, in Muir's estimation. In fact, police officers who were conflicted about the exercise of such bullying tactics were not going to be capable of handling some types of details. As long as police officers did not bully for inappropriate reasons—as long as their bullying was "principled"—they could be effective at doing their jobs and obtaining desired behavior from citizens.

An illustration is in order. When a police officer threatens an obnoxious drunk at the ballpark with arrest and gets the man to go home and sober up, an important little task has been accomplished. When a group of rowdy juveniles is harassing patrons at a convenience store and the police get them to disburse by suggesting that they do so "or else," another detail has been handled appropriately, without either arrest or violence. Principled bullying was an important tool of the police, as Muir pointed out, and not all officers were comfortable with this reality. Thus, his group of officers was divided into those who possessed what he called an **integrated** understanding of the morality of principled bullying and those who were **conflicted** about it. This is how he defined and applied the concept of passion in order to create his typology. By passion, then, Muir meant the ability to threaten in the name of doing good (Muir, 1977: 50–51).

Perspective

Muir then suggested that another differentiation among his police officers was equally critical. He called it **perspective**. His group of officers was also divided into two groups with regard to this concept. There were those who had the **tragic perspective** of life and those who had the **cynical perspective**. He clearly believed that the tragic perspective was optimal.

Muir began his discussion of people (police officers) who had a tragic perspective of life by suggesting that this included a feeling for the suffering of others. All people yearn to be treated with some sort of dignity, no matter what they might have done criminally. Important was a sort of "religious understanding," that no person was worthless. Everyone deserved some sort of deference due to their value as a "soul" in the world. There were three specific elements to the tragic perspective.

First was an understanding of what he called the **unitary experience** in life. All people share a common reality. They all struggle against the odds, suffer tragedies, and are capable of doing both good and evil. This is true of everyone, no matter what their specific circumstances. The police officer who had this perspective attempted to understand even those suspects who had perpetrated the most heinous of crimes—to search for a way to empathize with the injustices suffered by everyone (Muir, 1977: 178).

Second, the tragic perspective included an understanding of the **complex causal patterns of life** (Muir, 1977: 179). Deviance was the product of chance and necessity at times, and did not always evolve out of free will. Yes, some people looked at alternatives, made calculations, and *decided* to steal or to murder. They exercised free will in making such decisions. But life was not always that simple. Chance played a part in deviance, and so did necessity. The causes of crime are complicated and numerous—sometimes it is produced by poverty, tragic circumstances, and even bad luck. A person (police officer) with the tragic perspective took the time to look for the complex causal patterns behind whatever type of deviant behavior they faced.

Third, a person with this perspective understood the **precariousness and necessity of human interdependence**. Human solidarity and community were absolutely critical to the meaning of life (Muir, 1977: 180–181). We humans are communal animals, and it was essential to understand that the maintenance of community and interaction is the way in which humans have not only been able to live

TABLE 8.1

MUIR'S CLASSIFICATION ACCORDING TO PROFESSIONAL POLITICAL MODEL		
	Morality of Coercion	
	Integrated	**Conflicted**
Tragic perspective	Professional	Reciprocator
Cynical perspective	Enforcer	Avoider
Source: Delmar/Cengage Learning		

together, but to conquer nature and rule the planet. Humans only accomplished this through their collective and cooperative efforts. Maintaining relationships—person to person and even police officer to person—was a necessary condition of the human experience.

The cynic held opposing views in each of these directions (Muir, 1977: 225–226). The cynical perspective denied that everyone struggled with life's tragedies and adverse circumstances; the cynic believed that there were, quite simply, good people and bad people. Life did not involve a unitary experience. The cynic, therefore, believed that there was nothing complicated at all about deviance; bad people chose to be bad and that was all there was to it. The cynic was involved in individual fault finding and moralizing. Trying to discover and understand people's motivations and tragic experiences was a complete waste of time. There were no complex causal patterns, only simple-to-understand villainy. Furthermore, the cynic insulated himself or herself from psychic harm by denying interdependence. Cynics make themselves invulnerable by spurning civility and denying there is any moral conflict in the world.

Muir's police officers thus divided themselves into those driven by the tragic and those driven by the cynical perspectives. He then took the several sets of differentiations involved and used them to construct a four-part table of police officer types (see Table 8.1). Again, the types were divided by different sorts of passion and perspective.

We will now consider the four types of police officers Muir found operating out on the beat (Muir, 1977: 57).

Other than Professional Officers

Before moving on to engage Muir's professional directly, we will briefly discuss his other three types. Officers who were conflicted about coercing others, uncomfortable about bullying, and had a tragic perspective of life were labeled **reciprocators.** These officers operated on the street with a passive resistance to deviance. Since they were conflicted about coercion, they used reciprocal power as often as possible. In order to work their beats, reciprocators worked at developing relationships where citizens owed personal obligations to the police. Favors were exchanged in an effort to build up a level of gratitude that could be depended on in the future. Reciprocators even allowed minor illegality to proceed without sanction, in order to make the public believe that they were "nice" officers deserving of the public's cooperation. This propensity to allow crime to proceed without notice was particularly disturbing for Muir.

Those officers who had an integrated understanding of coercion—who had no trouble bullying people, but a cynical view of humankind—were labeled **enforcers**. These officers tended to be Dirty Harry–like. They were impatient with people and unenlightened about the causes of deviance. Theirs was a world driven by the idea that it was the job of the police to use force to punish those citizens who were naturally bad people. It was even acceptable to use two different standards in police work; there were different rules applied to good people and bad people. The inconsistency in treating people with two different sets of rules was lost on enforcers. Enforcers used their words to incite people rather than to probe and discover insights into motivations and causes.

Those officers who possessed a conflicted attitude about coercion and a cynical perspective of life were labeled **avoiders**. Avoiders were passive and ineloquent. They were lifeless and unresponsive to human suffering. They viewed the job as something to be done without ever really becoming engaged in the endeavor. They did as little as possible, not becoming interested in people's lives, motivations, or in doing good work of any kind. Muir was given particular credit by practitioners for observing the fact that there were avoiders in police work. Most outsiders have always taken the stereotypical view that the police are all aggressive, domineering, and boisterous personality types. As anyone who has ever been a police officer knows, this is not true. Avoiders *are* present on the job, and they make more work for those who actually do their jobs honestly.

REVIEW CHART 8.1

MUIR'S POLICE OFFICER TYPES

- *Enforcers:* Overly aggressive and proactive; nonverbal; driven to exercise the violent power of the law
- *Reciprocators:* Followers of the path of least resistance; in developing mutual relationships with citizens, they even allow illegality
- *Avoiders:* Ineloquent; not interested in becoming involved in the problems of citizens; a "soldiering" attitude
- *Professionals:* Gregarious, people oriented; teachers; mentors; use their motivational powers to teach citizens that much can be gained by living by society's rules

The Professional

It is now time to consider what Muir considered to be the optimum police officer personality set: those officers who had an integrated understanding of the morality of coercion and who at the same time possessed the tragic perspective of life. These were the **professionals**. The professional was gregarious and worked at teaching people on the street, not by asserting the naked power of the law, but by shaping events with their words so people would understand that there is a great deal to be gained by living within the legal framework and behaving themselves. Professionals were not afraid to explain things to citizens. In fact, they were comfortable with the idea that making explanations about what was being decided and how the law worked (and so forth) was a central part of what the police were supposed to do.

Clearly, Muir thought the professional to be the optimum police officer. Given the importance of the police officer role, Muir's insight adds weight to several points that have been made along the way in our discussions. Ideally, police officers should be open and gregarious, people-oriented individuals. There is no place in police work for the "strong, silent type" who does not do well with people. Police officers should enjoy just shooting the breeze with citizens, as this not only opens up lines of communication in general, but may develop into obtaining important information. They should want to go out proactively and engage with people's problems, and do the best they can to help create solutions. The avoider does none of this.

Police officers need to respect the dictates of the law. They need to possess an ethical framework to deal with the delicate balance of moralizing for people and using force. While putting life into the law with their discretionary decision making, police officers must nevertheless understand that the law is not something to be played with. They must avoid the type of behavior in which reciprocators engage when they allow some people to get away with criminal conduct in an effort to appear to be "nice guys" (or "nice gals"). Certainly, the professional officer needs to avoid the Dirty Harry–like aggressive and even abusive excesses of the enforcer.

Muir gave us a more individual officer-focused idea of professionalism. It is obvious that the modern COP movement aims to foster development and take advantage of Muir's professional officer. The police leader's role today involves encouraging the development of the professional officer, as defined by Muir.

 ## ETHICS AND DECISION MAKING

When police officers exercise their discretionary decision making powers, they make moral judgments about the behavior of others. Because this is so, our discussion in this chapter about ethics is of critical significance in the modern police world. The days of the "dumb flatfoot" are gone. Police officers are no longer bouncers with reasonably clean records. That era was long ago. Today's officers bear a set of responsibilities that are substantially different from those days of yore.

Defining the Law

As we discussed with regard to police discretion, the law as it is written can be seen to be the skeleton of justice; the decisions made by police officers put muscles and sinew on the framework. No matter what the law says about any particular type of deviant behavior, what the police *do* on the streets is definitive of what the law truly means. And how they behave—what they do—is inexorably linked to their individual and collective understandings of right and wrong conduct, personal and collective responsibility, and justice.

We are almost chanting a mantra in this chapter, over and over again, to make the point that police ethics are center stage in the arena of justice on the streets. This is because we simply cannot over-emphasize the importance of police ethics.

Moralizing for Others

From one perspective, police work is largely about making moral judgments about the behavior of others. As we have taken some pains to point out and noted by virtually everyone who has ever studied the police in America, police discretionary decision making power is of crucial import in the lives of millions of citizens. When the police make an arrest/no arrest decision, they are moralizing in a direct way. When deciding that someone is going to jail, the police officer is saying that they *deserve* to go to jail. When the handcuffs go on, the citizen loses his or her freedom. This differentiates him or her from all those citizens who have been left alone by the police to exercise their constitutionally guaranteed freedoms. Those who go to jail deserve it, and those who stay out on the street do not deserve it.

How is this decision made? The answer is not "that's what the law dictates." Something else is going on. The police officer is drawing from an ethical frame of reference that involves his or her own personal ethic. No amount of sanctimonious intention to be objective and impartial can change the reality that police decisions to arrest or to use force are related directly to the individual officer's own personal world view.

Character as a Driving Force

Understanding that the determining factor in the arrest/no arrest decision is the police officer's personal ethic brings us to a crucial focal point of this chapter, the concept of **character**. The character of the individual police officer drives such decisions directly. A person's ethical frame of reference is a part of their character, to be sure. It is a critical part. We cannot simply make such an assertion without embracing a debate about the nature of character, ancient in its history and importance. Taken together with Muir's conceptualization of the modern professional officer, we will have an excellent model for what it is police leaders are attempting to encourage in their subordinates.

BOX 8.3

EXERCISING DISCRETION IS MORALIZING

One reason why police ethics are so important has to do with the exercise of police discretionary decision making powers. It might appear obvious to some, but it is important to note that when police officers make an arrest/no arrest decision, they are often doing so on the basis of a *personalized* sense of morality. This doesn't tend to be the case with felonies, because probable cause to make a felony arrest almost universally results in a suspect being taken into custody. But with infractions and misdemeanors, when the police decide to cite a person or take someone into custody, they are making the moral judgment that the person in question "deserves" to be sanctioned. Thus, police decision making is often about moralizing for others. The critical question then becomes, of course, who merits going to jail and who does not? And, even more important, what criteria will the police use to make such decisions?

THE IDEA OF CHARACTER

Everything we are and do is informed by our character. Or is it the other way around? Is our character informed by what we do? It would appear that it has to be one or the other, right? Why is this question important? It is important because police work is a profession where we consistently talk about character. When we talk about police selection procedures, we are "looking for good character" in the candidates. When we talk about police behavior on the street, we talk about having good character because often the decisions police officers make are late at night with no one watching. For a moment here, we must visit a debate that has gone on for more than 2,400 years: does character determine behavior, or does behavior determine character?

Character and Virtue

One view of character suggests that a person's character is completely determined by their actions. No matter what a person says they believe, no matter what they think they believe, no matter what they announce to the world to be their personal philosophy, their character is determined completely by what they do. If a person behaves in a despicable way on a regular basis, then how could we say they have good character? If a woman worked in the Nazi death camps it would certainly be difficult to suggest that "deep inside, she is a good person." Key in this school of thought is the idea that *the* most important trait in life is the substance of how one comports oneself. This seems to be logical, and the one way people ought to organize their lives, correct?

Well, there is a school of ethical thought that suggests a person's character is independent of their actions. Aristotle was the inventor of this idea, about 2,400 years ago, that character is hard to fathom. It is a difficult to understand quality, hidden deep within the individual. Aristotle talked about attempting to behave like exemplars or role models. His idea was called the ethics of **virtue**, which suggested that if you organized your life to attempt to live it in an exemplary fashion, the impact of your actions were irrelevant. As we will see shortly, this debate informs several schools of thought that make up the classic ethical frameworks.

Character refers to one's inner make-up, those traits that indicate a person's habitual moral qualities or defects (the composite of virtues and vices). When we ask if people have good character, we are asking if they are honest, if they possess the moral strength to do the right thing, if they are courageous, if they have a solid understanding of what constitutes the good in life, and if they possess integrity. Integrity is a part of good character of particular importance in police officers.

Integrity is that characteristic of wholeness, unity, and completeness that means a person is well rounded in his or her approach to life. It is crucial that police officers have integrity because they must possess multiple sets of skills, areas of substantive knowledge, practical understanding of the real world, and physical/athletic abilities. Ethics and integrity thus play off of each other in a mutually dependent way. To draw together all the characteristics, knowledge, and skills necessary to make up a competent, professional police officer, one needs the interweaving "glue" of an ethical perspective. A thoughtfully developed ethical perspective is essential to personal integrity; no amount of intelligence or physical ability will suffice. Put more bluntly, you cannot be a good police officer without having good character. All the rest is wasted if officers do

REVIEW CHART 8.2

ARISTOTLE'S VIRTUES

Area	Defect	Mean	Excess
Fear	Cowardice	Courage	Recklessness
Pleasure	Insensitivity	Self-control	Indulgence
Money	Stinginess	Generosity	Extravagance
Honor	Small-mindedness	High-mindedness	Vanity
Anger	Apathy	Gentleness	Short temper
Truth	Self-deprecation	Truthfulness	Boastfulness
Shame	Shamelessness	Modesty	Terror

Source: Aristotle, *Nicomachean Ethics*, translated by J. A. K. Tomson, 1955.

not underwrite their training, skill, and experience with an understanding of the ethical implications of life.

Moral Judgment

Moral judgments, or judgments about right and wrong, good and evil, are best understood as a class of judgments about possibilities. The natural setting of such judgment is within personal deliberations where, either publicly or in the privacy of our own minds, we compare and evaluate possibilities. This deliberation happens in families, in offices, on job sites, or wherever people meet to discuss or argue about how to get along.

Much of what police officers do deals with people in conflict. Procedural justice encompasses the rules of the game for regulating the inevitable conflict between different perspective, expectations, and tolerances in people's lives. The police officer's job does not include attempting to make people's conflicting expectations come together and agree within some overarching conception of what is good (the good in life). Rather, the job involves, where possible, finding ways to enable people to coexist. Police officers cannot solve all the problems of the world that are created because of diverse opinions, experiences, and possibilities. But they can and must attempt to deal fairly with the conflict that arises.

Justice and the Good

The moral notion of good grows naturally out of a basic human experience, not a belief or theory that all people know and universally accept. People have very different ideas, for example, of how important education, financial security, exercise, and entertainment are to living a good life. They not only value these concepts to different extents, but they also possess different definitions of them altogether. In a free society, ferociously held interests and passions are often reconcilable or compromised through rational calculations.

But ferociously held concepts of the good, and right and wrong, are not reconcilable. No mechanism of rational choice can help in moral conflicts, as they might with conflicts over competing interests. The idea of justice, then, is embedded in an unavoidable predicament: the necessity of agreement by discussion—without force or outright surrender—between antagonistic people who have clashed because one or both are not getting their way due to different concepts of the good.

The police are caught in the middle of such arguments. It is important for the individual officer, and more so for the police leader, to understand that these types of esoteric arguments are often at the heart of the struggles they confront. It must be in the back of the minds of police officers, lest they miscalculate the passion involved and be caught off guard by unexpected violence and vehemence.

With these brief discussions about character and justice as a prelude, it is time to turn to a consideration of the philosophical schools around which police officer ethics revolve.

BOX 8.4

PREDETERMINING CHARACTER IS IMPOSSIBLE

One of the paradoxes—in fact, the most important paradox—of the police selection process is that, while the most important element involves attempting to determine the character of police officer candidates in advance, no foolproof test exists to determine that ahead of time. How could we possibly know in advance if a person will take advantage of the opportunities for corrupt behavior that are presented to police officers on the street—such as the chance to steal from or shake down citizens and/or businesses? How could we possibly know in advance if a person will acknowledge the importance of and weigh with appropriate significance the powers with which they will be entrusted as a police officer . . . or abuse them?

ETHICAL FRAMEWORKS

Before presenting the reader with our ideas about the "ethic to live by," which Moore has created for today's police officer, we will begin our discussion of ethical frameworks with a consideration of two classical schools of thought. Perhaps the most often discussed and utilized ethical frameworks in all of human history are the absolutist ideas of Immanuel Kant and the utilitarian principles of John Stuart Mill. We will discuss these theoretical constructs before attempting to put them together into a coherent whole that informs the contemporary police officer's life on the street.

Ethical Formalism: Kant

People who take conscience to be their guide are essentially Kantians. Whether they realize it or not, these people believe that the right, the obligatory, the morally good, is determined by only one thing: the intention that lies behind an action, or the reason for which it was done. In focusing exclusively on intention, ethics formalists believe there is an absolute principle upon which ethical choices must be based. Kant pointed out there are many factors involved in successfully accomplishing something. Over most of these factors, a person exercises no direct control. A person may not have the skill, knowledge, or luck to accomplish something. But morally speaking, doing something for the right reason is all that matters.

We agree with Kant in this: there are other considerations that make an action right, good, or obligatory besides the goodness or badness of its consequences (the outcome). We agree that certain features of an act itself make it right—for example, the fact that it keeps a promise or is just. We might also agree that sometimes other facts about an act make it right or obligatory—for example, that it is commanded by God, our political beliefs, or our patriotism. Kant's view, then, is an absolutist view of the world of ethics. Kant's philosophy of ethics focuses on the intention behind people's acts. It considers their consequences uncontrollable and, thus, irrelevant. He means to infuse into people the idea that their duty is absolute. Right is right, and it is right all the time.

Most police officers agree with Kant to some extent—as do most Americans—because, as a people, we tend to understand that our history includes an appreciation for limited government. We tend to rail against the tyranny of our government (or big corporations) because of the power it exerts over us. And, when we consider the discretionary power that police officers exercise over people, even if we are police officers ourselves, we tend to understand the fact that people will resent too much police power. We want governmental power limited, and one way to do that is to make hard and fast rules and make sure that everyone—the government included—sticks to them. This is the central strength of Kant's absolutism.

But Kant presents us with a problem. When we carry his idea to its logical extension, it becomes possible for an action, or rule of conduct, to be morally right even if it does not promote good over evil. That is, the logical extension of focusing on a person's intention is that the morality of an act is not measured by the difference for good or ill it makes in the life of anyone. A police-related example might involve citing a teenager who is found out after curfew. The child was driving home from seeing her ill grandmother after a Tuesday night high school basketball game in which she played. She has a clean record and is cooperative. Kant would say that the child should be cited, irrespective of the consequences for her. The curfew law is the law, and no amount of rethinking it would be morally defensible. There are other problems with Kant, but let us just say that this is a particularly troublesome difficulty with making absolute rules.

Utilitarianism: Mill

Another important and classic conceptualization of ethics is termed **utilitarianism**. This theory—developed by John Stuart Mill—holds that the sole, ultimate standard of right and wrong is the principle of utility. In everything we do, we are to seek the greatest possible balance of good over evil in the world. Taking this perspective, when judging what is the right or the wrong thing to do in life, the only criterion to be considered is the good or evil consequence that a choice would bring. Utilitarianism is very democratic in a sense. Utilitarians believe that in deciding ethical questions, a calculation must be made regarding which choice would maximize the good for the greatest number of people.

There are some important and attractive consequences to behaving in this utilitarian way. But doing one's duty can sometimes create hardship, pain, and even tragedy. Sometimes the police keep starving people from food because it doesn't belong to them. Sometimes the police ignore dishonesty in businesses and corporations, actions that hurt large numbers of citizens, because such actions involve torts and not crimes. Sometimes the police ignore upper-class drug use, upscale prostitution, and white collar crime and pursue lower-class offenders because their crime is more visible, it is easier to pursue to conviction, and that is what they are told to do by politicians and administrators. In these and any number of other ways, the police are doing their duty (sticking to the law as written and following their orders in an absolute way), but are perhaps participating in perpetuating misery for society's most downcast members.

Instead of constructing absolute sets of principles that must be acknowledged and followed at all times and under all circumstances (as Kant would do), Mill suggests ethics are situational. Either in focusing on the general good of the community or on the good of the individual citizen, this school underwrites police discretion directly. It suggests that, most of the time, the police ought to calculate what they think is the best course of action. When making their individual, particularized, situationally driven decisions, the police use their own logic, pursue their own understandings of the good, and exhibit their character. Thus, an idea that has been flowing through our entire discussion is once more given support; the police are the law, and their personal ethics are critical to the generation of justice.

For all of its strengths, utilitarianism has its own drawbacks. First, there is the problem of making calculations that often cannot be made accurately about the relative amount of good and evil an act might bring into the world. Second, there is an even bigger problem: what if an act is evil in and of itself, but it brings substantial good into the world? Utilitarianism would suggest that it is good. Here is a classic example from the world of criminal justice.

REVIEW CHART 8.3

KANT AND MILL ON ETHICS

Kant's ethical formalism emphasizes:
- Consistency in one's maxims—circumstances are ignored
- Reason is the most salient feature of morality
- Focusing upon the will/the intention of an act; Kant succeeds in taking people more seriously than Mill

Mill's utilitarianism emphasizes:
- Taking situations into account when deciding what is right
- Calculating what would produce the greatest good for the greatest number of people
- Focusing on consequences; right acts are those that, in their application, promote good over evil; thus, Mill takes the good more seriously than Kant (Perez and Moore, 2002: 94)

The deterrent effect of capital punishment has been argued for generations now, and there is no definitive answer to solve the argument (in fact, a great deal of evidence suggests that it does *not* work to deter homicide). But suppose, for the purposes of argument, it were to be proven beyond a shadow of a doubt that publicly executing people for the crime of homicide worked effectively to deter other homicides—lots of them. It then follows that, in the best interests of the vast majority of people, executing a person or two, now and then, is a good thing for the community. But what if the person executed were not guilty? To a strict utilitarian, it would appear that Mill would think it did not matter. The deterrent effect would be the same, whether the people who were executed were actually guilty or innocent. Kant, of course, would say that to execute an innocent person would be immoral to the extreme.

An Ethic to Live By

With the two most often studied classical schools of ethics behind us, it is time to consider a particularized form of ethics developed for police officers. It is called an **"ethic to live by,"** and it was developed by J. Alan Moore (Perez and Moore, 2002). Moore's idea involves making a ethical frame of reference by putting together a combination of the strengths of Kant and Mill.

Moore began his combining of Kant and Mill by discussing the limits of each. He then suggested that a police officer should endeavor to maximize the good (a Mill-like concept) while doing so in a just way (a Kant-like concept). He suggested that the central principle of his theory should be what he termed "beneficence." This principle involved doing good and preventing evil. Moore wrote:

> The reason we call this the principle of beneficence and not the principle of benevolence is to remind ourselves that it asks us actually to do good and not evil, not merely to want to do so. Benevolence means "good will, charitableness, kindliness." To be benevolent is to think well of people and to attempt to act well toward them. It is, in a Kantian sense, intentional—it is all about the general attitude toward others of having good will.
>
> But beneficence means more. Beneficence involves doing good deeds, acting charitably, and behaving in a kindly manner. In other words, beneficence is active and not intentional. It is not enough, in our discussion of ethics, for police officers to think good thoughts and wish people well. The police must engage in doing good and preventing evil. They cannot stand on the sidelines in life and merely have good will. Police officers are umpires or referees, not merely spectators in people's lives. (Perez and Moore, 2002: 104)

As Box 8.5 indicates, in the end, Moore translated his ethic down into four simple rules of thumb for police officers: inflict no evil or harm, prevent evil or harm, remove evil, and do or promote good. Finally, Moore decided, between our two forms of justice discussed earlier in the book, he favors the distributive justice

BOX 8.5

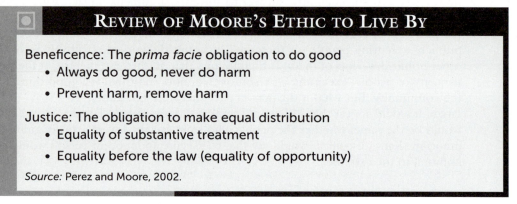

REVIEW OF MOORE'S ETHIC TO LIVE BY

Beneficence: The *prima facie* obligation to do good
- Always do good, never do harm
- Prevent harm, remove harm

Justice: The obligation to make equal distribution
- Equality of substantive treatment
- Equality before the law (equality of opportunity)

Source: Perez and Moore, 2002.

principle that "justice is fairness." In making this decision, he reminds us that it is not the job of the police to make people's lives equally good.

After pulling together two classical schools of ethical thought and combining them into an ethic to live by, we now have a generalized set of ideas to apply to police work's complex and sometimes contradictory requirements. One of the driving realities of police work is the concept—visited in Chapter 2—that the goals and functions of the police are multiple, conflicting, and vague. Of course, the key concept here is this idea of conflicting goals, as it drives so much in the way of confusion and frustration for police officers and citizens alike. Even in our discussions of philosophical underpinnings of police ethics, we cannot avoid this omnipresent conflict.

JUDGMENT CALLS

Though Moore put together an ethic that attempts to be of practical use to the everyday police officer, even his model can present conflicting suggestions to the officer on the street. Because this is so, the application of his "ethic to live by" involves making judgment calls. Here are two important conceptualizations of how such judgment calls present themselves and how they might be resolved.

Kant vs. Mill

It seems when the police perform the role of law enforcement officers, they are Kantians. They must be absolutists because they are dealing with people's freedom. When they decide to take away that freedom, they must apply absolute legal principles, procedural rules, and substantive laws. Similarly, it seems when police officers are operating in the order maintenance mode, they often use an utilitarian frame of reference. When maintaining order and not dealing with law enforcement–oriented decisions, police officers spend their time calculating what is in the best interests of the state and all the people. When dealing with drunks, the homeless, parties, loud music, groups of juveniles, family troubles, and a host of other order maintenance types of details, the police consistently calculate what to do with an eye toward what they understand to be fair and equitable in the local community.

Because of the confusion between these types of ethical perspectives, brought out by the multi-faceted, conflicting, and vague nature of the police officer role, Moore created his "ethic to live by." But even in applying that ethical perspective, the police are sometimes confronted with judgment calls. One kind of judgment call occurs when beneficence conflicts with justice. When this occurs, beneficence becomes paramount. This might put the police officer in a bind sometimes, but dealing with such binds (by making discretionary decisions) is a central reality of police work. Standing up for what is ethical and doing the right thing under such circumstances are actions the officer with good character takes and embraces willingly.

Dealing with the bind created when justice conflicts with beneficence involves understanding something that we addressed in our initial discussion about justice. Treating people fairly does not mean treating them exactly the same way. Doing good for people may very well involve treating them differently. As long as competent, ethical officers understand in their hearts that they would treat other citizens similarly situated in the same manner, then our ethic does not require equal treatment.

A second type of judgment call relates to what Mill called the **harm principle**. All societies must strike a delicate balance when they decide how much power the agents of the state should possess. A classical liberal, such as Locke, would say that individuals should be left alone to live their own lives without interference from the state or government (Locke, 1689). A classical conservative, such as Edmund Burke (who led opposition to the ideas of liberalism 300 years ago in England), would say that people cannot be trusted with their own decisions. Burke called for strong government, tight laws, and increased police power. He believed that the people, being ignorant and stupid, need to be controlled using any means possible (Parkin, 1965).

In his famous essay "On Liberty," Mill suggested a formula for how much power belongs in those hands. Mill said the individual should only be answerable to society for conduct that directly harms another. This is called Mill's harm principle and it is important for all police officers to remember, as it provides a good yardstick for making judgment calls. Often, police officers must decide whether to invoke the law, arrest, and/or become involved in solving a problem that might otherwise be solved if people were simply left alone. When this occurs, it serves the police well to remember Mill and ask themselves whether someone is directly harmed by the actions of another. If there is no direct harm to others from deviant behavior, why worry about it?

BOX 8.6

MILL'S HARM PRINCIPLE

The quintessential statement of individual liberty was crafted by John Stuart Mill in 1859. Mill suggested that there is an imaginary balance in life that is made between the freedom of the individual to do whatever he or she wants to do and the necessity of the state—all people taken together—to control dangerous behavior. The tipping point, or the place where the individual's freedom can be taken away from him or her, is where that freedom presents direct harm to others. This is called the "harm principle," and it is an important part of the utilitarian school of ethics.

Solving Ethical Dilemmas

We must make a critical differentiation here between an ethical question and an ethical dilemma. An ethical question suggests a choice between doing something that is good, proper, and ethical, and doing the easier or short-term thing. Sometimes we pass an ethical test if we do the right thing, and sometimes we fail if we choose the easy way out. For example, a police officer is angry about the attitude of a carload of obnoxious teenagers. But the kids have done nothing illegal. The officer is faced with the option of either taking some marginally legal (or even illegal) action in order to "teach them a lesson," or doing the right thing and letting them go. To pass the ethical test would entail just saying to oneself, "Well, I'll get 'em next time."

An ethical dilemma involves something different. It presents the individual with a choice when both alternatives represent ethically defensible decisions. For example, should a mother steal food to feed her starving children? If she does, she is breaking the law and the social contract, but she is living up to her duty to her children as a mother. If she does not, she is living up to her responsibility to society as a citizen, but she is letting down her children. In either case, she is doing something ethically defensible. Thus, she is in a dilemma.

Life presents us all with ethical questions on a regular basis. It is obvious that police officers are visited by more of these dilemmas than the average person, given their roles as peacekeeper and referee. Especially in an era of COP, police officers are confronted on a regular basis with situations where they balance conflicting interests—those of society as a whole, the community, the citizen-victim, the citizen-suspect—and must make decisions in the best interests of justice. Often, cleaving to the law as written can create problems related to order maintenance. We visited this idea in Chapter 3 and now see it in specific relief once again.

The point here—*the* point of this entire chapter—is that an officer's personal ethic, as a part of their character, informs the decision making element of the job.

If the police define the law with their decisions, then the law, to some extent, becomes defined by police ethics. That is why police competence absolutely cannot be divorced from police ethics.

THE MANAGER'S LEADERSHIP

So, the ethics of the police define and inform the law. It is that simple, and it is that important. While in past eras it appeared that police ethics presented a sideshow to the police leader, today we know that they are center stage. It is not possible to be a good police officer and not be an ethical police officer. By translation, it is not possible to be a good, competent, effective police leader without being engaged with the ethical problems and dilemmas presented to subordinates on a regular basis. Nothing—no other single part of the complex and diverse job of leading police officers—is as important as the leader's role of being a sort of "ethical guru" to his or her young officers.

Having an Ethic

First and foremost in importance for the police leader is to encourage the formulation of a personal ethic by every officer under his or her charge. This responsibility presents a bifurcated reality to the leader. On the one hand, some young officers—fresh from the college campus—will readily embrace this idea. They are conversant with the rhetoric involved when they are encouraged to create such an ethic, and are neither intimidated nor cynical about its formation. Well-taught criminal justice ethics courses will prepare the young officer for this endeavor and even give them a leg up in doing so. After a short period of time out on the street, it is not at all difficult to motivate this type of officer in the direction of personal ethic construction.

On the other hand, older officers, especially those with limited educational backgrounds, are more than a bit reluctant to embrace this idea. Supported by locker room naysayers, older officers can not only rail against the idea of having a personal ethic but motivate others—especially younger officers who respect their experience—to ignore this entire area of concern. Developing a personal ethic can be labeled by this type of good ol' boy to be a "book learning" sort of exercise that is an unproductive waste of time.

With regard to the development of a personal ethic, the police leader today must be motivated in three different directions. First, the leader must approach the college educated officer with the professional attitude that presumes an understanding of the importance of personal ethic creation. Second, with the type of older officers who are responsive to modern, professional ideas, the contemporary leader might very well want to aid in this creative endeavor with appropriately placed discussions about ethics that relate to specific details. In "coaching mode," the leader can take the tack that suggests deference to the experienced officer while at the same time exert confidence in the importance of the process. Here, the leader is a teacher, plain and simple. Third and finally, if the good ol' boys will not participate in such processes, the leader must be prepared to countermand the type of cynicism and negation that some of the most jaded officers will attempt. This is an ongoing problem in the police world, of course; the thoughtful and creative leader should be conversant with how to deal with naysaying. As we have noted in several places in our discussions, a leader must be ever vigilant when confronted with the potential impact of the omnipresent cynic.

Teaching Personal Ethic Construction

How is a personal ethic constructed? Does one read Plato and Aristotle and take a course on philosophy? The answer to that question is, why not? While it certainly is not what most officers will do, the world of policing has changed so dramatically in recent years that it is no longer bizarre or unheard of to find officers who know their philosophy and are interested in discussions about it.

The leader's role here is to encourage the individual officer to practice "the ability to discern, through moral reasoning and individual values, what the right thing to do is and the will to do it" (Donnithorne, 1993: 62). Thinking in ethical terms is not an instinctual thing. It's not something that even the most intelligent and educated officer does naturally. It is something that must be practiced, like everything else worth learning in life. The leader encourages this, utilizing whatever motivational and intellectual resources he or she possesses. Engaging the subordinate in the three different modes discussed, and responding in a way that does justice to the individual's career path, is the ongoing role of today's leader.

BOX 8.7

MAKING THE HARDER RIGHT: FROM *THE WEST POINT WAY OF LEADERSHIP*

Cadets are expected to behave morally—not to mention professionally—in all instances. Most people agree that leaders should always do the right—as opposed to the expedient, pragmatic, or the popular—thing. West Point asks cadets to do this, and then to go one step further and reach for what we call the "**harder right**." Before a leader makes a decision, she must imagine her range of influence as a circle. "The harder right" is usually the decision that most positively affects the widest possible circle . . . [A]t West Point we urge that our leaders draw the circle ever wider, and take into consideration not just those nearest to them, but those in the Army, the community, the nation, the world (Donnithorne, 1993: 61).

A Personal Ethic Cannot Be Forced

Regardless of the above points, it must be made clear that only so much in the way of motivation will work here. An officer who pronouncedly resists this process, whether a member of the good ol' boys or not, will present a frustrating reality because it is demonstrably true that no one can construct a personal ethic for another. This is an individual endeavor that requires more than just the tacit participation of the individual officer. It requires the officer to take center stage in the process, merely directed and motivated by the leader.

A TYPOLOGY OF POLICE MISCONDUCT

Before concluding this chapter and moving on to a consideration of systems designed to investigate allegations of police misconduct, we must briefly discuss and analyze what forms misconduct takes. In constructing a typology for police misconduct, the table accompanying this section was developed by Perez and Moore (2002: 127–140). The labels in the table's four boxes are determined by asking two questions about the nature of police misconduct. The first question is, was the misbehavior done in the name of personal gain? That is, did the police officer profit personally from the misconduct? Whether it takes the form of money, goods, or services, when police officers misbehave they are either looking to enhance their own material well-being or not.

The second question is, did the misconduct involve the misuse of the officer's legal authority? That is, did the officer "sell the badge" in exchange for something? Whether it involves protecting criminals from arrest or arresting certain criminals to enhance the business of others, police officers sometimes use their state-granted authority as a bargaining tool to get something accomplished that is improper. The answer to these questions requires a simple yes or no.

Once these two questions are answered, police misconduct can be classified into its five major types. Four of the types are shown in Table 8.2 and one exists outside of that table. This may seem to be just an academic exercise, but it is not. The consequences, methods of investigation, punishment, and political fallout associated with these five types of misbehavior are different—sometimes very different—from each other. Let us discuss these types individually.

Corruption of Authority

Police officers are guilty of what we label corruption of authority when they misuse their legal authority (badges) to obtain personal rewards. This takes several forms. Payoffs are sometimes obtained by police officers to protect certain criminal enterprises, such as gambling, prostitution, or drug sales. Money is handed over to the police, and arrests are not made. Shakedowns are sometimes undertaken, where police officers proactively demand money from people, normally small business operators.

TABLE 8.2

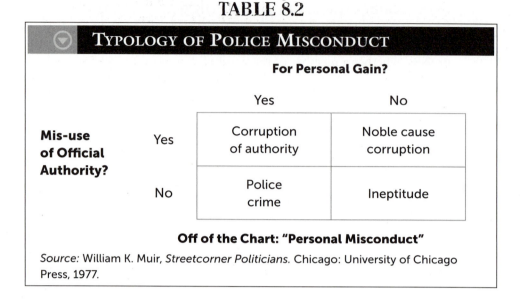

		For Personal Gain?	
		Yes	No
Mis-use of Official Authority?	Yes	Corruption of authority	Noble cause corruption
	No	Police crime	Ineptitude

Off of the Chart: "Personal Misconduct"

Source: William K. Muir, *Streetcorner Politicians.* Chicago: University of Chicago Press, 1977.

This is done in exchange for "letting them off easy" with regard to city ordinances and so forth. Graft is sometimes accepted for not administering the law in an impartial manner. Corruption of authority was the sort of misconduct that permeated police work before the reform era (Walker, 1997). This is the sort of misconduct to which most people refer when they use the generic term "police corruption."

Noble Cause Corruption

Here we are confronted directly by Dirty Harry. Some officers ignore the due process limitations of the law during investigations. They do this to get the job done (Caldero and Crank, 2009). To deter criminals and/or to prosecute people they believe are guilty of criminal deeds, police officers will write false reports ("creative report writing"), harass citizens, and/or use excessive force. When noble cause corruption involves lying on the witness stand to obtain a conviction, it is called "testilying." These behaviors involve police officers misusing their legal authority in inappropriate ways, but they are not doing it for personal gain. "Getting the bad guys behind bars" (rather than making money) is the rationalization here.

Police Crime

Sometimes, police officers will become involved in criminal activities while on duty that do not involve the use of their legal office. This is known as **police crime.** Officers will sometimes use the opportunities that being on duty (particularly at night) afford them, to burglarize businesses or residences. Sometimes,

BOX 8.8

POLICE CRIME

At a construction site where new homes were being built more than a mile out in the country and thus far away from prying eyes, several deputy sheriffs decided to take advantage of the fact that the site was left unguarded all night long. They began stealing hundreds of garbage disposals and microwave ovens that were kept at the site, still in their new boxes. Over the course of several months, the officers developed a thriving business selling these items to unscrupulous developers in other locations. When the theft ring was finally discovered, three officers went to prison for their thievery and three others were terminated for knowing about it and not taking action. This is an example of police crime. It is the product of greed and opportunity.

when a theft has already occurred, police officers will take extra merchandise or money and report it as part of the original theft. When this type of misconduct happens, the police are misbehaving to obtain personal gain, but they are not trading off their legal authority to do so (Kappeler, Sluder, and Alpert, 1998). Thus, this type of misconduct is considered to be different from either of the above two types.

Ineptitude

There are all sorts of transgressions against departmental general orders considered police misconduct that involve neither personal gain nor the misuse of police legal authority. This category is made up of such common violations as sleeping on duty, being habitually late, having sex on duty, drinking on duty, writing poor reports, failing to respond to calls, and ignoring orders. While these can be serious violations when investigated, they are neither criminal nor corrupt in nature. They are considered to be merely the product of **ineptitude**.

Personal Misconduct

In this category belongs the sort of personal (and sometimes even criminal) misconduct that reflects on an individual's image as a police officer, but occurs off duty. Examples include alcoholism, adultery, off-duty drunk driving, and so on. This category does not fit on our chart of types of misconduct because it does not directly relate to a person's on-duty actions as a police officer. However, we should not make the mistake of thinking that police officer behavior off duty is unimportant. It can have great significance. For example, when a police officer does not pay his or her bills it can have a tremendous negative affect on community confidence in the police. This is especially true in a small jurisdiction. A police officer can be found guilty of "conduct unbecoming an officer" even if the conduct has no relation to anything he or she does on duty. Perceptions held about the police are critical to maintaining legitimacy in any police organization.

 ## SUMMATION

The reader may be moved to say that we have used the word "critical" too often in this chapter. That may be so, and an unfortunate reality if true to such an extent that it falls on deaf ears at this particular juncture. For nothing we have discussed along the way—theoretical and pragmatic—is as "critically important" as are the ideas discussed in this chapter. Police decision making is driven by police officer ethics; thus, the meaning of the law in America is driven by police officer ethics. No amount of cynicism or foot dragging should be—*can be*—allowed to dissuade the modern leader from motivating young officers to take their personal ethic seriously.

Having discussed the complicated reality that surrounds police officer behavior and misbehavior, we now move to consider what to do about police misconduct when it occurs. When the officer's personal ethic either fails or was inappropriate to begin with, what should be done about it? Police accountability is next on our topical list.

DISCUSSION QUESTIONS

1. Discuss Muir's schematic for determining his four types of officers, engaging both the ideas of passion and perspective. Then, focus in particular on the enforcer type. Why is the enforcer the most difficult type of less-than-optimal police officer to control? (Hint: Dirty Harry is an enforcer.)

2. This book suggests that police officers "moralize for others." What do we mean by this? What are examples? How do officers make these types of decisions? What criteria do they use?

3. Discuss and debate two of the conceptualizations of justice that we consider in this chapter. Compare and contrast justice as fairness and justice as equity, using specific police work–related examples.

4. Compare and contrast Kant and Mill. What are the principles behind their ethical perspectives? What are some on-the-street examples of each being used appropriately by police officers?

5. This book differentiates between ethical questions and ethical dilemmas. What's the difference? What are some on-the-street, police-related examples of each that might be faced by an everyday beat cop?

KEY TERMS

Avoiders: Officers with a cynical perspective of life and a conflicted understanding of the morality of coercion.

Boys will be boys: The idea that police misconduct is understandable and acceptable.

Character: A person's beliefs, philosophy, and tenets.

Complex causal patterns of life: The idea that crime is not caused by simple, monolithic causes.

Conflicted about coercion: The idea that some officers cannot rationalize using coercion.

Cynical perspective: The idea that there are good and bad people, simplistic causal patterns in life, and human independence to the extreme.

Enforcers: Officers with the cynical perspective of life and an integrated understanding of coercion.

Ethic to live by: Moore's ethical framework developed for police officers.

Ethical formalism: The philosophy of Immanuel Kant, involving an absolute approach to ethics, with rules that are always immutable and constant.

Ethics: The science of moral duty.

Freebies: Goods or services given to police officers as gratuities.

Harder right: From the United States Military Academy, the principle that leaders must do more than merely be right, but must expand their horizons to consider their actions in community-wide, national, and worldwide perspectives.

Harm principle: Mill's idea that a person is only answerable to the state for conduct that directly harms another person.

Ineptitude: The type of police misconduct that involves no personal gain and does not involve the abuse of an officer's official authority.

Integrated about coercion: The idea that some officers can rationalize using coercion in the name of accomplishing good deeds in life.

International Association of Chiefs of Police (IACP): Organization centered in Washington, D.C., that involves police chiefs in research and political causes related to police work.

New blue line: Skolnick and Fyfe's idea that there is a new type of police officer in America today.

Passion: In the context of Muir's theory of professionalism, the ability to rationalize principled violence.

Personal ethic: The idea that each and every officer should develop his or her own view of ethics in order to be a competent police officer.

Perspective: A person's life view, either tragic or cynical; coined by William K. Muir, Jr.

Police crime: Police misconduct that involves personal gain but not the abuse of an officer's official authority.

Precariousness and necessity of human interdependence: The idea that humans are, by nature, interdependent and communal animals; part of the tragic perspective of life.

Principled violence: The element that makes for an integrated perspective of coercion.

Professionals: Officers who possess the tragic perspective and an integrated understanding of the morality of coercion.

Reciprocators: Officers with the tragic perspective of life and a conflicted understanding of the morality of coercion.

Quid pro quo: A tacit, unspoken understanding that an exchange of goods or services will transpire.

Tragic perspective: The view of life that includes the idea of unitary experience in life, complex causal patterns, and the precariousness and necessity of human interdependence.

Unitary experience: The idea that all humans share a basically similar life experience.

Utilitarianism: The ethical school of thought developed by John Stuart Mill that considers the end result of human behavior—rather than absolute rules—as critical to the construction of norms of conduct.

Virtue: Moral practice or action; moral principles; rectitude.

 EXAMPLE SCENARIOS

Ethics 101

Tom Chappel is the sheriff of Dogwood County in eastern Arkansas. He has been extremely successful in his first term of office, so he decides to begin trying his hand at private consulting. He has a pretty good background in training and developing training curriculum for law enforcement courses.

Recently, the local Indian reservation police chief requested some help in training his staff with a curriculum that he thought could best be developed by Sheriff Chappel. Chappel meets with the chief and discusses the needs for the reservation training and what the chief is looking for. They make an agreement for the sheriff to provide 40 hours of training on the process of CompStat, how to set up a CompStat program, and how to actually run the program, including the management of the sessions presented by the captains and lieutenants. The chief will pay the sheriff a consulting fee for his effort. The sheriff tells the chief this is okay because it is not a conflict of interest. It is related to law enforcement, and consultants do this as mutual aid all the time. The sheriff is merely acting as a mutual aid consultant.

To get this task done, the sheriff recruits one of his own lieutenants (known for his writing skills and training capability) and tells the lieutenant to get information on CompStat and help him get the details to the chief. The sheriff will pay the lieutenant a consultant fee for his involvement out of what the sheriff receives from the chief's agency.

Is all of this ethical? Why or why not? Would different ethical perspectives give us different answers to these questions? How about Moore's "ethic to live by"? What might it say about all of this?

A Big Problem?

Commander Joe Wilie is in charge of the police department investigation division, fraud and embezzlement unit. He has been working there for four years. During that time, he has met some very powerful people in the business community. One of the people he met is Tom Orca, a developer who rents the office space of the fraud/embezzlement unit to the police department.

Wilie is having some money problems. He tells Orca his problem and seeks some advice to help stave off a situation where he gets his paycheck garnished for money owed. A garnishment would mean a violation of the police department ethic of holding officers financially responsible in their private lives, as it might sully the good name and reputation of the agency.

Orca says Wilie can borrow some money from him at a favorable rate. Wilie declines but says he'll think about it. In the meantime, Wilie meets with his secretary and asks her to help him out. His idea is for her to borrow the money he needs from Orca. She will give the money to Wilie, and Wilie will pay her to pay Orca. This will then be a mere borrowing of some money from an employee and not raise any potential red flags.

Has this "sleight of hand" changed the nature of what is a departmental violation? Why or why not? And what about the regulation? Is it—in and of itself—ethical?

CompStat

Major Milton is the commander of Y sector of the Marsh City Police Department. Y sector is the most difficult area of the city to police. Over the last three months, Milton's investigative team has had some very low clearance rates on a rash of burglaries in several Y sector neighborhoods. Burglaries are up, and clearance rates are down. The inquisitors at CompStat (the chief and two assistant chiefs) have been very hard on Milton about his investigators not clearing more of the burglaries. The chiefs are getting a lot of heat from home owner associations about the problem, and the heat is also getting to the mayor and commissioners.

Just prior to his next three CompStat sessions, one of Milton's investigators makes an arrest on a local burglar, and the burglar confesses to 150 burglaries in the sector over the last three months. Milton knows that if he reports this one-man burglary team and the 150 cleared cases at one CompStat session and burglaries still continue in Y sector, he will have a really hard time settling the chiefs down. He and the burglary investigator decide to hold portions of the cleared burglaries as investigations not yet completed. They will take 50 of the burglaries to which the burglar admitted to each of the next three CompStat sessions and reveal them as cleared. This will make the monthly clearance rates go up and give the impression that investigations of burglaries are improving. After all, that's what really happened anyway, isn't it?

What do you think about this? Is it an example of creativity and logic or of unethical behavior? What would you do if you were the chief of police and you found out about it? Do any of our ethical frames of reference help you in analyzing this example?

ADDITIONAL READING

An introductory text in the field of ethics in general is Stuart Hampshire's *Freedom of the Individual* (Harper Row, 1959). For a historical treatment of the development of moral philosophy—from Aristotle through Kant and Mill to the present day—read Alasdair MacIntyre's *A Short History of Ethics, 2nd Ed.* (University of Notre Dame, 1998). The best introductory explanation of the philosophy of Kant, written in a very short and readable way, is Stephen Korner's *Kant* (Yale University Press, 1982). Each of these works provides a more readily understandable and useful view of these ideas than most readers develop if they read the philosopher's original works.

Joycelyn Pollock's *Ethics in Crime and Justice, 6th Ed.* (Wadsworth, 2010) discusses in greater detail the philosophical perspectives to which we have referred. It also includes numerous other schools of thought, such as those of natural law, religion, and the ethics of care in a way that our book has not. Other efforts in this vein include *Criminal Justice Ethics*, by Paul Leighton and Jeffrey Reiman (Prentice Hall, 2001) and *Morality in Criminal Justice: An Introduction to Ethics*, by Daryl Close and Nicholas Meier (Wadsworth, 1995).

John Crank and Michael Caldero's work *Police Ethics: The Corruption of Noble Cause, 2nd Ed.* (Anderson, 2004) is an important treatment of one type of police misconduct in depth. Perez and Moore's *Police Ethics: A Matter of Character* (Copperhouse Press, 2002) is a readable and police-specific text, but it overlaps a great deal with what is discussed here. And finally, an attempt at dealing with types, as well as prescriptive solutions in an international framework is *Corruption, Deviance, and Accountability in Policing*, by Maurice Punch (Willan Publishing, 2009).

CHAPTER 9

Accountability

INTRODUCTION

The topic of police **accountability** is one that brings out people's emotions in a unique way. No other police-related topic will so quickly illustrate how sensitive the American public is about the use of power on the part of agents of the state. Metaphorically speaking, our colonial roots, replete with concern for limiting the power of government, lie just beneath the surface of our skin. Americans who are generally pro-police and law-and-order oriented in their politics and individual life perspectives will often rail against the power of the state when they themselves are confronted by the police. This is especially true when the police exercise force out on the street.

In this chapter, we will consider some of the dynamics associated with attempting to hold the police accountable for their actions. We will remind ourselves that the police have multiple standards of conduct to which they must answer. Then we will spend significant time reviewing the subcultural, political, and legal limitations faced by any police review mechanism. Finally, we will examine the various review systems that attempt to hold police officers accountable to behavioral standards. That part of our discussion will include a comparative look at police review mechanisms in action.

This chapter's discussion is important for the police leader as it brings into specific relief a topic that is of critical importance to all Americans. One problem that haunts the police everywhere is, because they distance themselves from the public, officers can tend to become disconnected from the citizenry for whom they work. The police subculture, known for its isolation and solidarity, can work to protect officers psychically and physically, but also remove them from contact with average American citizens. It is a primary role of the police leader to avoid such isolation and steer subordinates away from it as well. Understanding how police accountability works, how it does *not* work, and how important it is to the public is critical for the police in a free society. Police leaders need to understand this in order to mentor, coach, and teach their subordinates a proper respect for the concerns of citizens. Furthermore, today's leader must focus on the progress that policing is making toward instilling a professional ethic into the fabric of the subculture.

THE GOALS: EXONERATION, TERMINATION, AND LEARNING

A police review system is, in essence, a miniature criminal justice system. It receives complaints about deviant behavior, decides which complaints to take seriously and which to handle informally, investigates those that appear to have some validity, and makes substantive decisions about the guilt or innocence of people accused of misconduct. It exonerates those found not guilty of misconduct and sanctions those found to be innocent. In the criminal justice system, the accused people are citizens and the deviance relates to criminal activity. With respect to a police review system, the accused people are police officers and the deviance relates (almost universally) to the violation of general orders.

It is important to keep this analogy in mind as we approach the topics in this chapter. The limitations faced by police accountability systems are similar to those faced by the criminal justice system. First, some accusations are false, misleading, and even purposefully dishonest. Those who make them sometimes have "axes to grind." Second, those who are accused of deviant behavior have procedural rights afforded to them by the system. They can often have cultural support (or subcultural support) for their misbehavior. Third, they can sometimes avoid being found guilty due to technicalities. Finally, those who complain almost always see themselves as being victimized unfairly to begin with, and doubly so if the system finds accused persons (officers) to be not guilty. No matter what the facts might be in reality, a review system will almost universally be perceived as unfair by those outside of its machinations.

Finally, as we are reminded in Review Chart 9.1, a police review system—as is true of the criminal justice system as a whole—has three over-arching functions. First, it must operate fairly, dispassionately, and thoroughly to do its investigating and decision making at the outset. It must operate to exonerate those who are found to be not guilty of deviant behavior. Their careers must not be tainted in any way by mere accusations or investigations that result in findings of not guilty. Second, it must work to rid the profession of those officers who are guilty of the sort of misconduct that is completely unacceptable. Some types of misbehavior are simply unforgivable for officers of the state, empowered to take away freedom and even the lives of citizens. An effectively run police review system must get rid of those who are guilty of conduct so egregious as to warrant their exit from the officer corps. Finally, a review system is charged with encouraging learning and change in a positive direction for those who are found to be guilty of misconduct that doesn't warrant termination. Just as the criminal justice system is supposed to correct convicts, the police review system must endeavor to teach errant officers.

REVIEW CHART 9.1

THE THREE FUNCTIONS OF ACCOUNTABILITY MECHANISMS (ANALOGOUS TO THOSE OF THE CRIMINAL JUSTICE SYSTEM)

- To exonerate officers not guilty of misconduct
- To terminate officers who are guilty of egregious violations
- To encourage different behavior/learning in officers guilty of minor offenses

At the outset of our discussion, we must consider this fact: the police have more than one standard of conduct to which they must be held, which creates a layered system of overlapping concerns for the review system as a whole and for the police leader in particular.

ACCOUNTABLE TO WHAT?

When we say that people must be held accountable, we imply a set of standards to which they must be held. Put another way, for there to be misconduct, there must acceptable standards of conduct. For there to be deviance, there must be norms. In a fairly constructed system, those rules of conduct and acceptable norms must be explicit. One of the principles of what is referred to by scholars as "the morality of the law" is that laws (rules) must be explicitly, clearly written down and made available to those to whom they apply (Fuller, 1969). No accountability system (whether it seeks to hold the police or the citizenry accountable) can be fairly run unless the rules under which it operates are specifically focused, narrowly constructed, and easily understood.

The problem with respect to police accountability is that officers must answer to multiple standards of conduct. As was the case with the goals and functions of the police, so it is with these sets of standards; they are multiple, conflicting, and vague (Wildavsky, 1987). The police play three different types of roles out on the street. Each role brings with it a separate set of standards.

First, the police are legal actors. Everything they do must stand up to legal scrutiny. They enforce the law on a regular basis and must be held accountable to it themselves. The police are accountable to the substantive law, of course. In addition, they must apply the substantive law correctly, fairly, and objectively. With respect to the "catch-all sections" included in every penal code—sections such as disturbing the peace and loitering—the police must be particularly circumspect about arbitrariness and capriciousness. This much is obvious. But the police answer to procedural law too. The rules of the game, as determined by appellate courts at all levels, impinge upon the police mission on a regular basis. Unknown before the advent of the Warren Court of the 1960s, the police mission today is bracketed daily by court decisions about seemingly trivial and minor police procedures (Roberg, Novak, and Cordner, 2005).

Second, the police are political actors. They must answer to the public. Especially in an era of COP, the police must ascertain and then respond to the desires of the citizenry (Dempsey and Forst, 2010). Lip service alone will not serve. We have entered into a new era of American policing in the past two decades, and a central principle—which must be understood by contemporary leaders so that it is transmitted and translated into police behavior in the streets—is that the police are accountable to the people. This is not a some-of-the-time feeling. It is an ongoing, living and breathing principle of organizational life for the police today. It is part of the way policing must be accomplished in America.

Finally, the police are administrative actors. They must be held accountable to hundreds of general police practices, taught in academies and in-service training programs, and specific rules included in their general orders. It is this area of accountability that presents both the most important responsibility to police leaders and one of the most troublesome political problems for review systems. Because the overwhelming majority of incidents of police misconduct are minor violations of general orders and police practices, they are (and should be) handled informally by immediate supervisors. How those problems are handled can have an important impact on local politics if police leaders are effective, fair, and understanding of political opinion.

On the other hand, the public often misunderstands police procedures. Most people are not lawyers or police officers, and don't fully understand the law or police training. They often have totally unreasonable expectations for accountability mechanisms and a perspective on police review that is ignorant of practical reality. This colors the perceptions of legitimacy that are held about review processes (especially internal affairs procedures) outside of the police organization. In fact, this combination of ignorance and misunderstanding drives the call for civilian review.

The most important problem here is that these three sets of standards can conflict with each other. Members of the community or a neighborhood group can ask the police to do things that are not legal. People have a distinctly no-nonsense approach to the generalized desire to have the police clean up the streets. The public does not care how this is accomplished. People want lower crime rates, guns out of their neighborhoods, gangs off the streets, and an end to drug trafficking. The average citizen does not care one iota about the constitutional or legal processes that may stand in the way of the police accomplishing these tasks. They want action, not excuses.

In demanding action, people can ask the police, directly or indirectly, to behave like Dirty Harry. The public will usually support any tactic that works. For example, even if they know *for a fact* that the police are harassing known gang members or planting evidence on suspected drug dealers, most people will not care. This support for Harry can interfere with attempts to hold the police accountable to legal and

REVIEW CHART 9.2

MULTIPLE ACCOUNTABILITY SCHEMES

- *The law:* As legal actors, the police must cleave to procedural law while applying substantive law appropriately and fairly.
- *The people:* As political actors under COP, the police must respond to citizens, neighborhood groups, and community leaders.
- *Professional standards:* As administrative actors, the police must observe professional regulations and follow standard operational procedures.

departmental standards. It is doubly difficult to fight noble cause corruption when it is applauded by the citizenry. So, in the public's mind, the definition of police misconduct is up for debate. There is, in some sense, nothing that anyone inside or outside of police work can do to bring together the differing perceptions and perspectives of the public and the police.

This is just the tip of the iceberg where the limitations of accountability are concerned. Because it is such a central element of what police leaders do, and it is where the "rubber meets the road" with regard to the perceptions among the public about how the police behave themselves, we must take a substantial amount of time to consider a number of other limitations that impinge upon accountability.

THE LIMITS OF REFORM

Before we engage in a comparative discussion of the forms which police review takes, we need to consider the severe limitations that are placed upon police accountability in America. There are police subcultural and American political limitations on the process of holding the police to answer. Then, too, there are multiple layers of procedural protections afforded to the police officer who is accused of misconduct. Investigations into allegations of misconduct can be cumbersome and legally complicated because of the same dynamics that trouble the criminal justice system as a whole. Because of these limitations—cultural, political, and legal—those who are factually guilty of police misconduct can end up going unsanctioned.

Subcultural Rationalizations

To begin with, we must note that the subculture can actually lead to police misconduct in several ways. Furthermore, it can also limit any accountability mechanism's effectiveness due to rationalizations that protect officers. Here are a couple of subcultural norms of police conduct that can work in both of these directions—to create misconduct and rationalize it after the fact.

First, with regard to the use of force, police officers tend to cleave to what is a perfectly understandable and yet unacceptable norm, that of overkill. The police are invariably outnumbered on the street. They face crowds of people on a regular basis. Theirs is a role within which intimidation is a paramount skill. It is crucial that they be able to handle large groups of what are sometimes angry and antagonistic citizens. As Muir tells us when he talks about the paradox of face, if the police carry with them a nasty reputation, they rarely have to prove their nastiness (see Chapter 2). The more "badass" their "rep," the less badass they have to be—the less often they have to use force. Putting these realities together, the police logically arrive at the idea that when they are attacked, they must win and win big.

A locker room axiom among police officers is this: "If they assault one of us, they go to jail. If they hurt one of us, they go to the hospital." This is the idea of overkill with regard to the application of force. Whether they know it or not, when espousing overkill police officers as a group are arguing that they need to work consciously on creating a nasty reputation in their own best interest and even in the best interests of the criminal justice system. They are utilizing the paradox of face to work for them. When this dynamic is present, limiting the police use of **excessive force**—even attempting to make the police circumspect about it—can be quite a difficult challenge.

Second, as has been found to be the case with criminals, the police can sometimes rationalize corruption of authority and/or police crime (Sykes and Matza, 1957). Research has found that police officers involved in misconduct for personal gain will offer up several standard rationalizations for it (see Box 9.1). Some officers will suggest that they have a tough job and it is only right that they take full advantage of the opportunities presented to them. Some will argue that they "get no respect" out on the streets, and they should receive money in lieu of the respect they do not receive. Sometimes their argument is, "If I don't take it, somebody else will." Then, too, officers will sometimes deny the status of the victim (Barker and Carter, 1994). If money is taken from a pimp, for example, the argument is that the pimp had no right to the money in the first place. Since the money was ill-gotten, the pimp is denied the status of victim.

Third, there is Dirty Harry–like behavior. Almost everywhere in America, modern policing has moved beyond the time when corruption of authority was rampant. Today, that type of misconduct is a rarity. However, noble cause corruption is quite another matter. Even though the overwhelming majority of police officers in the field today would never become involved in corruption of authority, many *will* involve themselves in noble cause corruption. This is because Harry is perceived to be "getting the job done."

But even though the number of officers who will become involved in noble cause corruption is limited, many officers will support Harry-type corruption indirectly by refusing to cooperate in its pursuit by police accountability systems. Large numbers of officers who would never become involved in noble cause corruption themselves will look the other way when Dirty Harry is active. Even in today's professional era, many officers who will cooperate with investigations into corruption of authority will *not* do so with investigations into noble cause corruption.

The rationalization here is logical enough. When an officer is investigated for **framing** a case around a bad guy, there are several potential outcomes for that investigation. If the erring officer is found to be not guilty of misconduct, the bad guy stays behind bars and the police officer continues working. If the officer is found guilty of framing a suspect (by testilying, as an example), the police officer goes behind bars and the bad guy goes free. Many modern, professional officers will simply not become involved in an investigative process that involves noble cause corruption.

Fourth, another axiom in the subculture has to do with those occasions when officers make mistakes. Police officers often agree that they should "never explain yourself, never apologize" to citizens. In what is clearly a macho type of subculture, many officers believe that to do either is to show weakness and refuse either to explain or apologize, no matter what the circumstances.

BOX 9.1

POLICE TECHNIQUES OF NEUTRALIZING DEVIANCE

Neutralization techniques, first defined by David Matza and Gresham Sykes while studying juvenile delinquency in the 1950s, are a mechanism people employ when they break the law. The theory states that offenders "drift" between illegitimate and legitimate lifestyles, and retain their personal moral code, by utilizing specific techniques.

Sykes and Matza's Neutralization Techniques	Verbalization	Techniques in the Police Context
* Denial of Responsibility	"They made me do it."	Police use of excessive force in arresting a citizen who challenges police authority.
* Denial of Injury	"No innocent got hurt."	Police use of perjury to justify an illegal search.
* Denial of Victim	"They deserved it."	Failure of police to uncover drugs during an illegal search of a "known" drug dealer is rationalized because he didn't have drugs "this" time.
* Condemning the condemners	"They don't know anything."	Police rejection of legal and department control and sanction of deviant behavior.
* Appeal to higher loyalties	"Protect your own."	Police perjury to protect another officer, destruction of evidence, using punishment for personal justice.

Source: G. M. Sykes and D. Matza (1957), "Techniques of Neutralization," *American Sociological Review,* 22, 664–670.

This is a troublesome reality for several reasons. To begin with, explanations tend to develop empathy and support. In any arena in life, a thoughtful explanation can bring people into agreement. When the police explain their actions, there is reason to believe they will receive more support in general. Also, as has been known in the world of medicine for some time, when doctors and nurses take the time to apologize for a mistake, they inhibit the propensity for patients to sue them for malpractice. This is not an intuitive feeling, but fact based on a steadily growing body of research (Wojcieszac, et al., 2007). Therefore, this subcultural "wisdom" actually works directly against the best interests of the police themselves. When they refuse to explain or apologize, officers exacerbate the propensity of citizens to file complaints and feel enmity toward the police.

Fifth, there is a general principle that goes back to police roots during an earlier, more unprofessional era of policing. The police in general have always tended to cleave to a **blue code of silence** (we will discuss this code more later in the chapter). Noted by dozens of observers and scholars over time, there is a propensity in police work to protect brother and sister officers from investigation by remaining silent when allegations of misconduct surface (Perez, 1994). While the heretofore rock-solid operations of this so-called code have been slowly exiting the subculture over the course of the past several decades, the blue code still lives on in some places. Especially with respect to noble cause corruption, the blue code can still protect officers guilty of misconduct.

There is an unfortunate side issue concerning police unions. Regrettably, the history of the response of police unions to attempts to hold officers accountable for misconduct is universally unsupportive, no matter what type of egregious behavior is alleged. This type of explicit support for police misconduct can only work to encourage those few genuine miscreants who make it through the selection gambit and into uniform. Furthermore, as noted elsewhere in our discussions, until and unless this changes over time—led by police leaders at all levels—police professionalism will be slow in coming. This should not be read as "union bashing." The argument here merely points out that modern police leaders—*including union leaders*—can have an incredibly important, positive impact on the future of the profession.

American Culture

There are also American cultural realities that can negatively impact the propensity for police to misbehave. In several ways, American culture works to create and rationalize police misconduct. The first way has to do with the police use of force. The police, of course, are licensed to use force. Furthermore, they *must* do so as a part of their responsibility to control crime on the street. They must use enough force to overcome the illegal use of force.

What is perhaps not so clear is that this guarantees the American police will be the most violent police anywhere in the industrialized world. This is neither an anti-police assertion nor an anti-American assertion. American society is the most violent, weapons-toting society in the industrialized world (Harries, 1997). To overcome this level of violence, American police must necessarily be the most violent police in the developed world. However, when the police use any force, there is always the perception on the part of some citizens that they are guilty of misconduct. There are large numbers of force complaints lodged against the American police on a regular basis. The more often force is used, the more often it will be perceived that misconduct has occurred.

A second cultural reality has to do with the level of crime in general, economic stratification, and hopelessness in today's society. The crime rate in the United States is slightly higher than in other industrialized nation, the homicide rate is higher than that of any industrialized nation (save several former states of the Soviet Union), and the rate of incarceration in America is *far* greater than anywhere else in the world. Economic stratification in the United States—the gap between the rich and the poor—also is greater than anywhere else in the developed, industrialized world (Judd, 1994). This not only produces more stress between the economic classes in the United States, but consequently more crime. Of course, the police work out on the street amid the strain and frustration that such realities produce and, again, the consequent crime. When they confront these inequities, the police in America will often be accused of repressing the underclass in favor of society's elites. They will, through absolutely no fault of their own, be accused of this more often than the police will be in more equitable societies. If police leaders in America are to understand and even improve police work, they must engage such facts with an open mind.

Finally, there is a political reality at work here. In America, in the long run, the "people get the policing that they want." We live in a democratic society and, over time, what the police do will mirror what people want them to do. If a great deal of support exists for noble cause corruption—which we know, in fact, it does—then the police are being motivated to misbehave in some sense. Since this motivation is often mirrored within the subculture, there is an amplification of problematic dynamics going on here. Both the police and the populace tend to be supportive of certain types of misconduct, especially those associated with noble cause corruption.

BOX 9.2

PEOPLE LOVE DIRTY HARRY

A police officer finds that an elderly man's home has been burglarized by a local ne'er-do-well who became an assailant when the old man came home to find the burglar there. The burglar pushed the 90-year-old man down a set of stairs and almost killed him. At the very moment when the police officer and the old man's neighbors were hearing the story, the assailant happened to come walking around the corner. The police officer lost his temper and pummeled the assailant in front of about a dozen citizens— and the citizens *applauded* the officer's actions. (This is a true story.)

The point here is that when citizens support Dirty Harry–like behavior in such a graphic and overt way, it is next to impossible to dissuade police officers from becoming involved in this sort of "noble cause."

These are some **subcultural rationalizations** for police misconduct and some dynamics operative in the dominant American culture that work to create misconduct and/or rationalize it after the fact. These dynamics, in turn, inhibit police accountability. But we have not even begun to consider the legal limitations to the accountability process, and it is toward this discussion that we now turn.

Due Process

Police leaders are familiar with the fact that there are both criminal investigations into police misconduct and **administrative investigations** (Perez, 1994). Criminal investigations about police officer misconduct are legally the same as those investigations for which citizens can be the focus. In the end, the potential sanctions are fines, imprisonment, or even death. Because this is so, the procedural rights afforded to police officers who are being investigated criminally are exactly the same as those afforded to accused citizens (Aitchison, 2004). But the police are almost never investigated criminally. The overwhelming majority of misconduct investigations are administrative in nature, not criminal.

For administrative investigations, the rules are different. When they are the subject of administrative investigations, police officers have some procedural rights, but those rights are limited. As one appeals court put it when handing down a ruling about an officer's rights, no one has "a constitutionally guaranteed right to be a police officer." Of particular importance is the fact that an accused police officer has no right against self-incrimination. Police officers under investigation must make truthful statements to investigators. It might appear that because of this particular procedural rule, police officers are at a distinctive disadvantage when being investigated administratively. As we shall see in a moment, this is not necessarily the case.

Law Enforcement Officers' Bill of Rights (LEOBR)

Beginning several decades ago, a movement to "protect" police officers who are under investigation for misconduct began to crystallize. The idea eventuated in the passage of what are now called **Law Enforcement Officers' Bills of Rights**, state level legislative acts that allow police officers far more procedural safeguards than they were previously allowed under existing case law (Aitchison, 2004). Today, more than 22 states have enacted such legislation and there is even a movement to enact a nationwide federal bill.

Some LEOBRs contain provisions that allow police officers to be represented when they are interrogated. Others contain limitations on the length of interrogations. Some disallow the use of the polygraph, and some limit the time of day when interrogations may occur (such as "during the officer's normal waking hours"). Some LEOBRs state that an officer under investigation must be advised of the nature of the investigation before interrogation, and others attempt to limit the ability of citizens to complain. Several allow that police officers under investigation have the right to be informed of the identities of all witnesses against them.

Citizens who know this might fear officer retaliation and decline to complain. Several LEOBRs even require complaining citizens to notarize their statements. These two provisions effectively chill the right of citizens to "petition their government for redress of grievances." Finally, in several states, LEOBRs will not allow investigations into anonymous complaints. Taken together, LEOBRs substantially limit the ability of investigations to find police officers guilty of misconduct (Perez, 1994).

Local Contracts

Collective bargaining agreements between police unions and their municipalities have always included provisions about a host of issues relating to working conditions. In recent years, such agreements have also begun to include provisions relating to how members of the local police union must be treated when they are investigated for misconduct. As an example, in some locations officers have the right to be represented by counsel and that counsel is even paid by the municipality doing the investigating. Such collective agreements provide still another layer of procedural safeguards for accused officers. So, there are normal, court-allowed due process safeguards afforded to accused officers, additional safeguards created within LEOBRs, and still more safeguards instituted by collective bargaining agreements.

Civil Service Review

Regulations vary from municipality to municipality, of course, but it is almost universally true that when an officer is given any substantial punishment for misconduct, the local civil service commission has the responsibility to review the case. The rationalization here is simple: because it is civil service that officially hires police officers, civil service must also officially fire them. Of course, civil service was invented in order to ensure that those who work for the state are hired, fired, managed, and disciplined in a fair and nonpolitical manner. This is its function.

REVIEW CHART 9.3

OVERLAPPING LAYERS OF PROTECTION

Police officers who are accused of misconduct can be shielded from being found guilty, even if they *are* factually guilty, by:

- Due process rights afforded them by case law decisions
- Rights afforded them by Law Enforcement Officers' Bills of Rights
- Rights afforded them by local collective bargaining agreements
- Civil service review

Such a **civil service review** process may seem to be just a formality; one might think that civil service commissions would tend to rubberstamp decisions made by police administrators. Often, this is not the case. Driven by the desire to be tough on crime and to support their local police officers, civil service commissions regularly restore fired police officers to their positions or reduce the severity of punishments handed out by the chief (Perez, 1994). This is certainly disconcerting to chiefs of police, and it provides still *another* layer of protection—of procedural rights—for accused police officers.

Taken together, all of these safeguards place severe limitations on the ability of any review system to find the police guilty of misconduct, no matter what the circumstances. The contemporary police leader must be pragmatic about these limitations. Knowing that they exist and that they construct a veritable minefield through which any review system must pass, the leader must be doubly motivated to understand any effective behavior modification is likely to fall upon his or her shoulders, instead of being the responsibility of official review mechanisms.

THE USE OF FORCE: A PARTICULAR CASE

Among all the other issues that make up the penumbra of police accountability debates, the use of force is paramount. It is the most critical issue to most citizens. It is the most critical issue to activists in favor of civilian review. It is perhaps the most important issue to police officers and leaders. So important is this one issue that it behooves us to take a moment to consider several crucial realities about the use of force that do not apply to other issues in this arena.

Excessive Force: Multiple Causes

Excessive force is the area of police misconduct that most elicits a visceral reaction on the part of American citizens (Nelson, 2001). Excessive force is troublesome due to its multiple roots. First, some excessive force is caused by bigotry on the part of the police. This form of misconduct is labeled as ineptitude in our typology from the last chapter. Fewer modern police officers make it through the selection gauntlet and into uniform possessing pronounced levels of racial bigotry or homophobia. But it is an unfortunate reality that there are still police officers who seek to "punish" certain groups. This is one cause of the use of excessive force.

Second, some excessive force is produced as an offshoot of corruption of authority. That is, excessive force is utilized by corrupt officers to maintain control over their nefarious enterprises. In order to corral "their" pimps or maintain control over "their" drug dealers, some corrupt officers utilize the power of brute force. Equally, they sometimes use force to protect their comrades in crime by visiting it upon competitors on the street. This is "just business," and it involves protecting stores or markets with violence.

Finally, some excessive force is Dirty Harry–related. This can occur when officers wish to obtain information from suspects or when officers want to punish "bad" citizens directly, on the street. Under such circumstances, sometimes even modern police can become involved in issuing curbside justice driven by the rationalization that the system will not do it. Concern about excessive force often underwrites calls for civilian review and, in turn, creates a gap between police and civilian expectations for police review systems.

Lack of Definition

Police leaders must wrestle with a central reality about excessive force that is virtually inexplicable to anyone else. The problem (outlined briefly in Box 9.3) is that there is no definitive understanding of what "excessive" entails. Is it excessive to use mace on a suspect who is ranting and raving? Is it excessive to use a nightstick on someone who is wielding a knife? Is it excessive to draw a firearm on someone who is brandishing a shovel as a weapon? The odd thing about excessive force is that people—even police officers—have no consensus about what it means. People know when they are outraged by it, but they do not know how to define what excessive force is in any *specific* way. Without specificity, any rule, law, or regulation lacks moral authority.

Here is an example of this dynamic. When people saw the Rodney King videotape many years ago, many reacted by saying (as surveys at that time noted) that the officers' conduct was outrageous and excessive. Excessive force was something of which it was accurate to say they "knew it when they saw it." On the other

BOX 9.3

KLOCKARS'S IDEAS ABOUT FORCE POLICIES

In a famous article published in 1992, Carl Klockars made a point that has now become widely understood within American police circles. In that article, Klockars pointed out that the biggest problem with controlling the use of excessive force is that there is no definitive understanding of what it is; what "excessive" means goes largely undefined. Thus, the only thing that can be done in attempting to control the use of force by the police is to pontificate about how they should be circumspect about their application of force. Since existing "force escalation" policies allow even a passive confrontation on the street to be elevated into a lethal situation, they effectively do nothing to limit the use of force in a substantive sense. Klockars pointed out that nothing definitive can be accomplished until a specific policy is developed that differentiates acceptable and unacceptable levels of force in everyday police–citizen encounters.

hand, millions of other people attempting to be pro-police at the time suggested they were "not sure" about whether they had seen something excessive or not. What constitutes excessive force is, truly, in the eye of the beholder.

Escalation-of-Force Policies

What the above example suggests is that some sort of policy needs to be put into place that differentiates levels of force in particular ways. This has been attempted in most police departments over the years. **Escalation-of-force** policies attempt to define what level of force is appropriate when the police face hand-to-hand combat, when they face a knife, when they face a firearm, and so forth.

But, as Klockars pointed out, even this does not help much. He noted that under policies that allow the use of force to escalate, an officer might pull over motorists for a simple speeding violation and end up using lethal force upon them. Nothing in most escalation-of-force policies makes a bottom-line, definitive rule about what types of details require what types of use of force *in the end*. That is because the scale moves. There is no hard and fast rule that says, "It is the responsibility of police officers to make sure that when they have made a simple vehicular stop for an infraction they do not, under any circumstances, end up using lethal force." Since no such rule (or set of rules) exists, escalation-of-force policies are rather hollow and worthless attempts to define the use of force. They are of no more substantive utility than asking officers generally to be circumspect about their force decisions.

After setting the groundwork here, it is time to move to an analysis of comparative police review systems. We will begin this discussion with a quick review of the type of police department–operated systems best labeled "non-judicialized." These are the several forms that police accountability can take when it is being kept out of the limelight, out of the public glare, and is not moving in the direction of anything that might be reviewed in a court of law.

NON-JUDICIALIZED ACCOUNTABILITY MECHANISMS

Before we discuss systems that make all the headlines—to compare the operations of internal affairs with those of civilian review boards—it is important to consider the **non-judicialized accountability mechanisms** that operate on a regular basis. This is for two distinct reasons. First, this is where and how most police misconduct is handled. It is done informally and throughout the police officer's individual professional experience, from academy through to retirement. Second, it is within this process, or set of processes, that the overwhelming majority of police leaders have their most obvious and ongoing chance to make a difference in the world of police accountability. Only a small percentage of police leaders have much to do with the police review systems we will next evaluate—internal affairs in particular. But every modern police leader has a great deal to do with the more informal systems toward which we now turn our considerations.

BOX 9.4

THE CREATIVE LEADER

Some years ago in a medium-sized sheriff's department, a rather wild "cop party" occurred involving numerous young deputies in "questionable" conduct. The behavior was not violent nor was it made public. But it was undoubtedly the sort of misconduct that could embarrass the department if it were to reoccur. Upon hearing rumors about the outlandish behavior involved, a thoughtful watch commander decided to respond in an informal manner. He quietly called in several of the young officers involved and, one by one, gave them a dressing down.

The commander (who would eventually rise to become sheriff) told each of the young men that, while he understood being young and energetic, he nevertheless also knew they could do permanent damage to their careers if they persisted in this type of behavior. By simply acting as an older, fatherly figure, he made a deep impression upon the young officers, and they never again were involved in such shenanigans.

This type of creative leadership contrasts with how many leaders might approach such rumors, with officiousness and the machinations of internal affairs. Had that type of officiousness been visited upon the young officers, they might very well have reacted with diffidence and self-righteous indignation, buoyed up by the fact that the misconduct did not ever embarrass the department or become public.

The Academy

Historically, the police experience has not included much in the way of accountability for cadets. Until very recently, an extremely high percentage of cadets made it through academy training. Today, this has changed. In some places, for example, 10 to 15 percent of the academy class fails to graduate. There can even be a higher rate of dropout, such as the 20 percent reported in New York in 2008 (*New York Post*, March 24, 2008). The relevance here, of course, is that the process of holding officers accountable to behavioral standards deemed appropriate by police leaders begins early on.

Of course, officer shortcomings are not the only reason for academy dropout rates. Some officers drop out because they discover some of the realities of police work and decide they are not a good fit. Also, in the past several years, due to the disastrous state of the economy, beginning police salaries have dropped in many locations. This has undoubtedly had an impact on retention problems. But the failure of recruits to make it through due to their own inadequacies was dropping steadily before that time frame.

It would be nice to think that increasing academy requirements and scrutiny might help in the ongoing professionalization of police work. But the reality is that, due to the startup costs of hiring cadets, there is likely to be less pressure exerted by academies to increase their selectivity in the near future. Perhaps when fiscal realities even out and things calm down in terms of the American economy, the drive to make the academy experience a genuine "weeding out" process can expand. For now, this is not a likely development.

The FTO

After the academy comes field training, accomplished with an **FTO** at the rookie officer's side. There are several standard formats for the FTO process, the San Jose model and the Reno model being the most prevalent (Roberg, Novak, and Cordner, 2005). The debate between them is rather esoteric and matters little to us here. What does matter is that the FTO ideal has grown into being a part of standard operational procedure in a vast majority of today's departments.

Several problems plague FTO programs. One is that experienced officers are given little financial incentive to participate. Furthermore, given the amount of time and paperwork involved, the average experience possessed by FTOs today has dropped to less than two years of seniority (Langworthy, Hughes, and Sanders, 1995). This is hardly the ideal level of experience to create a substantively effective program. Furthermore, as is true with police academies, the idea that the FTO process will be a genuinely difficult hoop through which rookies must jump is suffering from fiscal problems in contemporary America. It is hard to be choosy with rookies and "hold their feet to the fire" when municipalities must eschew being too selective because they have retention problems. So money, or a lack thereof, is driving several deleterious dynamics in contemporary American policing.

The modern leader needs to take the FTO process seriously, as it has been proven to be an effective tool in the overall professionalization process. Motivating experienced officers to participate is critical. Upper level leaders can be creative (utilizing choice assignments, vacation times, and so forth) to attempt such motivation. The "best and the brightest" veteran officers should be involved in the process. That has always been the idea. Immediate supervisors need to include FTO motivation in mentoring targets on the job. But having the FTO program be genuinely selective is troublesome, as the type of decision necessary to put such a policy in place is made at very high levels and even outside of police departments where city or county budgets are produced.

Field Supervisors

Police field supervisors (almost always sergeants) have their responsibilities with accountability as well. In fact, some would say that *the* critical person in any police accountability mechanism is the sergeant. We will spend a great deal of time later in our discussions focusing on the sergeant, and we have already suggested that the roles of coach and teacher are apposite to the position. In the last chapter, we pointed out that sergeants have a critical role to play in the creation of personal ethics for individual officers.

Today's sergeant can have a tremendous impact on police accountability in a positive direction. Discouraging the acceptance and continuation of some subcultural norms previously discussed is an obvious role for the contemporary sergeant. Teaching that it is acceptable to explain and apologize is important. Motivating officers to eschew the overkill idea is critical. Above all, generally nudging the subculture in the direction of achieving any and all of the elements of professionalism is a key ingredient in the sergeant's role today.

Police Department Review Boards

Some jurisdictions have their own in-house police officer review boards. Most of these boards are utilized for shooting-related incidents only. They involve using the expertise of experienced professionals to analyze incidents, make recommendations for training, and—sometimes—sanction errant officers. They operate independently of internal affairs in most places and, while their makeup is different from IA, they provide an overlapping layer of accountability.

Some police boards do include one important element worthy of consideration. Instead of having an adversarial approach to the consideration of accusations of impropriety, as is the case in IA, shooting review boards often take a more collegial approach. Led by experienced professionals, such as training division teachers and firearms instructors, the shooting review board is often a fact-finding, problem solving group, more interested in analysis and change than retribution and blame. As such, it provides an excellent future model for all police accountability mechanisms, including IA.

BOX 9.5

SOME BASICS ABOUT COMPSTAT

- *Assembling raw data:* Oversight, auditing, and inspection to ensure the accuracy of data
- *Data manipulation:* Compilation, tabulation, and analysis
- *Identification:* Strengths and weaknesses, competencies, skills, and routines
- *Strategizing:* Planning, reorganization, problem solving
- *Macro-analysis:* Promoting experimentation and innovation; setting and communicating goals

CompStat

Those who lead but are not out in the field (middle managers) are driven today in still another direction to be accountable. As noted earlier in our discussion, the invention of **CompStat** at the New York City Police Department some years ago was an attempt at developing day-by-day accountability for police leaders themselves. For those not familiar with it, CompStat is a computer-based system that generates timely data about crime in a quick and almost immediately analyzable way. Crime trends are plotted electronically, and middle managers are held responsible for the development of strategies on a weekly or biweekly basis. CompStat is highly technical, and it has its pluses. In particular, it has the attraction of being modern, computer driven, and state of the art.

But CompStat also has its detractors. When it was first instituted at the NYPD, it appeared to cause a profound drop in crime statistics. Changing its age-old philosophy from the watchman style to the legalistic style, the NYPD at the time utilized a very proactive and aggressive style of policing that dramatically increased the numbers of citations, misdemeanor arrests, and felony arrests. As the institutionalization of CompStat was reported to the police world, many accepted the idea that it had "caused" the parallel drop in crime.

Of course, there was something wrong with this analysis. Crime was dropping steeply everywhere in America, including where CompStat had not been instituted. Both violent crime and property crime were in decline. In several cities, most famously in San Diego, the institutionalization of COP was in progress and crime statistics looked even better (Roberg, Novak, and Cordner, 2005). The controversy over the effectiveness of CompStat—a debate that is still in progress today—was born. Suffice it to say, CompStat is probably here to stay. It represents still another part of the ever-complicated pattern that makes up the puzzle of police accountability today.

Now, as we move toward several types of police review systems that operate in America today, we must take a moment to consider exactly how a realistic and utilitarian comparison would be made. Given the highly complex and politicized nature of what review systems do, it is a complicated endeavor to attempt to set the various models side by side and make meaningful comparisons. How we might do so is the subject of the next section.

COMPARING ACCOUNTABILITY SYSTEMS

It is a very complicated process to compare police review systems. Nothing about it is straightforward. There are multiple issues involved: the judicial fairness of the process, the thoroughness of investigations, the objectivity of decision making, the political "sellability" of the system, and so forth. There are multiple personal interests involved. There are the rights and liberties of the complaining citizen, the accused officer, and witness citizens and officers. There are other, more widely defined sets of interests involved. There is the citizenry of the state and the people in general, the specific population of the jurisdiction in question, and the body of police officers of the local department. Finally, making a fair and objective analysis is troubled by perceptions—sometimes based in truth and sometimes based on prejudice and mythology—of individuals and collectivities in and out of the process. In analyzing the several types of systems that exist, the following set of criteria have been created (Perez, 1994; Walker, 2001).

Integrity

To begin with, any review system has to be evaluated as if it were a miniature criminal justice system (as noted above). It has a process for receiving complaints, and that process must be evaluated with respect to whether it is open and encourages genuine, honest petitions. It cannot be too complicated, inaccessible, or intimidating. It cannot "chill" the right of American citizens to petition their government for redress of grievances.

It must conduct investigations. Those investigations must be conducted in an objective, fair, and thorough manner. They cannot be accomplished with any preconceived ideas about the guilt or innocence of accused officers. The system cannot favor either complainant or officer. It must leave no stone unturned in its efforts to obtain the truth about what happened.

It must make decisions with regard to guilt or innocence that are (as with the investigations) objective, fair, and impartial. Whether conducted by police officers in an internal affairs section or by civilians on a civilian review board, the decisions must be judicially correct and observe procedural law and safeguards. Taken together, these are the issues investigated when considering what is called the **integrity** of the system.

Legitimacy

An issue of critical importance to anyone who wishes to compare police review systems is how people outside of the system perceive it to be working. No matter what the substantive reality of the system's integrity, people (especially in the community that is being policed) and the general police officer corps of the municipality must *believe* the system to have integrity. If they believe the system lacks integrity, that it favors the police or the citizen, then the system has problems. We call this criterion **legitimacy**, but it is, in fact, "perceived legitimacy" that is involved here.

Learning

Completely separate from our first two criteria is a concern that speaks to the third of our review system functions listed above, that of teaching errant officers to "mend their ways" and behave appropriately when guilty of minor misconduct. When officers are found culpable for transgressions, but they are not involved in misconduct for which termination is relevant, the system must operate to change behavior. Given the fact that almost all confirmed misconduct falls into this category, **learning** is perhaps the most important function of the overall accountability system.

BOX 9.6

THE (SLOW) DEATH OF THE BLUE CODE OF SILENCE

For generations, American police officers—both individually and collectively, as the subculture taken together—were known to cover for each other when any member of the group was accused of misconduct. Even after the invention of the idea of police accountability during the early years of reform, the police in America were known to live by the blue code of silence (Perez, 1994). This informal code suggested that no member of the police officer corps should ever cooperate with investigations into the misconduct of others.

This code, universally acknowledged, accepted, and observed for generations, has slowly fallen by the wayside in most places. Today, investigators into police corruption of authority find a substantial amount of support from the officer corps. When doing research into police review, one of the authors found any number of examples of police officers who had been fired from their positions on the strength of investigations into misconduct (the use of excessive force in particular) *that had been initiated by other officers*, not citizens.

Cost

Even though we would like to ignore the fiscal realities of administrative life, that type of thinking has brought America to the brink of a fiscal meltdown in recent years. Especially in the public sphere, where an inability to balance income with expenditures has visited disaster upon everything from schools to infrastructures to police departments, we must consider how much review costs. Despite all of its potential, civilian review is extraordinarily expensive to operate.

We shall now turn to several systems utilized in contemporary America that review the behavior of police officers when they are accused of misusing their power and/or being incompetent.

COMPARATIVE POLICE REVIEW SYSTEMS

Since the Wickersham Commission of the early 1930s (Wickersham, 1931), the idea of having someone other than the police themselves review allegations of police misconduct has been a central theme among those who call for more effective police accountability. First attempted in just a few places, and not with much staying power, civilian review boards have now been put into place in a substantial number of locations across America.

REVIEW CHART 9.4

CRITERIA OF EVALUATION FOR POLICE REVIEW SYSTEMS

- *Integrity:* Openness, objectivity, and fairness of systemic processes
- *Legitimacy:* Externally held perceptions of systemic integrity
- *Learning:* Propensity for errant police officers to change their behavior in a positive direction
- *Cost:* Fiscal impact of review upon local budgets

Of course, the overwhelming majority of allegations of police misconduct occur—and are dealt with—within the police organization itself (as noted above). These are allegations of ineptitude, and they are invariably handled by police leaders at the immediate supervisorial level (as they should be). But other allegations of police misconduct come from citizens. The study of police review systems is about analyzing who should deal with such citizens' complaints and how they should go about it (Walker, 2005).

There are three main types of review systems that accept, investigate, adjudicate, and impose appropriate sanctions regarding citizen allegations of misconduct. There are internal, police-operated review mechanisms, and there are civilian review boards. There are also **hybrid systems** that include elements of both the police and civilian-operated systems. Let us consider them each briefly here.

Internal Affairs

Internal affairs (IA) is a generic term that refers to all review systems operated by sworn police personnel within the police organization itself. The law requires that police departments have such a system in place for the acceptance and investigation of citizens' complaints. But most police organizations receive so few complaints of police misconduct that their case load of complaints is very small. Thus, most police organizations investigate citizen allegations of misconduct on an ad hoc basis. Such investigations are usually assigned by the chief of police to a trusted middle manager, usually a lieutenant. In only a few very large departments are there enough complaints to warrant having a separate body called IA.

IA processes are completely in-house. Allegations are accepted at police headquarters, initial statements are given to police investigators, investigations are done completely by the police, outcomes are decided by IA personnel (in consultation with the chief in most places), and sanctions are handed out by the chief of police when officers are found guilty. Everything is done by sworn police officers. These investigations are considered to be internal affairs in every sense of the words. They are done in secret and the results are kept from the public, even the complaining citizens (Perez, 1994).

There are several central rationalizations behind allowing the police to handle investigations into the conduct of their own people. First, it is assumed by most people in police work that because of their investigative expertise, police investigators will do the most thorough and effective job possible of investigating. Second, it is assumed that police investigators and leaders are driven by concerns of maintaining the "cleanest" organization possible. Not only with regard to individual cases, but with respect to keeping the image of the police department clean and professional, the idea is that the police are the best people to conduct such inquiries. Police investigators will consider themselves to be the guardians of the police department and police professionalism.

Third, it is assumed that no one from outside a police organization will be familiar enough with the multiple standards of conduct to which the police must be held. Only police officers will know the combination of the law, general police practices, and the specific regulations included in departmental general orders well enough to hold other police officers accountable. Fourth, it is argued that no one outside of a given police department will understand enough about the specific operational realties of how beats, high crime areas, and personnel issues are handled within that department.

A fifth reason in favor of internal review is that the chief of police must be given authority over such investigations and resulting discipline. Unless this is the case, it is not fair to hold the chief accountable for specific investigations or the operations of the department in general. Here again, we see the principle that "authority must parallel responsibility." Those who believe this type of review is best hold to a logical axiom: if the chief of police cannot be trusted with such investigations and with meting out discipline in a fair and appropriate manner, then the chief should be replaced. For this is, in essence, what a chief of police is hired to do.

Civilian Review Boards

Initially just an idea that was considered by those who distrusted the police, the concept of civilian review has grown pronouncedly in the past few years (Walker, 2001). Today, there are approximately 70 civilian bodies operating in America that share at least part of the responsibility for investigating citizen complaints against the police. While some of these organizations are, in fact, "hybrid" systems (see the next section), it is important to note that the expansion of civilian review is evolving quickly. As the name implies, **civilian review boards** are populated by non-police individuals who accept, investigate, and adjudicate citizens' complaints.

There are a number of logical reasons for civilian review boards. They offer the complaining citizen an alternate, civilian-run location for making their initial complaint. This is done because it is assumed that some citizens are intimidated by being required to go to police headquarters in order to file a complaint. So, one argument in favor of civilian review is that it is more accessible to the public. A second reason for civilian review is that its investigations are conducted by civilian, non-police personnel. It is assumed by proponents of this type of review that civilian investigators will bring more objectivity to the process. They will not conduct investigations with conscious or subconscious police subcultural bias at work.

A third rationalization for civilianizing police review has to do with the general openness of the process. Not only are investigative files made available to the public in most places, but public hearings are often conducted, bringing the issues involved out in the open. These are semi-judicialized hearings that include participants from both sides of the investigation, including the complainant, the police officer, and the police department.

The process of civilian review is done in the open and by non-police personnel, from beginning to end. One final twist to the process is that, in most jurisdictions,

BOX 9.7

POLICE EXPERTISE

A citizen walks into IA and wants to make a complaint. The woman says she was stopped for creeping through a red light and "about four police cars and eight officers showed up." She says this was unnecessary and intimidating. This is her complaint.

The IA investigator asks where and when the event occurred. She tells him. He immediately knows what happened and explains to her that the traffic stop occurred at the very end of a police shift—the swing shift—and near the police station. There were so many extra officers at the vehicle stop because they were all about to go off duty, and they simply stopped by to cover the traffic stop. The woman accepts the explanation. The IA investigator suggests that he talk with the supervisor of the shift in question and ask the supervisor to relate the incident to line officers and tell them to avoid such behavior in the future. The woman is satisfied. A complaint is avoided. The taxpayers are saved some money.

This is an example of one of the strengths of internal review. There is good reason to believe that such an immediate understanding of what had happened would not be made by a civilian investigator who did not work for the police department.

the chief of police is still the final determiner of what constitutes appropriate discipline for officers found guilty of misconduct. This is because of the logic just discussed above; the chief's job includes meting out discipline, and if the chief cannot be trusted with this power, then he or she should be replaced.

Hybrid Systems

There are important strengths to each of these processes, but each also has its drawbacks. In some jurisdictions, "hybrid" systems have developed that attempt to take advantage of the strengths of both internal affairs and civilian review boards, without sacrificing the integrity of the process. These hybrid systems are different in almost every location. The form differs, but the idea remains—to divide up the processes involved in police review and take advantage of the strengths of internal and external review.

One such system operates as the Office of Citizens' Complaints (OCC) in Kansas City, Missouri, and it is this system that we will discuss briefly (Perez, 1994). The OCC operates to allow citizens to make complaints either at a police station (any police station—there are several in Kansas City) or at the OCC office. Civilians interview complainants, outline allegations, and initiate complaint cases. The complaints are then handed over to the police department's IA for investigation. The OCC monitors these investigations. OCC civilians can suggest investigative strategies at the outset, and they can send back investigations when IA investigators complete them and the auditors at OCC are not satisfied. Complaint investigations that have been finalized are open to the scrutiny of the public—unlike IA systems, the OCC's investigations are available for the perusal of all people outside the police department.

Police officer guilt or innocence is determined by the director of the OCC. Reviewing complaints initially outlined by civilian personnel and investigated by police personnel, the director makes the initial decision about outcomes. The director then advises the chief of police about this decision. On those rare occasions when the director and the chief do not agree, they get together, review the investigation, and come to a mutual agreement. Thus, the OCC system is partly civilianized and partly operated by the police.

Analysis

Before we compare these systems to each other directly, it is important to note several research findings relating to police review systems. By comparing systems operating in parallel, it turns out that IA tends to find police officers guilty of misconduct slightly *more* often than civilian review. As counterintuitive as this may be, such findings have been reported in several jurisdictions. It has also been found that a large majority of police officers who work in jurisdictions that do not have civilian review are against the idea, driven by prejudgments about how unfair civilian review would be to officers. However, when officers who work in jurisdictions that *do* have civilian review are surveyed, they believe it to be a good idea—and by a large margin. It appears that real-life experience with civilian review in operation does not move police officers to reject its operations. With these counterintuitive findings in mind, let us turn to make a direct comparison of these systems.

There are several major strengths of the IA system. First, professional, experienced police investigators conduct the inquiries. They are conversant with the law, how police are trained, and the pragmatic operations of the local department, including beat differentiation, shift assignments, crime patterns, and so forth. So the systems have integrity. Second, today's internal police investigators tend to take their responsibility very seriously; they see themselves as the guardians of the police image and police professionalism. Rank-and-file officers take internal review seriously, too, because it represents review by their peers. Internal systems thus possess legitimacy in the eyes of the police. Investigated officers tend to learn from their mistakes if they are found to be at fault by other police officers. Third, the system allows the supervisorial staff complete authority over the process and thus it can be held accountable. The weaknesses of IA review are: it operates completely in secret, it suffers from the external perception that it is unfair to citizens, and it may conduct investigations with an inappropriate deference to subcultural values.

There are also strengths of the civilian review system. First, it is much more open to the public than internal review, operating to accept all complaints and uphold the right of citizens to complain. So, civilian systems also possess good integrity. Second, its investigatory findings are open to the public. Third, the decision making phase includes open hearings, which give not only complaining parties but the public in general an opportunity to witness the process. Both of these dynamics suggest that the civilian system possesses legitimacy in the minds of the citizenry. The weaknesses of civilian review are: sometimes its investigators are not conversant with police practices and local police operations; police officers tend to ignore its dictates, considering them to be irrelevant to their profession; and it is expensive.

The reason that civilian review is expensive is that it usually operates in parallel with internal systems in a genuinely independent way, completely removed from the police departmental apparatus. Because the law requires the police to do their own investigations, there are two systems operational—the internal one and the external one. The taxpaying public must foot the bill for both.

Which system is best? The answer seems to be that the balance between civilian review and internal review presented by the hybrid system is best. It enjoys several of the advantages of the internal system. Investigations are done by police officers. Rank-and-file officers who are sanctioned must respect the fact that experienced police officers have found them to be culpable. It leaves the disciplining to the chief and the chain of command. It possesses integrity. Research indicates that it is accepted and respected by police officers, too, possessing legitimacy among the police (Perez, 1994).

The hybrid system also enjoys several advantages of the civilian system. It is more accessible to receiving complaints at the input stage of the process. It is much more open than the internal system, allowing the public access to its findings.

BOX 9.8

CIVILIAN REVIEW: SOME SURPRISING FINDINGS

The extensive research reported in Perez's 1994 book *Common Sense About Police Review* included several counterintuitive findings with regard to the review of police conduct by civilian boards.

- Civilian review boards are actually slightly *less* prone to find the police guilty of misconduct than are internal affairs systems.

- While police officers who have no experience with civilian review are almost universally against it—feeling that it will be biased and unfair to police officers—those officers who *do* have experience with civilian review are not against it.

- Minority police officers—whether or not they have experience with civilian review—tend to support the idea of civilian review, and by a wide margin.

Source: Perez, 1994.

It is largely run by civilians, with a civilian administrator making final decisions in concert with the chief. Because there are not two systems operating in parallel, the hybrid system is not expensive, costing about as much to run as the IA process. The externally perceived legitimacy—what citizens think about it—of the hybrid system is greater than that of the IA process.

This discussion has attempted to simplify a complicated and politically volatile subject. There has been a wealth of research and debate over the topic for many years now. Suffice it to say, the hybrid system seems to utilize the strengths of each of the other major forms of police review, and it does so in a fiscally responsible way.

Having analyzed in a comparative way the several forms police accountability takes in today's world, we now engage two final paradoxes that circumscribe the role of the police leader where accountability is concerned.

TWO LAST PARADOXES

We have outlined the numerous limitations placed upon police review systems. It behooves us here at the end of the chapter to visit several pronouncedly important paradoxes associated with police accountability that are not legal, but pragmatic and political in nature.

Our first paradox has to do with the appearance of Dirty Harry in IA, as noted in Box 9.9. Calls to make internal accountability mechanisms as serious as possible about ferreting out police misconduct come from all directions, both within and without the police organization. Local politicos and community activists, those supporting internal review and those championing civilian review, citizens in general, police leaders, and even progressive members of the police officer corps all tend to support the idea that IA should be aggressive and unrelenting in its pursuit of misconduct.

What is oddly paradoxical is that on the trail of their "enemy"—the guilty police officer—the IA investigator can turn into an in-house Dirty Harry. Driven by the honest, energetic pursuit of their charge, investigators can be guilty of all the excesses into which Harry falls. In the furtherance of their noble cause, IA investigators can become what Muir calls an "unscrupulous enemy" (Muir, 1977: 250). From one perspective, we might be prone to applaud the IA Harry's exuberance. However, as is true with Harry on the street, the excesses of noble cause corruption can mean that the investigators become a law unto themselves. When that happens, the rule of law is suspended.

In turn, this means that one of the key elements of police leadership in modern America—teaching a profound respect for due process and the rule of law—is inhibited, if not defeated. If IA does not play by the rules, if the administration is not really serious about due process, if the chief is not a genuine champion of justice, and/or if the leadership of the department is not truly committed to the rule of law, then why should the men and women of the police officer corps be so disposed?

So, our first paradox—that of Dirty Harry appearing in IA—can work to create exactly the problem that IA seeks to deter. Police misconduct that comes with its own rationalization, or noble cause, can be encouraged and amplified by the operations of the accountability system itself.

A second paradox has to do with the influence of the almost ubiquitous subculture. An accountability system that works to instill police behavior with realistic, positive, and ethically defensible modes of conduct will not, *cannot*, be effective without obtaining the assent of the subculture in the long run. This is a principle that is analogous to one of the central rationalizations for COP. Among other things, that philosophy suggests that 800,000 police officers cannot deter crime or control its excesses in a country of 310,000,000. It takes a partnership between the citizenry and the police to accomplish that lofty goal.

So it is with police accountability. Police leaders and IA investigators alone cannot accomplish the goal of holding the police accountable to steadily expanding standards of conduct. As time goes on and constitutional law becomes ever more complex, as technology expands the horizons of forensics, and as the social sciences increase our understanding of the human mind and its motivational intricacies, the role of police officer will continue to become increasingly diversified and problematic. If, and only if, the police subculture's rank and file "comes along" with the movement toward professionalization and the institutionalization of COP will these goals ever reach fruition. Since the entire police subculture is populated with people who are experts at interrogation and investigation and also, whenever necessary, obfuscation and deception, it is effectively impossible for genuinely

BOX 9.9

DIRTY HARRY IN IA

As Muir points out, IA can come to be considered an "unscrupulous enemy" by the rank and file of police officers. This is because of the paradoxical reality that in pursuing the charge of cleaning up police work, those who work in IA can fall victim to the same types of dynamics that sometimes create Dirty Harry–like behavior in the average police officer. In an effort to "get the job done," IA investigators can twist reports, coerce witnesses, and generally lose sight of due process limits that are supposed to work to inhibit their job. When they do so, as is true with Harry, they become a law unto themselves and, paradoxically, part of the problem they are supposed to solve.

effective police accountability to develop without the participation of the subculture. So, the paradox is that control over the subculture's norms and values will never be effectively developed without the acquiescence of the subculture itself.

So, at the end of our discussion, we find two critically important paradoxes to add to the patchwork quilt of limitations that make police accountability such a touchy and difficult subject. For the police leader, this might very well be the most paradox-driven, troublesome, complicated, and, yet, potentially creative field of endeavor that he or she will ever engage in uniform.

SUMMATION

The purpose of this chapter has been to outline the debate over police review systems so the contemporary police leader understands the issues on all sides. This is of great importance for several reasons. Perhaps most importantly, the COP movement includes opening police accountability mechanisms up to more and more civilian scrutiny. Because this is true, police leaders and officers need to be understanding and accepting of this development. No amount of wishing it were different will change the future in this regard; police work will become increasingly open to public scrutiny, police policy making will become further politicized, and accountability will become more and more civilianized.

Amid such changes, the complicated role of police leader will change in two ways. It will become more difficult, complex, and replete with paradox, and at the same time it will develop even more opportunities for leader sophistication, responsibility, and creativity.

DISCUSSION QUESTIONS

1. The authors are very much in favor of police unions, as they are of unions in general (it is a historical fact that the union movement in America has kept us away from a genuine class revolution). However, police unions have historically fought against police accountability. Discuss this fact, and whether or not you think that it might be possible for police unions to become a part of the modern professionalization movement by working in favor of holding errant police officers accountable for their actions.

2. The right to have civil service review any major discipline meted out to police officers has often led to fired officers being given their jobs back, no matter how egregious their misconduct. Discuss this significant limitation to police accountability as a dynamic that is parallel to the support the public sometimes shows for Dirty Harry–like behavior.

3. Discuss Klockars's point that there is no generally accepted definition of "excessive force" and, therefore, when we talk about excessive force, we are blowing in the wind. The entire force debate is about nothing to some extent. Do you agree or disagree?

4. One critical question about police accountability is whether mechanisms create learning—behavioral change—among errant police officers. The text argues that internal, police-operated review systems tend to create more of this type of learning than civilian review systems. Why is this? Does this mean that internal affairs is "the only way to go" with regard to police accountability?

5. The text in this chapter includes a box (Box 9.8) that presents research findings which show that civilian review boards do not threaten police officers, they are not unfair to the police, and they even tend to support officers more often than internal systems. Given these findings, shouldn't intelligent, educated police leaders be in favor of civilian review, given that it is perceived by citizens to be more fair and open than internal affairs?

KEY TERMS

Accountability: The acknowledgment and assumption of responsibility for actions, products, decisions, and policies that include the administration, governance, and implementation within the scope of the role or employment position, and encompassing the obligation to report, explain, and be answerable for resulting consequences.

Administrative investigations: The investigation of a police officer or police personnel accused of the violation of the organization's administrative rules, policies, or procedures versus the investigation of the violation of law(s).

Blue code of silence: An unwritten rule among many police officers in the United States not to report on another colleague's errors, misconducts, or crimes.

Civil service review: A review by a body of government officials employed in civil occupations that are neither political nor judicial. In most countries, the term "civil service" refers to employees selected and promoted on the basis of a merit and seniority system, which may include examinations.

Civilian review boards: A municipal body composed of citizen representatives charged with the investigation of complaints by members of the public concerning misconduct by police officers.

CompStat: The name given to the New York City Police Department's accountability process, which has since been replicated in many other American police departments.

Escalation of force: The effect caused during a confrontation with a suspect where the original contact did not seem to indicate a necessity on the part of the officer to use force, but ongoing circumstances dictate that command presence; verbal commands may require hands-on force or use of a nonlethal weapon to control the event.

Excessive force: A law enforcement officer has the right to use such force as is reasonably necessary under the circumstances to make a lawful arrest. An unreasonable seizure occurs when a law enforcement officer uses excessive force in making a lawful arrest. Whether force is reasonably necessary or excessive is measured by the force a reasonable and prudent law enforcement officer would use under the circumstances.

Framing: To trap or set up a person for a crime or violation of rules or policies.

FTO: Field training officer; some agencies use the term "police training officer."

Hybrid system: A police review system that combines some of the elements of both civilian review boards and internal affairs review systems.

Integrity: A concept that has to do with perceived consistency of actions, values, methods, measures, principles, expectations, and outcome.

Internal affairs: A division of a law enforcement agency that investigates cases of lawbreaking by members of that agency.

Law Enforcement Officers' Bill of Rights (LEOBR): Legislated rights of due process given to police officers.

Legitimacy: A criterion of evaluation for comparing police review systems having to do with the perceptions of how a given system works that are held by those outside of the system.

Learning: A criterion of exavulation for comparing police review systems having to do with the police officer learning what does (or does not) eventuate because of the operations of the system.

Local contracts: Binding agreements mutually made between parties local to one another or within the same agency (union contracts).

Non-judicialized accountability mechanisms: Non-judicial, quasi-judicial, and neo-traditional accountability mechanisms designed and operated without sufficient consideration of their potential to contribute to the implementation and promotion of the rule of law.

Police department review boards: Internal agency review boards that examine misconduct, violations of rules, and/or actions taken by the department; a debriefing mechanism to determine best outcomes for problems developed within the organization (use-of-force review boards, accident review boards, etc.).

Subcultural rationalizations: A set of values, behaviors, and norms that set members off (deviates) from the mainstream culture and are considered the norm versus the mainstream culture.

Use of force: In police work, that force necessary to control an unruly or assaultive subject or to affect an arrest.

 EXAMPLE SCENARIOS

Errant Officer?

Detective Sergeant Smith is assigned to the Crime vs. Property unit. His usual investigations include burglary, selling or distributing stolen property, and theft. One day, he learns that a suspect he has been following closely for a last month may have stolen property in his possession. The tip he receives is anonymous. Based on the tip, he goes into the field seeking the suspect. After looking for several days, he finds the suspect driving a vehicle, but the vehicle is not the one described to him by the anonymous tipper. Nonetheless, Detective Smith makes a car stop and confronts the suspect.

The suspect has a proper driver's license and registration for the vehicle. Detective Smith, on a hunch, asks the driver if he can look in the trunk of the vehicle. The suspect says no. Believing the suspect has something to hide, Detective Smith yanks the keys from the ignition and opens the trunk anyway. In the trunk, there is property matching the description of property reported stolen on one of his burglary reports. He takes the property (seizes it) and arrests the suspect for possession of stolen property.

When the suspect is released from custody, he reports the incident to the police IA unit. IA conducts an investigation, finalizes its report, and forwards it to the investigation division commander. Only facts are in the report; no recommendation is provided for follow-up action.

Should this suspect have the ability to report an officer's conduct in this instance? What do you believe should be done about Detective Smith's actions? Should something be done at the chief's level? By IA? Is it appropriate to handle it at the division level? What sort of sanction might be appropriate?

Firefight

On patrol one evening, Officer Redding makes a car stop on a vehicle with four occupants. The stop is conducted because the vehicle has a right rear tail-light out, and Officer Redding thought that four adult males in a vehicle in this quiet neighborhood was unusual. She conducts the car stop by regulation, calling in the license number, location, and brief description of the vehicle with four occupants. Dispatch sends a cover unit as a routine measure.

As Redding walks toward the vehicle, the driver steps out, draws a weapon, and fires a round at the officer. Redding quickly moves to her left, draws her weapon, and begins firing at the suspect. The suspect jumps back in the car and drives off. Redding discovers she is wounded in the right leg and calls for help, describing the direction of the vehicle.

After the incident, Officer Redding is transported to the hospital, where she is met by both Crimes vs. Persons detectives and IA investigators. She is questioned by the detectives and subjected to investigative interrogation by the IA investigators. She is required to submit her weapon for testing and must provide the IA investigators with sample swabs of her hands to determine the gun residue from firing her weapon. She is temporarily placed on administrative leave with pay until further notice.

Are these actions on the part of the IA investigators proper, in your view? If yes, why? If no, why not? What might you do differently (or have them do differently)?

CompStat

Captain Spaulding is in charge of the county-wide task force, a unit that supports all other divisions of the agency he serves. His job is to ensure that any equipment or support other entities need is coordinated and delivered. This means motorcycles for extra traffic enforcement, mobile command centers if needed, aircraft for any county-wide need, and any other equipment, manpower, and resources he has in his command possession.

Captains are required by agency policy to attend and present data on their areas of command to the executive commanders every six weeks. This means the captains must have data, action plans for any problems they have encountered, and information available to inform the executive of their unit operation for the last six weeks. This is called a CompStat meeting, and the captains are subjected to rigorous questioning regarding the function of their command.

Captain Drummond is up for CompStat review this session. During his session, he presents his command very well. However, in one instance, he is queried about the effectiveness of a traffic control in his region. There have been many more accidents at a particular intersection of his region, and the stats show no improvement over the last session. One problem Captain Drummond says is causing his traffic unit trouble is the absence of available motorcycle units to help cite drivers disobeying the traffic controls at the intersection mentioned. When asked if he requested help from the county-wide task force, Captain Drummond says he did, but he has not yet received any support.

This review leads to the chief calling on Captain Spaulding to explain why he is not providing Drummond's unit with additional motorcycle traffic units. Spaulding says he does not have enough to help all the commands and would provide Drummond with a few if he could spare them.

The chief becomes angry because he views Spaulding's answer as irresponsible. As a result, Spaulding is directed to come to the chief's office when Drummond's session ends.

Why do you believe the chief was upset? Was his ire understandable? Do you think this sort of inquiry will build a better agency? Why or why not?

ADDITIONAL READING

There are several excellent works in the field of police deviance. Some that do an excellent job of covering how the subculture can rationalize misconduct are Barker and Carter's *Police Deviance, 3rd Ed.* (Anderson, 2002), Kappeler, Sluder, and Alpert's *Forces of Deviance: Understanding the Dark Side of Policing, 2nd Ed.* (Waveland Press, 1998), and Edwin J. Delattre's *Character and Cops: Ethics in Policing* (American Enterprise Institute, 2002). These works are synoptic efforts at developing a solid, wide-ranging introduction to the field of police deviance. With regard to the point made in our discussion that American society contributes to some police misconduct, Keith D. Harries's work *Serious Violence: Patterns of Homicide and Assault in America* (Charles C. Thomas, 1997) illustrates our point about American violence cogently.

The critically important study of the Dirty Harry problem is discussed in Caldero and Crank's *Police Ethics: The Corruption of Noble Cause, 3rd Ed.* (Anderson, 2009). This work is an insightful and thought-provoking treatment of this more specifically focused area in the field. Jill Nelson's *Police Brutality: An Anthology* (Norton, 2001) covers the most controversial of all police-related topics, the use of excessive force.

Police review is covered by two works that involve definitive treatments of the civilian review debate. Douglas W. Perez's *Common Sense About Police Review* (Temple University Press, 1994) is a research-oriented, comparative study of internal, external, and hybrid review systems. Samuel Walker's *The New World of Police Accountability* (Sage, 2005) includes an argument in favor of civilian review. Taken together, they give the student of police review a balanced approach to the subject.

CHAPTER 10

Discipline

INTRODUCTION

Even though we had a comparative discussion about police review systems in the previous chapter, we still must engage the topic of outcomes. What happens after investigations into police misconduct have occurred? What are the various options for police administrators and leaders at all levels? When officers are found not guilty of misconduct, what should be done? When they are guilty, what should be done? Furthermore, are there alternatives to the punitive sanctioning systems with which we are all familiar? The idea that punishment will instill discipline in others is age-old, with Biblical roots. It has long been taken on faith by billions of people that punishment is the one and only way for people to control errant behavior, by creating fear for the punitive consequences that would be visited upon them by their own error. One central theme for us here, and for police leaders over the course of the past generation, is to engage the idea that punishment might very well not be the "be all and end all" of discipline.

In this chapter, we will begin with a terse treatment of **burden of proof** and a typology of outcomes. These two sections will be followed by a classic debate about the different strengths and weaknesses presented by traditional, punitive types of disciplinary systems. We will then consider the potential of (relatively) new, no-fault disciplinary models. Amid that discussion, we will present alternatives to classical disciplinary patterns, such as **discipline without punishment**. Furthermore, we will engage in a brief discussion of **early warning (EW) systems** and other, more positive methods of behavior control that seek to avoid the counterproductive propensities of punitive discipline.

This chapter's set of discussions will draw together our three chapters about police behavior. Herein, we will focus on upper level police leadership alternatives because that is where the alternative philosophies suggested by **no-fault systems** must be debated and decided. We will also focus on middle management leadership, as that is where the administration of whatever system put into place is accomplished. Finally, we will discuss the leadership of the immediate supervisor, whose domain is where genuinely positive change can (and must) occur.

Let us begin with a treatment of the outcome options that are presented to police leaders by police review systems.

 OUTCOMES

Whether an IA system, a civilian review board, or a hybrid system of police review is in operation, the end results of the group's machinations are an official **outcome**. In those arenas where civilian versus internal review is debated, this point in the process presents one of the most contentious issues in the argument. It is here that the openness of the process is discussed, relative to how much (if any) information is made available to the public. Those who champion civilian review laud its openness and decry the secret nature of internal investigations. Indeed, even the name *internal affairs* is considered proof positive that the police cannot be entrusted with monitoring their own accountability; they clearly consider a complaint from a citizen as the property of the police and, thus, an internal affair.

For our purposes, we will avoid that discussion and focus on what police leaders should do with outcome-related information. However, we back up for a moment here and begin the process of analysis with a consideration of burden of proof.

Burden of Proof

For both internal and external systems, the debate is between the more classic burden of proof standard and a more controversial and tougher one. Of course, citizens are often confused to find that the standard is not "beyond a reasonable doubt." This is because, as we have noted several times in our discussions, citizens are not lawyers and do not know much about such standards. Since the type of investigation involved is administrative, not criminal, the debate begins with the classic burden for civil trials.

The civil standard is a **preponderance of evidence**, and we are all familiar with its meaning. What is controversial to some extent is the change in some locations to a tougher standard of **clear and convincing evidence**. Because it is tougher on the complainant (who *always* bears the burden of proof), this standard is more protective of the police. Those who are protagonists for civilian review favor the lighter standard of the preponderance of evidence (Walker, 2001). An interesting point to note here is that both civilian systems and police-operated systems vary with regard to which standard they demand. There is no definitive answer for the question, "Which should it be?"

Force Differentiations

Because force complaints represent the most controversial subject for any review system, we have presented some percentages in Table 10.1 of the rates at which each of the standard types of outcomes are achieved. In terms of the percentages of

TABLE 10.1

FORCE COMPLAINT OUTCOMES	
• Not-Sustained	34%
• Unfounded	25%
• Exonerated	23%
• Other (e.g. withdrawn)	9%
• Sustained	8%
Source: Bureau of Justice Statistics, 2010.	

complaints that eventuate in sustained outcomes, these force complaint figures—as is always true of force complaint figures—are low compared to the sustained rates for all types of investigations. Taken all together, the percentage of complaints that are sustained nationwide is about 10 percent (Pate and Fridell, 1993). As noted in this chart, a substantial number of investigations end up with **not-sustained** findings. Not-sustained makes up the largest single classification, and this is nearly always the case. In a moment, we will move to consider the dynamics associated with the various types, one at a time.

External vs. Internal Complaints

There is a practical reality that tends to be ignored by all of the literature chronicling the police review debate. A huge percentage of allegations of police misconduct are generated from inside the police organization. Internally generated investigations make up the bulk of what police accountability systems encounter in any organization. That huge number is almost invariably handled quietly and informally within the organization. Most misconduct is of the "ineptitude" sort and almost always first noted by police supervisors. Concomitantly, when such misconduct is handled, it is in a non-adjudicative manner, emphasizing lower level leadership and creativity. Since this is almost never the case with regard to use-of-force complaints—the most controversial form of police misconduct, whether real or imagined—this fact tends to be overlooked. The use of force drives police review arguments, conjures up all sorts of negative images in people's minds, and sells newspapers.

There is no way to know how much minor misconduct is handled in this way. Because of its very nature, this element of police accountability is buried. No statistics are kept (none *can* be kept) on what must be the thousands of occurrences each year, where immediate supervisors do their jobs and handle such issues. In a book about police leadership, we simply must note that how such accusations are handled—informally—is of monumental importance in the police world. For all of the important discussion contained here and in the literature about civilian review, in particular, the creativity of individual police leaders is what determines the effectiveness of police behavior control in the long run.

This is a good moment to point out that all of our discussions in the three chapters in Part Three have been important. Even though so much police misconduct is handled with informality by the leadership of immediate supervisors, it is important that modern leaders understand what is involved in the debate about civilian review. This form of review now exists in about 20 percent of all large jurisdictions, and it is on the way elsewhere (Walker, 2001). But even in those places where local politics do not favor the institution of civilian review, the debate is such a part of the fabric of urban American politics in general that it behooves all police leaders to understand the various arguments involved, their power and weakness, and the utility of both internal and external systems.

For the next several sections, we will focus on those complaints that are externally generated and make it into the formalized review process.

TYPOLOGY OF OUTCOMES

After considering the fact that so many police misbehavior–related allegations are handled informally, we will now consider the outcomes generated by formalized police review systems, either internal or external. No matter what the specifics of the process are, at the end of the deliberations of these miniature criminal justice systems, police review mechanisms come up with outcomes. They are not limited to guilty or not guilty. They are divided up into a four-fold typology as standard operational procedure. An additional category exists for the complaints that end up having something else happen: the "other" type.

Not-Sustained

The most common finding for police review mechanisms is also the most troublesome. When the not-sustained outcome emerges from the process, it signifies that neither the complainant's nor the officer's side of the story can be confirmed. Evidence is added up equally on each side of the debate, and there can be no definitive decision made. Put another way, it is a tie which cannot be broken with any independent information (evidence). Such investigations come along often and usually involve a citizen (or two) making statements to one effect and a police officer (or two) making contradictory statements. Again, a tie ensues. No amount of extra investigation will change that, as it is often the case that two opposing statements are all that exists as evidence.

BOX 10.1

THE NOT-SUSTAINED OUTCOME

No one is ever satisfied with a not-sustained outcome. Complaining citizens dislike being told that the system does not accept the validity of their statements. Accused officers invariably believe that the system should believe them, in lieu of "just some citizen," and they too are upset by this type of indeterminate finding. Furthermore, investigators from internal affairs are perhaps even more put off by a not-sustained finding, as it indicates that they have somehow been unable to do their job effectively.

None of this is news to an experienced police officer, let alone a police leader. Our point here is to note that the creative police leader must understand these realities and be prepared to work around them. That is to say, as long as misconduct is of a genuinely minor nature, to handle it informally is almost invariably the best alternative. The key issue is for the leader to understand that, under no circumstances, can he or she treat misconduct as minor. That is, in fact, not so.

This is the most troublesome outcome because it makes no one happy. Investigators are disappointed because they have been unable to develop independent information and, thus, they feel they have failed to some extent. Administrators feel the same unhappiness, not only because they want investigators to succeed at developing investigations with definitive outcomes, but because they must deal with the disappointment of the other parties involved.

Police officers, by and large, believe that police review systems should take their words as gospel. No matter how much education today's modern officer might have, there is a natural and understandable propensity for officers to expect their statements to be given more weight—be held as more valid—than those of civilians. As professionals, the police have an innate belief that because they do a difficult job with as much effectiveness as they can possibly muster, they should be believed by review systems. If there are two statements, one from an officer and one from a citizen, the officer believes that his or her statement should be considered to be definitive in an investigation.

An equal but opposite dynamic is operative on the other side of the formula. Citizens who come in and make complaints about police behavior think they should be believed. After all, the complainant rationalizes, "If I went to the trouble to come in and jump through all of the hoops and make a complaint, the system should consider my statement valid." From the perspective of the average citizen, this is totally reasonable. "Why would I make something up?" is the perspective of the complainant. The not-sustained outcome, implying that neither person involved is being believed, presents a no-win situation for everyone.

In an effort to avoid the troublesome dynamics associated with this "nobody wins, nobody is happy" outcome, some police departments and civilian review boards have created mediation procedures. We will not delve deeply into how mediation works in the places where it is practiced. Mediation of all sorts—marital counseling, labor relations, and so on—is pretty well understood by us all. But we will make a couple of comments about it here. First, mediation is aimed at developing support for the police among the citizenry when minor allegations surface. It is an effort to make people more accepting of the "lose/lose" nature of the not-sustained finding. Second, it is designed to do the same thing on the police officer side. Police officers who agree to go through mediation realize that this is a way to keep their records clean. That is usually why they agree to it.

Most important, mediation attempts to draw something out of the police officer that he or she is usually dislikes doing. Mediation is about explanation and apology. It is the general, practical idea that an explanation or apology can develop positive dynamics, written into administrative practice. As such, mediation is a newfound tool in most places and is largely public relations oriented. But this should not make us cynical about it and reject it. After all, if "politics is perception," then the politics of police accountability are all about the perceptions of those involved (officers and complainants). If mediation generates a more positive perception of police accountability processes, that is a good thing.

REVIEW CHART 10.1

TYPOLOGY OF OUTCOMES

- *Not-sustained:* The allegations cannot be proven one way or the other.
- *Unfounded:* The allegations were found to be untrue.
- *Exonerated:* The allegations were found to be true, but did not constitute misconduct.
- *Other:* The complaint has not ended in a resolution, normally due to it being withdrawn.
- *Sustained:* The allegations were found to be true, and they constitute misconduct.

Unfounded

We have suggested that the most troublesome outcome of the various possibilities is "not-sustained" because it satisfies no one. That makes perfectly good sense until we consider the **unfounded** finding, which says that what the complainant alleges has been proven to be false. Why is this not the most troublesome outcome? Given that it almost accuses the complaining citizen of lying, why is this not the most difficult outcome for police leadership?

The reason has to do with the politics of review, both inside and outside the police organization. On the inside, the unfounded investigation essentially sides with the police officer. There is never any problem selling such an outcome internally. Outside the organization, the unfounded complaint gives administrators grounds to suggest that a substantial number of complaints are just not true. Even though the specifics of complaint investigations are rarely opened up to public scrutiny if they are IA, the general circumstances surrounding unfounded complaints—the stories that were proven to be false—*are* often shared with civilians by police leaders whenever an appropriate venue presents itself. For example, when police leaders have a generic discussion about their accountability system and/or civilian review, it is always good for them to be able to punctuate such discussions with references to the number of unfounded complaints that come in to the organization. Furthermore, it can be politically effective for the police leader to spice up such a discussion with specific examples of particular, baseless, groundless complaints.

Exonerated

Then there is the **exonerated** finding. Clearly, because this finding determines that the police officer is not guilty of misconduct, it is easy to sell this finding in-house.

The police have acted in a legal and proper manner, and nothing could be better from the police leader's perspective. Two additional ideas must be visited here with regard to this finding.

First, on the police officer side of things, when either the exonerated or the not-sustained finding is the outcome, it is absolutely critical to the integrity of the system that the police officer who has been found not guilty of misconduct is held to be completely and thoroughly without culpability. That is, internal records that might in any way impact the officer's future in the department—moving up in rank or obtaining choice assignments—cannot be negatively impacted by an investigation that ends up with the exonerated finding. Furthermore, not even a combination of complaint investigations that end up being exonerated should be combined to imply anything negative. There is no way to defend any system that makes exonerated or not-sustained findings in some cumulative way into anything other than irrelevant to an officer's career. In essence, such findings must vanish for a review system to be fair to police officers.

Second, on the complainant's side of the formula, the exonerated outcome presents the police organization with an excellent chance to produce genuinely positive results. Consider the meaning of the outcome. It suggests that the actions of police officers were legal and proper, but it does not suggest that the allegations of the citizen were untrue. In essence, it agrees with the citizen. An example here might be that a citizen accuses a police officer of making an improper arrest when serving an arrest warrant. Investigation uncovers the fact that the arrest itself was proper, but the warrant was improperly handled by a court. The citizen is correct, but, equally, the police are not at fault. Under such a circumstance, a win/win situation is possible.

In our introductory discussion (Chapter 1), we considered the concept of "satisficing," first suggested 50 years ago by Herbert Simon. This is the perfect time to remind ourselves of this idea. When public administrators deal with citizens, they can make an explanation about an action taken by their bureaucracy in a way that creates acceptance in the mind of a particular citizen and positive public relations in the general population. We have only to focus on what the exonerated finding means to remember how satisficing works. The finding suggests that citizens were quite correct in their allegations (a good, positive thing); the satisficing explanation teaches citizens why the police are not arguing with them. Everybody wins.

The problem with satisficing is that the discretion involved can be abused. If the police are allowed—in some cases, encouraged—to explain away citizens' complaints, they might attempt to do so with important, valid complaints and not just when they are faced with minor complaints. The Christopher Commission, which studied the Los Angeles Police Department in the early 1990s, found just this sort of abuse. The policy allowing for satisficing was being used "to intimidate citizens from filing complaints. They sometimes made citizens wait for hours in solitary rooms if they wished to file complaints." The police even "characterized force complaints as 'minor'" (Perez, 1994).

BOX 10.2

ABUSING THE ABILITY TO HANDLE THINGS AS MINOR

One of the paradoxes of the citizen complaint process has to do with handling complaints in an unofficial manner. On the one hand, it is often a positive thing to allow the police the opportunity to handle minor complaints with satisficing explanations. This saves time and taxpayer money and, arguably, makes for a more satisfied complainant than an official (and officious) review process might.

On the other hand, as illustrated with the LAPD Christopher Commission, this latitude can be abused. When it is, the police are guilty of covering up misconduct in a dishonest and even illegal way. Such abuse can make things far worse than they were in the first instance. It can generate a lack of faith in the police that amplifies and spins into legitimacy problems for the police and the police leader.

Other

The "other" category can be disconcerting to police leaders because complaints sometimes end up in this category due to lawsuits or other extenuating circumstances that create frustration. However, complaints most often end up being labeled "other" because they are withdrawn. This can be because citizens give up on their quest to hold the police to answer or because they are the subject of a satisficing explanation. If a citizen has given up, this can be good or bad, depending on why they have done so. If this is the product of satisficing, then is it obviously positive.

The modern police leader is drawn to consider the importance of satisficing in relation to the almost universal propensity of officers to eschew explanation and apology. To some extent, this dynamic presents a graphic illustration of what the creative and thoughtful leader can do out on the street. Motivating young officers to explain and/or apologize—which effective leaders can do on a regular basis—is a short-term, immediate, and effective method of short-circuiting the review process's satisficing potential. Teaching young officers that complaints can be avoided in this way is a creative way of leading on the street. It is done in the world of medicine (noted in the previous chapter) and works equally well with police officers. After all, one of the things veteran officers learn to do over the years is to avoid obtaining complaints. It is, in fact, a skill of the veteran officer.

Sustained

The remainder of this chapter will discuss what to do about complaints of police misconduct that are **sustained**. The sustained finding is, of course, the optimum finding from the perspective of most complainants. Presumably, no one would complain who did not feel they have been wronged in some way, and this finding confirms that. Concomitantly, the sustained finding is the least positive outcome from the perspective of either the individual police officer or police leadership. Civilian systems tend to open up findings to the public; internal systems almost universally keep them secret. But aside from the substance of what was decided or the process through which the decision was reached, the sustained outcome leads us to a direct consideration of how disciplinary systems operate and/or should operate.

THE PUNITIVE MODEL

Everyone in the world is familiar with the **punitive model** of disciplining. We learn about this from the first moment we are able to communicate with other human beings in life. Organizational life mirrors the private sector in many ways; the types of disciplinary systems normally operational in complex organizations tend to be punitive in nature. Before we focus on traditional punitive disciplinary models, let us consider an idea that was brought into our discussions by Muir's work on power, first outlined in Chapter 2.

Recall that Muir, a political scientist, used a political definition of power. He suggested that power was behavior control, and there were three classic types of power utilized by anyone who attempts to influence the behavior of others. Whether we are talking about parents, presidents, or police officers, the only ways to control the behavior of others are exhortation, reciprocity, and coercion. In our discussion here and in the following sections, let us focus on the fact that when police officers misbehave, and yet have done nothing worthy of termination, there are three types of strategies that might be used to change errant behavior in the future.

Clearly, the punitive disciplinary system utilizes coercion (punishment for **transgressions**) to control behavior. But punishment is not the only method that might be attempted. Police officers might be exhorted to behave themselves. They might be motivated to do the right thing by their own personal ethics. Furthermore, they might be motivated to change their behavior through the power of barter or exchange. Reciprocity works, too. Changing the formula from one that threatens into one that rewards is not just some type of liberal "I'm okay, you're okay" nonsense from the 1960s. It is living possibility utilized in a steadily increasing number of private as well as public organizations.

Let us begin here by reminding ourselves of the nature of the punitive model: its rationale, strengths, and weaknesses.

The Dynamics of Punishment

Clearly, the idea of using punishment to change errant behavior is a fault-driven, coercion-related strategy. The formula is supposed to work like this. A police officer makes a mistake. The officer is found guilty of the mistake after going through some sort of investigatory procedure (the type of procedure doesn't matter). The officer is then punished for the transgression. Thereafter, the officer's behavior will change, and he or she will never do whatever it was again. The threat of future punishment—the fear of the stick in the carrot-or-the-stick metaphor—is controlling. It is the idea of punishment in general that punishing those who have erred in the past will motivate them to behave themselves in the future. When the erring individual is thus motivated, it is called *specific deterrence*; when people in general are deterred, it is called *general deterrence*. But the idea behind both is the same, and the limitations of such negative, punitive sanctioning is equally ineffective.

Several other topics come to mind here. For example, in the command-and-control way of operating a police organization, the punitive model is the most often attempted form of control. This martial approach to police leadership suggests that, as is true in the military, control over subordinates will be developed through implicit threats and ongoing fear of punishment. Similarly, the idea that coercion—and only coercion—is the one and only way to control police behavior is a rather paramilitaristic way of approaching police organization. These two ideas go hand in hand.

Also, a common American conservative political idea comes to mind here. In an era where politicians are allowed only brief sound bites to make their points in the media, political debate about crime and punishment has degenerated into an extremely simplistic dialogue. Labeled by some to be "the politics of blame," today's distilled political ideas are limited, facile ideas about the causes of crime and what to do about them. While any criminologist knows that crime has multiple causes, political dialogue today suggests that crime is caused in only one way: bad people choosing to behave badly. While this is certainly *one* cause of crime, poverty, stratification, racism, mental disorders, chemical imbalances, and a number of other causes come together to explain crime in our complex society. If one focuses on only one cause—people making conscious decisions to behave badly—then only

BOX 10.3

THE CLASSIC PUNITIVE MODEL (PUNISHMENTS IN ASCENDING ORDER OF SEVERITY)

- Oral reprimand
- Written reprimand
- Both of the above, and retraining assignments
- Time off without pay
- Demotion/loss of rank
- Termination

one solution is obvious: get tougher and build more prisons. So it is with today's politicians. Some of the counterproductive, money-wasting policies of the American criminal justice system today are produced by this simpleminded approach to a complicated problem.

As noted in Box 10.3, the standard formula for escalating levels of punishment begins with oral reprimand. The idea here, of course, is that a supervisor can make an adjustment in a subordinate's attitude and/or behavior (or can attempt to), without placing anything permanent into the record. Ideally, such a reprimand can be done in a positive way. Exhortation can be utilized in such an example and is how the majority of misconduct allegations are handled in the police world by leaders.

The next level of severity in punishment involves a written reprimand, which is put into an officer's file. The idea here is that either a combination of transgressions or one individual transgression may require something permanent be done. Now, written reprimands can be expunged from an officer's file. In many places, this is *supposed* to be how things work. This is an excellent idea, as it attempts to hold out the "carrot" to the officer that if errant behavior changes all will be forgiven. This is an effort to utilize reciprocity, in lieu of coercion. Unfortunately, there is quite a history in many jurisdictions regarding reprimands that were supposed to be expunged and never were. When this happens, the police subculture picks up on it, and the most vociferous naysayers come to the fore with their negative spin on "just one more example" of how the department is "out to get us all."

Next, either a combination of such lower level reprimands or a single, more substantial error can lead to retraining, if it is a reasonable option under the circumstances (if retraining is logically related to whatever problem is in evidence). After this level, punishment becomes quite serious; time off duty without pay (the next level) is tantamount to a fine. So substantial is this sanction that, in many places, so much as one day's worth of such punishment is immediately reviewable by the civil service commission. Next, there is the potential for demotion or loss of rank. Finally, there is termination. In a judicial sense, these last two options are similar. The consequences for police leaders and the organization are the same, in terms of the process involved in meting out these types of punishments, which can become cumbersome and lengthy. Civil service review is automatic, and police leaders do not always "win" under such circumstances (as noted in the previous chapter). Furthermore, termination can lead to lawsuits that take up significant amounts of time, money, and departmental and municipal resources.

One additional important topic here has to do with whether transgressions can be considered to be cumulative. Can a police organization take numerous minor violations and package them together to create something major? Most police leaders do not attempt to do this, for several reasons. First, there is the idea—congruent with that in the criminal justice system—that each and every transgression must be treated individually for a system to be fair. Second, adding errors together in this way opens the department up for legal action. This can be especially problematic if oral reprimands are considered to be a part of the pattern noted, because there is no paper trail with regard to the oral reprimand's specificity.

BOX 10.4

CREATING CIRCUMSPECTION WITH REGARD TO FORCE

Once again in our discussions, the late criminologist Carl Klockars is important here. With regard to the utility—or lack thereof—of the traditional, punitive system of discipline where the use of force is concerned, Klockars noted:

> The problem of getting skilled police officers to teach other officers to work in ways that minimize the use of force requires that such teaching be done under conditions in which the normal punitive and disciplinary orientation of police administration is suspended. Only under such conditions will officers be prepared to assume a reasonably receptive, non-defensive posture, and only then will experienced, skilled supervisors be capable of offering constructive criticism of officer conduct.

Source: C. Klockars, "The Only Way to Make Any Real Progress in Controlling Excessive Force by Police," *Law Enforcement News,* May 15, 1992, p. 12.

Usually, a great deal of discretion exists with regard to potential punishments. Immediate supervisors can choose oral or written reprimand, and supervisors above that level can choose anything on the list. The chief, obviously, is the final arbiter, especially with termination, loss of rank, or time off without pay. If civil service review and/or legal action is anticipated, the chief is the person directly involved. IA or immediate supervisors may make recommendations, but the chief is the authority on such substantial punishment.

In some jurisdictions today, there are "punishment matrixes" (Walker, 2005). These codified levels of punishment are constructed in an effort to be proactive and fair with officers. The analogy we have been dealing with for several chapters now, that of a police review system as a miniature criminal justice system, is complete here. Such a matrix proclaims particular punishments for specific transgressions as if it were a penal code.

The Punitive Model's Limitations

There are a substantial number of difficulties presented by the traditional punitive model. Any consideration of these drawbacks must begin with how difficult it is to find officers guilty of transgressions of any kind if the system operates in an adversarial way. As we took great pains to discuss in the previous chapter, there are many limitations on police accountability mechanisms of all kinds. There are subcultural limitations, American cultural limitations, due process limitations, Law Enforcement Officers' Bills of Rights limitations, police union limitations, and civil service limitations. If the system operates in a semi-judicialized fashion, these numerous limitations add up and create a situation where a substantial number of guilty officers end up not being sanctioned.

Collectively, these dynamics and limitations come together to create an atmosphere where the chance for change is minimal. We are referring to change in an individual police officer's behavior. People do not like to be coerced, and the propensity for police officers to become jaded, if not cynical, about organizational life is pronounced. The world of policing is filled with people who are prone to suggest on a regular basis that the department is "going to hell in a hand basket." It is an almost ubiquitous dynamic. Every pronouncement of the administration, every memo that comes across the watch commander's desk, and every development, large and small, is denigrated by the naysayers. When punitive discipline is employed, these merchants of negativity open up their treasure trove of reasons for everyone to be diffident and uncooperative.

This is not to say, of course, that such negativity does not exist in complex organizations of any kind. It lives in the corporate world, as well as public bureaucracies. In fact, it has been written about and commented on for generations now, especially with regard—in recent years—to new ideas about nonpunitive disciplining (Grote, 1995). In the long run, punishment almost never produces anything positive. In the coaching world, it has long been known that if an athlete has been disciplined too severely (especially in front of other athletes) you can "lose" that athlete. He or she may not literally quit, in the sense that they physically resign from the team, but a diffident athlete can become an individual problem and the center point for collective diffidence. Naysayers come from somewhere, and in police work they are not just motivated by the fact that police officers see the worst in people. Naysayers are also created, and this often happens because of the excesses of punitive discipline. In the police world—with its propensity for negativity—the likelihood of punitive disciplinary systems creating counterproductive organizational dynamics is exacerbated and amplified.

Since police accountability mechanisms are invariably run in a semi-judicialized, adversarial manner, it is perfectly logical for those who are accused of misconduct to employ the protection of attorneys or, at the very least, union representation. If accountability involves officers being charged by those who are interested in bringing negative, punishment-oriented sanctions to bear if misconduct is proven, then aggressively defending oneself would be (and is) the logical strategy. Here, the police union presents the individual officer with positive, unequivocal support at a time when that is needed.

If such an adversarial and negative relationship exists between officer and accountability mechanism, a cyclical dynamic can be created, where negativity and antipathy spirals and amplifies. If, on the other hand, treating alleged misconduct involves an honest exploration into the possibility of change in a positive direction and discipline that would not inhibit professional progress, growth, and income, then it might be that accountability could be accomplished in a collegial way. To be fair to police unions, under such circumstances, they might be more prone to take a positive approach and aid in creating accountability rather than working against it.

BOX 10.5

THE PARADOX OF OFFICERS GETTING OFF DUE TO LEGAL TECHNICALITIES

The study of police accountability in general is plagued by a not-so-subtle paradox that works to limit the ability of review systems to generate reform. Police officers tend to be more than a bit frustrated by the machinations of the American due process system when that system allows factually guilty criminals to go free (see Perez, 2010, Chapter 4). Driven as they are to focus on the substance of things—factual guilt—when they investigate crime, the police can lose patience with a system that allows procedural technicalities to get in the way of holding the substantive guilty to answer for their crimes.

Paradoxically, when they themselves are accused of misconduct, the police tend to cleave to the same sort of procedural rights that they ostensibly denigrate with regard to criminal investigations. Led by police unions, the American police cling to due process rights that sometimes allow officers who are factually guilty of misconduct to go free from sanction.

So, the problem with the traditional, punishment-oriented system is that police officers can and do often resent it. Instead of being motivated to change their errant ways when they are negatively sanctioned, guilty police officers can become diffident, cynical, and counterproductive. Anyone involved in disciplining others knows this. We are left with the question, "Is there any alternative to such a system?"

Might there possibly be some effective form of discipline that works in a positive direction or from the ground up? We noted in the last chapter with regard to ethics that too much emphasis in police academies and other training arenas focuses on "how not to mess up" when policing. We pointed out that such a focus is not acceptable to the thoughtful, educated professional. To avoid messing up is only obliquely related to ethics. In other words, being ethical is not the same as not being *un*ethical.

The idea here is similar. Instead of approaching discipline from the negative perspective, discipline might be looked at in exactly the opposite way. Perhaps when someone messes up, the way to attempt to change their behavior is through reciprocity or exhortation, rather than coercion. Those who focus on discipline without punishment suggest a change in perspective that mirrors some of what Muir had to say about power generally. People do not resent exhortation or reciprocity, because they like making the right decision themselves (being exhorted) or receiving something in exchange for behaving well (reciprocity). They invariably resent being coerced.

POSITIVE AND NO-FAULT SYSTEMS

In response to the problems associated with punitive discipline, several ground-breaking programs have been developed in both public and private complex organizations. One such program was constructed back in the 1960s by John Huberman, an executive at a lumber mill. What became known as the **Huberman plan** was, at first, just a set of musings about how there must be a better way to attempt to deal with employee misconduct. Huberman noted that employees almost never come back to being energized and positive if they are punished. While they might not quit their jobs, they usually—not some of the time, but almost *all* of the time—become listless and unresponsive. Furthermore, punitive disciplinary systems work to create saboteurs.

Huberman's musings led to brainstorming sessions with his fellow corporate leaders and eventually to a systematized plan of attack. Published in 1964 as "Discipline Without Punishment" in the *Harvard Business Review*, the plan quickly made the rounds of corporate America (Huberman, 1964). Huberman roamed the country as a speechmaker and corporate motivator. Along the way, several police leaders caught wind of his ideas. At the Contra Costa County Sheriff's Department in California, the sheriff heard about the idea, did the appropriate reading, and instituted the plan at that location.

The Huberman Plan in Action

There have been experiments in a limited number of jurisdictions with what are called no-fault disciplinary systems. First created in the private sector, the idea then made its way into the world of public bureaucracy. Even in police work, driven by subcultural conservatism and an innate reluctance about any sort of change, the literature about police administration began to talk about "discipline from the ground up" (Iannone et al., 2008). While we have few examples of this philosophy in action, it is an idea that is coming into the limelight in the police world.

Under the no-fault system, officers who have done something errant that does not warrant termination are subjected to less formalized sanctions. This type of system combines the written warning process with the idea of retraining as often as possible. When officers are "sanctioned" under such a system, they are given written explanations of what they did wrong, what retraining is in order, and what the errant officer is supposed to do to change their behavior in a positive direction.

The no-fault system has some interesting, positive twists to it. On the one hand, as is true of written warnings in the punitive system, constant, persistent, unchanging misbehavior can lead to termination if numerous episodes of misconduct are added together. The Huberman plan is very specific up front about how important patterns of behavior are that, over time, disregard positive suggestions and retraining. The entire philosophy is focused on exhortation (positively attempting to influence behavior) and reciprocity (rewarding change and evolution), in lieu of coercion. But when officers are not capable of introspection and change, it is designed to provide a written paper trail. It works to create patterns that are cumulative and legally defensible, if and when that becomes necessary.

On the other hand—and this is something officers like about such systems—if an errant officer *does* change their behavior, their disciplinary experience is expunged from their record after a prescribed period of time, usually six months to two years, depending on the severity of the misconduct. Being found guilty of misconduct may not ever impact an officer's chances for advancement and/or choice assignments. If they desist from misbehaving, all doors are open to the officer who grows and evolves in the direction suggested by leadership. Again, this no-fault idea is still an uncommon experiment. But it bears watching due to the propensity of police officers to become cynical and jaded regarding traditional disciplinary systems.

At the Contra Costa Sheriff's Department, officers took a very short period of time to become accustomed to locker room talk that referred to "being phased." This was because the plan as instituted put officers into various levels of gravity when it dealt with misconduct, and the levels were referred to as phases. So, any and all levity that the locker room's most creative minds could fashion revolved around the word "phase."

As per Huberman's original set of ideas, written records were kept of police officer misconduct investigations. The oral reprimand began to be eschewed, and this was perhaps unfortunate. It is certainly appropriate to keep most sanctioning informal in police work, and the plan—again, perhaps unfortunately—created more written records at the outset. Some effort had to be exerted to dissuade supervisors from resorting to writing too often. But that tendency settled down over time.

Whenever possible, counseling and training was the focus. Of course, counseling—written and oral—is always possible with regard to police misconduct. Training, on the other hand, is not always relevant. Put simply, there just isn't appropriate training for some types of misconduct. If an officer is using force improperly, he or she can be sent to defensive tactics classes. If an officer is writing poor reports, he or she can be given a course in that very skill. Poor driving can result in a defensive driving course. Officers who are rude to citizens can be sent to any number of interpersonal relations courses. But often, a surly or cynical attitude is at fault, and nothing in the way of training is relevant to such behavior. An officer who is sleeping or having sex on duty is not likely to respond to retraining. What sort of retraining would that involve, anyway?

Someone put into one phase initially could be moved up in phase level (to a more severe level) if they were guilty of some additional transgression. In the long run, even minor offenses could accumulate and become something quite serious. Again, this is good news for the police administrator who wants to have a defensible record of reluctance to change and become a more cooperative member of the organization on the part of an erring officer.

One operational norm that was considered by police officers to be extremely positive was the expunging rule. Any level of "phasing" could be overcome in the long run, and an officer with a spotty record could work his or her way out from

BOX 10.6

HUBERMAN'S EXPERIENCE AT CONTRA COSTA COUNTY

In the mid-1970s, the Contra Costa County Sheriff's Department (California) put into place a no-fault disciplinary system that was based on the model suggested by John Huberman. This system included several positive potentials for both police officers and leaders. On the officer's side, the system included the practice of expunging records of confirmed misconduct after proscribed periods of time, if errant police officers changed their misbehavior. On the police leader's side, the system allowed for the accumulation of minor offenses into a pattern that could lead to substantial sanctions, in lieu of the common practice of handling individual examples of misconduct separately.

under a cloud. This is of particular importance in light of the fact that most police officers obtain almost all of the citizen complaints that they ever obtain in the first few years of their careers (Perez, 1994). Most officers, as they move through their careers, not only become better officers in a substantive sense, they become more adept at avoiding complaints in a procedural way. Thus, the fact that a young officer could be guilty of misconduct and then, over the years, improve substantially was considered by officers to be of great importance. They warmed to this dynamic.

This brings us to consider how the officers of the sheriff's department reacted generally to the plan. The good news is that research was conducted into this topic, aimed at obtaining some knowledge about the system in process. What did the deputy sheriffs think about no-fault discipline?

Officer Response

When the Huberman plan had been in place for four years, researchers studied how the Contra Costa officers subject to the plan felt about it. According to self-reporting surveys, there did not seem to be much difference between the evaluations of the plan by officers who had been subjected to higher levels of discipline (higher phases) and officers who had few (or no) interactions with the plan. This was good news from the perspective of those who might want such discipline without punishment programs to work in a positive way. If there was little difference between the acceptance levels of those who had and those who had not been the subject of substantial discipline, then the system might very well be working in a positive way. And since acceptance in general was positive, there did not seem to be any diffidence being created by the plan in operation (Perez, 1994).

This finding needs to be juxtaposed against other research that found that officers subjected to traditional punitive disciplinary systems *do* tend to feel negatively about them. The more often they are sanctioned, or the more heavily they are sanctioned, the more negative are officers' evaluations of punitive systems (Perez, 1994). This is completely understandable and, in fact, is mirrored in other arenas in life. Research into all sorts of sanctioning mechanisms indicates the completely logical and intuitively understood idea that when a system punishes, it is resented. The Huberman plan did not seem to display this dynamic. It was not differentially evaluated by those who were phased and those who were not.

However, the paradox was that while individual, anonymous surveys indicated these deputy sheriffs accepted the system's fairness and effectiveness, locker room banter was as negative and cynical as ever. The police officer propensity to be dubious and fatalistic about programs—programs of any kind, from this type of no-fault disciplinary program to COP—was in clear evidence in the locker room. Perhaps all this illustrated was the propensity of some police officers to feel that being negative was essential in the locker room. There is no doubt about this tendency, of course, and it might very well be that the Huberman plan is well accepted in practice, but some police officers are just prone to protest and find fault with anything positive that comes along. This is something that must be understood by police leaders as an omnipresent dynamic in American policing.

Taken together, this particular example of an attempt to put into action a positive, no-fault disciplinary system in one jurisdiction must be considered to be a development of positive potential to police leaders everywhere.

OTHER ALTERNATIVES

Perhaps just as interesting as the Huberman plan experiment are several other attempts at innovation in the world of police accountability. As we have seen, the whole field is driven by two central problems relating to the limitations of reform relative to police review systems and the counterproductivity of traditional, punitive sanctioning systems.

Early Warning Systems

There can be no doubt that, in many police departments, a substantial number of citizens' complaints are received by a small number of "problem prone" officers (Walker and Katz, 2010). The Christopher Commission in Los Angeles found that a group of 44 officers were 13 times more prone to obtain excessive force complaints than all the other members of a 8,000 person department. In Kansas City, Missouri, it was discovered that 2 percent of the department obtained 50 percent of the overall number of citizens' complaints (*New York Times*, 1991). In an infamous example in Boston, two officers each received 24 force complaints in a nine-year period. When reporters from the *Boston Globe* looked into it, they found that 11 percent of the department's officers received 62 percent of the complaints there (*Boston Globe*, 1992).

On the strength of these and other findings—for this dynamic is by no means obscure or unusual—the idea of early warning (EW) systems was born about 20 years ago. To begin with, many chiefs of police created their own, intuitively based programs. They chose certain indicators to monitor, in an effort to predict which officers are moving toward behaviors that are deleterious for the interests of justice and the officers themselves. Box 10.6 suggests some ideas for the components that such systems might monitor in this endeavor.

Citizens' complaints, use-of-force reports, and involvement in civil litigation are reasonable indicators that any given officer might have a problem or be developing a problem with the use of force and/or their interpersonal interactions with citizens. Walker adds "Other indicators of performance problems" at the end of his **selection criteria** list. Here we might share with the reader some indicators that have been used by EW systems in some locations.

Resisting arrest charges are clearly relevant. Since this particular charge is often used as a "cover charge" (to cover the use of force), this is an important indicator to monitor. Solving certain types of details—such as those involving the homeless—with arrest, rather than informally, can indicate an increasing inability on an officer's part to handle one's job with tact. There are other generic indicators that an officer might be having personal or psychological troubles that could lead to trouble. Being late to work, taking excessive days off, or poor report writing are three examples. Having trouble with driving or a significant number of firearms discharge reports can also be illustrative of problems brewing. These and a host of other indicators have been put into "monitor these closely" lists by chiefs or IA directors in recent years. In fact, the EW movement shows so much promise that this is an area that begs for additional, substantial research to be done.

The Oakland Force Boards

In the early 1970s at the Oakland Police Department, Hans Toch, Douglas Grant, and Raymond Galvin conducted an experimental program that looked into the use of force by Oakland's particular group of "problem prone" officers. Later the subject of the book *Agents of Change*, this program took the creative approach of utilizing those officers who obtained the most force complaints as the agents of change. They themselves were put in charge of developing a program aimed at lowering the amount of force used on the street and, in turn, the number of citizen's complaints.

These officers became quite creative in their approach. They initiated their own early warning program. They contacted officers who showed up on their indicators and proactively got these officers involved in group counseling sessions about the use of force. They utilized individual mentoring as well. They came up with example scenarios for role-playing exercises. The effect of it all was pronounced. Not only did the force complaint numbers for these problem officers go down, but those for the department as a whole did, too. This was in every sense a peer-driven early warning and review system.

BOX 10.7

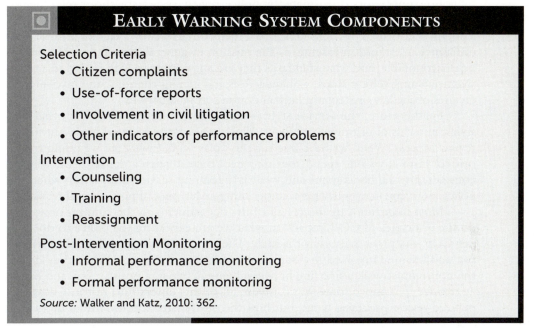

EARLY WARNING SYSTEM COMPONENTS

Selection Criteria
- Citizen complaints
- Use-of-force reports
- Involvement in civil litigation
- Other indicators of performance problems

Intervention
- Counseling
- Training
- Reassignment

Post-Intervention Monitoring
- Informal performance monitoring
- Formal performance monitoring

Source: Walker and Katz, 2010: 362.

Nearly a decade later, after this experimental program had been terminated, the Oakland chief of police was still operating his own self-created EW program. This program was pronounced creative and bold by several social scientists doing additional research at the OPD (Muir, 1977; Perez, 1994). Taken together, the long-term potential for such EW programs and the type of creativity shown at Oakland are great. Especially in our current, genuinely professional, COP-driven era of policing, it will be important for thoughtful and outside-the-box police leaders to innovate along similar lines.

DISCIPLINARY OVERVIEW

As we near the end of Part Three and three chapters about police behavior, it is appropriate that we take a moment to gather together several principles suggested by our discussions about ethics, accountability, and discipline. Here is a summation and review that attempts to accomplish that task.

Clearly, one principle that must be observed by the conscientious police leader is that discipline must be consistent with the organization's mission. We are suggesting that serious consideration be given to the style of policing agreed upon by any given department before the ethos of the accountability mechanism is created. It should be obvious that discipline cannot be accomplished in a watchman-style department as it is in a legalistic department. These two types are, to some extent, the obverse of each other. As such, they should not be monitored either informally by police supervisors or formally by police review systems without reference to their different priorities. The proactive or reactive nature of the department's philosophy is critical. This translates into a focus on arrests or a lack of arrests. This difference in definition extends to the mission in general, how police officers are held accountable, and what standards they are answerable to with regard to aggressively pursuing vehicle stops, making arrests and issuing citations, and invoking the dictates of the law or stepping back and monitoring situations.

Furthermore, the service style is completely different from the other two styles, in terms of priorities and focus. This cannot be considered irrelevant to any review process. When we have free time to "play with," what are we going to prioritize? How does one spend routine patrol time in such a department? What is considered to be harassment and what is a genuine service orientation when the police intervene in events where, under other styles, they almost never intervene?

Most important, in about half of the departments in the country now, how do the principles of COP impact on what we are expecting the police to do? Under COP, the proactivity factor is high. The expectation is that the police will go out and become involved in people's problems on the street. When they do so, the police must walk a fine line between being active in a positive way and overly aggressive in inappropriate ways. Again, all of this enters into not just how formalized review processes work, but how the on-the-street police leader motivates, teaches, and coaches on a day-to-day basis.

Another important principle is that any ethically defensible police accountability system must be aimed at positive learning for the individual officer. The learning factor being key to police accountability for the majority of incidents of police misconduct, how well is the system doing at positively influencing future behavior? The ability of police leaders to have any direct impact on individual officer behavior increases down the organizational chart. The immediate supervisor has a tremendously important role to play in officer behavior. The middle manager has less of an impact, and the police manager might have little indeed. Thus, some of what we have had to say about individual mentoring becomes less relevant to police upper level leadership.

As we go up the chain of command, we find the responsibility of policy development increases. To civilianize the review system or not presents upper level managers with a cogent debate that cannot be resolved by immediate supervisors. To institute EW or not is another such question. To create peer review boards or not involves taking collective risks that only those in upper management are empowered to take. And so on.

Another idea is important here. Aside from this individual officer focus, an appropriate system should be aimed at the creation of positive morale for the police group as a whole. This principle cannot be overstated, and is only obvious to those who are close enough to police complaint review systems to understand the overall focus and the minute-by-minute job accomplished by such systems. Police misconduct is troublesome for several reasons, as we have pointed out often, and almost universally misunderstood by citizens. But there is something else regularly included in the debate over the importance of police review, something misunderstood by even some of the most ardent champions of civilian review.

Citizens complain about the police on a very rare basis. Cities of 40,000 may receive a dozen complaints in a year. Cities of half a million might receive 250. Large cities receive even fewer complaints per capita. In fact, the overwhelming majority of cities in America do not have anything in their police organizations that is called "the internal affairs bureau" because there is not a sufficient case load of complaints to warrant such a bureau. The point here is that we are not exaggerating when we say (1) the overwhelming majority of incidents of accused misconduct are handled informally and (2) the key people with regard to police ethics and accountability are the immediate supervisors. This is just the way of things, and the modern leader, therefore, must take seriously the responsibility this reality presents to him or her.

Finally, our optimum system must be aimed at engendering professionalism. In Chapter 8 we argued that ethics cannot be divorced from competence. So, too, we argue that everything done by sergeants, middle managers, and chiefs of police, everything accomplished formally by semi-judicialized police review systems and informally mentored and coached into the hearts and minds of young officers—all of this—must be done with an eye toward instilling a professional ethic into the police officer corps of the future. This statement sounds romantically filled with platitudes. But that does not make it any less true or important. The responsibility born by those who lead today's police will bear fruit down the line if, and only if, the American police eventually achieve professional status. That is the ultimate truism of what confronts police leaders today.

BOTTOM LINE PARADOXES

As we have done at several points in our discussions, it is now appropriate for us to bring together a brief summation and review of several of the paradoxes involved in the topics of this chapter.

The first paradox is that the severe limits placed on the review systems we visited in the last chapter, and this chapter as well, discourage the development of genuinely effective accountability in police work. All of the concerns of those who debate the internal/civilian review issue, the time spent creating and maintaining review systems, and the honest effort spent by police managers in creating meaningful police accountability can be limited by extraneous variables out of the control of police leaders. Put another way, police review systems have a very limited impact on police behavior.

The second paradox is that traditional, coercive punitive systems don't work. They do not tend to modify police misbehavior in a positive way. They do not usually teach errant police officers to behave themselves. In fact, they have a propensity

BOX 10.8

BOTTOM LINE PARADOXES

- Formal police review systems have very little impact on police behavior.
- Traditional punitive disciplinary systems do not work; they actually create police misconduct.
- Holding the police accountable is more of an art than a science; it is almost impossible to engineer.

to create counterproductivity and diffidence in the police officer corps. They have the opposite effect on police behavior than intended.

Finally, no matter how much time and analysis are spent on police accountability as a topic, creating police behavior that is responsive to constitutional limitations and sociological and political realities is more of an art than a science. It is an art that must be practiced by individual, creative, professional police leaders on a one-on-one basis as they interact with their charges out on the streets of America.

SUMMATION

In this chapter, we have visited the various types of outcomes developed by police review systems and considered some dynamics relating to how useful they can be for the police leader. We have examined the strengths and weaknesses of traditional, punitive type disciplinary procedures. We have briefly discussed some alternatives to the traditional option and several cutting edge experiments that hold great promise for the future development of police accountability and professionalism.

The last paradox we should visit in this discussion is this: it turns out that, in the long run, the actual system used to attempt to control police behavior is not very important. Creative, honest, effective leadership accomplished by men and women of integrity will tell the tale. Police leaders who have the temerity and intestinal fortitude to motivate and coach young officers to do what is right, in the face of subcultural and traditional norms that work against the new professionalism, are going to make the difference in the 21st century of American policing.

DISCUSSION QUESTIONS

1. Discuss burdens of proof. Begin by differentiating between the criminal law burden of "beyond a reasonable doubt" and the civil law standard of a "preponderance of evidence." Then differentiate between our two sets of standards for misconduct investigations, the preponderance standard and "clear and convincing evidence."

2. Discuss the dangers inherent in allowing too much latitude to those who investigate citizen complaints. Consider how allowing satisficing explanations, as is true with allowing supervisors to handle complaints informally, might end up in allegations of abuse of authority.

3. Why doesn't punishment work? Why do those who are treated with coercion and punitive sanctions invariably end up being diffident, antagonistic, cynical, and even rebellious?

4. Consider the Huberman plan's "counseling and training" approach to discipline. Wouldn't this type of "touchy-feely" program invariably lead to cynicism and derision in the police locker room? If so, is the approach doomed to failure? Or is it possible that such a program could be used to bring about positive change in the hands of creative and thoughtful police leadership?

5. Consider how the Oakland P.D. boards put "the asylum into the hands of the inmates." Why did this work so well? Why was it effective to put those who were guilty of using excessive force in charge of limiting the use of force? Does this idea have a future elsewhere?

 ## KEY TERMS

Burden of proof: A duty placed upon a defendant or plaintiff to prove or disprove a disputed fact.

Circumspection: The mental ability to understand and discriminate between relations.

Clear and convincing evidence: The level of proof sometimes required for the plaintiff to prevail; the level of proof sometimes required is higher than "a preponderance of evidence" for the plaintiff to prevail.

Disciplinary overview: Oversight of the disciplinary process and its outcomes.

Discipline without punishment: Discipline that does not incur any form of punishment, only corrective action. Example: An officer is found to have violated a policy. The supervisor is allowed to conduct written counseling explaining the act, the violation, and what the officer must do to correct the behavior within a given period of time. The officer does not receive any punishment, just guidance to correct the behavior. He may receive punishment if he violates the same policy again within the grace period.

Dynamics of punishment: The outcomes experienced by an officer of the punishment incurred when she/he is found to have violated policy or rules. Example: An officer receives two days off without pay for crashing a police vehicle. The officer becomes bitter against the department and the managers for loss of pay for what she views to be an unavoidable action.

Early warning system: Known as EW in police organizations, a data system that tracks officer complaints and misbehaviors, and gives managers some foresight into who may demonstrate regular negative behaviors or activities. This foresight allows police managers to address negative officer behavior before it becomes a problem.

Exonerated: Absolved; freed from any question of guilt.

External complaints: Complaints against officers from sources outside the organization.

Force differentiations: The differences between use-of-force complaint outcomes versus other types of complaints against police officers. Most often, the outcomes (sustained) of complaints against police officers with regard to use of force are far lower than other types of complaints.

Getting off due to legal technicalities: When an offender (police officer, suspect) is found not guilty of a violation due to a technicality and not due to the "clear and convincing evidence" or "preponderance of evidence."

Huberman plan: A corrective action program developed by John Huberman in the 1960s, where corrective action against an employee is taken without punishment; a no-fault process where the employee receives written action regarding the negative act, the violation committed, and what action the employee must take to correct the behavior within a specific time frame. Sometimes known as "no-fault" discipline.

Internal complaints: Complaints against officers from inside the organization.

Intervention: To alter; an action or development.

No-fault systems: Systems of corrective action that favor written reminders, counseling, and phases of time to correct aberrant behavior versus punishment such as days off without pay, demotion in rank, or termination from employment.

Not-sustained: The allegations cannot be proven one way or the other.

Officer response: The outward behavior an officer demonstrates in reference to corrective action brought against him/her, either positive or negative.

Outcomes: The result(s) of an action.

Positive systems: Corrective action systems that focus on positive types of corrective action (how to improve behavior), rather than the negative (punishment).

Post-intervention monitoring: Tracking and observing the behavior of an officer who has received some form of corrective action (intervention) to determine if his/her behavior improved or declined after the corrective action was initiated.

Preponderance of evidence: The level of proof required to prevail in most internal affairs cases.

Punitive model: A model of corrective action based on punishment for violations of organizational policy, rules, or the law.

Selection criteria: A carefully chosen or representative collection of people or things.

Sustained: The allegations were found to be true, and they constitute misconduct.

Transgressions: The violation of a law, a duty, or moral principle.

Unfounded: The allegations were found to be untrue.

EXAMPLE SCENARIOS

Violation of Conduct Rule

While conducting a review of data in old investigation files, Detective Commander Olson discovers one of his detectives has been "sandbagging" cases and reporting them later than discovered. He notes the cases were closed but not reported as such. Further, he discovers the detective held some cases in abeyance and then released information in sets each month for about 10 months. Commander Olson suspects that the detective held the cleared cases to report them in batches each month so it looked like he was clearing cases at a steady rate. This action would give the impression that the detective was working steadily each month, and it inflated the number of cases he claimed to have cleared.

Commander Olson launches an investigation, and as a result, the detective is suspended without pay for violation of department policy that all cases cleared for the month must be reported that month and not held to be reported later to make the records look more favorable for clearances.

What type of investigation did the commander launch? What model of discipline was used? Could there have been a different approach to corrective action in this case?

Violation of Conduct Rule #2

The same event occurs again in Detective Commander Olson's unit. In this instance, he launches an investigation and the same outcome is found. The detective had violated policy and was determined to have "sandbagged" cases, reporting them later than policy dictated.

The commander decides to place the detective on probation for six months. The detective receives written documentation that he violated the organizational policy when reporting the clearance of cases investigated. He is advised, in writing, what is expected of him for the next six months, with the stipulation that if he again violates the policy, he will receive at minimum a suspension without pay and possible termination.

What type of investigation did Commander Olson launch? What model of discipline was used?

The Citizen/Witness

Two police officers attempt to pull over a drunk driver in the middle of the night. After the blue lights are turned on, the driver continues for several blocks before deciding that he cannot get away from the police and pulls over. He immediately exits the vehicle, and berates the police officers on the sidewalk. He uses arm gestures and raves at the top of his voice about "fascist pigs" and so forth. One officer attempts to put handcuffs on the suspect, and the melee is on. The suspect is drunk enough that it does not take long for him to be subdued.

While one officer is handcuffing the suspect on the front lawn of an adjacent residence, the owner of the residence comes out on his porch in his bathrobe, wanting to know what is going on. The officer not involved in the handcuffing procedure turns to the man and yells at him to "shut the f---- up!" The man, who is on his own front porch in the middle of the night, simply wanting to know why he and his family have been awakened, is then confronted by the officer, who proceeds to attempt to handcuff him, too. The man gives marginal resistance, and the officer takes out his flashlight and hits him numerous times over the head. The homeowner ends up in the hospital in intensive care from his police-inflicted injuries.

So egregious was the behavior of the second officer that the first officer, and one other who showed up in the middle of all this to cover the arrest, storm into the police locker room at the end of their shift, raving about how out of line the officer was who assaulted the citizen. They are so loud in their protests about "what bull---- this is, putting an uninvolved citizen in intensive care" that the watch commander overhears it and comes into the locker room to listen.

How should this event be handled in our modern world of policing? What responsibility does the watch commander have? He is confronted by two officers who are outraged by what another police officer has done. Should he instigate an investigation? What about the two protesting officers? Do they bear a positive responsibility to file a complaint? Even if the citizen does not complain, what should happen in our contemporary police world, where the professional police bear the responsibility to operate under an internalized, personal, and professional ethic?

 ## ADDITIONAL READING

The classic work in the field of police administration, which treats the reader to the oft-cited rationalizations for traditional, punitive disciplinary systems is O. W. Wilson's *Police Administration*. This work has been changed and molded into many editions over the course of more than 40 years, most recently published by McGraw-Hill in 1997, with the co-authors of James J. Fyfe, Jack R. Greene, William F. Walsh, and Roy McLaren. *Fallen Blue Knights: Controlling Police Corruption*, by Sanja Kutnjak Ivkovic (Oxford University Press, 2005) presents a more contemporary explication of the traditional approach to the question of what to do about police misconduct.

Contemporary, synoptic, introductory textbooks about police work in general that include good, albeit brief, treatments of both the traditional and no-fault systems and explications about police administration, as well, are *Police and Society, 3rd Ed.*, by Roy Roberg, Kenneth Novak, and Gary Cordner (Roxbury Publishing, 2005), *The Police in America, 4th Ed.*, by Samuel Walker and Charles M. Katz

(McGraw-Hill, 2002), and *An Introduction to Policing, 5th Ed.* by John S. Dempsey and Linda S. Forst (Delmar Cengage, 2010). A brief treatment of the idea of EW is included in the Walker and Katz work.

Outside the field of criminal justice studies, Richard C. Grote's *Discipline Without Punishment* (AMACOM, 1995) gives the student a look at no-fault disciplinary systems. Grote's work is being utilized everywhere in the fields of business and public administration. As noted in the text, experiments with this type of system are growing in contemporary American police work. Iannone, Iannone, and Bernstein approach this same idea—labeling it "upward discipline"—in *Supervision of Police Personnel, 7th Ed.* (Prentice Hall, 2008). Their work points out the pluses and minuses of what may very well be the police disciplinary system of the future. And finally, John Huberman's "Discipline Without Punishment," *Harvard Business Review* 42: 62–68 (July–August, 1964) was the article upon which the Contra Costa experiment was based.

PART FOUR

The Challenges of Leadership

In these last two chapters, we will bring together the various elements of police leadership into a coherent whole. Chapter 11 divides police leadership into specific tiers and engages in a discussion of the separate requirements and responsibilities involved in leading as a sergeant, a middle manager, and a chief. Chapter 12 ends our journey with an attempt to construct a set of cumulative lists for the police leader. As has been true along the way, the focal point is police professionalism under the umbrella of COP.

CHAPTER 11

The Three Tiers of Leadership

INTRODUCTION

So far, our investigations into the theories and practice of police management have focused on the term "leader" in a generic way. We have made no differentiation between the immediate supervisor, who leads lineups, develops one-on-one relationships with beat officers, and goes out on the street as a uniformed police officer, and the chief executive officer (CEO) of a police organization, the chief or sheriff. While there are minor differences between chiefs and sheriffs, there are substantial dissimilarities between immediate local leaders and upper level management. Thus, we must take the time to focus on the specific challenges that face these diverse leaders.

Before differentiating in this way, we will remind ourselves that there is no single, particular way to lead, in general. We will suggest that the goals of police management present the leader with a set of challenges that present a moving target of sorts. This can be considered either a frustrating and futile reality or one of the more important selling points for a career as a police leader. The fact that the target does move as one progresses through one's career can drive the achievement-oriented individual to be engaged and motivated by the profession as a lifelong commitment to excellence.

At the end of the chapter, we will visit for the last time a thread drawn through all of the text: police professionalism. The drive to generate a genuinely professional attitude and approach among the police officer corps in America, and achieve the concomitant status of professionals, lies directly in the hands of today's police leaders. Ever since the change from the early, corrupt era of American policing into the reform era—mislabeled at the time to be the arrival of professionalism—progress has been slow and halting. Policing as a profession has been frustrated in some places by reluctant politicos and a recalcitrant subculture. But, in recent years, the pace of advancement has accelerated. Today, it is almost within our grasp.

Let us begin by reminding ourselves of the tools available to the police leader in contemporary times.

ONE TYPE OF LEADERSHIP?

We have noted several times that an important element of learning in the life of the young police officer involves realizing there is no single way to accomplish any particular type of police detail. If this is true for the young officer, then it is most assuredly true for the police leader—there is no one way to lead and no one direction in which to lead. The point made here is both substantive and procedural.

Charisma and Creativity

On the process side of this is an idea that we engaged several times in the last chapter. The lot of the police leader is such that he or she must be thoughtful and innovative, resourceful and imaginative, original and inventive. All of this must be accomplished in a way that avoids making it appear that he or she is confused. Naysaying having the power that it does in police work, it can be devastating to the ability of leaders to impact police behavior if analyzing how something ought to be done is perceived to be an inability to make up one's mind. This is, of course, true in all areas of leadership in the world. When a politician takes the time to analyze something, there are always those on the other side of an issue who are ready to attack, waving a flag that says "lost and confused."

We will not reiterate points made in our chapter on assessment, but merely remind the reader that charismatic authority can be critical to police leadership, and it is not transferable from one person to another. Some elements of creativity can be taught and learned—methods of analysis and problem solving—but nothing can be done to create charismatic authority in those who do not naturally possess it.

A Moving Target: Courage Required

Then there is the substantive side of leader creativity. When we speak of courage, we almost universally refer to physical courage, such as charging into gunfire or burning buildings. With regard to the police, we know that on occasion they are faced with challenges similar to those of combat soldiers in the military. Of course, we don't want to emphasize a Hollywood-type view of how exciting and dynamic police work is. The sort of violence and danger that Hollywood portrays is seldom a part of the police experience. But it does happen. Sometimes, officers are faced with life and death situations that require them to go beyond the norm and risk their lives. Under such circumstances, physical courage is indeed required.

REVIEW CHART 11.1

COURAGE

The modern police leader must understand there are three different forms of courage. This is crucial because their subordinates must be motivated (and expected) to exercise all three.

- *Physical courage:* The ability to confront fear of death and/or injury and nevertheless do one's duty
- *Intellectual courage:* The capability to question what one thinks one knows, and alter one's mindset when evidence indicates that attitudinal change is warranted
- *Emotional courage:* The propensity to care about people in general, even in the face of personal heartache and/or negative experiences

But there are other types of courage, and we seldom associate them with police work. There is **emotional courage**. This is the courage to care about people, to empathize or sympathize with others. Even if people have been let down by those they have shown care, they can still extend themselves and be caring. In the face of numerous failed relationships, people sometimes show an emotional courage when they once again try to love. Why does it take courage to behave in these ways? Because—particularly in cultures or subcultures where macho, toughness-oriented behavior is the norm—to be empathetic or sympathetic can be considered a sign of weakness. So it is in police work. While all humans possess empathy and the ability to sympathize to some extent, the dynamics of the police subculture tend to mollify these natural propensities. It takes emotional courage for the police leader to keep in touch with his or her own ability to empathize and sympathize. A leader must also encourage the same things in subordinates.

Then there is **intellectual courage**. As they get older, people tend to be conservative in life. They decide on their own personal philosophy and stick to it. All people learn about the world and develop their own personal ideas and philosophical tenets when they are young. Often, they then cleave to notions and philosophies no longer related to reality when they get older. The world changes, sometimes profoundly. The reality that young people experience can morph into something entirely different when they get older. The person with intellectual courage has the ability to question what they think they know. Such a person exhibits the propensity to continually re-analyze incoming information and then reconstruct their perception of what is going on in the world.

Because police work is in a period of change that presents the most dramatic and dynamic challenges in a century, today's leader has to adapt "on the fly," to some extent. The police officer and the police leader need to have the intellectual courage to question their own world view as they receive data that might be opposed to their understanding of the world and how things work. This is akin to one of the most often cited mottos in the American military, "adapt and overcome."

Adapt and Overcome

As recruits hear in the military, police work is driven by the idea that education and training are accomplished to prepare an officer to face all sorts of problems, crises, and contingencies. Then, out on the street, real life gets far more complicated than anticipation allows. What eventuates is the necessity to adapt and overcome. That is, what was long ago labeled the **"fog of war"** overcomes people and changes anticipated events into something different. No matter how much training has been accomplished, and how rational the leadership is in its efforts to prepare the rank and file, once guns begin firing and dust and smoke prevail, battle becomes something unanticipated. Thus, the axiom in the military is not to ignore training, but be prepared to adapt and overcome. Even though supervisors are universally available in combat, the individual soldiers/officers should still be capable of reshaping their mode of thinking and accommodating ever-changing events on the ground.

Today, the final turn is being made in the direction of police professionalism, after a century of aiming at a goal that was, at one time, considered nothing more than a pipe dream. Police leaders must be prepared to lead, rather than follow, the drive toward change. Pre-service educational requirements are rapidly expanding toward the four-year college degree. Hiring practices are morphing in the direction of requiring numerous pre-service skills and experiences. Training is expanding, in terms of substance and duration. Post-academy training is also expanding and—where it is fiscally possible—FTO programs, as well. Accountability mechanisms are changing and, in some places, evolving into hybrid forms.

While all of this is happening, the police officers of America must continue on with their work. They must be led by those who understand these changes, accept them, and buy into the reality that, while the target is moving, is not necessarily something about which negativity, jadedness, or cynicism can (or should) develop. The institutionalization of COP requires that the target—ethical, effective, and modern police professionalism—is, in fact, ever-changing.

THREE LEVELS OF LEADERSHIP

There are as many tiers of police leadership as there are ranks. One can argue that every level of supervision is unique and presents different challenges, responsibilities, and opportunities. But it is rational for us to logically analyze various levels of management and distill them down to their essence. In such an analysis, three levels suggest themselves: sergeant, middle manager, and chief.

The Sergeant

As is true with teachers and coaches, the most important leader in the life of the individual police officer is the immediate supervisor, or the sergeant. When conducting research into the police officer's experience, Muir asked officers about the influence exerted by various actors in the departmental hierarchy. Muir found that "the chief, the deputy chief in charge of the Patrol Division, and the watch commander were, in comparison, remote and minute men, seen from afar and infrequently. The patrol officer saw none of them as being so crucial to his own development, for good or ill, as his sergeant" (Muir, 1977: 235).

The Sovereignty of the Sergeant We have danced around an issue that now takes center stage: how and why sergeants maintain their critical importance in the lives of individual officers. In some places, sergeants have input into the process of assigning officers, not only to particular beats, but particular shifts and teams as well. When doing so, they exercise a level of power within the organization that is paramount in the lives of individual officers. Depending on the size and diversity of the jurisdiction, such assignments can profoundly impact any officer's professional life. This is just the beginning of the influence that the immediate, local supervisor can have within the organization.

BOX 11.1

THE SERGEANT'S PARADOX: BEING ONE OF "US" AND BEING ONE OF "THEM"

In order to be effective at their charge, sergeants must be in touch with their subcultural roots. They must remember and understand subcultural wisdom in general and local history in particular. Their leadership must be influenced by a realistic grasp of how the rank and file see the organization and its machinations.

On the other hand, the sergeant cannot be a member of the subculture. He or she must remain aloof from its prejudices and ignore some of its norms and values—those that tend to move officers in the direction of overkill with regard to use of force, as an example. It is a fine line that must be walked between membership in and being divorced from the subculture.

We have talked about the creative leader utilizing reciprocity to construct circumstances where the individual officer is motivated to behave in a positive direction. The sergeant is close enough to the individual officer to provide a pat on the back for positive behavior. In a profession largely populated by people who often expect the worst and experience negative evaluations from the public on a regular basis, the sergeant can bestow respectability on an officer. He or she can help with letters of application, vacation assignments, and days off. Even extra overtime hours can be tendered by the sergeant, indirectly awarding extra pay.

When the sergeant assists in solving particularly risky or delicate encounters, he or she actually impacts the safety of officers. The sergeant can take "heat" from above when negativity rolls downhill. In departments where there are implicit quotas ("targets") for arrests and/or citations, the sergeant can steer new officers in the direction of "**duck hunting ponds**." Taken together, the sergeant can bestow "skills, knowledge, safety, self-respect, freedom from blame, friendship, better jobs, extra money, and even a sense of moral context" (Muir, 1977: 240).

Of course, there are limits to what a sergeant can do. But such limitations tend to be less important in medium and large size departments. While limitations might come from the administration or the "**good ol' boys**" ("the old guard"), even these entities possess a limited amount of restrictive power. Since civil service does the promoting and hiring, the sergeant has as much of an impact on advancement from officer to sergeant, and sergeant to lieutenant, as those do above him or her—which is to say, not very much. As is true of the work done by individual police officers, it is virtually impossible for the administration to control the work done by an individual street sergeant. Furthermore, while the potential power of the old timers might be great, in theory, they aren't often motivated to become overtly active. While major changes—such as those that accompany the movement to COP—can be, and sometimes are, resisted by the good ol' boys, the positive influence exerted by sergeants on individual officers is rarely opposed. The nature of the good ol' boys is such that they are willing to accept the status quo, as long as they are not sanctioned personally in a negative way. So when a sergeant "takes care of" the young, active, educated, vibrant, dynamic officer, the old guard will rarely have much to say about it. They do not care enough to make the effort to limit the power of the sergeant under such circumstances.

Allowing for Mistakes/Developing a Personal Ethic At several points in our discussions, we noted that the police leader should allow for innovation and tolerate mistakes on the part of subordinates. Here is where the sergeant can "protect" the younger, learning, growing, maturing officer from "harm." Again, the administration is just too far removed from the street officer to have much of an impact on day-to-day operations. Add this to the fact that most mistakes are never brought to light, and the sergeant has a great deal of latitude within which to operate how he or she wishes, without much fear of interference.

In Chapter 8, we spoke of the importance of officers creating a personal ethic. Furthermore, we discussed what the sergeant can do to facilitate this important process. As with allowing for mistakes, we simply want to remind the reader once more of this dynamic.

Teach and Persuade William K. Muir, whose ideas we have discussed at several points, often tells his students that when writing, one should endeavor to "**teach and persuade**." In written work, one seeks to teach the reader about the subject matter involved and persuade them in one direction or another. What better phrase could there be for a contemporary sergeant to utilize to help with his or her focus when dealing with subordinates?

Sergeants provide the glue that keeps things together (Muir, 1977). While those above them occupy important roles too, police sergeants are the only supervisors who continue to go out on the street and work as police officers in uniform. Police officers know and respect this reality. When the "s--- goes down," the sergeant is out there, on the street, working and struggling "with us." This is the perspective of the average line officer.

Sergeants are the critical link that brings together upper level policy developers and the rank-and-file officers who actually go out on the street and interact with the populace. Their efforts at coaching, mentoring, and teaching beat officers bring meaning to the otherwise sterile dictates of the law and police policy. Here are some teaching dynamics that the effective and creative sergeant must be familiar with.

Perhaps the most important teaching job required of sergeants is that they nurture an understanding and feeling for the paradoxes of police work in subordinates. While many sergeants do not necessarily label them as such, they understand a great deal about these paradoxes. In their roles as teachers and mentors, it is essential they prepare young officers for the on-the-beat frustrations that stem from the paradoxes. Only if officers understand, in an intellectual sense, some of the paradoxes operable on the street, will they be able to avert the emotional stress that accompanies experiencing the limitations presented by these paradoxes.

A second critical piece of teaching for the sergeant relates to the use of power and force. Since there is no definitive understanding of what appropriate force is—what does "excessive" mean? (Klockars, 1992)—the sergeant is the key person in developing the circumspection police officers must have about the use of force. With empathy and compassion for the difficulty of the job, the sergeant must illustrate how critical the use of force is; police officers must think about this a great deal, and come to terms with the paradoxes involved. In particular, the sergeant needs to work consciously on the subcultural norm of **overkill**. The immediate supervisor must understand the paradox of face, and why police officers tend to accept the idea that they have to "win and win big" when confronted by citizen violence. The sergeant must attempt to dispel the idea that excessive force has any place in police work.

Third, and in conjunction with the above point about force, the sergeant needs to do everything possible to dissuade police officers from cleaving to those subcultural norms most deleterious to the best interests of justice. Aside from overkill, the sergeant must endeavor to lessen the distance between the police and the public. Nothing good ever comes from the "us against them" focus. In particular, a good sergeant will teach police officers that to explain or apologize is neither a sign of weakness nor counterproductive to the interests of the police. The contemporary police officer must understand that COP requires a closely knit, ongoing relationship between police and public. In order to create and maintain this relationship, explanations of how the police are operating should be offered up to citizens whenever possible. In the long run, this is productive in facilitating cooperation and respect for the police among the citizenry.

Finally, the sergeant must do everything possible to aid the young police officer in avoiding one of the difficulties often presented to anyone who works with people in a bureaucratic capacity. In the helping professions, there is a tendency for workers to treat citizens as "cases." So many individuals pass through the bureaucratic system, they can become dehumanized. The objectification of people can be a tendency into which doctors, nurses, social workers, and a host of other helping professionals can fall.

On the one hand, the propensity to make people into cases can be a positive thing. It can be utilized to lessen the tension sometimes experienced by doctors or nurses in the operating room, for example. It can be positive if it helps police officers be more objective, correct, and just in their decision making. But, on the other hand, the objectification of citizens can also be a negative dynamic if it leads the professional to lose touch with their humanity and become jaded and cynical. The propensity for professionals to make people into cases can be a profoundly troubling dynamic about which the creative sergeant must warn the young police

BOX 11.2

ALLOWING FOR MISTAKES

A young police rookie shows up at the scene of a domestic disturbance. When the rookie suggests to an irate husband that he must quiet down or he'll have to be "taken out of here," the husband responds with indignation and states, "If you think you're man enough." The young officer immediate takes offense to this challenge to his manhood and grabs the man by the shirt. The man responds by grabbing the officer by his shirt.

The rookie's sergeant arrives at that exact moment. He calms down the husband who, in fact, is not really any threat to the police. He separates the two, and handles the detail without incident or arrest. Later, the sergeant sits the young officer down and talks him through the event, suggesting a number of alternative strategies for its resolution. The sergeant believes that the rookie has performed poorly and made several important mistakes, but he understands the macho mentality of the young man. He remembers how young and inexperienced the rookie is and handles the entire situation informally, in a "just between you and me" manner. In this way, the sergeant acknowledges the rookie's mistakes, encourages learning, and at the same time develops a level of trust he can depend on in the future. The sergeant has allowed for mistakes without being too officious or judgmental. He has probably taught the young officer several important lessons.

officer. Guarding against such "us and them" cynicism is something that rookie police officers, in particular, need to accomplish. It is the job of the sergeant to help them do so.

Our discussion has focused on the substance of what the sergeant must teach. We have also talked about empathizing with subordinates and allowing for experimentation and error, critical in a procedural sense. There is still a final element to our list of the tasks that confront the sergeant.

A sergeant cannot be a member of the subculture. The requirements of leadership will not allow for such an attitude. The sergeant must be firm and resolute, while, at the same time, empathetic and understanding, a difficult mix of characteristics to achieve. The sergeant must be circumspect about his or her own behavior, not just on the street, but also in social situations involving other officers. The integrity of sergeants is the most important relationship between what they teach and do. Something that all coaches know is our final coaching axiom: you cannot give speeches to athletes about commitment, punctuality, loyalty, intensity, focus, or proficiency if you do not live up to them yourself.

The Middle Manager

Caught between the proverbial rock and a hard place, the middle manager faces a tough challenge. Our discussion about middle management will be brief because this topic involves an entire field of police study that is growing more complicated all the time. Along with the changes instituted in the advent of the COP movement, police middle management has become replete with a host of programs aimed at making the development of strategies, implementation, and evaluation more effective. We cannot do justice to this broad set of developments in a survey of the entire field of work, such as this text.

We will examine the middle manager's role in two ways. The leader serves as the glue that holds together upper level policy makers and the line officers on the street. Policy is developed above and flows down the chain of command to the middle manager. Middle managers help develop day-to-day strategies that aim at implementing policy developed above—in our current COP era, they do this as facilitators who aid teams in this effort. Then, as the second part of their job, middle managers evaluate implementation strategies; they evaluate and assess individual officers, as well.

Total Quality Management (TQM)   In the modern era, with COP strategies being instituted around the country, the role of the middle manager has expanded. It still includes some of the basic elements of command and control, of course. When policy is decided on above, the middle manager is still charged with implementing it below. The middle manager is also responsible for generating police accountability systems that assess officer productivity. This much is the same as it has always been. But, under COP, there is much more. Today's middle manager must learn to implement the sort of management systems that have come into vogue in the police world. We will briefly mention the system most often utilized around the country, **Total Quality Management (TQM)** (Peratec, 2009). First brought into police work from the private sector, this system seeks to inculcate some of the basic principles of COP by creating more specifically targeted strategies and developing measuring instruments (Walsh and Vito, 2007). TQM is attempted at thousands of police departments around the country.

The qualitative dimension of TQM includes several key concepts that are equally part of the COP movement. First and foremost, middle management is about teamwork. Managers are required to seek lower level expertise and input before they make decisions. The best way to improve work quality is to seek such input. Top-down, command-and-control management is discouraged. Today's middle manager is meant to play the role of **facilitator**. Gathering input from those at the lower level who actually meet the public, middle managers become the leaders of groups of decision makers, but are not necessarily the primary decision makers themselves.

Second, where discipline is concerned, leaders are encouraged to spend their time focusing on the management of the 95 percent of their subordinates who are not the troublemakers. The focus of management in the past has often been on the 5 percent who *do* cause problems. TQM encourages prompt and fair dealings with problem employees, but suggests that little time should be spent in this negative direction.

Third, TQM emphasizes allowing and encouraging creativity in subordinates. As we have mentioned with regard to sergeants, the middle manager should coach, motivate, and facilitate. He or she should allow for honest mistakes and understand errors will be made if subordinates are being creative and attempting to come up with alternative strategies.

Fourth, TQM's qualitative dimension involves a focus on citizens as **customers**. Evaluating whether customers are obtaining what they want is critical

REVIEW CHART 11.2

PRINCIPLES OF TOTAL QUALITY LEADERSHIP (TQM) IN MADISON, WISCONSIN

- Believe in, foster, and support teamwork.
- Make a commitment to the problem solving process, use it, and let data drive decisions.
- Seek employees' input before making key decisions.
- Believe that the best way to improve working quality or service is to ask and listen to employees who are doing the work.
- Strive to develop mutual respect and trust among employees.
- Have a customer orientation and focus toward employees and citizens.
- Focus on the behavior of 95 percent of employees, not on the 5 percent who cause problems; deal with the 5 percent promptly and fairly.
- Improve systems and examine processes before placing blame on people.
- Avoid top-down, power-oriented decision making whenever possible.
- Encourage creativity through risk taking, and be tolerant of honest mistakes.
- Be a facilitator and coach; develop an open atmosphere that encourages providing for and accepting feedback.
- With teamwork, develop with employees' agreed-upon goals and a plan to achieve them.

Source: Couper and Lobitz, 1991: 48.

here. This is, of course, also true of COP. Surveys are done to ascertain citizen feedback; the information obtained is taken seriously and included in further decision making. Citizens' complaints are understood not as individual problems, but as departmental feedback that brings more data into an organization's decision making process.

The quantitative dimension of TQM involves the use of research and statistical techniques in evaluating organizational effectiveness and efficiency. Here, middle managers are supposed to focus on data-driven problem solving. This is done in lieu of making decisions based on emotion or tradition. As in the paragraph above, both departmentally generated surveys and citizens' complaints provide data upon which decisions should be made. One example of the type of new statistics involved in TQM is the idea that counting numbers of "problems solved" is more important than focusing on arrests and citations.

Of course, as is always the case, there are problems with TQM. Hundreds of types of surveys have been attempted in different locations, some generating results of questionable value. Evaluating "problems solved," for example, is difficult, given the amorphous nature of the rubric. Then, too, police officers must accept and buy into creative and innovative ways of doing things. Often, this is not the case. The surveying and generalized research orientation of such systems can be seen to be a waste of time at best, and can constitute an unwarranted addition of extra work and angst at worst. Line officers sometimes complain that TQM has turned the police department into a survey research center.

Authority and Responsibility In Chapter 4, we engaged the idea that today's middle managers are often placed into an awkward reality. Under this new philosophy, middle managers tend to feel they have lost the authority to command those underneath them and yet are still held responsible for the actions of subordinates. Today's middle managers are caught in an odd position, and that makes their position an extremely difficult one.

This brief discussion has merely scratched the surface of a set of issues. Our efforts here have only been aimed at pointing out the existence of evaluation and implementation systems such as TQM and, in addition, to note that the progress of such systems is problematic, at times. The paradox presented to middle managers is, during the past generation of American policing, they have operated within a sea of change; while being expected to embrace this change, they can often be left rudderless. Middle manager can feel as if they are lacking the sort of clear-cut focal points they used to enjoy under the command-and-control model.

Aloof, Yet Available Given this in-between sort of existence, the middle manager must walk a thin line. COP attempts to create a much more open and direct relationship between middle manager and individual street cop. In the past, the lieutenant, and certainly the captain, had such a removed persona from the individual officer on the street that they sometimes did not even know the names of all of their charges. Insulated (as noted above) by the sergeant and geographic realities, the middle manager was just too aloof to have much to do with the street. Today, that is still a part of the reality of the relationship, and understandably so. If we want the sergeant to play the role of mentor, coach, and teacher—which we do—an "authority figure" must exist within the departmental milieu; the middle manager is that person.

However, it is equally true that this officer-lieutenant/captain relationship has changed today. If we truly want there to be collegial problem solving under COP, with middle managers and sergeants as facilitators and resources for today's empowered agents of change on the street, then the middle manager cannot remain aloof, as was previously the case. The change has been toward the middle manager being a parent-like figure in the individual officer's career. That is, the middle manager must be capable of being supportive and understanding (motivational) or being swift and ruthless (coercive) whenever either is required. Middle manager creativity is required to perform the balancing act of both at once, of course.

The Chief

For several hundred pages, we have focused on police leadership as the exclusive realm of the immediate supervisor. At this point, we will finally consider the position of authority most responsible for the general steering of the "ship" that is the police department.

Vulnerable and Corruptible William Muir's work included an important discussion of the role of the chief of police. Muir suggested that the chief is "vulnerable and corruptible." In this section, we will examine what Muir meant by this. In general, the chief of police lives a **"fishbowl"** existence. His or her decisions, and even personal behavior, are viewed with both interest and skepticism from inside and outside the police department. Because of the power that others can exercise over the chief's **tenure,** the chief is vulnerable to being removed from office at a moment's notice. This does not often occur, but it is legally and politically an ever-present possibility.

Because of this vulnerability, the chief can become corruptible. We do not mean to say that the chief may tend to fall into corruption of authority. Almost everywhere, the time when that was true has long exited the stage in American policing. But chiefs of police are susceptible to noble cause corruption. Just as it is true of beat officers, the chief can be the recipient of requests to do anything to get the job done. Because they occupy such a vulnerable position, chiefs can be prone to respond to such requests even when they are totally inappropriate.

A Word About Tenure Chiefs of police are vulnerable in that their tenure is not guaranteed in any way. Chiefs are appointed by mayors, city councils, boards of selectmen, or even city managers. While they are civil servants during the rest of their careers, when they move up to the head position, they are not afforded civil service protections. They serve **"at the pleasure of"** whomever appointed them.

BOX 11.3

TOO MUCH POLICE CHIEF POWER

We have made the point that most chiefs of police enjoy such a limited tenure that they are vulnerable to corruption and even coercion. But that is not always the case. A generation ago, the Los Angeles Police Department had a chief who was in place for so long he developed a sort of independence from *anyone's* control. Daryl F. Gates was the chief in L.A. for 14 years, and during that time his way of doing things gave the LAPD a black eye and led to the reconstruction of the city charter and how chiefs in L.A. enjoy tenure.

Gates operated a secret spy organization that began with the rationalization it was looking into communist organizations. The Public Disorder Intelligence Division (PDID) had over 200 people assigned to it. Over time, Gates had them spy on and investigate local politicians, religious leaders, media operations, and record companies. Anyone and everyone whom Gates thought suspicious was targeted. In the end, Gates was forced to retire and the city reorganized how it deals with police leaders. This example of police power run amuck illustrates just how politically controversial and volatile the power of police leadership can become (Gates, 1992; Rothmiller and Goldman, 1992).

This means they do not have to be removed for good cause. They can be removed whenever the powers that installed them decide they are no longer effective. Such decisions can be made using whatever grounds these powers decide are reasonable to make such a determination. Thus, chiefs are vulnerable to being discharged at any time. A major corruption scandal, a controversial political fight over police policies, or an individual incident involving police misconduct of some egregious sort—these are just a few examples of the sorts of events that might lead to the firing of a chief of police.

In some places, because of these troublesome dynamics, there have been attempts to create a more solid level of stability for the chief. Understanding the various pressures that make the position vulnerable, some jurisdictions have sought to allow some sort of tenure to the chief. The idea is to place the chief executive police officer on more sound footing and thus make it possible for the chief to do the ethical thing when confronted with elements in the community that may lobby for the expedient and inappropriate thing. In Los Angeles, for example, the city charter has been modified to allow the chief of police a five-year contract, renewable only once. During the five years of the contract, the chief is only removable for cause. Again, this is an effort to free the chief from political powers that sometimes operate against the just and professional decision (Rothmiller and Goldman, 1992).

Sheriffs, on the other hand, are elected, usually in nonpartisan elections. The American sheriff administers the county's policing as long as he or she continues to be popular. Because of this requirement to do what is popular, the sheriff is also vulnerable. Of course, this is true only in a once-in-a-while, political sense. Sheriffs enjoy a sort of tenure denied to chiefs, because of how seldom elections are held. But they too often receive calls to do things that are inappropriate and even illegal.

The important point here is that both chiefs and sheriffs can be responsive to calls for inappropriate, overly aggressive, and even illegal police action. Much as the individual officer is sometimes responsive to calls for Dirty Harry–like behavior, police leaders too can compromise their integrity in an effort to create a more stable work situation for themselves.

Police executives can be vulnerable in a political sense. Unfortunately, this is just the beginning of the list of characters to which the chief must respond.

Media Influence The media in America tend to be very supportive of the police, in general. But when controversy occurs, the media will pounce on it. Controversy means increased television ratings or newspaper sales, or that is how the media perceive things. Police executives must operate to manage their image in the local press. Since this involves keeping away from controversy, chiefs of police tend to work at public relations management constantly. They work at comforting local politicos. They work at appearing to be tough and effective at fighting crime. They work at polishing their individual images.

This is usually an easy enough task. But it can become impossible when anything out of the ordinary occurs. One operational norm to which chiefs cleave is that of the **"rotten apple syndrome"** (Perez, 1994). This idea suggests that when misconduct of any kind becomes manifest enough to be covered in the press, the police executive's internal review system must find a culprit. That culprit is always an individual officer, or group of officers, not the police administration itself. Individual officers are "sacrificed," to some extent, by being sold to the media as "rotten apples." This metaphor suggests that the barrel full of good apples—the police department as a whole—is clean, effective, and ethical. Whatever problem exists lies with a few rotten apples that might "spoil the barrel." IA systems thus work to do two things at once. They get rid of such rotten apples and, coincidentally, avoid having to deal with larger questions about executive level competence. In other words, by discharging officers involved in misconduct and labeling misconduct as unusual, the chief avoids questions about whether the roots of misconduct might lead to the chief's office. Here again, the chief can become involved in noble cause corruption in order to covet the favor of the local media.

Police Unions An odd paradox faced by chiefs of police is that they are supposed to be in command of police organizations and, at the same time, they can be vulnerable to being controlled by the very people they are supposed to manage—line officers. Modern police unions can possess substantial amounts of political power (Delord et al., 2008)—so powerful in some locales they can operate to get the chief discharged. There are numerous examples of this happening. Being aware of this possibility, chiefs of police can sometimes be required to placate union leadership. This reality can work to dissuade the chief from taking actions that would otherwise be considered logical and progressive. Thus, where unions have obtained a substantial amount of political power and independence, the chief's job is made more vulnerable by the very officers he or she is supposed to control.

Personal Life Chiefs of police must maintain unsullied personal lives. They cannot avoid their fishbowl-like existence. They must behave in a way that is irreproachable. Chiefs must pay their bills—and on time. They must pay their taxes—and on time. They must sleep with their significant others—and no one else. They must avoid the police subcultural propensity to become involved in public drinking. In these and a hundred other ways, chiefs of police must be circumspect about their own behavior and image. If it is true, as pointed out above, that the police sergeant's role becomes to some extent boring because of how circumspect such leaders must be about their own personal lives, then it is even more critical for chiefs to behave themselves.

Sending Out Messages Being so far removed from the individual police officer, the chief executive of a police organization can have the single greatest effect on specific officers when **sending out messages** to the organization, both direct and implicit in content. To be sure, the sergeant is the most important teacher in an

BOX 11.4

THE "CORRUPTIBLE" CHIEF

When Muir suggests that chiefs of police are corruptible, he does not mean to suggest that today's modern chief is prone to take money from members of criminal organizations or become involved in police crime. In a country that has over 20,000 police organizations, those propensities may very well surface on occasion. But what is a genuine danger in today's police world is noble cause corruption.

If, for any number of reasons, individual police officers on the street can sometimes become motivated to behave like Dirty Harry—as they are—then so can the chief of police. Hearing requests from local politicos or community leaders to get the job done regardless of how it is accomplished, chiefs of police may very well be persuaded to use draconian (and yet politically acceptable) tactics, such as random sweeps of public housing projects, returning to the days of "suppression teams," and so forth.

organization, interacting with the line officer on a daily basis. The middle manager, in our era of COP, can also have a teaching impact, when team-related decision making occurs and they interact with the line. But given how seldom the chief interacts with even sergeants (much less line officers), what can the chief to do influence the future of the department as a teacher? Here are a couple of ideas about the substance of several proactive subjects that can by dealt with by the chief in an important, long-term way.

Legality and Democracy   The chief of police must operate within yet another ongoing paradox: having to teach democracy and legality at the same time. Muir points out that both of these concepts are critical to modern policing (Muir, 1977). Police officers must be hired, trained, and disciplined on a regular basis with an eye toward ensuring they have an appreciation of the law. Everything they do must be done legally, and this must be a serious principle that drives the organization.

The police must also have an appreciation for democracy or the rule of the people. Especially in an era of COP, they must understand they serve the citizens of their community and need to be as responsive to public concerns as possible. Thus, as pointed out in previous chapters, the police must be both legal actors and political actors. To do both things at the same time is sometimes impossible. The people will sometimes call for the most outrageous police actions. To ignore calls for illegal action from the citizenry and thus ignore the principle of democratic rule, is to adhere to the law. This can produce even more angst in the world of the chief of police. Obeying the law and doing what is right become a political liability.

Affirmative Action   From the 1960s until the 1980s, the federal government had an **affirmative action** policy in place. This policy required that local, state, and federal hiring procedures take cognizance of race as a part of their process (Kellough, 2006). This policy applied to all governmental jobs, including positions in police work. If a systematic pattern of discrimination had been in place in any jurisdiction, the discriminating entity—a local police department, a state-run school system, or a federally run parks department, as examples—had to attempt to undo that discrimination by prioritizing the hiring of whatever race had been the target of discrimination. At the federal level, affirmative action is no longer required, but some states and major cities still have affirmative action policies in place. We will take the time to discuss affirmative action here, not only because it still determines part of the selection process in some places, but because it was a critical element involved in the changes in American policing that have occurred in the past generation.

This is not a constitutional law text, so we will not spend time flushing out all of the intricacies of affirmative action—how it came into being, how it was made operational, and the debate that surrounded it. For our purposes, it is only important to note that a part of the formula that defines the "model police officer" in some jurisdictions can include the race, gender, or sexual orientation of prospective police candidates, and there are logical reasons for this. As noted above, there is

BOX 11.5

BROWN V. BOARD OF EDUCATION (1954)

In terms of its impact on American society and the lives of millions of individual Americans, the Supreme Court's most important decision of the 20th century was *Brown v. Board of Education*. In this case, the Court reversed an 80-year-old decision that allowed the state to discriminate on the grounds of race, as long as the separated races were treated equally. The "separate but equal" doctrine went by the wayside in *Brown*. Later cases required any level of government systematically discriminating along racial grounds not only stop such discrimination, but to use "affirmative action" to undo the harm caused by discrimination. Applied to police work, this has meant profound changes in terms of the demographics of American police departments all across the country.

good reason to believe it is important for the demographics of a police department to reflect the demographics of the city it polices. Until affirmative action came along in the late 1960s, many cities had almost all-white police departments in populations made up of a majority of non-white citizens. In Oakland, for example, the police department had over 600 officers in the mid-1960s, and all but one were white males. This organization policed a city with a population that was more than 60 percent black and Latino. The idea behind affirmative action was, and still is, that this imbalance was not good for police–community relations in general, and could also be troublesome for the delivery of justice on the streets.

So affirmative action came to the city of Oakland. By the late 1970s, with a non-white population of more than 70 percent, the police department had a patrol division that almost replicated the percentage demographically. Why is this important? There is every reason to believe a racial disparity between police officers and citizens can produce a great deal of citizen–police (and police–citizen) enmity. As was pointed out by the riot commissions of the 1960s, one of the reasons for the riots was this very tension between the races.

Of course, affirmative action has its own paradox. In attempting to do away with a history of systematic discrimination, the tool used is systematic discrimination (Anglin, 2006). That is, in turning an all-white police department into one that is largely black and Latino, there have to be many academy classes made up of almost all non-white cadets. During the years when this changeover occurs, it is extremely difficult for a candidate to be hired if he or she is white. No matter how much we might accept the logic of affirmative action in theory, it has been difficult for white males, in particular, to avoid the feeling that it involves **reverse discrimination**, the application of racial prejudice to selection processes in a way that prioritizes candidates of diverse ethnic backgrounds over white candidates. The fairness of the civil service system is thus circumvented by affirmative action (Moran, 1988).

Affirmative action was first aimed at the black/white dichotomy, but later was utilized to integrate Latinos, women, Asians, and gays into many police departments. Has it worked? Has affirmative action led to a lessening of tensions between the police and the public? The answer is that it is hard to tell. There is a great amount of "testimonial" evidence that having a police department that mirrors the ethnic diversity of the community it polices tends to mollify antipathy toward the police and encourages the development of good police–community networking. But there is little empirical evidence to this effect. Several studies indicate there is a short-term, positive impact that comes from affirmative action. On the other hand, some long-term studies find that statistical data does not necessarily support this conclusion. We are left to ponder whether it only *seems* logical that affirmative action has worked in positive ways with regard to tension between the races.

As for women in policing, some interesting findings have been observed in recent years. In the beginning, many male officers felt that women could not handle the physical requirements of policing. Therefore, there was a great deal of angst about affirmative action bringing more women into the profession. But over time, several things have been proven about female officers that are truly fascinating. Female officers get far fewer citizens' complaints than their male counterparts. They are very rarely the subject of excessive force complaints and seldom get into altercations with citizens. Women are better at dealing with children and rape victims. Taken together, it is clear the addition of women into the ranks of the patrol officer corps has had a positive impact in many places and many ways.

The same can be said of homosexual police officers. It has been found that opening police work up to openly homosexual officers not only had no deleterious effects for the public, it generated a substantial amount of normalization on the part of straight police officers for their gay comrades (Belkin and McNichol, 2002). This, in turn, may create even more acceptance of gay people in general among the police.

Affirmative action has changed the face of American policing. There is reason to believe that the changes brought into effect have narrowed the distance between the police and the public, in the inner city in particular. Of course, we must remember that these changes have been hard on the white male candidate from the "dominant" culture.

Whether or not their particular jurisdiction has an affirmative action policy in place, we have taken some time to note its positive potential for police CEOs. It is possible, even without it being official policy, for the chief of police to institute a limited affirmative action policy utilizing the Rule of Three in civil service selection. In some locales, where affirmative action has been done away with, this can be a good example of what the chief can do to become a creative and forward thinking police leader.

Sergeants, Ethics, and IA We have argued for several points about ethics in our discussions. First, it is critical for the individual officer today to develop a personal ethic for application on the street. Second, it is important that the sergeant encourage and take part in the creation of such an ethic. Third, everyone else in the departmental milieu should take such ethical issues seriously. Finally, it should be considered impossible for an officer to be competent without being ethical. The two are interchangeably linked.

Two extraordinarily creative ideas for the chief have to do with these points about ethics and I.A experience. These ideas came from the former chief of the Oakland PD, John Hart. In an effort to ensure all of the above are operative dynamics within the police organization, the chief can do two important things. First, when a person makes it to the sergeant's level, there is an open window to the machinations of IA. In every department except in the largest organizations, it is possible for the newly minted sergeant to spend a week or so in IA. Even if that experience merely involves being shown around and interviewing a complainant or two, the idea is to make sure—in the long run—that every sergeant in the entire department understands two things: how the IA process works and how important the chief believes it to be.

Second, in order to send out an important, no-nonsense message about how the department is run and what is prioritized, the chief should endeavor to put the "best and brightest" investigators into IA. In police work, it is traditional to put the most intelligent and fast-rising people of the organization into homicide and/or robbery as they pass through the ranks on their way up. This is why investigators from those bureaus or divisions are often referred to as the "**varsity**" by uniformed officers. Well, the same can be done with regard to IA. If the chief takes care to place such people into IA on a regular basis, the subculture will learn that the chief is serious about what goes on in IA. Putting the best and the brightest into IA on a consistent basis will accomplish an important task without the chief having to emphasize it. The police officer corps will note and remember this when they see it.

These two points are not small ones. Over time, Chief Hart of Oakland did, in fact, send out the message that IA was to be taken seriously. It was not a backwater assignment for investigators, and its processes were understood by every sergeant in the department. Again, over time, everyone at the OPD learned (if there had ever been any doubt about it before) that under Chief Hart, the machinations of internal affairs were to be taken seriously. There was to be nothing tongue-in-cheek or semi-serious about IA and ethical conduct.

GENERATING PROFESSIONALISM

The entire endeavor of leading police officers may be fairly said, in a substantive sense, to focus on police professionalism. Every leader at every level can have an impact. Before we spend a moment more on this most important police goal, let us briefly refer to the history of policing in America in an effort to put today's parallel movements (toward COP and professionalism) into proper perspective.

REVIEW CHART 11.3

THE CHIEF'S STRESSFUL EXISTENCE

Chiefs of police must respond to and are often controlled by:
- Politicos who appoint them
- Public opinion in general
- The electronic media (television/radio news)
- The print media (newspaper/magazine news)
- Police unions (in some jurisdictions)

A Note about Police History

In most policing textbooks, an entire chapter is spent covering the history of policing. While some of the content of such chapters is interesting, most of it is irrelevant to the development of an understanding of today's police. So, in this work, we will simply list the historical eras of policing and note how our above threads are related to these eras (see Box 11.6).

When the American police first materialized, they were controlled directly by political "machines." We call this the "political era" of policing (Lyman, 2004). Corruption was rampant, morale was low, effectiveness was limited, and the police enjoyed little status in America. Begun during the progressive era of American politics (Diner, 1998), calls for reform eventuated change. In an effort to make the police more effective and efficient, and to do away with the police corruption of the times, the second era of policing, the "reform era," was instituted (Lyman, 2004).

Reform did not come all at once. Indeed, corruption scandal by corruption scandal, American policing was changed into a different type of institution. Civil service examinations were instituted, police academies were invented, and police accountability was taken seriously for the first time. In general, police organizations were made more responsive to the law and the interests of justice. The methods utilized to introduce these changes involved altering police work in the direction of paramilitarism. There was good news and bad news associated with these changes.

The good news was that the paramilitarism of the reform era did away with corruption almost everywhere. The tactic worked. Almost immediately, the police began to obtain more status in the minds of American citizens. Unfortunately, after several decades of such paramilitaristic policing, people began to rail against its excesses. People began to dislike the aloofness of the police and their rigid, occupying-army carriage. Business owners did not like that they had no ongoing relationship with their local beat officers, and minorities distrusted the

BOX 11.6

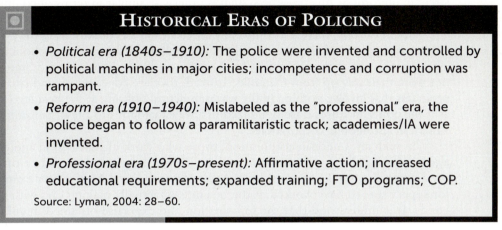

HISTORICAL ERAS OF POLICING

- *Political era (1840s–1910):* The police were invented and controlled by political machines in major cities; incompetence and corruption was rampant.

- *Reform era (1910–1940):* Mislabeled as the "professional" era, the police began to follow a paramilitaristic track; academies/IA were invented.

- *Professional era (1970s–present):* Affirmative action; increased educational requirements; expanded training; FTO programs; COP.

Source: Lyman, 2004: 28–60.

paramilitaristic police almost more than they had distrusted the police of the political era. Hence, further changes were in order.

The modern era, the professional or community-oriented era, evolved out of the excesses of the paramilitarism of the reform era (Lyman, 2004). Driven by concerns about the skyrocketing crime of the 1960s and 1970s, the inner city riots of that era, and the drawbacks of paramilitarism, people began to call for something new and different. Out of this set of concerns came the impetus to create a new philosophy. The pressure exerted by those who called for change eventually drove police scholars and practitioners to develop community policing. It is within the professional or community-oriented era of policing that we now abide.

What Needs to Happen?

The sort of professionalism the police seek today includes several major elements. An advanced academic experience introduces the professional to a systematized body of knowledge unknown to laypeople and collegial problem solving. Furthermore, it includes self-regulation, self-disciplining, and an internalized professional ethic. We have noted the police are "almost" professionals with regard to this definition. Where does the police leader go from here to participate in the development of professionalism? What remains to be done? In this section, we will first consider the European model of police professionalism and then offer several suggestions about future directions for the American system.

The European Model In many European countries, those who police the streets in uniform have similar backgrounds and training as American police officers. Although the training process has reached a genuinely professional level—as one example, it takes two full years of academy training to be put on the street in uniform in Austria—the system is otherwise similar in terms of command structures, FTO requirements, and so forth (Das and Dolu, 2009).

But in Europe, there is a completely different way of administering the police. The entire upper level command structure is educated at the graduate school level. Those who work at the equivalent level of above captain in the United States do not work their way up from the ranks. Instead, they are educated in graduate level programs that involve nothing in the way of practical policing at the beat level. It is as if the police in Europe are organized in a way analogous to the organization of American automobile corporations.

In such an American corporation, those who work in supervision and management are college educated and rarely, if ever, have any experience on the production line. It is not considered necessary at General Motors, for example, for supervisors to have worked at the business of actually making cars with their hands. It is understood that the information and expertise obtained in college, majoring in business administration, is sufficient. If managers know about budgets, personnel administration, organizational theory, and marketing, they are well suited to supervise and make corporate policy. So it is with the police in Europe. Police commanders are sent through graduate schools in order to obtain the equivalent of master's degrees and Ph.D.s in police management. Then they take their places in the police hierarchy and supervise those who police on the streets.

In America, policing has always worked under the assumption that, to be an effective supervisor, it is necessary to have worked on the beat and have made one's way up through the ranks. Is this truly necessary or might an effective route to professionalism in American policing be to change our view in this European direction? This is not likely to happen, given the strength of the police subculture and more than 150 years of history. But it does give us an interesting point of reference for our discussions here. We can muse about how effective it might be to keep the American lower level police system the way it is and change the upper management structure to bring in experts in managing police systems in the way that corporations or public bureaucracies are managed. Would this accelerate the development of professionalism and COP in America? Would it be better for the public or more in the interests of the delivery of justice on the streets? Who can say? One thing we *can* say for sure is the police CEO can open up his or her mind to the idea of bringing in certain types of experts who might be of great value to the organization, but have never worked on the street. The European model suggests this can work and can work well to inculcate the police world with certain types of expertise that tend to be lacking.

The Research Component How scientific is police work? How much of what the police do is because police officers, administrators, or scholars have systematically collected evidence that is effective and efficient? For police work to be professionalized, it would have to be more research driven and scientific. Much of what police officers do is because of tradition and police intuition. The practical

BOX 11.7

THE EFFECTIVENESS OF ROUTINE PATROL

In 1974, a report was issued about the first and perhaps single most important piece of police research ever done. In Kansas City, Missouri, an experiment was constructed to ascertain the effectiveness of routine patrol. Long believed to deter crime, the movement of patrol vehicles around the streets of the city was found to have a negligible impact on crime. This, of course, changed our understanding of the importance of routine patrol. But it also ushered in today's era of constant research into police effectiveness.

applications of police officers on the street tend to be effective because they make common sense, they have worked in the past, or they follow the dictates of police traditional lore.

In the past several decades, policing has become more scientific due to knowledge created by a wealth of research projects (Caiden, 1977). Police professionalism has expanded dramatically because about 30 years ago social scientists who had been studying the police from the outside looking in began to be embraced by police leaders. Instead of resenting such outsiders, many police leaders in the late 1960s and early 1970s had the foresight and courage to open up their operations to dozens of studies. Just about everything in police work has now been studied or is being studied. The information garnered in these studies has advanced the cause of professionalization rapidly. All of this works to increase the scientific nature of the systematized body of knowledge possessed by the police.

In 1965, spurred on by several riot commissions that called for more scientific policing and police education, federal funds were committed to police research under the **Office of Law Enforcement Assistance (OLEA)**. Hundreds of millions of dollars were committed to this effort (Roberg et al., 2005). COP in particular was partly driven by research that questioned paramilitarism, the effectiveness of random and reactive patrol, the need for rapid response, and the effectiveness of criminal investigations. The police began to understand that utilizing research in order to solve problems was more logical and effective. Not only has police procedure been dramatically changed, but our understanding of the causes of crime and what to do about it generally has expanded. This research component of modern policing has been one of the reasons that genuine professionalism is within reach.

Police Review The genuine professions enjoy the privilege of disciplining themselves. This is because of the latitude society grants, due to their academic experience and substantive knowledge base. Such latitude has never been granted to the police. In contemporary times, the call for the civilianization of police review has expanded. Research has discovered that civilian review is not abusing of police officers (Perez, 1994). At the same time, several studies suggest that it enhances the externally perceived faith in police operations. Therefore, external police review is expanding rapidly (Walker, 2005).

While civilian review has its drawbacks, as noted in Chapter 10, hybrid systems seem to afford both an effective accountability mechanism and an efficient use of taxpayer dollars. And there is something else: police professionalism is underwritten by such open review systems because they generate more citizen support for the police in the long run. On the police officer side of things, opening up review to a more broadly based point of view can instill a more COP-oriented view of who should control the police and why. The partnership ideal of COP is moved closer to fruition by civilianized review.

COP Many of the problems associated with the fact that the police have not yet achieved genuine professionalism in America is addressed by the movement toward COP. We need only remind ourselves that COP encourages more logical, scientifically defensible police operations. It suggests more collegial problem solving and decentralization, which empower the individual police officer. It inspires police officers and managers to behave in any number of intelligent and educated ways, emblematic of a genuine profession. Everything about COP influences the drive toward genuine professionalism in a positive way.

These are the types of programs and movements operating today that encourage and develop police professionalism. Progress in this direction, incremental and halting for several generations, has now escalated. There is good reason to believe the genuine professionalization of the police is within the grasp of its practitioners.

THE LIMITS OF REFORM

Having already visited some of the roadblocks of the movement toward police professionalism, we will merely remind ourselves, very briefly, what they are.

Media Imagery

The media tend to sensationalize police work, focusing on anything negative when it appears. While day-to-day coverage is positive, the amplification of police misconduct and occasional failures can create backsliding in the drive to professionalize the police. This is because part of the achievement of genuine professional status will be in the eyes of the public. The media sell inaccurate images to the American populace that mitigate a feeling of respect in the minds of citizens. Then, too, the media are so focused on the elimination of crime that they do not care how it is achieved; they can even demand noble cause corruption.

American Cultural Resistance

American citizens are born and raised with a penchant to be against governmental power; the public will always be reluctant to ascribe to police the sort of professional status they extend to doctors, nurses, teachers, engineers, architects, and so forth. Also, as is true with the media, the public tends to demand that the police accomplish the job of minimizing crime and creating safe streets, no matter what it takes. So, noble cause corruption is accepted and at times even encouraged and applauded by the public.

Paramilitarism

Keeping aloof from the public through the machinations of paramilitarism only exacerbates the propensity for people to denigrate the police and refuse them professional status. Even though paramilitarism has its place in police work on some limited, extraordinary occasions, it can create a feeling of separation in the hearts and minds of not only the police, but the citizenry as well. This feeling works against the achievement of professional status. Paramilitarism also works against the sort of interactive and partnership-oriented approach toward the citizenry that professionalism demands.

The Good Ol' Boys

Those in police work who operate with the "old-school thinking is best" mentality are of no help whatsoever here. For obvious reasons, the good ole' boys operate in an unprofessional manner, are not apologetic for this, and work directly against all efforts at professionalism. While this sort of policing is becoming an anachronism, it still impacts rural policing in particular and inhibits the growth of status and respect for all police officers everywhere.

Subcultural Resistance

There is little *overt* resistance to professionalism within the police subculture. After all, achieving the status accompanying this achievement would mean increased respect and fiscal stability for all police officers. The sort of subcultural resistance that exists is latent. It takes the form of support for Dirty Harry and grass-eating misconduct, subcultural norms regarding overkill and never explaining oneself, resistance to police accountability, and resistance to the changes involved in COP. In these ways, the police subculture actually works against the interests of the police in general by standing in the way of the professionalization movement.

In this brief section, we have visited numerous roadblocks that inhibit the development of police professionalism. But this is not meant to imply that these roadblocks will inhibit the fruition of the dream of professionalism forever. Police professionalism is on its way, and in the long run, nothing is likely to stop it.

BOX 11.8

⊙ CENTRAL PARADOX: HERDING CATS

Of course, we are being tongue-in-cheek here in analogizing leading police officers to herding cats. But this suggestion was made on the very first page of our endeavor and it bears remembering as we come to the end. Perhaps *the* central paradox of all of the paradoxes that can frustrate or confuse the issue with regard to managing the police is this one: no matter how hard we work at making the leadership role one that is done scientifically and how much charismatic authority the police leader may be lucky enough to possess, the physical isolation of the individual police officer from his or her supervisors, combined with the power and solidarity of the police subculture, can work to make almost everything we try ineffective.

SUMMATION

Our travels through the world of police leadership have led us full circle to a central issue outlined in the introductory chapter: the parallel development of police professionalism and COP. As we differentiated between sergeant, middle manager, and chief in this chapter, we have consistently stuck to the idea that *the* most important goal of them all is to institute these changes. Nothing else remotely approaches the importance for today's police, the officers of the future, and the American public than the fruition of these long sought after goals.

For the sergeant today, the roles are multiple and challenging. One can either be frustrated and conflicted by their multiplicity or absorbed and engrossed by the challenge they present. One platitude is certainly apposite: to be the best sergeant one can be in today's police world is to be involved in a level of commitment that is a lifelong career path—a path that most certainly involves the individual in the world of the professions. For the middle manager, too, though the road is replete with paradoxes and complexities, being a part of what is happening in modern American police work involves the individual in a dynamic and exciting set of trials.

Finally, for the chief, the road can also be frustrating, given the host of powerful agents arrayed before him or her. But, equally, to participate in the creation of a profession out of an occupation can be rewarding and satisfying. What better way could there possibly be to spend one's working years in life?

DISCUSSION QUESTIONS

1. Discuss the idea from the text that there are several types of courage in the world. What are examples of courageous actions that police leaders might take that do not relate in any way to physical courage?

2. What does it mean to suggest that sergeants must allow their subordinates to take chances and make mistakes? How can leaders do this without making individual officers and/or the police department vulnerable to legal attack?

3. Discuss this idea that chiefs of police are vulnerable. What does this mean? How are they vulnerable? To whom? To what? What about the paradox that, in some ways and places, the chief's authority is actually limited by the police officers he supervises?

4. Our discussions about generating professionalism in today's police officer corps include some suggestions about what needs to happen before the police become genuine professionals. Review this list in light of the definitions of professionalism that we have visited. Can you add to or subtract from the list of what needs to happen before the police enjoy the type of status that is enjoyed by doctors, lawyers, teachers, and so forth?

5. Consider the good ol' boys. Who are they? Where have you experienced them? Do you agree that they can have a tremendously negative impact on progress in contemporary American police work? How can the creative police leader deal with good ol' boys in a reasonably creative and positive way?

KEY TERMS

Affirmative action: Policies that take race, ethnicity, or sex into consideration in an attempt to promote equal opportunity or increase ethnic or other forms of diversity in the workplace; *Brown v. Board of Education:* Undo harm caused by discrimination.

Aloof, yet available: A term used for executive police leaders who learn to keep themselves above the rank and file but are available to them periodically; not completely separated by rank.

American cultural resistance: The notion or accepted ideal that Americans are resistant to governmental power.

At the pleasure of: A term used in government and business denoting that appointed officials "serve at the pleasure of" the commissioners, a board of directors, a CEO, etc.; the official can be dismissed from the position without cause.

Customers: A term used in Total Quality Management circles representing the people, organizations, or entities the business or public safety agency serves. Example: When an officer responds to a citizen's call for service, he is "attending the customer."

Duck hunting ponds: Locations where criminal activity and traffic violations are frequent and regular. Officers looking for arrestor citation activity go to these locations to improve their statistics.

Emotional courage: Having the internal ability to take action when one is not sure of the outcome. Example: To stand up and confront a boss who has given a directive you know will be destructive to the organization.

Facilitator: Someone who helps a group of people understand their common objectives and assists them to plan to achieve them.

Fishbowl: A term used to illustrate how a leader is viewed and lives his/her life during their tenure. They are seen by the public from the outside looking in.

Fog of war: A term used to describe that, while soldiers are fighting a war, they are oblivious to any activity outside the battlefield. Sometimes leaders are so busy focusing on their own problems and concerns they miss other activities that may impact their organization in a negative way.

Good ol' boys: A term used for a group of officers or leaders who are related to each other through social means or friendships and who back each other up.

Intellectual courage: The ability of a person to question what they think they know about others, themselves, cultures, religions, etc.

Media imagery: Impressions created by the media through articles, stories, or filmmaking, true or otherwise.

Media influence: The ability of the media (print or film) to directly sway or affect the opinions or notions of those they reach.

OLEA: Acronym for the former Office of Law Enforcement Assistance.

Overkill: Police propensity to use excessive force when they are attacked.

Research component: That part of an agency devoted to conducting qualitative and quantitative research on activities within the agency to determine whether those activities were of benefit or detriment.

Reverse discrimination: A denial of equal protection of the laws, generally viewed as discrimination of members of a dominant or majority group in order to promote members of a minority or consistently disadvantaged group.

Rotten apple syndrome: This metaphor suggests that the barrel full of apples (the police department) is clean, effective, and ethical; the problem (whatever problem) lies in a few rotten apples that might spoil the barrel (Perez, 1994).

Sending out messages: A method of messaging from an executive officer to the rank and file about an issue or concern he/she wants addressed. This may be done through policy changes, memoranda, or through the "grapevine" (direct, implicit, or indirect). In modern day policing, sending out messages can also be done via the organization's newsletter, bulletin, or website. The purpose is to make the issue well known.

Teach and persuade: A phrase that suggests when one wants to influence others they should teach them about the subject and persuade them in a specific direction.

Tenure: Permanence of position based on specific established conditions.

TQM: An acronym standing for Total Quality Management. A method utilized by some police agencies to develop quantifiable methods toward continuous quality improvements of the agency's operations.

Varsity: A term used in some police agencies describing officers who are tenured and have risen through the ranks by their placement in high profile divisions, such as internal affairs and/or homicide.

EXAMPLE SCENARIOS

Emotional Courage

Chief Joe Safire is in charge of a moderate-sized police department. The department has been a significant challenge for him since his appointment as chief. Not only was he not the person the police union wanted in the position, but he was challenged by a group of citizens who wanted another person to be the police chief.

Almost all his efforts to bring positive change to the agency have been met with challenges from the union president. In spite of those challenges, Chief Safire has persevered. His personal sentiment about the union president is the guy is a malcontent, a naysayer who has only himself in mind, not the mission of the organization or the community. His feelings almost border on hatred. But the chief always presents himself as a professional to the president and never makes disparaging comments behind closed doors about his feelings.

Then the union president contracts a serious untreatable disease. He is terminal and has about a year to live. Chief Safire searches inside himself and buries his negative feelings about the union president and decides to help him by keeping him on board in the department as a regular officer so his family can receive benefits offered to an officer who normally retires. He also takes time to visit the president regularly to keep track of his condition, both physically and mentally. The chief does not have to do this. He could require the president to switch to long-term disability and miss the opportunity to pass his salary on to his family.

Is this appropriate behavior? It costs the city money, since a spot is kept essentially unfilled in the department. It might be interpreted to be a romantic notion not commensurate with the responsibilities of a chief of police. What would you say about it if you were on the city council? What would you do about it if you were in upper level police management?

Vulnerable and Corruptible

Sergeant Ronald Dill works in a small Midwestern agency. He has worked hard to get to his position. He considers himself to be on the way up in his department. His belief is that he is smarter than other officers and leaders, and better equipped to be in charge. He made a pledge to himself he would do whatever it takes to move up the organizational ladder.

Dill is very good friends with one of the district commissioners, Jay Fulsteen, who intends to become mayor someday. He has expressed this intention to Dill, who pledged his support to Fulsteen. One day, Fulsteen contacts Dill and says he has information that a citizen who is announcing his candidacy for Fulsteen's district commission seat has some bad news in his personal background. Fulsteen tells Dill he heard that the guy was involved in some criminal activity, but the information was sealed and is not available for public viewing. He wants Dill to check this out using the department's records base and Dill's resources to get to the data. He promises Dill support in the future for any endeavor he seeks. Dill searches for a way to get the information somehow so it won't be tied to him.

Can this behavior be rationalized as "just politics"? How might it look from the outside? What problems do you foresee for the commissioner and the department if it were to go public? Is this just a "little favor" or something important and a major problem? Does the history of the department—how it's run, and how closely the police are related to local politicos—make a difference? Why or why not?

Reform?

Lieutenant Chris Mantle is known for his technical abilities with data and computers. He has been interested for some time in setting up a system of indexes that can help his police department quantify some the information that would help it demonstrate its achievements to the public, as well as the board of commissioners.

He has developed a program to measure Part I crimes and clearance rates that has an easy data entry process and calculates numbers and percentages for comparison in real time. This system would enhance the investigation and patrol division's ability to problem solve activity in their zones, as well as help them establish proactive activities to potentially predict future criminal activity.

He presents his information program to the commander of the investigative division, who views computers and electronic devices as a waste of valuable resources and money. The commander thinks he could better use money to hire an administrative assistant to produce his memos and complete his paperwork. Mantle knows his program has great potential, but he seems to be fighting a battle of organizational ignorance and resistance to promising reform. He sees the commander—as do other younger, more educated members of the department—to be one of the good ol' boys.

What should Lieutenant Mantle do? He does not want to violate the chain of command, but he sees himself as a member of the "new blue line" and a professional. He sees his program as essential to the development of departmental professionalism. Should he shop his idea around the department? Should he wait until he has more power, later in his career? Should he look for allies?

ADDITIONAL READING

As cited elsewhere (several times, to be sure) Weber created the quintessential definition and analysis of charismatic authority (of all three types of authority, for that matter), more than 100 years ago. The Gerth and Mills work (cited in the text of this chapter) is the original source on this.

With regard to the importance of the sergeant, many police management books work on this premise. But important, classic social science textbooks which reflect upon it are Egon Bittner's *The Functions of the Police in Modern Society* (National Institute for Mental Health, 1970), George Berkley's *The Democratic Policeman* (Beacon, 1969), Edwin Dellattre's *Character and Cops* (American Enterprise Institute for Public Policy Research, 1989) and Dorothy Guyot's, *Policing as Though People Mattered* (Temple Unversity Press, 1991).

An important set of reflections on the multiple stresses placed upon the chief—and how creative chiefs might respond—was written and analyzed at the end of the oft-cited work by our friend Muir, *Police: Streetcorner Politicians* (University of Chicago Press, 1977).

Finally, we refer in several chapters to the critical research component of the drive toward professionalization. Two organizations fund all kinds of research and, in addition, are spurring the drive in general. They are the Police Executive Research Forum and the International Association of Chiefs of Police. They can be found—and many citations regarding research of all types into police operations and practices, as well—at www.policeforum.org and www.theiacpfoundation.org.

CHAPTER 12

Bringing It All Together

INTRODUCTION

This chapter is an epilogue of sorts. It is a summation and review, composed of a catalogue of the issues we have been concerned with during the course of our entire endeavor. It has no discussion questions, key terms, example scenarios, or additional reading at the end. This final chapter is meant to bring together some of the most important points in our discussions and focus on them as a whole. It presents a set of distillations, in list form, that can be taken from the book. Hopefully, these lists will be useful to police managers everywhere who confront and engage the paradoxes of police leadership on a daily basis.

DEALING WITH INDIVIDUAL OFFICERS

On one level, the police leader must interact with the individual officer in his or her charge. We have given the reader dozens of ideas about how to manage this interaction; here are some reminders and paradoxes that are of critical importance when dealing with subordinates in the world of police leadership.

Police leaders must:

- Remind themselves of the paradoxes faced by the rank and file on a daily basis.

- Recall that some officers will believe in the positive utility of noble cause corruption. Too many supports exist within the subculture and American society for Dirty Harry to be completely defeated.

- Exercise positive discipline whenever possible. Traditional, punitive systems never, under any circumstances, work to change behavior in a positive way in the long run.

- Teach and encourage the use of common sense and be cognizant of the limitations of the search for any one, definitive way to handle any given type of detail.

- Emphasize openness and honesty—not just in interactions with subordinates, but also between individual police officers and citizens.

- Encourage and facilitate the formation of a personal ethic by every police officer in America.

- Deal with the requirement to construct a personal ethic in a positive way, and not with the traditional "don't screw up" type of approach.

- Understand that while Americans hear so much about intelligence quotient (IQ), an officer's social or emotional quotient is more important.

DEALING WITH THE POLICE POPULATION AS A WHOLE

On a different level, the leader must deal with groups of officers and/or the subculture. Sending out messages to the collectivity of police officers presents a slightly different set of considerations. Here are several ideas from our discussions about multiple-officer concerns.

Police leaders must:

- Be cognizant of the mission, focus on it, and work consistently to stay on track in everything they and their subordinates do.
- Balance command responsibilities with COP-type decision making and modern, professional administrative methods.
- Emphasize creativity, innovation, and adaptation.
- Set a no-nonsense tone with regard to integrity, ethics, moral decision making, and discipline.
- Remember that the police are licensed to use force to overcome the illegal use of force. This makes the police, in some ways, violent people; nothing a leader can do changes this reality.
- Be cognizant of the changing times through which today's police are moving toward COP and modern professionalism.
- Recall that while virtually everyone outside of police work considers the police to be powerful individuals, police officers understand and are often frustrated by the paradoxes of coercive power.
- Remember that the conflict between law enforcement and order maintenance is an ongoing, everyday occurrence—especially in urban and college environments.
- Understand that no matter how honest and hard-working police leaders might be, the power and solidarity of the subculture can mitigate even their best efforts at control and professionalization.
- Acknowledge that unlike any other type of complex organization, discretion in police work increases at the very bottom, making leadership difficult in a unique way.
- Recall that police work is driven by several conflicting definitions of justice and each is morally defensible.

SERGEANTS

The police leader can interact with the individual officer as a mentor, protector, benefactor, teacher, compatriot, and even friend. In fact, so diverse can this set of roles be that the local leader needs to be careful to some extent. As with coaching, watching police officers out on the street involves seeing into their souls. The essence of a person's soul is revealed when they deal with being outnumbered, threatened, ostracized, and so on. This makes the role of sergeant an intimate one and different from that of other leaders in important ways. Trust is critical in a way that is absent for leaders at other levels.

Sergeants must:

- Recall that though the police must deal with citizens in a civil and deferential way, confrontational skills are still of critical importance.

- Remind themselves of the limitations of command and control, even though it is the traditional and expected method of leadership in most places.

- Remember the coaching paradox that everyone must be treated in the same way even though everyone is different.

- Be ever vigilant with regard to how naysayers possess an inordinate amount of power and influence.

- Remember that less than 20 percent of the officer corps causes virtually all of the problems, but leaders must endeavor to avoid spending all of their time with those problem officers.

- Remember the critical limitations there are when attempting to teach circumspection with regard to the use of force. There is, in effect, no definition of excessive force.

- Remember that while leaders must stay close to their charges, they are no longer "one of the gang."

- Recall that the goals of the immediate supervisor often constitute a moving target that can be frustrating if it is not acknowledged.

 ## MIDDLE MANAGERS

Crucial differences exist for middle managers. These organizational actors live and operate in a nether world of sorts. They are halfway between the police subculture on the street and the executive level, where the most important policy is developed.

Middle managers must:

- Utilize accountability initiatives while at the same time avoiding bureaupathology.

- Acknowledge the positives of the watchman style. Remember that its reactive, passive, "hands off" style is preferred by many Americans, driven as they are by an appreciation of individual liberties and limited government.

- Be wary that while many in the police world admire the strengths of the legalistic style, it appears in operation to be racist to the freedom-sensitive American mind.

- Recall that they must take great care when constructing organizational subgoals, as bureaupathology can rear its ugly head.

- Remember that in training, there is an almost universal propensity for leaders to create paranoia in the officer corps due to concerns about potential violence.

- Remember that while almost everything about paramilitarism is negative, the police *do* have to be ready to morph into an army-like operation instantly, under certain circumstances.

- Understand that collegial problem solving is not "lead-able."

- Remember that assessment is an inexact science, because the essence of police work—what we want to accomplish, who the best officers are, etc.—is largely unquantifiable.

 ## CHIEFS OR SHERIFFS

All of the points above are important for the top brass, along with one more layer of critical realities. Unlike other executives, those who head up police organizations are involved in delivering an oddly paradoxical, multiple, conflicting, and vague "product" that is not easily quantifiable. Thus, their concerns are many and they are of a decidedly different nature than other leaders.

Chiefs or sheriffs must:

- Keep a clear focus on the real elements of police professionalism and COP in order to make continuing progress and keep naysaying in check.

- Be aware that middle managers—whose support is absolutely crucial to their endeavors—can tend to be frustrated by COP due to the apparent lack of congruence between authority and responsibility.

- Remember that no matter how hard chiefs/sheriffs work at making officers circumspect about the exercise of their authority, they will eventually tend to feel they "are the law."

- Remember that while all police executives "talk service," only a limited number of departments can and do prosecute this particular style. Take care to understand the public relations–orientation of the service style, and how it is sold to the public.

- Remember that no matter how hard they work or how logical the system they put into place, most of the work in complex organizations is accomplished informally and most information is passed through informal chains.

- Keep themselves aloof from focusing on multiple power points that are, in fact, out of their control.

- Recall that when they are crafting subgoals they need to be aware of bureaupathology.

- Remember how it is next to impossible to predetermine character.

- Not be threatened by civilian review because the police are never abused by it. In fact, they should embrace this idea because it can help create better police–community relations.

- Remember Muir's admonition to teach democracy and legality.

WHAT CAN WE EXPECT OF OUR OFFICER CORPS?

Weber suggested that the role of the exceptional bureaucrat/politician involved forging together a warm passion with a cool perspective. We have visited Muir's ideas of passion and perspective, and this is what Weber meant. We want our charges to have an integrated understanding of the morality of coercion. They cannot be conflicted about the exercise of power in the name of accomplishing good things. Furthermore, we want them to have a tragic perspective of life. We hope they are curious about discovering the causes of deviance and how every person is driven by a yearning to be treated with some modicum of dignity.

We want officers to be gregarious and enjoy "shooting the s---" with people. There is precious little room in police work for the "John Wayne, strong, silent type." Effective police officers need to be people persons, and, as a leader, one needs to bring that out of the reticent officer. Of course, an individual's natural personality cannot be changed, but the effective leader needs to motivate, teach, and coach officers to engage with the public openly and often.

As always, we want officers to be as aware and educated as possible about the paradoxes of police work. No one can completely inoculate himself or herself from the frustrations the paradoxes present, or be sufficiently prepared to deal with the negative side of the human experience confronted on the street. Keeping a consistent focus on these paradoxical realities is important. It is the best thing we can do for our subordinates.

Perhaps, of all that has ever been written about the police, Muir best sums up what we would wish our modern, professional officers to understand. He suggests that the individual police officer needs to have an appreciation for:

> The suffering of each inhabitant of the earth, a sensitivity to man's yearning for dignity, and, ultimately, "some kind of faith" that no individual is worthless. In short, the professional … developed a cognitive efficiency, a "perspective," a capacity for seeing rich implications of meager cues. He developed an inner understanding of the motives of men, a sense of life's rhythms of cause and effect, and a self-suspicion that drove him to find out for himself when what he had been told by frighteners and flatterers did not square with his inner "knowledge of tragedy" (Muir, 1977: 51).

WHAT CAN WE EXPECT OF OURSELVES?

Much has been made here, and in other works by other authors, about what we should expect of the men and women we lead. But what about ourselves? What should police leaders expect from police leaders? In attempting to be as tough on our own working personalities as those of our subordinates, what are the foci?

The police leader must be conversant with nuance and subtlety. Ours is not a profession where there is room for a black-and-white view of the world. Things are never as clear out on the street as Hollywood or the average American would like them to be. All is accomplished in shades of gray, and all must be understood with an eye toward the need to possess a delicate and refined sensitivity to the human condition. Bullishness and single-mindedness, normally considered to be positive traits in the military, are anathematic to the police experience on the street.

Equally, the police leader needs to be able to tolerate ambiguity and appreciate the importance of irony. Paradox, in particular, can be hard to fathom; how can two sides of something both be true at the same time? Anyone who cannot wrestle with such ideas, who wants to plow through complicated circumstances quickly and without thinking (in the name of simplicity and specificity) is going to have a difficult time of it in police work. As is true in life for the sophisticated adult, being comfortable with paradox and ambiguity is essential, for reasons we have attempted to make clear throughout the discussions in this book.

Modern police leaders need to possess the tragic perspective. They need to have an appreciation for the unitary experience of life: all people go through a similar search for dignity and freedom. They need to understand how complicated causal patterns operate to make life's complexities confusing. Deviance, in particular, faces police officers and leaders on an almost minute-by-minute basis; it is not caused merely by "bad people deciding to behave badly." The modern leader cannot accept such silliness. It is simplistic and even dangerous to do so. Finally, the modern leader must understand the necessity of human interdependence—the nature of how and why community is so critical to life for all of the people with whom they interact.

At the end here, please allow us to wax poetic for a moment. The authors genuinely believe that police work is, quite literally, the most honorable of all professions in America. Policing the streets of our society requires courage, honesty, and commitment. It requires a sense of duty, obligation, and responsibility. To do it well involves a lifelong pledge to the citizens of our communities that the police officer and the police leader will do all they can to be as objective and professional as is humanly possible while pursuing justice on the street corners of America.

As we finish a text about how police leaders should comport themselves and what we should expect from police officers in general, we would like to share with the reader our firm belief that doing good works is what lies at the core of the police role. Furthermore, we do not believe it too clichéd or hackneyed to suggest that all police officers—every last one—have the potential to do good works, achieve great things, and even be heroic on occasion. All of us are capable of cowardice and heroism, of doing great things and of shirking our responsibilities. The value of a person's life is weighed in the light of this reality.

Here is how John Steinbeck put it when reflecting upon the human condition in *East of Eden*:

> I believe that there is one story in the world, and only one, that has frightened and inspired us. . . . Humans are caught—in their lives, in their thoughts, in their hungers and ambitions, in their avarice and cruelty, and in their kindness and generosity too—in a net of good and evil. I think this is the only story we have and that it occurs on all levels of feeling and intelligence. There is no other story. A man, after he has brushed off the dust and chips of his life, will have left only the hard, clean questions: was it good or was it evil? Have I done well—or ill?

We hope all police officers and all police leaders embrace the idea that doing good and thwarting evil is their solemn responsibility out on the streets of America. This is not a romantic platitude of the authors, but a living, breathing reality.

WORKS CITED

Aamedt, Michael G. *Research in Law Enforcement Selection*. Boca Raton, FL: Brown Walker Press, 2004.

Abrahams, Jeffrey. *The Mission Statement Book*. Berkeley: Ten Speed Press, 1999.

Adams, John. *The Massachusetts Constitution, Part the First, Article XXX*. 1780.

Adams, Scott. *Dilbert and the Way of the Weasel*. New York: Harper, 2003.

Adams, Thomas F. *Police Field Operations*, 7th Ed. Upper Saddle River, NJ: Prentice Hall, 2006.

Aho, James. *This Thing of Darkness*. Seattle: University of Washington Press, 1995.

Aitchison, Will. *The Rights of Law Enforcement Officers, 5th Ed*. Labor Relations Information Systems, 2004.

Albrecht, Karl. *Social Intelligence: The New Science of Success*. Hoboken, NJ: Pfeiffer Publications, 2009.

Albrecht, Steve. *Surviving Street Patrol: The Officer's Guide to Safe and Effective Policing*. Boulder, CO: Paladin Press, 2001.

Alpert, Geoffrey P., and Roger G. Dunham. *Understanding Police Use of Force: Officers, Suspects, and Reciprocity*. New York: Cambridge University Press, 2004.

Anglin, Kirklin. *The Affirmative Action Dilemma*. BookSurge Press, 2006.

Aristotle, translation by J. A. K. Tomson. *Nicomachean Ethics*. New York: Penguin Classics, 1955.

Baker, Stephen A. *Effects of Law Enforcement Accreditation: Officer Selection, Promotion and Education*. Santa Barbara, CA: Praeger, 1995.

Baker, Thomas E. *Effective Police Leadership*. Looseleaf Law Press, 2005.

Balko, Radley. *The Rise of Paramilitary Police Raids in America*. Washington, DC: Cato Institute, 2006.

Banks, Cyndi. *Criminal Justice Ethics: Theory and Practice, 2nd Ed*. London: Sage, 2008.

Barker, Thomas, and David L. Carter. *Police Deviance, 3rd Ed*. Albany, NY: Anderson, 1994.

Belkin, A., and J. McNichol. "Pink in Blue: Outcomes Associated with the Integration of Open Gay and Lesbian Personnel in the San Diego Police Department," *Police Quarterly*, 5:63–95 (2002).

Berg, B. L. "First Day at the Police Academy: Stress-Reaction Training as a Screening-Out Technique," *Journal of Contemporary Criminal Justice*, 6:89–105 (1990).

Berkley, George. *The Democratic Policeman*. Boston: Beacon, 1969.

Blakeman, J. D. *Interpersonal Communications Skills in the Correctional Setting, Instructor's Guide*. Washington, DC: Capitol Communications Press, 1969.

Blakeman, J. D., T. Keeling, R. M. Pierce, and R. R. Carkhuff. *IPC: Interpersonal Communication Skills for Correctional Management*. Amherst, MA: HRD Press, 1997.

Black, Donald. "The Social Organization of Arrest," *Stanford Law Review*, 23: 1087–1111 (1971).

Blum, Laurence N. *Force Under Pressure: How Cops Live and Why They Die*. Brooklyn, NY: Lantern Books, 2000.

—. *Stoning the Keepers at the Gate: Society's Relationship with Law Enforcement*. Brooklyn, NY: Lantern, 2003.

Bolton, Ken, Jr. *Black in Blue: African-American Police Officers and Racism*. New York: Routledge, 2004.

Boston Globe. "Wave of Abuse Claims Laid to a Few Officers," October 4, 1992, p. 1.

Bouza, Anthony. *The Police Mystique: An Insider's Look at Cops, Crime, and the Criminal Justice System.* Jackson, TN: Perseus, 2001.

—. *Police Unbound: Corruption, Abuse and Heroism by the Boys in Blue.* Amherst, NY: Prometheus, 2001.

Brogden, Mike, and Preeti Nijhar. *Community Policing: National and International Models and Approaches.* London: Willan Publishing, 2005.

Brown, M. K. *Working the Street: Police Discretion.* New York: Russell Sage Foundation, 1981.

Bruner, Jerome S., Jacqueline J. Goodnow, and George A. Austin. *A Study of Thinking.* New York: Wiley, 1956.

Burris, John L., and Catherine Whitney. *Blue vs. Black: Let's End the Conflict Between Cops and Minorities.* New York: St. Martin's Griffin, 2000.

Caiden, G. E. *Police Revitalization.* Lexington, MA: D.C. Heath, 1977.

Carkhuff, R. R. *The Art of Helping.* Amherst, MA: HRD Press, 1973.

Caldero, Michael A., and John P. Crank. *Police Ethics: The Corruption of Noble Cause,* 3rd Ed. Albany, NY: Anderson, 2009.

California, State of. Commission for Peace Officer Standards and Training. Bulletin 95-9, May 12, 1995.

Carroll, Lewis. *Alice's Adventures in Wonderland.* 1865.

Carter, Lycia, and Mark Wilson. "Measuring Professionalism of Police Officers," *Police Chief* (March 2009).

Chambers, Harry. *My Way or the Highway: The Micromanagement Survival Guide.* San Francisco: Berrett-Koehler, 2004.

Chandiramani, Ravi. "Talking PR Crap? The Village Is on Hand to Help You." Posted on www.thevillagelimited.com., November 30, 2009.

Close, Daryl, and Nicholas Meier. *Morality in Criminal Justice: An Introduction to Ethics.* Belmont Shores, CA: Wadsworth, 1995.

Connor, Greg, and Gregory Connor. *Vehicle Stops, 3rd Ed.* Champaign, IL: Stipes Publishing, 2000.

Cohen, Bernard, and Jan M. Chaiken. *Police Background Characteristics and Performance.* Lanham, MD: Lexington Books, 1973.

Cohen, Howard S., and Michael Feldberg. *Power and Restraint: The Moral Dimension of Police Work.* Santa Barbara, CA: Praeger, 1991.

Cook, Leah. "Police Stress: Learning Through Experience, Research, and Observation." Research paper, San Jose State University/Department of Anthropology (2003).

Cordner, G. "Community Policing: Elements and Effects." In R. G. Dunham and G. P. Alpert, eds. *Critical Issues in Policing, 5th Ed.* Long Grove, IL: Waveland Press, 2005.

Couper, D. C., and S. H. Lobitz. *Quality Policing: The Madison Experience.* Washington, DC: Police Executive Research Forum, 1991.

Crane, Thomas G., and Larissa Nancy Patrick. *The Heart of Coaching, 3rd Ed.* Poway, CA: FTA Press, 2007.

Crank, John P. "The Influence of Environmental and Organizational Factors in Police Styles in Urban and Rural Environments," *Journal of Research in Crime and Delinquency*, 27(2) (1990).

—. *Understanding Police Culture.* Albany, NY: Anderson, 1998.

Dantzker, M. L. *Understanding Today's Police.* Monsey, NY: Criminal Justice Press, 2005.

Das, Dilip K. "Police Training in Ethics: The Need for an Innovative Approach in Mandated Programs," *American Journal of Criminal Justice*, 11(1) (1986).

Das, Dilip K., and Osman Dolu. *Cross-Cultural Profiles of Policing*. Palo Alto, CA: CRC Publications, Stanford University, 2009.

Davey, J. D., P. L. Obst, and M. C. Sheehan. "Developing a Profile of Alcohol Consumption Patterns of Police Officers in a Large Scale Sample of an Australian Police Service," *European Addiction Studies*, 6:205–212 (2000).

Davis, Kenneth Culp. *Police Discretion*. Eagan, MN: West Press, 1977.

Delattre, Edwin J. *Character and Cops: Ethics in Policing*. American Enterprise Institute, 2002.

Delord, Ron, John Burpo, Michael Shannon, and Jim Spearing. *Police Union Power, Politics, and Confrontation in the 21st Century*. Springfield, IL: Charles C. Thomas, 2008.

Dempsey, John S., and Linda S. Forst. *An Introduction to Policing, 5th Ed*. Clifton Park, NY: Delmar/Cengage, 2010.

Diner, Steven J. *A Very Different Age: Americans of the Progressive Era*. New York: Hill and Wang, 1998.

Donnithorne, Larry. R. *The West Point Way of Leadership*. New York: Currency/Doubleday, 1993.

Durkheim, Emile. *Suicide*. New York: Free Press, 1997.

Edwards, Charles J. *Changing Policing Theories for 21st Century Societies*. Annandale, NSW, Australia: Federation Press, 2005.

Farson, Richard. *Management of the Absurd*. New York: Simon & Schuster, 1996.

Fogelson, R. *Big City Police*. Cambridge: Harvard University Press, 1977.

Fleishacker, Samuel. *A Short History of Distributive Justice*. Cambridge: Harvard University Press, 2005.

Fletcher, Connie. *Pure Cop*. New York: Pocket Books, 1991.

Freidman, Robert R. *Community Policing: Comparative Perspectives and Prospects*. New York: St. Martin's Press, 1992.

Freidson, Eliot. *Professionalism: The Third Logic*. Chicago: University of Chicago Press, 2000.

Fuller, Lon L. *The Morality of Law*. New Haven: Yale University Press, 1969.

Gardner, Gerald W. *Common Sense Police Supervision: Practical Tips for the First-Line Leader*. Springfield, IL: Charles C. Thomas, 2008.

Gates, Daryl F. *Chief: My Life in the LAPD*. New York: Bantam Books, 1992.

Geison, G. L., ed. *Professions and Professional Ideologies in America*. Chapel Hill: University of North Carolina Press, 1983.

Gelder, Ken. *Subcultures: Cultural Histories and Social Practice*. New York: Routledge, 2007.

Giles, Howard, ed. *Law Enforcement, Communications, and Community*. Amsterdam, NL: John Benjamins Press, 2002.

Glantz, Aaron, ed. *Winter Soldier: Iraq and Afghanistan: Eyewitness Accounts of the Occupation*. Chicago: Haymarket Books, 2008.

Glenn, Russell W. *Training the 21st Century Police Officer*. Santa Monica, CA: Rand Corporation, 2003.

Glennon, Jim. "Surviving the Streets," Lombard, Illinois, Police Department. PoliceOne.com, 2009.

Goldstein, Herman. *Problem Oriented Policing*. Columbus, OH: McGraw-Hill, 1990.

Goleman, Daniel. *Working with Emotional Intelligence*. New York: Bantam, 1998.

—. *Social Intelligence: The New Science of Human Relationships*. New York: Bantam, 2006.

Goodsell, Charles T. *The Case for Bureaucracy*. Washington, DC: C Q Press, 2003.

Cooper, L. *The Iron Fist and the Velvet Glove*. Berkeley: Center for Research on Criminal Justice, 1975.

Greene, J. R., and S. D. Mastrofski. *Community Policing: Rhetoric or Reality*. Santa Barbara, CA: Praeger, 1988.

Groeneveld, Richard F. *Arrest Discretion of Police Officers: The Impact of Varying Organizational Structures*. LFB Scholarly Press, 2005.

Grote, Richard C. *Discipline Without Punishment*. New York: AMACOM, 1995.

Grupp, Jeffrey. *Corporatism: The Secret Government of the New World Order*. Joshua Tree, CA: Progressive Press, 2007.

Guller, I. B., and M. Guller. *Candidate and Officer Personnel Survey Technical Manual Revised*. Oakland, NJ: The Institute for Forensic Psychology, 2003.

Haberfield, Maria R. *Critical Issues in Police Training*. Upper Saddle River, NJ: Prentice Hall, 2002.

Haider, James T. *Field Training Police Recruits: Developing, Improving, and Operating a Field Training Program*. Springfield, IL: Charles C. Thomas, 1990.

Handy, Charles. *The Age of Paradox*. Cambridge: Harvard University Business Press, 1995.

Hansen, Randall S. "The Five-Step Plan for Creating Personal Mission Statements," www.citeHR.com. DeLand, FL: Stetson University School of Business, 2006.

Harries, Keith D. *Serious Violence: Patterns of Homicide and Assault in America*. Springfield, IL: Charles C. Thomas, 1997.

Hays, Kraig, Robert Regoli, and John Hewitt. "Police Chiefs, Anomie, and Leadership," *Police Quarterly*, 10:3–22 (2007).

Hennessy, Stephen M. *Thinking Cop, Feeling Cop: A Study in Police Personalities, 3rd Ed*. Center for Applications of Psychological Type, 1998.

Hersey, Paul. *The Situational Leader*. Escondido, CA: Center for Leadership Studies, 1997.

Hickman, M. J., and B. A. Reaves. *Local Police Departments*. Washington, DC: Bureau of Justice Statistics, 2000.

Hill, Stephen M., Randall R. Beger, and John M. Zanetill. "Plugging the Security Gap or Springing a Leak: Questioning the Growth of Paramilitary Policing in U.S. Domestic and Foreign Policy," *Democracy and Security*, 3(3) (2007).

Hrenchir, Tim. "Miranda Readings Lack Hollywood Spin," *Topeka Capital-Journal*, January 25, 1999.

Huberman, John. "Discipline Without Punishment," *Harvard Business Review*. 42:62–68 (1964).

Hunt, Robert C. *Beyond Relativism: Comparability in Cultural Anthropology*. Lanham, MD: AltaMira Press, 2007.

Iannone, Nathan F., Marvin D. Iannone, and Jeff Bernstein. *Supervision of Police Personnel, 7th Ed*. Upper Saddle River, NJ: Prentice Hall, 2008.

International Association of Chiefs of Police (IACP). *Leadership in Police Organizations, Vol. I., Areas I and II, 2nd Ed*. Boston: McGraw-Hill, 2002.

—. "Ethics Training in Law Enforcement." *Police Chief* (January 2009): 14–24.

Ivkovic, Sanja Kutnjak. *Fallen Blue Knights: Controlling Police Corruption*. New York: Oxford University Press, 2005.

Jefferson, Tony. *The Case Against Paramilitary Policing*. Columbus, OH: Open University Press, 1990.

Johnson, D. R. *American Law Enforcement: A History*. St. Louis: Forum Press, 1981.

Jones, Laurie Beth. *The Path: Creating Your Mission Statement for Work and for Life*. New York: Hyperion, 1998.

Judd, Kenneth L. "The Growing Gap Between Rich and Poor." *Hoover Digest: Research and Opinion on Public Policy, #2*, 1997.

Kalish, Carol B. "International Crime Rates: Bureau of Justice Statistics, Special Report." Washington, DC: Bureau of Justice Statistics, 1988.

Kaminsky, Glenn F. *Field Training Concepts in Criminal Justice Agencies*. Upper Saddle River, NJ: Prentice Hall, 2000.

Kaminsky, Robert J. "Police Minority Recruitment: Predicting Who Will Say Yes to an Offer for a Job as a Cop," *Journal of Criminal Justice*, 21(2) (1993).

Kappeler, Victor E., Richard D. Sluder, and Geoffrey P. Alpert. *Forces of Deviance: Understanding the Dark Side of Policing, 2nd Ed.* Long Grove, IL: Waveland, 1998.

Kelling, George. "Juveniles and Police: The End of the Nightstick." In Frances X. Hartmann, ed., *From Children to Citizens, Vol. II: The Role of the Juvenile Court*. New York: Springer-Vertag, 1987.

Kelling, George, and Catherine M. Coles. *Fixing Broken Windows: Restoring Order and Reducing Crime in Our Communities*. New York: Free Press, 1998.

Kelley, Robert. *The Power of Followership: How to Create Leaders People Want to Follow and Followers Who Lead Themselves*. New York: Currency/Doubleday, 1992.

Kellough, J. Edward. *Understanding Affirmative Action: Politics, Discrimination and the Search for Justice*. Washington, DC: Georgetown University Press, 2006.

Kleinig, John. *The Ethics of Policing*. Cambridge, UK: Cambridge University Press, 1996.

Klockars, Carl. "The Dirty Harry Problem," *Annals of the American Academy of Political and Social Science*, 452(2):33–47 (1980).

—. *The Idea of Police*. London: Sage, 1985.

—. "The Only Way to Make Any Real Progress in Controlling Excessive Force by Police," *Law Enforcement News*. May 15, 1992.

—. *Thinking About Police*. Columbus, OH: McGraw-Hill, 1983.

Klockars, Carl, Sanja Kutnjak Ivkovic, and M. R. Haberfeld. *The Contours of Police Integrity*. London: Sage, 2004.

Krantz, Sheldon. *Police Policy Making: The Boston Experience*. Lanham, MD: Lexington Books, 1979.

Kraska, Peter, and Victor E. Kappeler. "Militarizing American Police: The Rise and Normalization of Paramilitary Units," *Social Problems*, 44(1) (1997).

Kratcosky, Peter C., and Dilip K. Das. *Policing Education and Training in a Global Society*. Lanham, MD: Lexington Books, 2007.

Kurke, Martin I., and Ellen M. Scrivner. *Police Psychology into the 21st Century*. London: Psychology Press, 1995.

Lane, Roger. *Policing the City: Boston, 1822–1882*. Cambridge: Harvard University Press, 1967.

Langworthy, R., T. Hughes, and B. Sanders. *Law Enforcement Recruitment, Selection and Training: A Survey of Major Police Departments in the U.S.* Highland Heights, KY: Academy of Criminal Justice Sciences, 1995.

Larson, Magah Sarfatti. *The Rise of Professionalism: A Sociological Analysis*. Berkeley: University of California Press, 1979.

Lawrence, Regina G. *The Politics of Force: Media and the Construction of Police Brutality*. Berkeley: University of California Press, 2000.

Lazear, Edward P. "The Peter Principle: A Theory of Decline," *Journal of Political Economy*. Chicago: University of Chicago Press, Vol. 112 (S1), pp. S141–S163, February 2004.

Leighton, Paul, and Jeffrey Reiman. *Criminal Justice Ethics*. Upper Saddle River, NJ: Prentice Hall, 2001.

Leinen, Stephen. *Gay Cops.* Piscataway, NJ: Rutgers University Press, 1993.

Locke, John. *Two Treatises of Government.* 1689.

Long, Carolyn N. *Mapp v. Ohio: Guarding Against Unreasonable Searches and Seizures.* Lawrence, KS: University of Kansas Press, 2006.

Lonsdale, Mark V. *Raids: A Tactical Guide to High Risk Warrant Service.* Specialized Tactical Training Unit, 2005.

Lovell, Jarret S. *Good Cop/Bad Cop: Mass Media and the Cycle of Police Reform.* Monsey, NY: Criminal Justice Press, 2003.

Lyman, Michael D. *The Police: An Introduction, 3rd Ed.* Upper Saddle River, NJ: Pearson/Prentice Hall, 2004.

Lyman, Michael D., and Vernon J. Geberth. *Practical Drug Enforcement.* Danvers, MA: CRC Press, 2001.

Macdonald, Heather. *Are Cops Racist?* Chicago: Ivan R. Dee Press, 2003.

Maguire, Edward R. *Organizational Structure in American Police Agencies: Context, Complexity, and Control.* Albany, NY: SUNY Press, 2003.

Maier, Norman Raymond Frederick. *The Study of Behavior Without a Goal.* Santa Barbara, CA: Greenwood Press, 1982.

Mayer, William G. *The Changing American Mind.* Ann Arbor, MI: University of Michigan Press, 1993.

Mayzer, Marla. "A Guide to Surviving Workplace 'Backstabbers,'" *Washington Post*, January 18, 1999.

Megargee, Edwin I. "Minnesota Multiphasic Personality Inventory-2." *Criminal Justice and Correctional Report.* San Antonio, TX: Pearson Publishing, 2001.

Merriam-Webster. *New Collegiate Dictionary.* Cambridge, MA: G. and C. Merriam Co. Press, 1949.

Meese, Edwin, and P. J. Ortmeier. *Leadership, Ethics, and Policing: Challenges for the 21st Century.* Upper Saddle River, NJ: Prentice Hall, 2003.

Megathlin, W. L., and S. Day, "The Effects of Facilitation Training on Corrections Officers." Washington, DC: United States Bureau of Prisons. JIC Grant # JIC- 21.767, 1969.

Miller, Laurence. *Mental Toughness for Law Enforcement.* Flushing, NY: Looseleaf Law Press, 2007.

Miller, Linda S., and Karen M. Hess. *Community Police: Partnership and Problem Solving.* Florence, KY: Wadsworth, 2007.

Miller, Linda S., Karen M. Hess, and Christine M. H. Orthmann. *Community Policing: Partnerships for Problem Solving.* Clifton Park, NY: Delmar/Cengage, 2010.

Miller, Wilbur R. *Cops and Bobbies: Police Authority in New York and London, 1830–1870.* Chicago: University of Chicago Press, 1977.

Monkkonen, Eric H. *Police in Urban America, 1860–1920.* Cambridge, UK: Cambridge University Press, 1981.

Moran, T. K. "Pathways Toward a Nondiscriminatory Recruitment Policy," *Journal of Police Science and Administration*, 16:274–287 (1988).

Morley, Patrick. *Beyond No Comment: Speaking with the Press as a Police Officer.* Chicago: Kaplan Press, 2009.

Muir, William K., Jr. *Police: Streetcorner Politicians.* Chicago: University of Chicago Press, 1977.

Mumford, Michael D. *Pathways to Outstanding Leadership.* Mahway, NJ: Lawrence Erlbaum, 2006.

Musto, David F. *The American Disease: Origins of Narcotic Control.* New York: Oxford University Press, 1999.

Navarro, Joe, and Marvin Karlins. *What Every Body Is Saying: An Ex-FBI Agent's Guide to Speed-Reading People.* New York: Collins Living, 2008.

Nelson, Jill. *Police Brutality: An Anthology*. New York: W. W. Norton, 2001.

New York Times. "Kansas City Police Go After Their 'Bad Boys,'" September 10, 1991.

O'Donnell, Tim. *American Holocaust: The Price of Victimless Crime Laws*. Bloomington, IN: IUniverse, 2000.

O'Halloran, Richard, and David O'Halloran. *The Mission Primer: Four Steps to an Effective Mission Statement*. New York: Mission Inc., 2000.

O'Keefe, James. *Protecting the Republic: The Education and Training of American Police Officers*. Upper Saddle River, NJ: Prentice Hall, 2003.

Oliver, Willard M. *Community Oriented Policing: A Systematic Approach to Policing, 4th Ed*. Upper Saddle River, NJ: Prentice Hall, 2007.

O'Neill, J. L., and M. A. Cushing. *The Impact of Shift Work on Police Officers*. Washington, DC: Police Executive Research Forum, 1991.

Parkin, Chares. *The Moral Basis of Burke's Political Thought*. Cambridge: Cambridge University Press, 1965.

Pate, Anthony M., and Lorie A. Fridell. *Police Use of Force, 2 vols*. Washington, DC: The Police Foundation, 1993.

Patterson, Jeffery. "Learning the Lessons of History," (1995) available at www.lectlaw.com/files/cjs07.htm (accessed September 20, 2010).

Peak, Kenneth J. *Policing America, 6th Ed*. Upper Saddle River, NJ: Prentice Hall, 2008.

Peak, Kenneth J., and Ronald W. Glensor. *Community Police and Problem Solving, 5th Ed*. Upper Saddle River, NJ: Prentice Hall, 2007.

Peratec Ltd. *Total Quality Management*. New York: Springer, 2009.

Perez, Douglas W. *The Paradoxes of Police Work, 2nd Ed*. Clifton Park, NY: Cengage, 2010.

—. *Common Sense About Police Review*. Philadelphia: Temple University Press, 1994.

Perez, Douglas W., and J. Alan Moore. *Police Ethics: A Matter of Character*. Thomson Wadsworth, Belmont, CA, 2002.

Perrow, Charles. *Complex Organizations: A Critical Essay*. Glenview, IL: Scott, Foresman, 1972.

Peter, Laurence J., and Raymond Hull. *The Peter Principle*. New York: Bantam, 1969.

Peters, Tom. *A Passion for Excellence*. New York: Random House, 1985.

Pinizzotto, Anthony J., Edward F. Davis, and Charles F. Miller. "Officer's Perceptual Shorthand," *The FBI Law Enforcement Bulletin*, July 2000.

Pollock, Joycelyn. *Ethical Dilemmas and Decisions in Criminal Justice, 6th Ed*. Belmont Shores, CA: Wadsworth, 2008.

Poteet, Lewis, and Aaron C. Poteet. *Cop Talk: A Dictionary of Police Slang*. Bloomington, IN: IUniverse, 2000.

Pound, Roscoe, and Ron Christenson. *Criminal Justice in America*. Piscataway, NJ: Transaction Press, 1997.

Prince, H. T., J. Halstead, and L. Hesser. "Expectancy Theory of Motivation and Goal Setting Theory," in *Leadership in Police Organizations, Vol. I, Lesson 5*, New York: McGraw-Hill, 2008.

Punch, Maurice. *Corruption, Deviance, and Accountability in Policing*. London: Willan Publishing, 2009.

Rahtz, Howard. *Understanding Police Use of Force*. Berkeley: Criminal Justice Press, 2003.

Richardson, Reed. "How to Handle Workplace Gossip," *Business 24/7,* available at www.smallbusinessonlinecommunity.com (accessed September 20, 2010).

Roach, Kent. *Due Process and Victims' Rights: The New Law and Policies of Criminal Justice.* Toronto: University of Toronto Press, 1999.

Roberg, Roy, Kenneth Novak, and Gary Cordner. *Police and Society, 3rd Ed.* Los Angeles: Roxbury Press, 2005.

Robinson, Cyril D., Richard Scaglion, and J. Michael Olero. *Police in Contradiction: The Evolution of the Police Function in Society.* Santa Barbara, CA: Greenwood Press, 1993.

Rothmiller, Mike, and Ivan G. Goldman. *L.A. Secret Police: Inside the LAPD Elite Spy Network.* New York: Pocket Books, 1992.

Satterfield, Brian. "How to Find and Stop the Workplace 'Snitch,'" www.HRWorld.com, December 5, 2009.

Sampson, S., J. D. Blakeman, and R. R. Carkhuff. *Social Skills for Law Enforcement Officers.* Amherst, MA: HRD Press, 2006.

Schnaubelt, Angela. "Mission Statement Examples: Samples and Uses of Effective Statements for Your Organization," www.Suite101.com, August 1, 2007.

Schneider, David J. *The Psychology of Stereotyping.* New York: Guilford Press, 2005.

Schultz, David A., and Robert Moranto. *The Politics of Civil Service Reform.* New York: Peter Lang, 1998.

Scott, Eric. *Calls for Service: Citizen Demand and Initial Police Response.* Washington, DC: U.S. Government Printing Office, 1981.

Schur, Edwin M. *Victimless Crimes.* Upper Saddle River, NJ: Prentice Hall, 1975.

Seddon, John. *Freedom from Command and Control.* London: Productivity Press, 2005.

Sherman, Lawrence. *Quality Police Education.* Hoboken, NJ: Jossey-Bass, 1978.

Sherman, Nancy. *The Fabric of Character: Aristotle's Theory of Virtue.* New York: Oxford University Press, 1991.

Signorelli, Walter P. *The Constable Has Blundered: The Exclusionary Rule, Crime, and Corruption.* Durham, NC: Carolina Academic Press, 2010.

Simon, Herbert. *Administrative Behavior.* New York: Macmillan, 1957.

Skogan, Wesley. *Disorder and Decline: Crime and the Spiral of Decay in American Neighborhoods.* New York: Free Press, 1990.

Skolnick, Jerome. *Justice Without Trial.* New York: John Wiley and Sons, 1966.

Skolnick, H. Jerome, and David H. Bayley. *The New Blue Line.* New York: Free Press, 1988.

Slovak, Jeffrey. *Styles of Urban Policing: Organization, Environment, and Police Styles in Selected American Cities.* New York: New York University Press, 1988.

Stack, S., and T. Kelly. "Police Suicide," in D. J. Kenney and R. P. McNamara, eds. *Police and Policing: Contemporary Issues, 2nd Ed.* Santa Barbara, CA: Praeger, 1999.

Stamper, Norm. *Breaking Ranks: A Top Cop's Expose of the Dark Side of American Policing.* New York: Nation Books, 2006.

Stark, Rodney. *Police Riots.* Florence, KY: Wadsworth, 1972.

Sternberg, R. *Successful Intelligence.* New York: Plume, 1997.

Sudnow, David. *Normal Crimes.* New York: Irvington Publishers, 1993.

Sykes, Gresham M., and David Matza. "Techniques of Neutralization," *American Sociological Review,* 22:664–670 (1957).

Taylor, Frederick S. *The Principles of Scientific Management.* Harper Brothers: New York, 1911.

Terrill, William. *Police Coercion: Application of the Force Continuum.* El Paso, TX: LFB Scholarly Publishing, 2001.

Thompson, Victor A. *Modern Organizations*. New York: Knopf, 1961.

Thorndike, E. L. *The Elements of Psychology*. New York: Seiler Publications, 1905.

Thornton, Sarah. *The Subcultures Reader, 2nd Ed*. New York: Routledge, 2005.

Toffler, Alvin. *Future Shock*. New York: Bantam, 1984.

Truxillo, Donald M., Suzanne R. Bennett, and Michelle L. Collings. "College Education and Police Job Performance: A Ten Year Study," *Public Personnel Management*, 27(2) (1998).

United States Controller General. "Impact of the Exclusionary Rule on Federal Criminal Prosecutions." Report #GGD-79-45, April 19, 1979.

United States Federal Bureau of Investigation. *Uniform Crime Reports*. Washington, DC: 2005, 2007.

United States Department of Justice, Bureau of Justice Statistics, www.ojp.usdoj.gov.

—. Office of Community Oriented Policing Services.

—. "Special Report: State and Local Law Enforcement Training Academies, 2006," Bureau of Justice Statistics.

Walker, Samuel. "Broken Windows and Fractured History: The Use and Misuse of History in Recent Police Patrol Analysis," *Justice Quarterly*, March 1984.

—. *A Critical History of Police Reform*. Lanham, MD: Lexington, 1977.

—. *The New World of Police Accountability*. London: Sage, 2005.

—. *Police Accountability: The Role of Civilian Oversight*. Florence, KY: Wadsworth, 2001.

Walker, Samuel, and Charles M. Katz. *The Police in America, 7th Ed*. Columbus, OH: McGraw-Hill, 2010.

Walker, Tom. *Fort Apache: New York's Most Violent Precinct*. Bloomington, IN: iUniverse, 2009.

Walsh, William F., and Gennaro F. Vito. *Strategic Management in Policing: A Total Quality Management Approach*. Upper Saddle River, NJ: Prentice Hall, 2007.

Wambaugh, Joseph. *The New Centurions*. Boston: Little, Brown, 1971.

Weber, Max. *From Max Weber: Essays in Sociology*, ed. and trans. H. Gerth and C. Wright Mills. New York: Oxford University Press, 1946.

Weisenand, Paul M. *Supervising Police Personnel: The Fifteen Responsibilities, 6th Ed*. Upper Saddle River, NJ: Prentice Hall, 2006.

Wechsler, D. *The Measurement of Adult Intelligence*. Baltimore: Williams and Wilkins, 1944.

Wells, Sandra, and Betty Sowers Alt. *Police Women*. Santa Barbara, CA: Greenwood, 2005.

The Wickersham Commission on Law Observance and Law Enforcement. Washington, DC: U.S. Government Printing Office, 1931.

White, Michael D. *Current Issues and Controversies in Policing*. London: Pearson, 2007.

Wildavsky, Aaron. *Speaking Truth to Power*. Piscataway, NJ: Transaction Publishers, 1987.

Wilson, James Q. *Varieties of Police Behavior*. Cambridge: Harvard University Press, 1968.

Wilson, James Q., and George Kelling. "Broken Windows," *The Atlantic*, March 1982.

Wilson, O. W., and R. C. McLaren. *Police Administration, 4th Ed*. New York: McGraw-Hill, 1977.

Wojcieszac, Doug, James W. Saxton, and Maggie M. Finkelstein. *Sorry Works!* Bloomington, IN: AuthorHouse, 2007.

Wrobleski, H. M., and K. M. Hess. *Introduction of Law Enforcement and Criminal Justice, 7th Ed*. Belmont Shores, CA: Wadsworth, 2003.

Zhao, Jihong "Soloman," and Kimberly D. Hassell. "Policing Styles and Organizational Priorities: Retesting Wilson's Theory of Local Police Culture," *Police Quarterly*, 8(4) (2005).

INDEX